# shaping neighbourhoods

*Shaping Neighbourhoods* challenges the conventional approaches to brownfield and greenfield development. It encourages all the relevant parties to work together to plan localities as if people and the environment really mattered. This guide provides the most detailed, comprehensive and practical advice covering issues of social inclusion, health, community, economic vitality, transport and urban design, biodiversity, and use-diversity, sustainable energy, food and water.

This guide has been produced under the auspices of the European region of the World Health Organization Healthy Cities movement and is backed by CABE, RSPB, LGA, HBF and CDF.

Neighbourhoods can have an enormous influence on our health, well-being and quality of life. *Shaping Neighbourhoods* builds on the concepts and principles previously explored in the WHO handbook *Healthy Urban Planning*, providing a comprehensive and practical guide to creating local environments which respond to our daily demands. It should prove an invaluable resource for city practitioners and communities everywhere.

*Agis Tsouros, Director, WHO Healthy Cities and Urban Governance Programme*

CABE welcomes this publication for the helpful guidance it provides to everyone involved in neighbourhood planning. We are particularly pleased that it underlines the Government's emphasis on the importance of strategic spatial design and masterplanning.

*Stuart Lipton, Chairman, CABE*

There are very few texts that bridge the gap between community planning and spatial planning. *Shaping Neighbourhoods* is the exception, and is essential reading for communities seeking to influence the planning process.

*Alison West, Director, CDF (Community Development Foundation)*

*Shaping Neighbourhoods* will be of great value to local authorities seeking to translate the principles of sustainable development into everyday practice on the ground. Its focus on best practice is exactly what members and officers need.

*Celia Cameron, Chair, UK LSG (Local Sustainability Group)*

This guide provides a valuable basis to enable the public and private sectors to enter into productive discussions about how to secure sustainable development in a proactive and collaborative way.

*Jo Hanslip, HBF (House Builders' Federation) Regional Planner, Southwest and Midlands*

# shaping
# neighbourhoods

## a guide for health, sustainability and vitality

Hugh Barton, Marcus Grant
and Richard Guise

Spon Press
Taylor & Francis Group

LONDON AND NEW YORK

First published 2003
by Spon Press
11 New Fetter Lane, London EC4P 4EE

Simultaneously published in the USA and Canada
by Spon Press
29 West 35th Street, New York, NY 10001

Reprinted 2004 (twice)

*Spon Press is an imprint of the Taylor & Francis Group*

© 2003 Hugh Barton, Marcus Grant and Richard Guise

Designed and typeset in Linotype Ergo by
Joan Roskelly, Bookcraft Ltd, Stroud, Gloucestershire
Printed and bound in Great Britain
by St Edmundsbury Press, Bury St Edmunds, Suffolk

*British Library Cataloguing in Publication Data*
A catalogue record for this book is available from the
British Library

*Library of Congress Cataloging in Publication Data*
A catalog record for this book has been requested

ISBN 0-415-27852-X (hbk)
ISBN 0-415-26009-4 (pbk)

# the authors

**Hugh Barton** conceived and led the *Shaping Neighbourhoods* project. He is a town planner and Reader in Planning at UWE. In the early 1980s he founded the Urban Centre for Appropriate Technology – now the Centre for Sustainable Energy.
He is Executive Director of the WHO Collaborating Centre for Healthy Cities and Urban Policy. His publications, as co-author or editor, include the DoE good practice guide on *Environmental Appraisal of Development Plans* (1993), *Sustainable Settlements* (1995), *Sustainable Communities* and *Healthy Urban Planning* (both 2000).

**Marcus Grant** is a landscape architect and research fellow in the WHO Collaborating Centre at UWE. With a first degree in ecology, he has over fifteen years' consultancy experience dealing with a wide range of land use issues in sustainable development. He specialises in stakeholder working for sustainability using consensus building processes and collaborative strategic planning.

**Richard Guise** is an architect-planner and Award Leader of the MA Urban Design at UWE. He has been instrumental in the emergence of the innovative joint course in Architecture and Planning. He is advisor to the Urban Design Panel of the Royal Town Planning Institute and works actively with local authorities. He was co-author of *Sustainable Settlements* (1995).

# contents

Chapter 1

## ORIENTATION AND PRINCIPLES

'Neighbourhood' is a contested concept. This chapter draws critical distinctions and sets out the planning principles that are used throughout the guide. It also outlines the context of official policy.

Chapter 2

## NEIGHBOURHOOD CHECKLISTS

Some users of the guide will be concerned with producing an integrated community plan, but many will be concerned with specific newbuild or regeneration projects that affect a locality. This chapter gives sustainability checklists for both. It also acts as a summary of the guide.

Chapter 3

## A NEIGHBOURHOOD PLANNING PROCESS

Local Agenda 21 and the new-style 'Community Strategies' encourage neighbourhood-level integrated plans. This chapter is about the process, not the product, of such plans. It tells you how to go about collaborative decision-making, and how to ensure that policies are properly aimed at sustainable development.

Chapter 4

## PROVIDING FOR LOCAL NEED

Here the emphasis is on spatial policies that promote health, equity and accessibility. The chapter explores who lives in a locality, and how to increase the level of local choice in housing, jobs, services, open space and movement.

Chapter 5

## RESOURCES

This chapter deals with policies and design for environmental sustainability at the local level. It covers the key resources of energy, water, food, materials and wildlife.

Chapter 6

## URBAN DESIGN SYNTHESIS

While the two previous chapters are topic-based, this one provides integrated guidance on the physical development of neighbourhoods in terms of density, shape, use-mixing, and community at the different scales.

# acknowledgements

**Very many thanks are due to ...**

**WHO Healthy Cities**
Agis Tsouros and Claire Mitcham

**Participants of the reference group**

Philip Bisatt (Advisor RTPI Transport Panel
and City and County of Swansea)
Amanda Brookman (The Recycling
Consortium)
Robert Brown (North Hertfordshire District
Council)
Caroline Brown (SPECTRA at UWE)
James Bruges (The Southern Trust)
Barbara Carroll (Enfusion Ltd)
Gillian Clark (Bath & North East Somerset
Council)
Richard Copas (Environment Agency)
Patrick Devine-Wright (Institute of Energy
and Sustainable Development)
Linda Ewles (Avon Health Authority)
Martin Fodor (Local Government
Association & Bristol City Council)
Andy Fudge (Prowting Homes South West)
Oona Goldsworthy (Bristol City Council)
Adrian Gurney (Ove Arup & Partners)
Jo Hanslip (House Builders Federation)
Christine Hine (Avon Health Authority)
Janine Michael (Centre for Sustainable Energy)
Philip Smith (Land Use Consultants)
Mark Southgate (Royal Society for the
Protection of Birds)

**Staff from the Faculty of the Built
Environment at the University of the
West of England (UWE)**

Caroline Brown, Jim Claydon, Isobel Daniels,
Colin Fudge, Paul Revel, Vincent Nadin, Kim
Seaton, Julie Triggle, Gillian Weadon

**Others that helped**
through correspondence, discussion and
debate, both at the University of the West
of England and in the wider world,
including many staff and students at UWE,
short course attendees, and in particular
Matthew Frith (English Nature), Mike King
(Energy Services Association), Robin
Wiltshire (BRESCU)

**Origins and funding**

*Shaping Neighbourhoods* is in direct line of
descent from the acclaimed guide to
*Sustainable Settlements* (Barton, Davis and
Guise 1995) which was jointly published by
the University of the West of England and
the Local Government Management Board.

The new manual has been produced by the
WHO (World Health Organisation)
Collaborating Centre for Healthy Cities and
Urban Policy – based in the Faculty of the
Built Environment at UWE – and under the
auspices of the European region of the
WHO Healthy Cities movement.

**We are very grateful to the Southern
Trust, Marks and Spencer and UWE
itself for providing the resources which
allowed this project to come to fruition.**

*Author credits*
*All diagrams, charts, maps and
photographs, unless explicitly sourced in the
text, are copyright to Barton, Grant and
Guise, and must be properly credited in any
subsequent use or adaptation.*

*Ordnance Survey*
*The following figures are based on material
reproduced from Ordnance Survey mapping
with permission given on behalf of The
Controller of Her Majesty's Stationery office,
Crown Copyright MC 100018918:*

*Figures 1.10, 1.11, 1.12, 1.13, 1.15, 1.16, 3.9,
3.10, 3.11, 3.12, 3.13, 3.15, 4.10, 4.31, 4.32,
5.15, 5.27, 5.28, 6.38, 6.39, 6.40, 6.41, 6.44*

# foreword

**by Jonathon Porritt**

Jonathon Porritt is a Programme Director of Forum for the Future and Chairman of the UK Sustainable Development Commission

More and more, we're urged to celebrate the fact that we live in a more 'connected world'. Telecommunications, the internet, cheap air travel, increased car ownership: we certainly don't lack the means when it comes to staying in touch. Yet at the same time, there's growing evidence that people feel less connected to their local community or neighbourhood, less tied into that network of relationships and responsibilities that secure the 'social capital' on which we depend.

That loss of connection with locality can impoverish our lives and prejudice the integrity of local and global ecosystems. Urban problems of traffic congestion, pollution and health are in no small part due to the breakdown of neighbourhoods. Whilst many people feel little connection with their immediate locality (relying on work, leisure activities and social contacts far from home), others have little choice but to depend on declining local services, trapped in unsupportive, ill-served communities with little prospect of 'escape'.

Both planning and design are critical elements in addressing such dilemmas, as is powerfully reaffirmed in *Shaping Neighbourhoods*. Hugh Barton's text is very much 'of the moment', ensuring that the issues of health, social inclusion, economic vitality and sustainable use of resources are fully integrated. As such, it is likely to be an indispensable guide for students of and professionals in local planning. It should be required reading for all public sector investors, private developers and councillors whose decisions affect the future of neighbourhoods.

All across the world, innovative projects are now clearly demonstrating the huge potential for neighbourhood sustainability strategies that encompass housing, local facilities, rewarding livelihoods, green spaces, community development, food, energy, water and biodiversity. Such strategies can reinvigorate local communities whilst simultaneously playing a part in reducing the threat of global climate change and other pressing environmental and social concerns. All this is exactly in line with government aspirations: here in the UK, national policies for health, regeneration, transport energy and town planning all emphasise the importance of getting things right at the neighbourhood level.

*Shaping Neighbourhoods* manages to set a lot of important technical material in the context of an inclusive collaborative process, and provides clear signposts to involving local partners and people in the development of neighbourhood sustainability strategies. In that respect, it has the potential to make a profoundly empowering contribution to this critical debate by helping community groups to become even more focused and effective in their campaigns for better places to live, work and play.

# how to use this manual

## ITS PURPOSE AND SCOPE

This neighbourhood guide is designed as a desktop manual for planners, designers, developers and community groups. It provides an integrated picture of sustainable, healthy neighbourhoods, with a wealth of specific detail that can help local decision-makers, and people who are concerned about those decisions, get to grips with the issues.

The guide is radical, in that it tries to take the principle of sustainable development seriously, recognising the profound shift in practice that needs to occur. But it is not a utopian tract. It suggests policy options that are potentially implementable now – practical idealism.

### The focus is on the physical fabric of neighbourhoods

The guide is concerned with how the planning, design and management of the physical environment can enhance quality of life, promote social inclusion and husband natural resources.

Two themes run through this guide:
- the neighbourhood as the local human habitat, providing a healthy, sustainable, convivial living environment
- the management of that habitat by voluntary co-operation between the various public, private and community stakeholders that affect it

It is not about social programmes (health, education etc.) or economic regeneration policy as such, but does deal with their implications for and interactions with space and place.

### Converting rhetoric to reality

There is rarely one best answer for sustainability. The guide represents a staging post in a learning process. It cannot provide you with everything you need to know and makes no claim to infallibility. It tries to set out clearly the direction of change that is desirable, and the choices open to achieve it, allowing users to reach their own conclusions.

Equally, however, the guide attempts to distill the best knowledge and experience – from Europe and elsewhere, as well as the UK – and to synthesise diverse perspectives into coherent, integrated strategies for planning and design.

Its advice is generally consistent with government policy and has been prepared in consultation with a wide range of environmental, community and development agencies. If there is to be more than mere lip service paid to the goals of sustainable development and healthy communities, then this guide provides a challenge and a test.

*SYMBOLS USED IN THE GUIDE*

*SEE ALSO*

*BASIC PRINCIPLE*

*CASE STUDY*

| Scope of the guide | Chapters | 1 | 2 | 3 | 4 | 5 | 6 |
|---|---|---|---|---|---|---|---|
| *Theory* | Neighbourhood planning principles | ■ | | | | | □ |
| | Ecosystem approach | ■ | | | | □ | |
| *Processes* | Collaborative decision-making | □ | □ | ■ | | | |
| | Spatial planning frameworks | □ | □ | □ | □ | | ■ |
| | Design briefs and masterplans | | □ | ■ | | | □ |
| | Sustainability project appraisal | | ■ | | □ | □ | □ |
| | Urban capacity studies | | □ | | | | ■ |
| *Policies* | Housing and community issues | | □ | | ■ | | □ |
| | Local work and facilities | | □ | | ■ | | □ |
| | Planning for movement | | □ | | ■ | | □ |
| | Energy, water and other resources | | □ | | | ■ | □ |
| | Biodiversity | | □ | | | ■ | □ |
| | Mixed use and density | | □ | | □ | | ■ |
| | Green space and recreation | | □ | | □ | ■ | □ |
| | Detailed urban design | | □ | | □ | | ■ |

**Pathways to follow through the guide**

- **The contents pages** are designed for quick but precise pathfinding

- **The index** at the end of the book provides a finer topic net

- T**he community checklist** in Chapter 2 gives a summary of the contents and an entry point for neighbourhood planning

- **The investors' checklist** in Chapter 2 gives a summary of the contents and entry point project design and appraisal

- **Cross-referencing** is given linking one topic to another

- **Page layout** assists quick flicking through to find a section

- **Follow-up reading** is suggested in the side column and at the end

**The guide is relevant to ...**

- existing urban neighbourhoods
- market towns
- urban regeneration projects
- new urban extensions
- new settlements
- town and district centres

**... and is useful to**

- local authority planners and designers
- public and private sector service providers (e.g. health, education, energy, water)
- commercial developers, house builders and housing associations
- planning, environmental and design consultants
- district, parish and town councillors
- community and environmental groups

**The guide can help you with**

- defining what neighbourhoods are, or could be
- clarifying the full health and sustainability agenda
- working out a collaborative process for a Community Strategy
- preparing a spatial plan for an urban district or country town
- understanding the links between policy areas
- preparing development briefs and masterplans
- appraising the sustainability of development projects
- planning the natural ecology of settlements
- tackling problems of social exclusion, unhealthy lifestyles and mental illness
- reducing the impact of human settlements on climate change

# orientation
# and principles | chapter 1

## introduction

### 1.1   REINVENTING NEIGHBOURHOODS

 Neighbourhoods are the localities in which people live. They imply a sense of belonging and community, grounding our lives in a specific place. Aspirations for neighbourhoods are surprisingly consistent amongst people with very different lifestyles. We want neighbourhoods that are attractive, safe, healthy and unpolluted, with high-quality local facilities, access to green spaces, and excellent connections to other areas. We would like the opportunity for convivial social activity and friendship. There is a recognition that for some people – particularly the old and young, and those who are home-based throughout the day – the neighbourhood is vitally important for health and well-being.

#### MAKING PLACES THAT ARE HEALTHY, SAFE AND SUSTAINABLE

This guide is about enhancing the quality of neighbourhoods as places to live, work and play. It advocates an inclusive, environmentally responsible model of neighbourhoods:

- a socially balanced population, and varied housing opportunities which are suited to a range of incomes and types of household;
- diversity of use – housing, business, shopping, social, cultural and health facilities, offering easy accessibility, opportunity and choice for all;
- pedestrian, bicycle, public transport and road networks within the neighbourhood, linking to the wider city and region, creating a permeable and connected environment with real transport choice;
- a pedestrian-dominated public realm to facilitate healthy social life and provide an attractive, safe, human-scaled environment;
- ecologically responsive development principles consistent with social inclusion and cutting resource use and pollution;
- a greenspace network that provides accessible open space, with effective water, energy, wildlife and climate management;
- aesthetic identity that is rooted in the collective identity of the region, reflecting characteristics valued by the local community;

*Cross references: § denotes discussion in other sections as numbered*

# 1.1

■ a fine-grained neighbourhood, structured around public transport accessibility, with varied densities, providing opportunity for gradual renewal and adaptation to new needs;

■ the opportunity for active and frequent participation of all sectors of the population, commercial interests and voluntary groups in the planning and design of the area.

## RECOGNISING THE DIFFICULTIES

The reality is often rather different, and there is widespread concern about the future of neighbourhoods. High mobility and economic change have undermined the significance of locality in people's lives. Where once children played on the street and there was a close local community, people now travel out by car to disparate activities or rely on virtual connections. As a result, local shops and facilities cease to be viable. While the changes represent greater choice and opportunity for some, others find their lives impoverished. Our lifestyles have become less healthy at the same time as we are using resources in unsustainable ways and threatening the stability of global ecology.

### Public policy: sometimes part of the problem

These trends are in part the response of the market to perceived consumer preferences, but they have been reinforced by official policies for schools, hospitals and post offices that demote the significance of local accessibility. In addition, planning authorities in alliance with developers have been promoting single-use residential estates and business parks, at relatively low densities, which are innately car-dependent, land-hungry and polluting. The trends not only affect the quality of the environment, but also exacerbate problems of social exclusion, discourage exercise and restrict the potential for local economic activity. A linked problem is the sense people can have, particularly in run-down areas, of powerlessness to influence the decisions that are progressively degrading their own environment.

### Signs of hope

Suggestions of the death of neighbourhoods, however, are premature. Despite rising car dependence, 30 per cent of trips are still less than 1 mile, and most of those by foot. Even in outlying suburban estates with very high car ownership there is a perhaps surprising level of use of local facilities where they exist. And in some urban neighbourhoods the fabric of local community networks remains strong (Gilchrist 2000). In many areas, therefore, it is not a matter of recreating neighbourhoods from scratch, but reinforcing and building on current patterns of activity.

## NEIGHBOURHOOD RENAISSANCE

In this context, the recent shift in Government policy towards a more sustainable and locally responsive approach is immensely welcome. The planning of safe, convenient and attractive

*Neighbourhoods have been written off by sociologists for many years:*
*'Neighbourhood is a largely nostalgic idea having that flavour of ideological beatification.'*

NORMAN DENNIS 1968

*For further evidence about the use of local facilities see*

**4.8 Access to local facilities** ➔

neighbourhoods is seen as an essential part of the Government's sustainable development strategy, and a key to urban renaissance. It is also advocated as part of the UK public health strategy and the WHO Healthy Cities movement.

Yet local authorities (and the development industry) are finding it difficult to change tack. A new survey of neighbourhoods across Britain finds alarmingly few innovative schemes (McGill 2001). Change is hampered, particularly at the neighbourhood level, by the absence of integrated and coherent policy guidance, by the diverse perspectives of different stakeholders, including the local communities themselves, and by the dearth of local authority resources available for local planning.

The neighbourhoods of the future need to reflect cultural shifts and new technology. We cannot return to the (supposedly) cosy localism of the past. Rather, neighbourhoods will be open, varied, egalitarian and connected places – providing more choice, opportunity and beauty but without undesirable impacts on health and ecology.

### THE ROLE OF THIS GUIDE

This guide is designed to bridge the gap between rhetoric and action. It adopts a radical and challenging stance in terms of the search for effective neighbourhood strategies, taking health, sustainability and vitality as the touchstones of success. In terms of local decision-making the guide takes an inclusive approach, recognising that neighbourhood initiatives may stem from a range of sources including community groups, private investors and the local authority. Collaboration between local partners, leading to synergy in the design and management of the built environment, is a hallmark of sustainable development. The guide is concerned with reality, not vain hopes. It is about socially and economically feasible policies for commonplace, everyday neighbourhoods.

## 1.2 AIMS FOR NEIGHBOURHOOD PLANNING

The three basic goals of health, sustainability and vitality provide the starting points for planning and design:

### ▪ Health and quality of life

Health in this context is a state of physical, mental and social well-being. The physical environment of neighbourhoods affects health and well-being both directly, through the quality of housing and public space, and indirectly, through impact on behaviour and the sense of community. A key theme is the degree to which neighbourhoods provide for all groups – young and old, rich and poor.

### ▪ Environmental sustainability

The ecological footprint of settlements in terms of resource use and pollution is great, continues to grow in certain respects, and ought to be greatly diminished. There is local, neighbourhood, responsibility for the health of the global commons – climate, land, biodiversity. Planning sustainable neighbourhoods means reworking the development conventional of the recent past.

### ▪ Economic and civic vitality

Localities should not be mere dormitories. Their rejuvenation as healthy and sustainable neighbourhoods can only be achieved if there is the local will and energy. Part of the energy comes from the vitality of the local economy, investing in people and places; part comes from local political commitment, and effective partnerships between community, voluntary, public and private sectors.

## 1.2

### TWELVE KEY OBJECTIVES

There are at least twelve good reasons for the intentional planning of neighbourhoods. These provide the positive incentive for action. The range of interests represented means that it is possible to build a powerful coalition of public and political support. The list below is organised around social, economic and environmental perspectives.

| **Objectives** | | **Policy directions** |
|---|---|---|
| *Social* | | |
| 1 | to enhance local community | create opportunities for local social groups and networks |
| | | promote mental health through supportive social environments |
| | | strengthen social and cultural life |
| 2 | to increase equity | diversify housing opportunities and affordability |
| | | promote accessible local facilities |
| | | enhance movement options – especially walking, cycling and public transport |
| 3 | to promote healthy living | improve local air quality |
| | | encourage an active life-style (e.g. walking, sport) |
| | | facilitate access to local fresh fruit and vegetables |
| 4 | to improve safety and security | reduce the chance of accidents |
| | | reduce the likelihood (and fear) of street violence |
| | | encourage a sense of ownership and belonging |
| 5 | to enhance freedom of choice | diversify opportunities for local facilities, work and social contact |
| | | open up life-style and movement options |
| 6 | to increase local decision-making | build local social capital through the participatory process |
| | | create local partnerships and trusts |
| | | increase user control of local systems |
| *Economic* | | |
| 7 | to promote wealth creation | diversify local entrepreneurial opportunities |
| | | recycle financial resources locally |
| | | promote urban regeneration and renewal |
| 8 | to promote employment | ensure diverse local employment opportunities |
| | | enhance further education and training opportunities |
| | | ensure good public transport, walking and cycling connections to the wider area |
| *Environmental* | | |
| 9 | to enhance environmental quality | create an attractive public realm |
| | | promote local distinctiveness and value local heritage |
| | | reduce noise and vandalism |
| | | create robust, adaptable and high-quality buildings |
| 10 | to promote wildlife and open country | enhance habitat diversity within the neighbourhood |
| | | realise urban 'brownfield' potential thus reducing countryside loss |
| 11 | to safeguard natural resources | manage water resources sustainably |
| | | reduce demand for non-renewable resources |
| | | close local resource loops (re-use and recycling) |
| 12 | to cut greenhouse gas emissions | increase energy-efficiency of buildings |
| | | promote renewables and combined heat and power |
| | | reduce car reliance and the need to travel |

# the policy context

## 1.3 PROMOTING SUSTAINABLE DEVELOPMENT

The apparently divergent objectives set out above can be seen in the context of the integrating principle of sustainable development. Sustainable development is the watchword for UK planning policy – advocated by the National Sustainability Strategy (DETR 1998b); promoted by opinion-formers such as the Royal Commission on Environmental Pollution; actively encouraged through a series of PPGs and white papers. The Local Government Act (2000) further strengthens this commitment by giving local authorities the explicit power to promote or improve economic, social and environmental well-being.

### DEFINING SUSTAINABLE DEVELOPMENT

Despite over-exposure, and the consequent danger of the phrase losing resonance, sustainable development remains a valid and challenging goal for planning. It is often, wrongly, pigeonholed as a purely environmental goal, and therefore sidelined by those who have an economic or social agenda. But the classic Brundtland definition (see side column) makes clear that the focus is on people – on equity for current and for future generations. In this context, 'development' is concerned not only with economic success but also health, social inclusion, quality of life, quality of environment.

The Government's view of what is sustainable development has been clarified by the 1999 Opportunities for Change document. There are four broad objectives, and sustainable development means achieving all of them together:

- Maintenance of high and stable levels of economic growth and employment.
- Social progress that recognises the needs of everyone.
- Effective protection of the environment.
- Prudent use of natural resources.

Sustainable development is therefore about maintaining and enhancing the quality of human life – social, economic and environmental – while living within the carrying capacity of supporting ecosystems and the resource base.

### The need for an integrated approach

The biggest problem in interpreting such principles into practice is no longer, arguably, political will. It is the fragmented nature of knowledge and practice. Responsibility for different facets of local life – economy development, health, housing, environmental quality, planning, energy, social development, biodiversity – is divided between a host of public, private and voluntary agencies. The challenge is to make sense of these disparate elements. The government strategy is therefore to promote effective co-operation between the varied 'stakeholders' in any area, seeking for strength in diversity.

*Planning policy*

*This guide cites English Planning Policy Guidance notes (PPGs) throughout. There are equivalent 'National Planning Policy Guidance' notes in Scotland, 'Planning Policy Statements' in Northern Ireland, and 'Planning Evidence: Planning Policy' (1999) in Wales.*

*See websites in Sources*

*The Brundtland definition of sustainable development*

*'Sustainable development is development which meets the needs of the present generation without compromising the ability of future generations to meet their own needs.' (WCED 1987)*

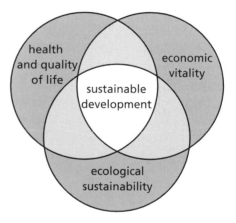

*Figure 1.1*
*Searching for sustainable development*

*The trefoil diagram does not imply a weak trade-off between social, economic and environmental priorities, but the need to find solutions that marry all three*

PLANNING POLICY AND RENEWAL

# 1.3

*Creating a better future*

*An example of the aims of a Community Strategy from Havant Borough Council:*

*Overiding aim: 'to improve the quality of life now and for the future in ways that do not cause irreversible harm to the environment'*

- *making a safer community*
- *strengthening our economy*
- *improving educational attainment and lifelong learning*
- *enhancing our environment*
- *promoting a healthier community*
- *promoting social wellbeing*
- *working to engage young people.*

*Official advocacy for neighbourhoods*

*DETR 1998c: Planning for Sustainable Development*
- *Promoting urban villages*
- *Pedestrian-based neighbourhoods*
- *ixed use and mixed tenure*
- *Density sufficient to support local facilities*
- *Community involvement*
- *A strong sense of place*

*Urban Task Force DETR 1999i: Towards an Urban Renaissance*
- *Promotes neighbourhoods 5,000–10,000 population*
- *District local catchment areas 400/500 m radius*
- *Gross densities of 150 people per ha*

*English Partnerships and Housing Corporation 2000: Urban Design Compendium*
- *Walkable neighbourhood units*
- *Distinctive local identities*
- *Permeable grid-based layouts*
- *Perimeter block development*
- *Graded densities*

## LOCAL AGENDA 21 AND COMMUNITY STRATEGIES

The Local Agenda 21 (LA21) initiative has been running since 1993 and seeks to encourage local authorities to develop collaborative programmes for sustainable development involving stakeholders from private, voluntary and private sectors. For some local authorities the emphasis has been on the neighbourhood or local community level, but often without effective participation by the agencies (such as the education department, the housing department, large local employers) who have a major influence on the locality.

### Local Strategic Partnerships

The new obligation – under the Local Government Act 2000 (England and Wales) – to form Local Strategic Partnerships (LSPs), is set to replace or transform LA21 and should make co-ordination much more effective. LSPs bring together at local level the various parts of the public sector as well as private, voluntary and community sectors so that diverse initiatives and services can be designed to support rather than contradict each other.

Each LSP has to produce a *Community Strategy*. This establishes a long term vision for the area, specific goals/priorities and an agreed action plan. The Office of the Deputy Prime Minister, (formerly the DTLR) sees the active involvement of neighbourhood and community groups as vital to ensure that diverse local needs and aspirations are recognised (DTLR 2001). Community strategies can thus provide a very helpful integrated policy framework for neighbourhood initiatives.

### Local spatial strategies

The *development plan* is, of course, the key document setting local authority policy for the physical evolution of settlements. The Community Strategy and the development plan have to be consistent with each other. Any neighbourhood level plans will need to be adopted by the local authority as supplementary planning guidance if they are to be effective.

A radical rethink of the form of development plans is underway (2002). The idea of a *local spatial development strategy* is to broaden local planning policy to incorporate transport, health and education agencies and work holistically towards sustainable development (Local Government Association 2000). It thus could provide the physical dimension of the Community Strategy. Neighbourhood level spatial frameworks could rest within the local authority-wide strategy.

## 1.4 PLANNING POLICY AND NEIGHBOURHOOD RENEWAL

Since 1997, UK government rhetoric and policy guidance in support of neighbourhoods has intensified. There are at least three important strands of advice:

### PLANNING POLICY GUIDANCE

The DETR's publication *Planning for Sustainable Development* (1998) set the agenda for a series of reviews of PPGs that could influence the character of localities, through the medium of
development plans. Some of the key themes emerging are:

- Enhancing the quality of the local environment – distinctive local character and sense of place (PPG1).

- Reducing the need to travel by promoting local facilities clustered around public transport nodes, and designing streets for pedestrians and cyclists (PPG13).

- Making best use of existing resources of urban land and buildings and thus regenerating decaying localities (PPG3).

- Reducing the stimulus to car use by rationing parking in housing and commercial/institutional developments (PPG3).

- Reviving rural market towns, by encouraging more local service provision and diversification of local economies (PPG7).

Many of these themes are given added impetus by the Urban Task Force report (1999) *Towards an Urban Renaissance*, which sets them in the context of urban regeneration, and the Rural and Urban White Papers (DETR 2000b and c).

### NEIGHBOURHOOD RENEWAL

The new policy for neighbourhood renewal, articulated in the National Strategy for Neighbourhood Renewal (SEU 2000 and 2001), is mainly concerned with the 'joined-up' delivery of public services in deprived neighbourhoods. The big changes from earlier schemes are:

- the emphasis on all localities in need of renewal, not just the most desperate; and

- the move to an integrated, unified approach involving public, private, voluntary and community sectors.

Local Neighbourhood Renewal Strategies (which should link with the Community Strategy) will set out a programme of action supported by all the key stakeholders in the LSP.

The policy is likely to have significant implications for physical change as well as for public services within certain neighbouhoods. Not only could it shape the pattern of facility provision in a more coherent way, but also it is targeted at housing improvement and the regeneration of hard-to-let or abandoned housing areas. The New Deal offers special project funding, and Neighbourhood Management can provide an integrated approach. Having said that, there is sometimes a policy divide between the service providers and the planners – a divide that this guide can help to bridge.

### Health Improvement Programmes

*Health Improvement Programmes (HImPs) are a vehicle for continually reviewing and improving local health and health services. Led by the local health authority, the HImP process seeks to involve a wide range of partners, including local authorities, in addition to the primary care organisations and NHS trusts.*

*In theory, but not yet seen in practice, the HImP process can be used to develop healthier neighbourhoods. The ideas and issues contained in this publication could be brought into the HImP process by the inclusion of local authority planning officers in the process. This could be facilitated by making the link between Local Authority community strategies and the local HImP.*

### Best Value

*'Best Value requires local authorities to make the best use of resources, obtain value for money, avoid waste and consider whether services meet the requirements of local communities.' (DETR 1999)*

*The 'key drivers' in Best Value include*

- *the use of performance indicators*
- *standards and targets*
- *public consultation.*

*NB: It currently (2001) only applies in England*

### Defining health

*'Health is not only the absence of disease but a state of physical, mental and social well-being. The enjoyment of the highest attainable standard of health is one of the fundamental rights of every human being, without distinction of race, religion, political belief, or economic and social conditions.' (WHO 1946)*

## PROMOTING PUBLIC HEALTH

Health Authorities are increasingly working in partnership with local authorities, both in service delivery and health promotion. But the broader view of health promulgated by the World Health Organization (WHO), and by the UK Government in the White Paper Our Healthier Nation (DHSS 1999), emphasises that public health is not just a matter of hospitals and health centres: amongst other influences, the planning/design of neighbourhoods has a vital role. Combating heart disease, respiratory problems and mental illness, for example, relies on factors such as healthy exercise, air quality, fresh food and local social networks, all of which are influenced by the physical nature of localities.

## BEST VALUE DRIVER

The wide spectrum of official support for the planning of healthy and sustainable neighbourhoods remains largely in the realms of rhetoric (McGill 2001). But the mood is changing. The introduction of Best Value into local authority decision-making could be a powerful motor. Best Value replaced Compulsory Competition Tendering in April 2001 and means that instead of going for the cheapest option, authorities should be looking for quality – value for money. In that frame of mind they may be motivated to pursue the cross-cutting agenda of sustainable development and be more responsive to neighbourhood-level initiatives. The Community Strategy could be the vehicle for co-ordinated policy-making and management.

## 1.5  HEALTHY CITIES

The UK's commitment to local sustainable development is reinforced internationally by a wide range of UN and EU policies and programmes. One of particular relevance to this guide is the WHO Healthy Cities programme, which provides a model for an integrated approach to neighbourhoods. Launched in 1988, the programme has grown from a handful of cities to a movement of over 1,000 cities and towns in 29 European countries (and more globally). Healthy Cities is about changing the ways in which individuals, communities, private and voluntary organisations and local authorities think about and make decisions about health. It seeks to improve the physical, mental, social and environmental well-being of people living in urban areas.

## TOP-DOWN AND BOTTOM-UP PROCESSES

Healthy Cities emphasises the need to take a strategic approach, with explicit political commitment at the highest level of the municipality, and co-ordinated programmes across different departments and agencies. But there is also the understanding that 'top-down' commitment must be matched by the active involvement of local groups in decision-making and implementation if the initiatives are to be productive. Neighbourhood-level projects are central to Healthy City programmes and demonstrate the potential of the integrated community approach.

## INTEGRATING HEALTH AND URBAN PLANNING

The concept of 'healthy urban planning' is being promoted by WHO to draw attention to the need for planners, public health professionals and others to work together to plan places that foster health and well-being. The Healthy Cities principles of equity, intersectoral co-operation, community involvement and sustainability underpin the idea of healthy urban planning.

The initiative is gaining momentum in Europe. In 2000 a book entitled Healthy Urban Planning was published on behalf of WHO, and provides an introduction to many of the issues explored in this guide. Subsequently a group of twelve cities across Europe has formed to elaborate the concept in terms of practical programmes at the neighbourhood and city-wide levels.

## HEALTH AS THE TOUCHSTONE FOR SUSTAINABILITY

The principle of health can provide common ground, to draw different interests into support for sustainable development at the neighbourhood level – a core value everyone can 'buy into'. It also helps tie the human purpose of neighbourhoods with the ecosystem approach:

- the health and wellbeing of individuals
- the health of the local community
- the health of the local economy
- the health of the local environment
- the health of the bioregion
- the health impact of the neighbourhood on the wider world.

A healthy neighbourhood, with equity of access to housing, work, local facilities, good food, green environment, safe streets, exercise and diverse social opportunities, together with a concern for the well-being of future generations, is likely to be a sustainable neighbourhood.

*Determinants of health*

| Social and economic | Environmental | Life-style | Access to services |
|---|---|---|---|
| Employment | Air quality | Physical activity | Education |
| Social inclusion | Housing | Diet | Health services |
| Social capital | Water quality | | Leisure facilities |
| | | | Transport |

*Figure 1.2*
**The influence of the spatial environment on health**

*SOURCE: BASED ON DHSS 1999*

# 1.6

*Advocates of the ecosystem approach to settlements*

*McLoughlin (1968) Urban and Regional Planning: A Systems Approach*

*Odum (1971) Environment, Power and Society*

*Barton, Davis and Guise (1995) Sustainable Settlements*

*EU Expert Group on the Urban Environment (1995) European Sustainable Cities*

*Hough (1995) Cities and Natural Processes*

*Tjallingii (1995) Ecopolis: Strategies for Ecologically Sound Urban Development*

# the neighbourhood as habitat

## 1.6  THE ECOSYSTEM APPROACH

The ecosystem approach provides a coherent philosophy to underpin the principle of planning for health and sustainability. The neighbourhood is an ecosystem in the sense that it is the essential local habitat for humans, providing not only shelter but also a network of social support and opportunities for a wide range of leisure, cultural and economic activities. It is also a natural habitat, where humans and other species live in a symbiotic relationship. Physical systems – part natural, part constructed – control energy and water flows, affect soil and air quality, and influence climate.

The idea of the settlement as ecosystem has a long heredity. Plato used the idea (if not the phrase) with remarkable insight when describing the decline of Greek settlements in the fourth century BC (Critias). In the modern era, Ebenezer Howard's Garden City of Tomorrow was essentially based on an ecosystem model, relating the town to the land.

*Figure 1.3*
**The settlement as an ecosystem**

SOURCE: FOREST OF DEAN 1998

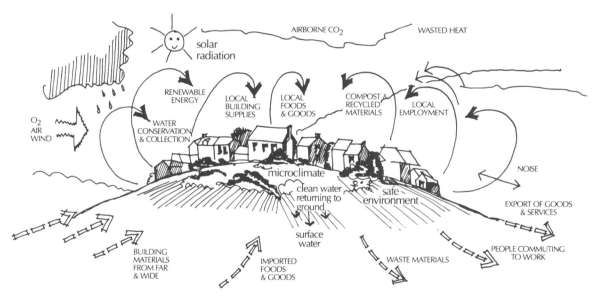

## ECOLOGICAL NICHE AND SYMBIOSIS

The neighbourhood can function as a complex ecosystem in supporting a diversity of ecological niches within the locality for different groups and activities that are living more or less in harmony with each other.

It is important to recognise the diverse needs in a locality – different ages and life stages, different income levels, varied ethnic, household and family groupings, different cultures, lifestyles and levels of mobility – and to encompass not only the needs of residents but workers, providers, visitors, those running businesses and those just passing through. There is no such person as an 'average' neighbourhood user. Rather, there are many people with specific demands: the kids playing on the waste ground, the people drinking in their local, the elderly couple next door.

People are responsible for satisfying their own needs, but the spatial design of the neighbourhood can either support this self-reliance or restrict and frustrate it. So a key principle of neighbourhood planning is to open up choice, providing a congenial and sustainable habitat for everyone, while protecting it from destructive forces.

## THE NEIGHBOURHOOD ECOSYSTEM MODEL

 For this guide we have developed a new conceptual model of the neighbourhood, which integrates the ecosystem approach (with its emphasis on the bio-physical environment) with the social focus of health and well-being. The model carefully distinguishes between human society (spheres 1, 2 and 3) and the human habitat (spheres 4 and 5). It encourages analysis of the impact of one sphere on another – a constant reminder of the importance of each layer of reality.

## THE USE OF THE MODEL

The model can be used for quite specific processes of analysis or evaluation. Different spheres can be taken as the starting point depending on the issue being examined. For example:

### Sphere 1: Analysing health impact

In line with Brundtland's definition of sustainable development (see p. 5), the model has people at its heart (sphere 1). Each of the outer layers (2–5) have an impact on people's health and well-being, as illustrated by Figure 1.5. The model helps to structure the analysis and ensure a consistent approach.

### Sphere 2: Analysing factors affecting 'social capital'

A later chapter discusses the important of community networks and local social groups (see Section 4.3). Whether or not a local community can be said to exist depends not only on individual and household choices but the degree to which people meet in local schools, shops, pubs and clubs, enjoy chatting on the street, feel at home in the neighbourhood.

### Sphere 3: Analysing the needs of an activity

Local activities (or the absence of activity in a dormitory settlement) help define the nature of a neighbourhood. It is instructive to take an activity defined as a problem (such as young people loafing about) and assess what kinds of places can provide for it most appropriately; or to take an activity conspicuous by its absence (children cycling to school, for example) and assess the social, educational and physical changes that might be needed to effect change.

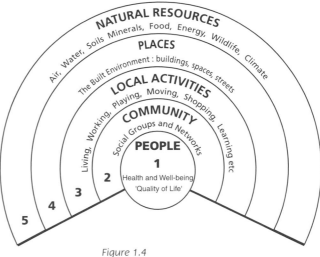

*Figure 1.4*
**Ecosystem model of a neighbourhood**

*This model is adapted from models on the determinants of health by Whitehead and Dahglen (1991) and on neighbourhoods by Barton (2001). It provides an integrating motif for the guide.*

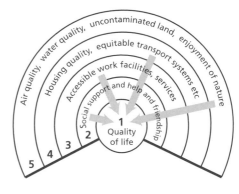

*Figure 1.5*
**The neighbourhood determinants of health**

# 1.6

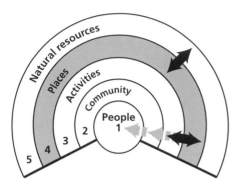

*Figure 1.6*
**The influence of physical planning**

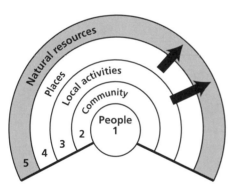

*Figure 1.7*
**The impact of activities and the built environment on the neighbourhood ecological footprint**

### Sphere 4: Analysing the impact of development projects

This is the most important use of the model in the context of this guide. The model gives a clear agenda for evaluating planning policies and specific development projects:

- What natural resources (energy, land, water, materials) does it use, and what resources (such as air quality and biodiversity) does it impact on?

- How will it directly or indirectly affect the character and function of the place?

- What local activities will it provide for or affect (including its impact on transport?)

- How is it likely to affect community groups/networks by either direct physical change or by impact on activities?

- How, in the light of these other impacts, is it likely to affect the health and quality of life of people?

### Sphere 5: Analysing the ecological footprint of a neighbourhood or town

The outermost sphere constitutes the natural environment, which provides essential life-support functions for the people of the neighbourhood. As Figure 1.7 suggests, it is not so much the number of people, but the activities they indulge in and the character of the buildings and streets that impact on the sustainability of those life-support systems. For example, local air quality is affected by traffic, heating systems and industrial activity. The model reminds us of our dependence on the biophysical environment.

## IN SUMMARY

The health of the neighbourhood as ecosystem is measured by the degree to which it sustains:

- a good quality of life and environment for everyone

- vital and viable services and economic processes

- the carrying capacity of the supporting natural systems and resources.

The model of the settlement/neighbourhood as habitat can help establish common ground, a context within which specific interests can be placed, and assess the overall health of the neighbourhood.

## 1.7  NEIGHBOURHOOD DESIGN PRINCIPLES

### THE NEED FOR ROBUST PRINCIPLES

The neighbourhood objectives presented earlier in this chapter (1.2) set up formidable aspirations for neighbourhood planning and design. In themselves, the objectives are difficult to argue with, but many people would see great tension between them – they would seem to be difficult or impossible to achieve all at the same time.

Equivalently, the ecosystem philosophy presented above (1.6) may seem admirable in theory, providing a holistic and integrated approach, but difficult to interpret in practice. Some would even question its relevance.

It is for these reasons that we believe it is important to try to identify robust principles of spatial planning and design that cut right across the divergent objectives and demonstrate the practicality of the ecosystem approach. We have identified six such principles that seem to stand every test we have subjected them to. They underpin the detailed advice given in the guide.

*Neighbourhood design principles*

1  *Stakeholder involvement*

2  *Increasing local autonomy*

3  *Connectivity*

4  *Diversity*

5  *Response to place*

6  *Adaptability: the life-time neighbourhood*

| OBJECTIVES | DESIGN PRINCIPLES | | | | | |
|---|---|---|---|---|---|---|
| | Stakeholder involvement | Increase local autonomy | Connectivity | Diversity | Response to place | Adaptability |
| **Social** | | | | | | |
| 1. Community | ● | ● | ○ | ○ | ○ | ○ |
| 2. Equity | ○ | ○ | ○ | ● | | |
| 3. Healthy living | ○ | ● | ● | ○ | | |
| 4. Safety/security | ○ | | ● | ○ | | ○ |
| 5. Choice | ○ | ● | ● | ● | ○ | ○ |
| 6. Local decision making | ● | ● | ○ | | ● | ● |
| **Economics** | | | | | | |
| 7. Wealth creation | ○ | ○ | ● | ○ | | ○ |
| 8. Employment | ○ | ● | ● | ○ | | ○ |
| **Environmental** | | | | | | |
| 9. Environmental quality | ○ | | | ● | ● | ○ |
| 10. Wildlife and countryside | ○ | | ○ | ● | ● | |
| 11. Natural resources | ○ | ● | | | ● | ● |
| 12. Greenhouse gases | ○ | ● | ○ | ○ | | |

*Figure 1.8*

**Matrix of design principles and objectives**

*Note the degree to which each principle helps to achieve many objectives.*

*The objectives are those from Section 1.2.*

## 1.7

*'Local authorities
should develop a
shared vision with
their local
communities'*

*PPG3 (DETR 2000)*

### 1  STAKEHOLDER INVOLVEMENT

The active involvement of all the locally relevant interests in the process of decision-making is widely recognised as essential if sustainable development is to be achieved in a pluralist society. One objective is to gain the backing of all stakeholders for a consistent and integrated programme; another is to build the capacity of the community (particularly less vocal segments) to take action.

Mechanisms need to be developed which ensure that all the main stakeholders (public, private, and community sectors) are consulted and involved when their interests are at stake. Inclusive processes aim to achieve mutual knowledge and understanding along with opportunities for collaboration and joint projects. These mechanisms have to be adaptable to different circumstances, such as community-led initiatives, major development projects, and the preparation of local plans. (See Chapter 3.)

### 2  INCREASING LOCAL AUTONOMY

The principle of increasing the degree to which localities provide for themselves runs counter to powerful trends but is key to the achievement of many of the objectives – supporting accessible employment, choice of local facilities, the opportunity for healthy exercise and the development of local community networks. At the same time, it can lead to reduced pollution and reduced need for the import of energy, water and materials.

The basic principle is that services/activities should be managed at the lowest feasible level. In some spheres that may mean changed practices at the level of the individual building – for example, in relation to energy efficiency. In others the home-patch or housing cluster is a practical level – say for toddler playspace, or water-demand management. The neighbourhood provides the appropriate level for primary schooling, local park, shops and pubs, while the township can satisfy services requiring higher population thresholds – such as library and leisure centre.  *§ 4.8–4.13; Ch.5*

### 3  CONNECTIVITY

Supporting greater local autonomy does not imply isolation of one neighbourhood from another. On the contrary, connectedness between as well as within localities is essential for vitality, viability and choice. Rather than a fragmented, agency-by-agency pattern of provision it is the links between activities and between places that help ensure their success. The principle of connectivity applies across many areas of policy:

▓ the management of resources (see Figure 1.9)  *§ 5.2*

▓ the provision of retail, social and leisure facilities  *§ 4.9*

▓ the permeability of the street network  *§ 4.15*

▓ the interdependence of adjacent neighbourhoods  *§ 6.12*

▓ the network of wildlife and water corridors.  *§ 6.9*

### 4  DIVERSITY

The principle of diversity is in response to the failures of conformity. The tendency has been to seek economies of scale in the process of urban development, and segregate uses to safeguard environmental quality. The result has been zoning strategies that create huge single-use, single-class estates, with local employment opportunities squeezed out, social polarisation and exclusion rife, and visual monotony.

The solution is to value diversity over conformity – and apply the principle of reasonable diversity to most aspects of neighbourhood planning:

- diversity of housing type and tenure (social inclusion) *§ 4.4*

- diversity of local work and service opportunities *§ 4.6, 4.8*

- diversity of modes of movement (choice) *§ 4.14*

- wildlife habitat diversity *§ 5.17*

- variety of aesthetic character. *§ 6.2*

Reasonable diversity across a neighbourhood does not exclude small-scale homogeneity or imply that 'bad neighbour' uses should be allowed.

## 5   RESPONSE TO PLACE

A central facet of connectivity is connection to place. The ecosystem approach requires recognition of, and response to, the unique heritage of each locality: its location, resource base and cultural landscape. but what we have had too often has been the application of standard development solutions irrespective of the ecological and cultural characteristics of the place concerned. This can lead to resource inefficiency, characterlessness and functional isolation. Rather, we should:

- capitalise on the specific environmental resources (e.g. streams, woods, slopes) *§ 6.9, 5.5, 5.19*

- build new developments to reflect the best of what is already there, cultivating 'local distinctiveness' *§ 6.2*

- judge development policy according to the area's location, links and character. *§ 6.11, 6.12*

## 6   ADAPTABILITY: THE LIFE-TIME NEIGHBOURHOOD

Neighbourhoods, like wildlife habitats, are not fixed and unchanging. People come and go; initiatives are born, grow, mature, and die; buildings are extended, used for different purposes, redeveloped. The human habitat has to adapt to changing conditions or decay. The aspiration for every neighbourhood is that it should evolve steadily and 'naturally', at an unforced rate, providing a healthy, convivial environment for residents and users at all stages. In terms of planning and design this means:

- adaptable building forms (designed for varied uses) *§ 6.15*

- extendable buildings, adaptable streets *§ 6.16*

- encouraging gradual renewal *§ 6.4*

- evolving heritage, not mothballing it *§ 6.3*

- keeping transport options open *§ 4.14*

- making space available for next-generation households and businesses

- avoiding fixed edges and barriers.

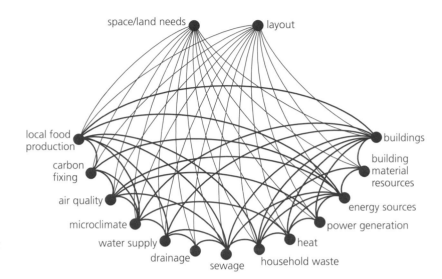

*Figure 1.9*
**The interplay of resource management and spatial planning**

SOURCE: BARTON ET AL. 2000

# the neighbourhood in focus

**1.8 DEFINING NEIGHBOURHOODS**

### NO EASY ANSWER

There is no generally accepted basis for defining neighbourhoods. If a local authority or a community forum wishes to identify different urban localities for purposes of public debate and planning then they will first need to agree the criteria.

Neighbourhoods may be defined:

- **administratively**: by ward or parish boundaries
- **aesthetically**: by distinctive character or age of development
- **socially**: by the perceptions of local residents
- **functionally**: by catchment areas for local services; and/or
- **environmentally**: as traffic-calmed areas where through traffic is excluded and the quality/safety of the living environment is paramount.

Given these varied interpretations, it is vital for stakeholders to agree the main purposes of the neighbourhood exercise before defining areas on the ground. At the end of this chapter we suggest a consistent categorisation, which is then used in the rest of the guide.

### ALTERNATIVE CRITERIA (AS LISTED ABOVE)

**1    Administrative convenience**

Using existing ward or parish boundaries is a pragmatic, simple way of defining localities. It has the advantage of tying into local democratic processes and thereby clarifying political responsibility. The local ward councillors, the parish or town councils are given clear obligations and added legitimacy.

Wards and parishes are also the units for census analysis and 'state-of-the-environment' or 'quality-of-life' reports. Assessing problems, measuring progress and comparing different areas thus becomes relatively straightforward.

The major disadvantage with reliance on administrative boundaries is that they may be historical accidents unrelated to people's own perceptions, functional linkages or aesthetic character. If so, then reliance on them can compromise both the level of public involvement and practical value.

**2    Areas of distinctive character**

These may be defined by analysis of maps and aerial photographs supplemented by personal knowledge. Typically age and dominant building form give the distinctive character: for example,

*It is sometimes difficult to see where neighbourhoods start and stop*

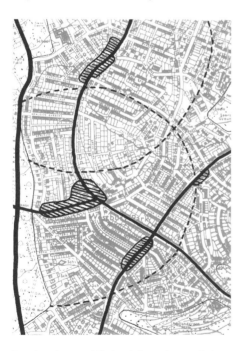

*Local centres and their catchment areas help articulate form*

Figure 1.10
**Defining neighbourhoods**

Edwardian terraces or late-twentieth-century estates. Such areas may not conform at all to social or functional definition of neighbourhoods – in smaller settlements and inner cities they may be quite small – but they can be valuable for analysis of physical change and urban capacity (see Chapter 6).

### 3    Residents' perceptions

Social surveys and/or community workshops can be used to find out what the people living in an area perceive as their own neighbourhood. The Ipswich study shown here (undertaken as part of the city expansion project) illustrates a surprising degree of resident consensus. While residents had varying views about neighbourhood size, the boundaries they chose provide a strong pattern, often following barriers formed by rivers, railways, main roads and open space. For the most part the perceived neighbourhoods were not centred on local shops and facilities. Rather they were bounded by them, because retailing was concentrated along main roads. Local centres can thus be the place where people from different neighbourhoods mingle.

### 4    Local catchments

The conventional image of a neighbourhood – derived from many new estates and new towns – is that of a local catchment area, with residential areas grouped around a local service centre or primary school. The Harlow plans illustrate this principle at the township scale, shaping the pattern of the settlement.

Catchments may be identified empirically by pedestrian surveys and time/distance mapping. One study has coined the term 'ped-shed' (like 'watershed') for the area within a 5- or 10-minute walk of the local centre (Llewelyn Davies 1998). Such ped-sheds are not normally the same as perceptual neighbourhoods. But they do offer a useful analysis, and a prompt for action where barriers or cul-de-sac layouts impede accessibility.

### 5    Traffic-calmed areas

These are areas where the local quality of environment takes precedence over the needs of traffic – similar to Buchanan's 'environmental' areas. According to Buchanan et al. (1963) traffic flows in such areas should not exceed 300 passenger car units an hour. Government advises maximum traffic speeds of 20 mph. These targets can be achieved by the careful planning of road hierarchies and traffic management. Traffic-calmed areas may approximate to perceived neighbourhoods, but not normally to catchments. The Ipswich planners used the residents' views of neighbourhood boundaries, which often followed main roads, to define environmental neighbourhoods used in traffic planning.

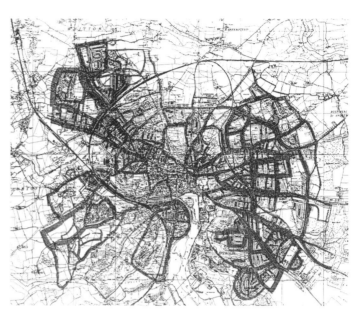

*Figure 1.11*
**Ipswich: Residents' perceived neighbourhoods**

*Note: thickness of line denotes the frequency of mention by residents*

SOURCE: SHANKLAND, COX AND ASSOCIATES 1968

*Figure 1.12*
**Ipswich: Neighbourhoods delineated by planners on the basis of the survey of residents**

SOURCE: SHANKLAND, COX AND ASSOCIATES 1968

# 1.9

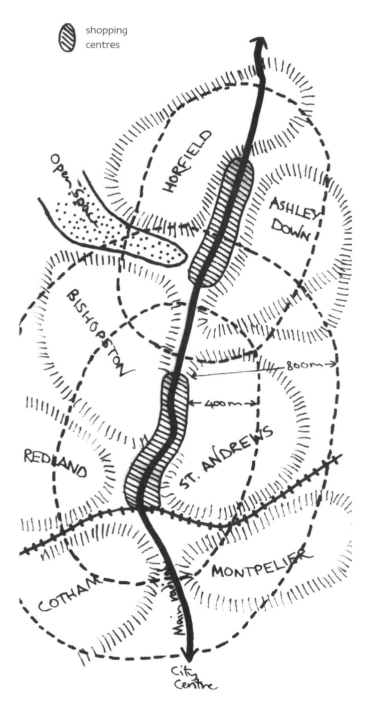

shopping
centres

*Figure 1.13*
**Named city neighbourhoods are not the
same as catchment areas**

In this guide we adopt criterion 3 (i.e. neighbourhoods defined primarily by the perceptions of residents), but complement that with larger catchment neighbourhoods which we call townships (see next sections).

## NEIGHBOURHOOD AND COMMUNITY

There are seeds of confusion in the way these two terms are used: they are not interchangeable, as neighbourhood is about place while community is about people. The neighbourhood, in terms of its streets, houses, facilities and greenspaces, may be consciously planned. Communities – in the sense of networks of mutual support and friendship – cannot be planned in the same way, but occur through people's choices and actions. Most communities are based around shared interest or identity rather than closeness. Many communities of interest (to do with work, education, leisure pursuits or politics) are spatially wide-flung, though most still have a specific local base somewhere. With high mobility, individual life-style choice and 'virtual' meetings, propinquity is not a prerequisite for community.

None the less, the locality still provides the focus for a number of overlapping interest communities and activities – children in school, scouts and guides, baby-sitting circles, surgeries, local shops, pubs, allotments, churches. Together with casual meetings in the street, these create the sense of a diverse, evolving local community. The opportunity for such communities to flourish is profoundly affected by public policy and design – for example through the provision of local facilities and the perceived safety of the streets. The existence of such communities is important for health and well-being, particularly amongst young families, retired people, and those out of work (for full discussion see Barton *et al.* 2000, particularly Chapters 1 and 9).

### 1.9   NEIGHBOURHOOD FORM

A clear and realistic view of neighbourhood form and function is a prerequisite for the effective planning of development so as to promote health, equity and sustainability. Central to such a view is the recognition that neighbourhoods are not separate units but interconnected parts of the urban continuum.

Neighbourhoods come in many shapes and sizes. There is an illuminating distinction to be drawn between old and new settlements. In many ways, traditional town patterns are working better than more recent models; the key variable is the degree of separation or integration.

## INTERCONNECTED NEIGHBOURHOODS

### Characteristics (see Figure 1.12)

- Typically older areas of mixed-use development.

- Often no clear boundaries between neighbourhoods, with one area blending seamlessly into another in a rather fuzzy pattern.

- Local centres normally in the form of 'high streets' along the main distributor road, acting as the meeting place between adjacent neighbourhoods.

- Bus routes and pedestrian/bike/car movement focused on these high streets, creating a congested but bustling atmosphere.

- Development generally at medium to high density, with some lower-density enclaves where infill has occurred in the last 80 years.

- Often socially quite mixed, reflecting diversity of housing stock.

- A general pattern of mixed use, with a wide range of services, some local offices and industries, though tending to become more zoned as 'non-conforming' uses are planned out.

### Advantages

- excellent level of local services

- flexible hinterland size according to different/changing commercial and institutional needs

- good connections for all modes of transport

- good potential for local community development because high level of local activity

- efficient use of land

- a reasonable choice of residential/commercial accommodation.

### Disadvantages

- congestion and pollution by traffic along main streets

- risk of blighted properties where fronting too close to heavy traffic

- risk of 'bad neighbour' uses

- small yards/gardens and a lack of open space in some areas.

## THE NEIGHBOURHOOD AS CELL

### Characteristics

- typically planned in the middle to late twentieth century in some new towns and suburban estates

- principle of semi-autonomous inward-looking neighbourhood unit

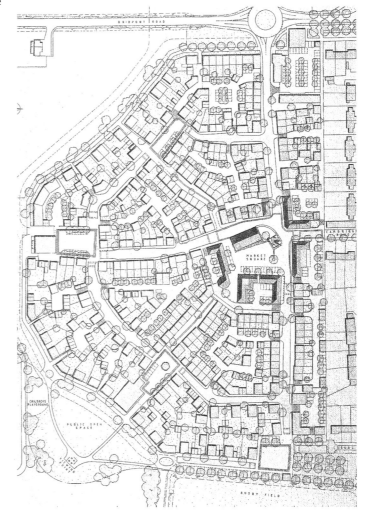

*Figure 1.14*
**Closed cell pattern illustrated at Poundbury, Dorset**

# 1.9

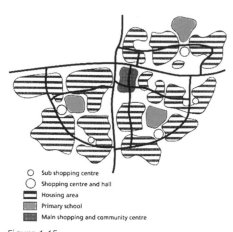

○ Sub shopping centre
◯ Shopping centre and hall
▤ Housing area
▨ Primary school
▦ Main shopping and community centre

*Figure 1.15*

**Harlow: neighbourhoods clustered around the district shopping centre**

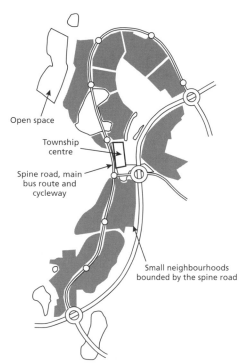

Open space

Township centre

Spine road, main bus route and cycleway

Small neighbourhoods bounded by the spine road

Total township population is about 30 000

*Figure 1.16*

**Linear concentration in Peterborough**

*For strategies implementing linear principles and for information on ways to overcome the disadvantages of the cell model see*

6.7 The spatial framework →

6.8 Renewal strategies →

- curvilinear or hierarchical road patterns of a cul-de-sac type, offering limited connections to surrounding areas, with no through roads

- neighbourhood centres as the nucleus of the cell

- low to medium densities with buildings all of similar age

- a zoned pattern of land use, with limited social variation.

## Advantages

- easily identifiable neighbourhoods

- simple to plan and build because few connections

- potential for a relatively traffic-calmed environment

- fits the neighbourhood into the hierarchy of road planning.

## Disadvantages

- poor connectivity to surrounding neighbourhoods

- fixed catchment over, too small to allow some facilities to succeed, and inflexible in conditions of changing commercial/institutional needs

- lack of visibility of local facilities to passing trade

- for the various reasons above, a poor level of local facility provision, with risk of vacant retail units

- bus services likely to be inefficient because absence of through routes

- limited choice of accommodation, lack of social diversity, and lack of aesthetic variety.

## Conclusion

The disadvantages of the 'closed-cell' model – particularly in relation to the viability and catchment-flexibility of local facilities – far outweigh the advantages. It is not, and never was, an appropriate form. Note, however, that many classic town plans from the last century avoided the pitfalls by creating 'open-cell' patterns, with distributor roads linking directly between neighbourhood centres (see Figure 1.14).

## NEIGHBOURHOODS IN LINEAR TOWNSHIPS

### Characteristics

- a planned pattern applied in a limited number of twentieth-century new or expanded towns, and also seen in some historic cities (such as Oxford)

- principle of seeing neighbourhoods in the context of public transport corridors and green parkways

- neighbourhoods normally bounded by a township spine road, which act as a 'uniting seam' (Lynch 1981) between them

- the spine road acts like a local high street and is the focus for pedestrian, bike, bus and (often) local car movement

- local retail, social and employment facilities may be clustered anywhere along the high street spine, and can be geared to whole-township catchments

- green parkways (often along water courses) provide the backcloth to the linear band of development, offering easy access to open space/countryside, sustainable water management and wildlife corridors

- densities are graded from high intensity along the high street to low intensity adjacent to open country.

## Advantages

- reinforces viability and quality of public transport

- encourages a high proportion of walking, cycling and public transport trips

- offers wide variety and flexibility in catchments, hence a good range of local jobs and services, and a sense of high street vitality

- gives good access to open space and a logical basis for the planning of open space, water and wildlife

- can provide (potentially) a sense of township identity, with connected neighbourhoods of varying character

- can provide for diversity of housing stock, social groups and land uses across the township.

## Disadvantages

- excessive trip length if not planned well in relation to the town as a whole

- risk of congestion along the main spine road.

### The Dutch twin-track strategy

Linear townships centred on tram routes radiate from the city centre, with green parkways for water management and recreation providing the backcloth. Tjallingii's model for an ecopolis shows this pattern well (Tjallingii 1995).

This linear strategy ties in well with the traditional form of interconnected neighbourhoods, and sustainability principles, and informs the advice given later in this guide.

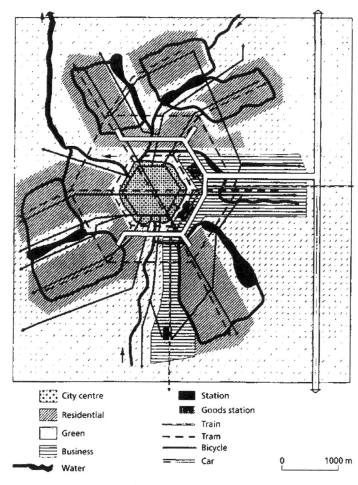

| City centre | | Station |
| Residential | | Goods station |
| Green | | Train |
| Business | | Tram |
| Water | | Bicycle |
| | | Car |

0          1000 m

*Figure 1.17*
**Ecopolis: a guiding model for the city**

SOURCE: TJALLINGII 1995

*Figure 1.18*
**Sustainable urban townships could have something**

## 1.10 TOWNSHIP, NEIGHBOURHOOD AND HOME-PATCH

**The need for a consistent approach**

Towns and cities vary tremendously in size, form, density and character. There is no universally applicable template for neighbourhoods. But some variables of identity, catchment and accessibility are sufficiently predictable to offer a basis for planning practice (Barton 2000). This guide structures policy at three distinct levels.

### 1 TOWNSHIPS AND MARKET TOWNS

The township is a sector or district of a city large enough to support in principle a full range of local facilities and a good level of employment opportunities. The median population is about 25,000. Facilities could include a district or town centre, one or more superstores, several secondary schools and, depending on local authority policy, a library, leisure centre and technical college. The figure of 25,000 is the population recommended by one UK report as the minimum viable size for a free-standing new settlement (Breheny *et al.* 1993). In practice, the population may vary widely, from, say 15,000 to 40,000.

This scale is equivalent to many rural or market towns, especially if the dependent hinterland population is taken into account. Many of the principles applicable to urban townships are also relevant to these small towns. Indeed, the principles are often clearer for the towns because of their physical detachment from other settlements.

Within urban areas, townships are rarely so distinct as in Peterborough or Tjallingii's Ecopolis. But the essential goal of providing accessible jobs and facilities to every part of a city is articulated by the township principle.

### 2 NEIGHBOURHOOD

They definition of 'neighbourhoods' adopted in this guide is one based on resident perceptions. As such they are normally residential areas of distinctive identity, often distinguished by name, and bounded by recognisable barriers or transition areas such as railway lines, main roads, parks, and the age or character of buildings (often associated with social or land-use differences).

Neighbourhoods thus defined vary in size very widely according to local circumstances, but a typical size might be 4,000–5,000. They are often large enough to include a primary school and some local shops. However, as noted in Ipswich, they may not coincide at all with local catchment areas. The local high street with its wider range of township facilities will sometimes be at the edge of the neighbourhood.

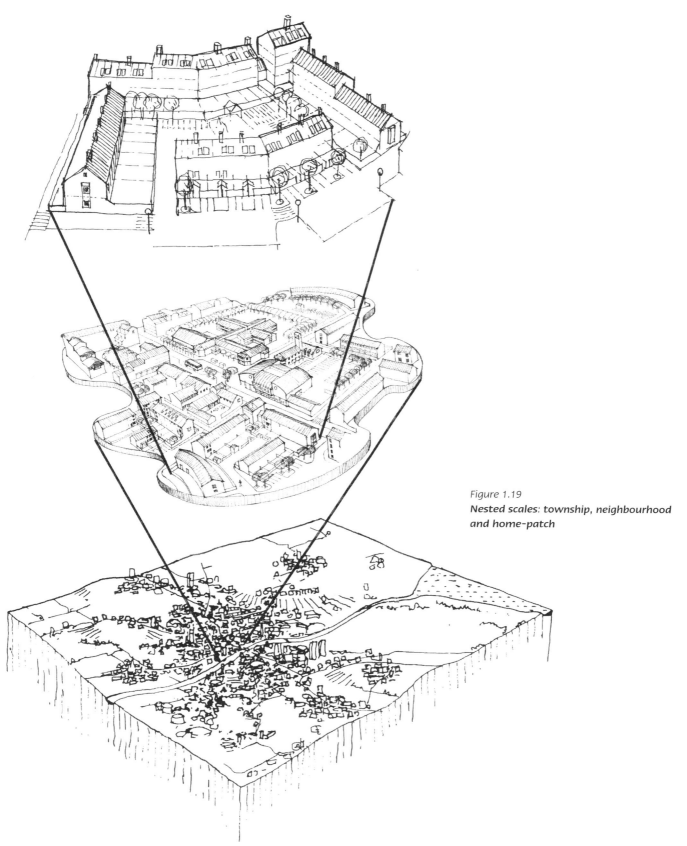

*Figure 1.19*
**Nested scales: township, neighbourhood and home-patch**

### 3 HOME-PATCH

The home-patches are the individual streets, squares, blocks or cul-de-sacs that make up the patchwork of the neighbourhood. As discussed in 4.3, the home-patch is critically important in residents' feelings of security or insecurity. Increasingly, the scale of the home-patch is seen as a useful unit for urban design – offering the potential for Dutch-style 'Woonerfs' or British 'homezones', where the safety of the streets for play and social exchange is paramount, and traffic is calmed to 5 or 10 mph.

**DEFINING TERMS**

| The three levels | | Typical population |
|---|---|---|
| Township | a sector or district of a town large enough to support a good range of job opportunities and local facilities including secondary school(s), large supermarket and leisure centre. | 15,000–40,000 |
| Neighbourhood | a mainly residential area of distinctive identity, sometimes named, which may coincide with either a local catchment area or an environmental area, and is geared to pedestrian/cyclist access. | 2,000–10,000 |
| Home-patch | a cluster of dwellings often developed at the same time, with shared identity or character, grouped round a common access (e.g. square, street, cul-de-sac or shared semi-private space), and ideally enjoying pedestrian priority. | 20–200 |

| Other useful terms | |
|---|---|
| Local catchment area | Zone of good pedestrian accessibility to local services such as primary school and shops, normally defined by threshold walking times (5 or 10 minutes) or distance (400–800 m). Note that catchment areas for different facilities will vary widely, according to their nature and location. |
| Environmental area | Zone where through traffic is excluded and the quality of the local environment takes precedence. Routinely achieved in new development though careful planning of road hierarchies. |
| Local community | A network of overlapping and interacting communities of interest and identity at the local level, providing mutual recognition, support and opportunities for friendship and co-operation. |
| Urban village | A medium- to high-density neighbourhood with a core of mixed uses and bustling pedestrian character. Normally applied to new development. |
| Urban quarter | A neighbourhood or district where uses are of a particular complementary character, such as the jewellery quarter in Birmingham. But also used more generally. |
| Homezone | Official UK term for a home-patch where special traffic management and environmental improvement policies are pursued to give residents a safe and pleasant environment, especially for children's play. |

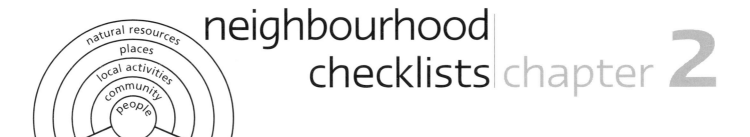

# neighbourhood checklists | chapter 2

## community checklist

This checklist is concerned with the health and sustainability of a neighbourhood, township or small town. The first section deals with the neighbourhood decision-making process that might be appropriate for the preparation of a local community strategy or spatial framework. Subsequent sections then work through the substantive issues, generally following the ordering of the guide, starting with people and community and ending with design.

The community checklist is intended for:

- community groups evaluating the current situation in their town or neighbourhood

- local councillors concerned with establishing partnerships and appropriate policy frameworks

- local planners trying to set a neighbourhood agenda, or compare different localities, or prepare a spatial framework

- community alliances wishing themselves to promote and be involved in a neighbourhood plan.

*Chapter 2 acts as a summary of the guide in the form of two complementary checklists. The community checklist provides a quick test of the overall health of a neighbourhood, while the investors' checklist provides criteria for judging the local impact of development proposal.*

**CONTENTS**

## 2.1

| 2.1 | **NEIGHBOURHOOD DECISION-MAKING** |

*Local communities are not masters of their own fate. Most development decisions within a locality are taken by private, public or voluntary sector organisations based outside the locality. The community interest is represented by the local planning authority through Local Plans and development control decisions, following consultation with parish or town councils.*

*However, there is potential for more active community involvement. This guide recommends the creation of neighbourhood plans at the level of the urban township or the country town. These can offer a sense of local identity while being at a practical scale for local provision and spatial planning. Plans could take the form of neighbourhood 'community strategies', contributing to district-wide Community Strategies that now have to be produced by every local authority. Or they could take the form of Supplementary Planning Guidance adopted by the local authority.*

*Community ownership of the process is very important. While in some areas local interests may be co-ordinated by parish or town councils, in others it will be necessary to establish new community forums. Community development trusts provide a possible model.*

*§ DENOTES DISCUSSIONS IN OTHER SECTIONS AS NUMBERED*

**CHECKLIST** ■

This checklist starts from the assumption that local community groups, working with town/parish councils, are interested in developing neighbourhood (or 'township') level of policy-making for sustainable development.

**Starting up** *§ 3.6*

☐ Is there an identifiable need for a town or township strategy?

☐ Is there already some form of sub-local-authority policy-making (e.g. within the Local Plan) that could provide the starting point for community planning?

☐ Is there a sufficient initial community of interest amongst a range of political/voluntary/public/ private sector groups to warrant launching an initiative? *§ 3.6*

☐ Are there widely recognised problems, opportunities and aspirations which can act as a motivator for other groups and interests to get involved?

☐ Is the suggested area on a scale large enough to address the problems, and defined so as to avoid, on the one hand, the premature exclusion of interested parties, and on the other, loss of focus by including too much?

☐ Is there a lead organisation (maybe the local authority itself, or a formal public/private/ voluntary partnership) which has a clear and accepted idea about what needs to be done, and in what way? *§ 3.6*

**Getting going**

☐ Is there a project brief, agreed by all the main stakeholders, which defines
  • the remit and the scope of the project
  • the way decisions are to be taken
  • how people are to be involved
  • programme of work
  • the intended outputs? *§ 3.7*

☐ Does the stakeholder group include all the relevant 'movers and shakers' in the public, private and voluntary sectors, together with effective representation of the interests of residents, vulnerable/marginal groups and the wider (global) public interest? *§ 3.4*

☐ Is there an inclusive and effective mechanism of public involvement (e.g. a citizens' forum or a focus group) that offers real participation without raising unrealistic expectations? *§ 3.5*

☐ Has a 'neighbourhood appraisal' been undertaken encompassing social, economic and environmental issues in a format appropriate for policy-making? *§ 3.8*

☐ Have major policy options been clearly identified and evaluated by stakeholders against fundamental health and sustainability criteria? *§ 3.9*

**Making it happen**

☐ Has a long-term spatial framework been approved which can work towards a healthier and more sustainable environment, providing an effective context for short-term decision-making? *§ 3.10*

Have influential agencies (such as the health authority the education authority, county highways, or major local firms) committed themselves to fulfilling their part in the overall strategy?

Are both the local authority planning department and the planning committee (or equivalent) fully on board?

Where there are major development sites, urban extensions or regeneration areas, have development briefs and masterplans been prepared as appropriate? *§ 3.10*

Are specific development proposals coming forward, and being evaluated, in the context of the spatial framework and other policy guidance? *§ 3.11*

Is the implementation, and subsequent management, of projects occurring on a sustainable basis?

## 2.2   PEOPLE AND COMMUNITY

*The starting point for any evaluation of the health of a neighbourhood or township is the people of the area: their quality of life, living conditions, social networks, and the issues that concern them. Even when the prime motives for a town/ township strategy are environmental or economic it is vital to put people centre stage. The benefits are awareness of all the different interests (including those of future generations), a holistic, human-orientated view, and legitimacy.*

*This section illustrates the kind of questions that need asking. They may be answered in a variety of ways, according to context:*

- *through professional appraisal of statistics, such as those in state-of the-environment reports or equivalent*

- *through social surveys*

- *through public consultation*

- *through collaborative policy-making processes.*

**CHECKLIST** ■

### People

Who lives in the area, especially in terms of social and racial groups, types of household, age groups, and income levels? *§ 4.2*

How is the population changing? Is there much in and out migration? If so, of what kind? And what factors (housing, for example) are causing it?

Is the population reasonably 'balanced' in terms of age groups, households and income levels? What are the trends in this respect? *§ 4.2*

What 'quality of life' is enjoyed (or endured) by residents? Key indicators include
- mortality rates (by ward and age group)
- the population of working-age people in work
- unemployment claimants
- the proportion of income-support residents
- recorded crime per 1,000 population
- families becoming homeless
- school education results (Key Stage 2)
- car ownership rates *§ 3.8*

Who else (besides residents) rely on the facilities of the neighbourhood (for example, entrepreneurs, workers, shop-keepers, people regularly socialising or playing in the area, visitors who value it)?

### Community and housing

Is there a thriving local community, especially in terms of the networks of association, mutual support and friendship that are vital for mental health and for groups such as children and retired people? *§ 4.3*

Is there a good mix of different types of housing in terms of tenure, size and affordability which can promote social inclusion and allow people to choose the location that maximises their own convenience and minimises the need to travel? *§ 4.4*

Are specific housing needs, identified by local surveys and Housing Authority lists, being provided for in such a way as to avoid the creation of ghettos and to recognise locational needs (such as sheltered housing close to a local centre)? *§ 4.5*

ACCESS TO LOCAL FACILITIES AND JOBS

## 2.3

| 2.3 | ACCESS TO LOCAL FACILITIES AND JOBS |
|---|---|

*Good local accessibility to retail, leisure, health and education facilities is critical to establishing healthy neighbourhoods. It means that people without access to a car have convenient options (often now denied). In addition it means that a higher proportion of trips will be on foot or bike, and those who do use cars can choose not to travel so far. This cuts pollution and energy use. Having more people on the street also increases safety and the opportunity for casual meetings, facilitating friendship networks and a sense of community.*

*The possibility of local work opens up choices for residents and is important for those wanting part-time employment. It also reduces the average length of the (normally motorised) journey to work and increases the number gaining healthy exercise.*

*Planning can support (or restrict) local work by attitudes to homeworking, small workshops and the provision of local facilities. More broadly, planning policy can be re-oriented away from the injudicious support of dispersed business parks (which are car/lorry reliant, energy intensive, land-hungry and socially exclusive) towards the development of mixed-use township and town centres.*

*§ DENOTES DISCUSSIONS IN OTHER SECTIONS AS NUMBERED*

### CHECKLIST ◼

#### Local accessibility

▪ What range of facilities (retail, civic, leisure, social, religious, healthcare, educational, etc.) are available within or close to the neighbourhood? *§ 4.8*

▪ How accessible (in terms of accepted distance standards) are different parts of the neighbourhood to key local facilities such as local shopping centres, schools, health centres, and parks/playgrounds? *§ 4.8*

▪ What are the perceptions of local people about what new facilities are needed? *§ 3.5*

▪ Is there a good range of jobs and training opportunities locally available, matching the needs of the population? *§ 4.6, 4.7*

#### Retail and business centres

▪ Can existing township/town centres or local high streets compete effectively with out-of-centre stores and/or regional shopping centres and provide a social hub for the community?

▪ Can potential entrepreneurs find appropriate locations for their business in the context of mixed-use centres at public transport nodes rather than edge-of-town business parks? *§ 4.6, 6.13*

▪ Is there a clear official planning strategy, in partnership with local stakeholders, to enhance the attractiveness and viability of local retail centres?

▪ Are new stores (especially supermarkets) being located so as to reinforce the quality and use of existing or planned mixed-use centres? *§ 4.9, 6.17*

▪ Are local retail outlets (especially in low-density suburbs and villages) being actively supported by market, voluntary and local authority action? *§ 4.10*

#### Schools and health centres

▪ Does the Education Authority give a high priority to local access to nursery, primary and secondary schools, with appropriate standards and procedures in place? *§ 4.11*

▪ Are schools run as community facilities with opportunities for a range of activities, or treated as exclusive fortress schools? *§ 4.15*

▪ Does the Health Authority support, or plan to achieve, a good range of accessible local health services? *§ 4.12*

#### Recreation

▪ Does the local authority have a strategy for local play, and a programme for rectifying gaps in provision where residents support this? *§ 4.13*

▪ Does the Local Plan have policies protecting/enhancing open space provision (parks, playing fields, allotments, informal greenspace) so that accessibility and continuity are improved? *§ 4.13*

▪ Is the maintenance and management of open space successful in offering quality and freedom with a sense of safety, thus inviting use by everybody?

| 2.4 | **PLANNING FOR MOVEMENT** |
|---|---|

*The aim of movement is not only to get to places but, at the level of the neighbourhood, it is also about enjoying the process of moving.*

*Objectives for local movement planning are*

- *encouraging healthier life-styles – more walking and cycling*
- *improving access to local facilities and to public transport, especially for those who do not use a car and for less-mobile people*
- *enhancing the viability of local facilities and employment opportunities*
- *reducing accidents, street crime and fear of crime*
- *reducing energy use, air pollution and $CO_2$ emissions.*

*Key to these objectives is getting people from all sectors of society to walk. Research shows that people's propensity to walk is significantly affected by how safe, convenient and pleasurable the experience of walking is. Safety is also a key factor in encouraging cycling, especially for children and older people. Public transport use is profoundly affected by distance to stops, reliability and the speed and comfort of service as well as frequency. Achieving these objectives requires close co-operation between transport providers, together with effective land-use planning.*

**CHECKLIST** ■

### General issues

- What is the current balance of different types ('modes') of movement –walking, cycling, bus, car – for particular purposes: for example, to the local shops, schools, work?

- Which streets are dangerous in terms of accidents and assaults and what has been done to reduce the dangers?

- What are the views of local people about the problems of and priorities for movement within the town/township and to the wider area?

### Walking and cycling

- Does the local authority have a strategy for the incremental improvement of conditions for pedestrians, for example through pavement

widening, crossings, new connections, safe routes to school? *§ 4.15*

- Has a safe cycle network (on and off street) been identified, together with a programme for implementation? *§ 4.16*

### Public transport

- What are the pattern and quality of public transport services, and how accessible are homes to good-quality services? *§ 4.17*

- Is there any plan for the improvement of public transport services, with key interests involved?

- Are new developments (housing, commercial, institutional) being closely linked to existing or new public transport routes and nodes?

### Traffic reduction

- Are the levels of traffic and of congestion rising or falling? *§ 4.18*

- Is there a coherent strategy, area-wide, for traffic reduction, with a programme of investment in traffic management and the promotion of alternatives?

- Is new development being classified (by relative accessibility) as car-free, car-limited or traffic calmed? *§ 4.18*

| 2.5 | **THE GREENSPACE SYSTEM** |
|---|---|

*Neighbourhoods, and urban areas generally, are not divorced from the landscape within which they sit, but part of it. They rely on the land for management of water, pollution and energy, and for local food production. The quality of the greenspaces in and around the neighbourhood is central to the quality of life for the residents. That quality is measured in terms of natural beauty, wildlife diversity, cultural heritage and recreational value. The effectiveness and quality of greenspaces is greatly enhanced if they are interconnected to form a system. For example, linear parks along streams can benefit wildlife, ease problems of water run-off, provide air-cleansing woodland and attractive walks. Yet in some urban areas where the amount of open space is well below official standards, some spaces are being sold off for development.*

ECO-DEVELOPMENT

## 2.6

### CHECKLIST ■

◻ Is there a long-term strategy for creating, enhancing and linking multifunctional greenspaces as part of an ecosystem approach to the area? *§ 6.9, 6.12*

◻ Are water courses, drainage systems and balancing ponds being planned as accessible aesthetic and biodiverse amenities? *§ 5.8*

◻ Have flood-plains been identified and plans for their protection/improvement been incorporated in Local Plans or Community Strategies?

◻ Are urban trees being planted and protected as part of a healthy neighbourhood strategy, with particular concern for their energy and pollution functions (e.g. windbreaks, carbon absorption, particulate cleansing) as well as visual, biodiversity and recreational functions? *§ 5.21*

◻ Are wildlife havens and corridors being planned/ enhanced as part of an overall biodiversity strategy? *§ 5.18*

◻ Is there potential to increase community composting and food production through partnerships and management of allotments, city farms and local parks? *§ 5.10, 5.11, 5.13, 5.16*

### 2.6    ECO-DEVELOPMENT

*A basic principle of sustainable development is that buildings and settlements should use resources at sustainable rates and avoid polluting their own or the global backyard. Key resources in this respect are energy, water, food, air, minerals, biodiversity and climate. Processes of urban development and renewal should ensure that assets are properly valued, used and re-used efficiently, with levels of wastes and emissions that can be satisfactorily absorbed by the environment. § 5.1*

*It is difficult to exaggerate the central importance of buildings in achieving sustainable development. Taking energy as an example, the energy used in buildings equals that consumed by transport and industry combined. Indeed, because of the dominance of housing in most neighbourhoods, it is likely that the heating, lighting and appliances of homes constitute the majority of local energy demand, with knock-on effects on the exploitation*

*of non-renewable reserves, on air quality and CO$_2$ emissions.*

*There are important social, health and economic issues as well as environmental. An effective energy efficiency programme can, in time, eradicate fuel poverty and premature winter deaths, while reducing costs for householders and businesses.*

*The checklist below may paint an over-ambitious picture of what can be achieved at the neighbourhood level. But in fact many aspects are technically and behaviourally much easier to achieve than reduced transport energy use/ emissions.*

*§ DENOTES DISCUSSIONS IN OTHER SECTIONS AS NUMBERED*

### CHECKLIST ■

**Energy**

◻ Does the local authority have an energy strategy in place, for all users and suppliers, working in concert with key energy agencies? *§ 5.4*

◻ Are there policies in place (in Local Plan or Supplementary Planning Guidance) which ensure that new developments are sited and laid out so as to reduce heat loss and maximise solar gain? *§ 5.5*

◻ Is there an effective programme of action for increasing the energy efficiency of the neighbourhood's older housing stock, particularly that occupied by low-income households?

◻ Are there any innovative energy schemes in the locality: for example, Community Heating with Combined Heat and Power (CHP), local sourcing of renewable energy, very low-energy solar buildings? *§ 5.6*

◻ Are buildings being constructed out of low-energy and/or locally sourced materials?

**Water**

◻ Is there available information about local water resources and a strategy (agreed between the water authority and the local authority) for their management? *§ 5.7*

◻ Are building renovations and new developments as a matter of course incorporating water demand reduction, grey water recycling and sustainable drainage systems (SUDS)? *§ 5.8, 5.9*

### Waste

▨ Are kerbside recycling collections available and any new developments/renovations constructed with space for household recycling? *§ 5.14*

### Food

▨ Is the potential for households to grow their own food at or very close to their dwelling being maintained, even in this era of low participation in vegetable gardening? *§ 5.10*

▨ Are new dwellings being planned with (for the most part) south-facing gardens? *§ 6.16*

## 2.7 URBAN FORM

*The most significant scale for the planning of local facilities, jobs and community development is not normally the neighbourhood (with a population of 2,000–10,000), but the urban township or district (20,000– 40,000). This level of population is sufficient to support a good range of retail, cultural, leisure and employment facilities, including for example superstore(s), technical college, library, leisure centre. It is roughly equivalent to a rural town of 10,000–20,000, plus its hinterland.*

*Yet many such areas are not well served, or are experiencing progressive decline as facilities migrate to bigger centres and dispersed car-based locations, with consequent impacts on accessibility, social inclusion, health, congestion, energy use and emissions.*

*We recommend developing a robust spatial framework for each urban township or country town. The purpose of such a framework is to revitalise, reshape, and provide a context within which individual development decisions can be properly taken. The framework also acts as focus for debate and partnership between local private-, public- and voluntary-sector stakeholders, working with the local planning authority. § 6.12*

*The social and economic health of neighbourhood may be judged indirectly by the incremental process of renewal – from ongoing maintenance of home and garden through to refurbishment of piecemeal redevelopment. This is mainly reliant on private householders and businesses, who will only reinvest if they and their bankers have confidence in the future of the area. § 6.4*

## CHECKLIST ■

### Spatial framework

▨ Is there a spatial framework for the township/ town, based on the principles of health, equity, environmental quality and resource efficiency?

▨ Does the framework have accessibility to public transport services (existing and planned) as its starting point, and the basis for land-use planning? *§ 6.12*

▨ Does the framework incorporate an open space strategy geared to recreational access and sustainable resource management? *§ 6.9*

▨ Is mixed-use development encouraged at appropriate locations, with good pedestrian connections between uses, and space-sharing where possible? *§ 6.5*

▨ Does density guidance (not only for residential development) reflect the level and quality of pedestrian accessibility? *§ 6.8*

### Urban regeneration

▨ Is there a gradual process of housing and business renewal and reinvestment across the area? *§ 6.4, 6.13*

▨ Is the potential for brownfield development and urban intensification properly assessed in relation to accessibility and environmental capital (or quality)? *§ 6.11*

▨ Does the strategy identify 'critical' areas where major intervention through urban regeneration projects is justified, and provide the policy context for those projects? *§ 6.13*

▨ Does the strategy also identify what might be called 'pre-critical' areas, where judicious investment by the local authority, housing associations, private sector or voluntary partnerships might assist revival? *§ 6.10*

## 2.8 URBAN DESIGN

*People identify with the 'neighbourhood' in the sense of a familiar distinctive locality, often with its own name. They also gain a sense of security (or insecurity) by the feeling of the street, square or block where they live (the 'home-patch').*

*If people feel safe and secure on their street then the chance of mental well-being is significantly increased. Equivalently, if traffic is calmed and non-intrusive, then the street can become the forum for conversation, play, and the development of local social networks. The design of home-patches is also key to solar access and the adaptability of the area to small-scale work and retail facilities.*

*§ DENOTES DISCUSSIONS IN OTHER SECTIONS AS NUMBERED*

*The streets, squares and courts knit together to create the public realm. The attractiveness of the public realm, its variety and local distinctiveness are central to the principle of a walkable neighbourhood.*

**CHECKLIST** ■

☐ Is there a strategy for maintaining and enhancing (or improving where necessary) the distinctive character and identity of each neighbourhood, with appropriate participation in the process by residents and/or residents' groups? *§ 6.2, 6.3*

☐ Has a townscape survey of the locality been undertaken, preferably with the involvement of residents, which identifies distinctive local character? *§ 6.2, 6.3*

☐ Is there a recognition of the importance of the area immediately around the dwelling (street, square, block) as a 'home-patch', helping to give a sense of security and local friendliness? *§ 6.14*

☐ Is there a programme for home-patch enhancement, particularly through traffic management, provision of local play facilities and landscaping (as in the DETR's 'homezone')? *§ 6.15*

☐ Where new or infill development is proposed, is this guided by the principles of facing and over-looking the street ('perimeter block development') so as to safeguard the aesthetic quality and the natural surveillance of the street? *§ 6.14*

☐ Is new/infill development geared to maximising passive solar gain and sunny back gardens while at the same time minimising materials use and heat loss by wall sharing? *§ 5.5*

☐ Do new blocks or streets incorporate a variety of built forms allowing for some diversity of user and adaptability between users (e.g. from house to corner shop or office)? *§ 6.15*

---

**Figure 2.1**

**PLACECHECK**

*Placecheck is a method of investigating how a place can be changed for the better. It consists of a checklist of 100 questions.*

*Placecheck focuses on*
- *people*
- *places*
- *movement*

*and the connections between these.*

*The method is designed for ease of use by community organisations and small groups of stakeholders. It can be used on all scales of development from single buildings to whole neighbourhoods.*

*The goal is to develop an understanding of place in preparation for responding to change.*

*A picture of a place builds up through responses to the series of questions posed in the checklist. Material collected can then assist in guiding documents which the council may be preparing, such as:*

> *a neighbourhood plan*

> *a development brief*

> *a design guide (or design code)*

> *a local plan review.*

*Placecheck is an initiative of the Urban Design Alliance, and is supported by the Department of Transport, Local Government and the Regions and English Partnerships*

*For further information visit: HYPERLINK http://www.placecheck.com*

# investors' checklist

| 2.9 | INTRODUCTION |
|---|---|

This checklist develops the principles of healthy neighbourhoods at the level of a specific site or project within the neighbourhood – for example a mixed-use renewal scheme, a new retail outlet or a new housing development. The checklist is intended to assist people making decisions about developments, assessing the extent to which a specific project, or alternative development options, fulfils health and sustainability criteria.

The checklist is indicative rather than comprehensive. It focuses on factors relevant at the neighbourhood level and does not deal, for example, with detailed building design. The first section works through the process of consultation and establishing partnerships with relevant agencies and the local community. The subsequent sections address the key substantive issues of need, location, context, site appraisal and design.

**Who should use this checklist?**

The checklist should be used by socially responsible developers and by anyone else evaluating the local impact of a development. It is linked to the established instrument of environmental impact analysis, extending the scope so as to include health and sustainability criteria more explicitly. It is potentially useful to:

- major landowners who wish to consider the future use of a site or influence a detailed local plan for an area in order to sell land

- the local authority as land owner and/or developer, who have to balance social/environmental responsibility with getting good financial return

- other investing organisations, public, private or non-profit, who wish to evaluate alternative investment options or refine a specific proposal

- project managers and designers charged with developing and implementing a project, negotiating with other interests and ensuring compliance with official policy

- development control officers, in pre-application discussions with developers and in evaluating planning applications

- local councillors charged with making decisions about new development proposals and networking with potential future investors

- community groups, responding to and commenting on proposals that affect their neighbourhood.

*Origins of the checklist*

*This checklist is based on that in the WHO publication* Healthy Urban Planning *(Barton and Tsourou 2000), adapted to reflect the neighbourhood emphasis*

*Smart growth*

In America, developers, the Environmental Protections Agency and communities are being drawn together around the banner of 'smart growth'.

This concept highlights the benefits to developers through embracing a more sustainable from of development.

- Better saleability of homes with good transport connections.

- Reduced liability and costs associated with using sustainable drainage systems.

- Improved marketing when wildlife is planned for in the landscape.

- Better fit with planning policies if development makes good use of existing features such as rivers, shelter belts, slope and existing buildings.

- Added value and market flexibility if homes are designed to facilitate future changes in use, changes in resident profile and additions/extensions.

| 2.10 | **THE PROCESS OF DECISION-MAKING** |
|---|---|

*Consultation is a necessary part of the decision-making process even for small house-holder development applications, but with larger projects it is often necessary to go beyond consultation if a co-ordinated and healthy scheme is to result. Other interests will be at stake. Action by a range of agencies (such as infrastructure agencies, service providers) is likely to be critical to the quality of the outcome.* § 3.2, 3.4

§ *DENOTES DISCUSSIONS IN OTHER SECTIONS AS NUMBERED*

**CHECKLIST** ■

### Establishing the need for the project § 3.6

▢ Is the purpose of the project clear?

▢ Is the project responding to needs identified in the development plan or community strategy for the town/township?

▢ Is there backing from the wider community for the principle of such a project?

▢ Is the project tied to the site by reason of its specific characteristics, or is it footloose?

▢ If footloose, then have alternative locations been properly investigated?

### Working with the relevant agencies § 3.4

▢ Is there a clear framework agreement at the outset between the project developer and the local planning authority which establishes who should be partners or consultees in the decision process, and how they should be involved, given the particular scale and nature of the project?

▢ Are the specific project development interests appropriately involved:
- land owners?
- developers?
- any current tenants in or users of the site?
- potential end users?

▢ Are relevant infrastructure providers involved:
- providers of transport infrastructure?
- operators of public transport?
- agencies for water supply, sewage treatment and drainage?
- companies providing gas, electricity and district heating companies?
- education, leisure, health, police and fire services?

▢ Is the community actively involved:
- neighbours?
- local community groups?
- urban social/environment/civic/economic lobbies?

**Mechanisms for co-operation** § 3.3

▢ Has an effective working partnership been established between all key stakeholders, with a co-operative attitude established so that issues and possible solutions can be properly recognised and evaluated?

▢ Are there close working relationships with organisations with whom potential joint development and operation could be desirable?

▢ Are community interests being effectively recognised through public meetings, focus groups, Planning for Real, citizens' juries or other appropriate means, on a practical time-scale and with participation of the key players, so that the results can be properly incorporated in the development proposals?

▢ Is the professional and technical work being staged in such a way that decisions are not reached prematurely and the health, social, environmental and economic context of the project and the site is fully taken into account?

▢ More particularly, does the project programme include the following stages:
- site, context and stakeholder appraisal?
- based on the appraisal, a development brief and/or master plan showing linkage with surrounding areas?
- in the context of a validated brief and master plan, detailed designs and construction programme?
- in the wake of construction, user involvement in on-going management and monitoring to ensure objectives are achieved?

| 2.11 | **CHOOSING THE RIGHT LOCATION** |
|---|---|

*This section looks at the question as to whether a given site is appropriate for development. The checklist could also be used to compare and evaluate alternative sites. The main issues raised are about the quality of the environment, safeguarding of resource quality, and the level of accessibility.*

*The criteria here relate to those used in the development potential framework. § 6.11*
*A possible site can be evaluated, for each question below, as being*

- *a priority for development, helping to solve wider problems and create quality*
- *satisfactory for development, with no particular impacts*
- *possible, subject to negotiated agreement to mitigate problems*
- *difficult, requiring fundamental shifts in approach or policy*
- *impossible, because essential local social/ environmental capital is destroyed.*

**CHECKLIST** ■

### Movement networks

Is the site well served by existing or potential walking and cycling routes that offer safe and convenient routes to local facilities and by public transport services? *§ 4.14, 4.15, 4.16*

Could the development of the site help to justify the improvement of public transport services? Could it contribute financially? *§ 4.17*

Is there reasonable road access to the site without exceeding the physical capacity of the network or causing environmental damage or increased danger? *§ 4.18*

### Accessibility

Would potential residents have good access to a wide range of jobs both locally and regionally without being obliged to rely on car use? *§ 4.6*

Would residents be within easy walking or cycling distance of a good range of local facilities, social, health, leisure, shopping, education and open space? *§ 4.8*

Would commercial uses be embedded within an urban area so that a good proportion of employees or clients could be within walking or cycling distance? *§ 6.12*

Would the development help reinforce the viability and vitality of local service centres by increasing their catchment population and/or by complementary commercial or social activities? *§ 4.9*

Do employment or social facilities have an appropriate degree of public transport accessibility to afford easy access from the surrounding area to

- local facilities on a main local bus or tram route?
- district facilities at a nodal point for local public transport services?
- city-wide facilities at the hub of services, including close to main-line rail services?

### Biodiversity and carbon fixing

Would development on the site affect a protected wildlife conservation area or valued wildlife habitat? *§ 5.18, 5.19*

Are woods and copses conserved and potentially enhanced by the development? *§ 5.21*

### Pollution and hazard

Is the site, or part of the site, subject to excessive levels of air pollution, noise, vibration, ground contamination or industrial hazard, beyond that which can be solved by good design?

Is the development liable to cause excessive levels of pollution, noise or danger for people in the vicinity, either directly through the nature of its activity or indirectly because of traffic generated? This applies most obviously to industrial or extractive activities in residential areas.

### Water resources

Does the proposed site avoid areas susceptible to flooding, and avoid exacerbating problems of excessive surface run-off? *§ 5.7*

Is it located where there is space capacity in the water supply system (or on-site catchment potential), avoiding areas where groundwater abstraction rates are not sustainable?

Is it located where there is spare capacity in the surface and wastewater drainage systems, or on-site potential to deal with these? *§ 5.9*

### Minerals, land and soil

Does it avoid high-grade soils, areas of organic farming and with intensive local food production (such as allotments)?

Does it safeguard potentially useable virgin or recyclable mineral resources?

35

# 2.12

Does it re-use or reclaim derelict urban land and thus reduce pressure on greenfields sites?

### Energy use

Is the site in a sheltered position, avoiding exposed hill crests? *§ 5.4*

Is the site level or gently sloping towards the sun, avoiding north-facing zones, so as to maximise the potential for solar gain? *§ 5.5*

Is the site in a position to benefit from the introduction of district heating and combined heating and power in the wider area, or to help justify the extension to the network which would benefit others? *§ 5.6*

### Built environment

Could the site potentially provide an attractive environment for people living, working and playing: safe streets, pure air, pleasing aesthetic (sound, sight, smell and touch)? *§ 6.2, 6.14*

Would it have the capacity to enhance the environmental quality of the neighbourhood preserving what is valued, including history, townscape and landscape, while regenerating dead, hazardous or ugly elements? *§ 6.3, 6.13*

Would development enable existing structures on site to be rehabitated or, failing that, their materials re-used?

## 2.12 SITE AND CONTEXT APPRAISAL

*Good analysis of the site and its context are necessary if the principles of sustainable development are to be converted into practice in the development scheme. It is critical that the developers (and their designers) engage with this appraisal and understand its significance. To encourage this, the local authority could oblige developers to submit a site appraisal in support of their development application. Such a submission could take the form of annotated maps and short statement of stakeholder consultations.*

*§ DENOTES DISCUSSIONS IN OTHER SECTIONS AS NUMBERED*

**CHECKLIST** ■

### Land use and character

What are the surrounding uses? Is there potential complementarity with proposed uses on the site,

especially in terms of pedestrian movement? *§ 3.9*

Can development on the site be used to trigger renewal or revitalisation on neighbourhood sites (thus enhancing the land values of both)?

What is the prevailing scale and character of surrounding development? Should the new development seek to reinforce this?

What locally distinctive architecture or townscape, reflecting the traditional materials and culture of the area, could be used as a starting-point for design? *§ 6.2*

### Movement and accessibility

What existing/proposed pedestrian or cycling routes, desire lines (routes people instinctively take through an open space) and rights of way could be affected (positively or negatively) by the project?

Where are the nearest bus, tram or rail stops, and how could access be gained most directly and safely to them from the site?

Where are the nearest schools, surgeries, shops, cafés, pubs, children's play areas, parks and playing fields in relation to the site?

How does the time or distance to these facilities compare with approved standards? *§ 4.8*

Do existing or possible pedestrian and cycling routes offer good quality in terms of
- road traffic safety?
- gradients and surface?
- ease of use by the less mobile?
- attractiveness?
- directness? *§ 4.14, 4.15, 4.16*

Do any specific new links need to be made to avoid a land-locked site and improve permeability?

Are the relative merits of different possible vehicle access points identified in terms of noise and danger (on and off site) and a permeable road network?

### Ground conditions and topography

Has the condition of the soil and ground been investigated to determine stability and bearing capacity?

Are there past (potential) mineral workings or areas of landfill on or adjacent to the site that might cause hazard?

Is the ground contaminated with any hazardous materials, and have radon levels been checked?

Have slopes been analysed in terms of gradient and aspect to guide design decisions so as to
- minimise cut and fill and retaining walls?
- minimise disruption of natural drainage?
- maximise solar gain or shade (according to climate)?
- avoid undue exposure?

### Microclimate, air and noise

Have the implications of prevailing insulation levels, wind patterns, diurnal air flows and frost risk been considered? *§ 5.5*

Have sheltered positions been identified, especially in relation to neighbouring buildings and tree shelter belts? *§ 5.5*

Is the site affected by sources of pollution or noise, especially major roads or factories?

Is there potential on-site or by agreement with neighbours for mitigating or reducing levels of pollution or noise?

### Water, and wildlife and landscape

Has the amount and quality of rainwater and its potential for use on-site been assessed?

Has information been gathered on infiltration, groundwater, watercourses (flow, pollution and wildlife interest)? *§ 5.7*

Has the potential for on-site treatment of grey and black wastewater been evaluated? *§ 5.8*

Is there potential treatment of polluted water-courses to enhance on-site health and biodiversity? *§ 5.9*

Has a wildlife survey been conducted, identifying habitats (often associated with watercourses) that are inherently valuable and could contribute distinctive character to development? *§ 5.20*

Have locally significant landscape features been identified (on or near the site) such as tree groups, streams or crests of hills?

Does the site contribute (now or potentially) to a green corridor important for recreation, wildlife or landscape? *§ 5.19*

### Re-use of buildings and local materials

Have existing unused/derelict buildings on sites been assessed for their historic/townscape value and the viability of retaining them?

If demolition is unavoidable, is there potential for re-using the materials?

Where buildings or plots within the project area still have tenants (often with low ability to pay rent) what potential is there for retaining/improving them?

## 2.13 NEIGHBOURHOOD SUSTAINABILITY IMPACT

*This section provides a checklist for evaluating the project brief, masterplan or concept stage of a development project. It is a form of project appraisal. Depending on the scale of the development, the questions have a different significance. On very major sites with a range of uses and perhaps 1,000 dwellings, the questions relate more to the internal arrangements. For smaller sites, the question is how they fit into the wider neighbourhood.*

**CHECKLIST** ■

### The mix of activities *§ 6.5*

Does the development contribute to a broad pattern of mixed use, with a rough balance of homes, jobs and services in any given locality, township or small settlement?

Does the development complement (rather than reproduce) the neighbouring activities, and link to them by easy, direct access so as to enhance viability and attractiveness?

If employment or services: does it avoid the creation of single-use or isolated facilities, instead contributing to clusters of mixed uses in local centres or high streets? *§ 6.6*

If housing: does it provide options for home-based work or subsequent change of use to local services? *§ 4.7*

**Housing balance** § 4.4

▢ Does the development contribute to ensuring there is a wide variety of types of housing (especially tenure and price) within a given neighbourhood or small town?

▢ If a large development (varies with the context: the normal UK threshold is 25 dwellings), does it include a proportion of social housing? **§ 4.5**

▢ Again, if a larger project, does it provide variation on site in relation to garden provision, built form and character, in order to offer options to people with different needs?

**Public transport access** § 4.17

▢ Is the land close to public transport used at an appropriately high intensity to facilitate access to public transport?

▢ If this is a major development: are the main magnets of pedestrian activity located close to tram or bus routes and every part of the development within striking distance (for example, 400 m) of a stop?

▢ Are any stops financed by the development conveniently located by principal users, well served by pedestrian routes, sheltered, visible and safe?

**Cycling** § 4.16

▢ Is the level of design appropriate to encourage potential cyclists?

▢ Do any cycle routes provided by the development link effectively with desire lines for the wider area?

▢ Are the cycle routes as direct as possible, with gradients, bends, kerbs and junctions designed correctly?

▢ Have potential areas of conflict between cyclists and vehicles or pedestrians been identified and effectively resolved?

▢ Has provision been made (if appropriate) for secure cycle parking?

**Pedestrian environment** § 4.15, 6.14

▢ Do pedestrian routes create a continuous and coherent network ensuring a permeable environment with ease of access to all neighbouring areas?

▢ Are gradients and the use of kerbs minimised to facilitate use by those with impaired mobility such as the elderly, partially sighted, wheelchair users, also by parents with pushchairs and children with skateboards or tricycles?

▢ Are the road-crossing points designed to give pedestrians effective protection from traffic, and the right of way wherever possible?

▢ Are the footpaths designed to give visually attractive and varied routes while ensuring good visibility and minimal risk of ambush?

▢ Are the public faces of buildings turned towards footpaths and squares so that they provide informal surveillance?

**Traffic and parking** § 4.18

▢ Is there a legible road hierarchy that allows ease of access for vehicles and reasonably direct routes (to minimise noise and pollution within and around the development)?

▢ Are roads in residential, shopping and central areas designed for 'natural' traffic calming, with 30 kmph design speed and priority for pedestrians, cyclists and buses clearly established?

▢ Is the level of parking provision as low as is realistic, given the use and the location of the development?

**Public greenspace** § 4.13, 6.9

▢ Is provision made for accessible and appropriate open spaces particularly satisfying local needs for meeting-places, children's play, kick-around, sport, allotments and recreational walks?

▢ Are green spaces designed with both beauty and a sense of safety in mind?

▢ Does green space in the development link into a wider network
  - encouraging circular walks and cycle rides?
  - providing a variety of wildlife habitats?
  - managing water resource sustainably?
  - managing the microclimate?
  - helping to control and reduce pollution?

**Privacy, security and gardens**

▢ Does the layout of external spaces around homes provide an appropriate level of surveillance and sense of user control, clearly distinguishing between public and private access? *§ 6.15*

In areas with lower density, are gardens shaped and orientated to assist home growing and composting?

In areas with higher density, are there balconies, roof gardens or patios, or communal gardens or allotments next to the buildings?

**Energy strategy** *§ 5.5, 5.6*

Is the development designed to minimise the need for artificial heating or cooling, with appropriate solar orientation and natural ventilation?

Has the landscape around the buildings been designed to reduce wind speed, provide summer shade and allow winter sun?

Is the heating/cooling system (if needed) the most environmentally economical available: for example, in northern climes, combined heat and power using renewable fuels?

**Water strategy** *§ 5.7, 5.8, 5.9*

Does the proposed development catch and purify rainwater to provide for at least some uses on site?

Are systems to be installed which encourage re-use of grey water?

If the existing capacity in centralised sewage systems is limited or none is accessible, will the development deal with its own sewage?

Will all surface water be allowed to percolate into the ground or reach local streams, with pollutants removed?

**Biodiversity strategy** *§ 5.20*

Does the development preserve and enhance the value of any special on-site habitats (for example, stream banks, trees and hedgerows)?

Does the layout provide green corridors or 'stepping stones' across the site, increasing the potential for wildlife infiltration?

In higher-density schemes has thought been given to providing nooks and crannies for wildlife colonisation?

**Noise and pollution**

Are the buildings laid out and constructed so as to minimise problems of noise between neighbours on and off site?

Have problems of airborne pollution (from neighbouring areas), on-site ground contamination, or watercourse pollution been identified and managed so as to reduce health risks to an acceptable level?

**Use of existing buildings and local materials**

Have existing buildings on site been incorporated in the development scheme?

Have local sources of traditional building materials (normally associated with low energy use) been identified and used where appropriate, to give more of a sense of place and continuity with the past?

*See overleaf for Building Research Establishment – Checklist for Developments.*

**Figure 2.2**

### BRE – CHECKLIST FOR DEVELOPMENTS

The Building Research Establishment (BRE) have published a common framework for specifying, analysing and checking sustainability issues in urban developments – for use by developers and planners for a variety of mixed-use and neighbourhood developments.

The checklist describes the practical steps that can be taken to specify and incorporate economic, social and environmental sustainability into a development.

Whilst recognising their interrelationships, issues are presented under eight headings:
- Land use
- Transport
- Energy
- Buildings
- Natural resources
- Ecology
- Community issues
- Business issues

Typical uses include
- writing development briefs or proposals
- demonstrating sustainability aspects of a proposed development
- specifying sustainability standards; and
- evaluating development proposals.

The checklist can be used at any of three levels, according to circumstances and need. One strength is its adaptability, which means it can take account of local conditions:

**Level 1** A comprehensive list of the issues to be considered

**Level 2** Guideline benchmarks and recommended levels of performance

**Level 3** A guideline scoring system

This guide is the result of a project jointly sponsored by the Department of the Environment Transport and the Regions and Industry, under the Partners in Innovation Scheme.

For further information visit www.bre.co.uk

# a
# neighbourhood planning process

## overview

### 3.1 PURPOSE AND SCOPE

This chapter is about how to consult, collaborate, analyse and take effective decisions at the neighbourhood or township level. It is therefore not so much about what to do but how to do it. It encompasses both the technical and political processes,

■ a collaborative process of decision-making and implementation;
■ an integrated and systematic appraisal of problems and policy.

These two processes are entwined but distinct. Effective collaboration between planners, investors and the local communities is indispensable to the implementation of co-ordinated strategies. But collaborative processes without dispassionate analysis can lead simply to negotiated agreements between established and vested interests. If the needs of under-represented groups and future generations are to be recognised, then political expediency must be married to inclusive rationality.

### WHOSE PROCESS?

The process described here is for a neighbourhood-level Community Strategy or spatial framework. The focus is on the physical development of the area. The process might be initiated by

■ a regeneration agency
■ the local authority
■ a development company; or
■ a community alliance.

The process is similar whoever takes the lead. The chapter is written to allow use by each of the partners. The different starting points are set out in Section 3.6: Stage 1 – Taking the initiative. Clearly in some areas there will be no or little impetus for an integrated neighbourhood strategy. Even in relatively stable areas, however, each modest incremental change is affecting the trajectory towards or away from sustainability. A strong spatially specific strategy, backed by the significant local players and the community, is desirable. The next two sections give an overview of the process. Section 3.2 explains the rationale for the collaborative approach and sets out the local partners in the process. Section 3.3 summarises the seven-stage process of neighbourhood planning, from 'taking the initiative' through to implementation. The rest of the chapter elaborates these themes.

## CONTENTS

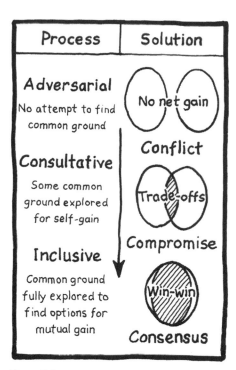

Figure 3.1
**Build on common ground**

*Adversarial approaches to development decisions can be counter-productive*

**A model to learn from**

*The WHO Healthy Cities movement has since 1987 provided a model for inclusive, collaborative working at the levels of both the neighbourhood and the municipality.*

## 3.2   COLLABORATIVE COMMUNITIES

**THE CO-OPERATIVE PRINCIPLE**
The creation of sustainable neighbourhoods depends on the active commitment of local stakeholders. Public, private and community sectors need to pursue common purposes. This co-operative principle is not about romantic community idealism; it is about co-ordination. It may mean working in partnership with other bodies, sharing ownership of a neighbourhood project, or it may simply mean open/effective information exchange and consultation.

**Reasons**

▢  *Health and sustainable development*
Collaboration is necessary in order to understand problems and to promote effective solutions. For example, a sustainable energy project, a regeneration scheme or a local healthy food strategy will rely on co-operation between many interests.

▢  *Human rights*
There are legal rights for households and businesses to be consulted about planning policies and decisions that affect them. These rights are being progressively extended into other spheres, for example council housing and education. In the context of the Human Rights Act it is arguable that obligatory consultation should be also extended to health services and leisure management.

▢  *Shifting attitudes*
Social and environmental objectives are promoted by the mutual education and consciousness-raising which can occur when different interests engage in dialogue. For example, a local wildlife trust or a black women's group can affect local authority attitudes and priorities.

▢  *Taking control locally, changing behaviour*
Businesses and households become more aware of shared communities of interest, and may be willing to alter their behaviour, when sustained public debate occurs – say in relation to safety on the streets or supporting the local post office or primary school. A collaborative community provides channels and forums where such concerns can be highlighted and joint action considered. It helps to establish new social norms of behaviour and foster individual behavioural change.

▢  *Strengthening local community networks*
The collaborative processes no doubt only involve a small minority of people in the neighbourhood, but the people drawn in will be reinforcing their commitment to the locality and to local community networks. New and often serendipitous local initiatives will be born. Stronger community networks will help support vulnerable people, reduce anomie and depression (Gilchrist 2000).

## THE LOCAL PARTNERS

A realistic map of local partners in neighbourhood/township development provides a means of assessing the appropriateness of any consultation or decision process. The simple map given here and elaborated later (Section 3.4) is specific to the spatial planning of an area, and distinguishes four groupings:

### The local planning authority

The planners are charged with guiding the spatial evolution of an area towards sustainable development. They produce the plans and policies but have little direct power of implementation, relying on the other partners, including service departments of the local authority (housing or education, for example) to play the game.

### Investors and providers

These are the private-, public- and voluntary-sector organisations who are the main agencies of change. This sector includes the major employers, the private developers, the non-profit developers (such as housing associations), and varied transport, health, education and social service providers. These agencies normally have quite specific remits, which they often pursue completely independently of neighbourhood participatory processes. In some localities there may also be a quango involved such as the Countryside Agency or a Regional Development Agency.

### The community groups

Local voluntary organisations include campaigning groups (such as civic societies), service-providers (the Citizens Advice Bureaux, for example) and a host of social, religious and recreational clubs and associations. Certain groups may see participation in community development projects as central to their mission, but most will not. Many will have a remit and catchment much broader than any specific neighbourhood. Politically active local groups are central to the development of a neighbourhood strategy. However, they do not necessarily provide an adequate proxy for the views/needs of the whole population.

### The people of the area

These are the users of the neighbourhood – the real owners. They include all the residents, together with local business people, workers, and those dependent on local leisure/retail/education/ health facilities but who live outside the area. Typically, about 10 per cent of local residents are members of organised groups – so 90 per cent are unrepresented except through the ballot box. Consultation processes often fail to reach (or motivate) the most vulnerable or marginalised groups.

*Figure 3.2*
**The four partners in neighbourhood planning**

*This simple map of the local partners forms the basis for subsequent guidance*

# 3.3

*Going local?*

*Guidance on area and neighbourhood governance is given in Hoggart and Kimberlee 2001*

## NEIGHBOURHOOD GOVERNANCE

The section above assumes there is the political and institutional will to achieve effective collaboration between local partners. This guide does not attempt to deal with the more formal methods of neighbourhood governance, but it is important to note the mechanisms, appropriate in different situations and with varying degrees of local democratic control, for example:

- *Parish and town councils*, directly elected, with powers delegated by the local authority.

- *Area or neighbourhood committees*, responsible for the co-ordinated delivery of local authority services.

- *Neighbourhood forums*, with cross-sectoral membership, creating potentially good conditions for partnership working.

- *Community Development Trusts*, with strong community representation, able to undertake development projects.

3.5 The ladder of participation →

### 3.3 THE SEVEN-STAGE PROCESS

**BASIC PRINCIPLES**

Any process of spatial policy-making or major development affecting a locality needs to be RITE:

- Rational, in the sense that there is a real attempt to understand the nature of the problems, to analyse the merits of different solutions, and learn from the process of implementation.
- Inclusive, in the sense that important stakeholders – whether they be local people, voluntary associations, private- or public-sector agencies – are actively involved.
- Transparent, in that information is readily available and verifiable and the sources of power and influence visible, open to challenge.
- Effective, in that decisions, once taken, are capable of being acted on – that responsibilities are clear, the programme realistic and co-ordinated.

## THE PROCESS IN OUTLINE

### 1    Taking an initiative

The initiative for a neighbourhood-wide project may come from the local authority, a major investing organisation or the local community. Effective and sustained leadership by the initiator is very important, but equivalently it is vital to recognise fully the other interests involved. Early and open consultation may well reveal opportunities or problems that lead to redefinition of the project. 'Scoping' should aim to answer these questions:

- What is the purpose and scope of the project?
- Is the initiating organisation capable of pursuing it?
- What stakeholders should be involved?
- Is the project consistent with broader goals and strategies?

taking the initiative

defining shared vision

learning lessons

understanding the locality

taking action

developing ideas

agreeing a programme

*Figure 3.3*
**The seven-stage process**

3.6 Taking the initiative →

## 2　Defining a shared vision

The first milestone in a collaborative neighbourhood planning exercise is the development of a shared vision. The vision must be both highly motivating and practical, so that potential partners want to 'buy into' it. The vision should then be reflected in a project brief which it sets out:

- the aims, scope and hoped-for outcome
- the way the project will be managed
- the collaborative and consultative process; and
- the process of appraisal and policy-making.

3.7 Defining the project →

## 3　Understanding the locality

A careful appraisal of the neighbourhood (or the project) and its context is essential before fixing on specific policies or proposals. This is to avoid blinkered solutions and open up the possibility of synergy/collaboration. A neighbourhood appraisal should if possible:

- be undertaken with other key stakeholders, to broaden the base of understanding and engender a sense of shared ownership of the initiative, using the appraisal to build community capacity

- involve a quick but systematic scan of all the levels of analysis in the neighbourhood model: people, community, activities, place, resources and the wider context

- link into and contribute to monitoring of the quality of life

- focus attention where there are real difficulties, tensions or uncertainties, bringing on board others who are involved, looking for opportunities as well as assessing problems.

3.8 Understanding the locality →

## 4　Developing ideas

It is important not to lurch prematurely into supposed 'solutions' to local problems. The established policies of service providers, developers and planning authorities have often failed (or not attempted) to deliver sustainable development. It is therefore vital to examine radically different options. Ideas may be triggered simply by the process of inter-agency collaboration, but also by a deliberate search for best practice in the field, learning from experience elsewhere. Techniques of visioning and brainstorming can help in the right context.

In some situations a formal evaluation process may be required. The purposes of such evaluation, and who should do it, are key issues for discussion. The checklists in Chapter 2 provide starting points for an evaluation framework. The process of evaluation should be seen as part of a creative process, pushing ideas forward, not an end in itself.

3.9 Developing ideas →

## 5　Agreeing a co-ordinated programme

A local neighbourhood plan – whatever form it takes – serves not only to identify policies but also to win commitment from the key implementing organisations. The process of gaining political support and influencing investors is critical. Without backing the plan will flounder.

The core document is therefore a programme rather than a plan. It needs to be explicit about the agreed vision for the area, the development priorities, and the way in which the often-unpredictable process of implementation is to be handled. The roles and tasks of contributing agencies need to be spelt out and agreed, with staging posts for co-ordinated review. Desired outcomes should be stated.

3.10 Agreeing a co-ordinated programme →

In the context of such a programme individual agencies produce their own policy documents. Specifically the Planning Authority should produce the spatial framework which will shape the physical evolution of the area.

**6   Taking action**

The best-laid plans can fail. Implementation is an incremental and often disjointed process over an extended timespan. Effectiveness depends on

- long-term consistency of vision and strategy

- a creative, pro-active stance from the planning authority setting the objectives and parameters for the development of specific sites (with development briefs, for example)

- seizing opportunities when they emerge, for example when land ownership changes bring forward sites unexpectedly

- responding to concerns and sharing problems by flexibility in design solutions, and networking with other stakeholders

- maintaining the sense of shared ownership and decision-taking, through regular information exchange and meetings

- cultivating community and councillor support.

Effectiveness also depends on subsequent management. It needs to be crystal clear in the neighbourhood plan: who is going to manage any community facilities? Is the local authority able to pick up the tab? If not, does a Community Trust or residents' management committee exist which could manage on behalf of users?

*3.11 and 3.12 focus on particular tools of design and implementation: masterplanning, design codes, development briefs and planning applications*

3.11–3.12 Taking action ➜

**7   Learning lessons**

On-going monitoring and review works on three levels:

1   Assessing policy impact – i.e. how far have policies been implemented and with what success? If there are undesirable side effects, or hiccups in delivering the policy, then what can be done?

2   Assessing health and sustainability outcomes – i.e. what are the trends in quality of life for residents/workers in the area? How is the neighbourhood changing? Has the plan as a whole addressed the issues?

3   Assessing the effectiveness of the process – have the collaborative and policy-making processes worked? Could they be fairer, more inclusive, more efficient? What lessons for elsewhere, or next time round?

3.13 Learning lessons ➜

# the collaborative approach

### 3.4  DEVISING A PARTICIPATORY PROCESS

**BASIC PRINCIPLES**

Whatever the origin of a neighbourhood planning process – public, private or voluntary sectors – effective and appropriate collaboration with other local stakeholders is essential. Initial informal discussions with a wide range of interests can help define priorities and opportunities. Then a clear participatory strategy needs defining which is focused, transparent and deliverable.

### Reasons

Participatory processes are sometimes seen by local authority officials – and even more by local business leaders – as a time-consuming deflection from the main task of getting things done. But principles of community collaboration and partnership are nothing to do with political correctness or cosy utopianism. They are everything to do with effectiveness and ownership. One organisation by itself has neither the power nor the authority to deliver sustainable development. Working with stakeholders is necessary to ensure that:

- local expertise is tapped and local demands understood;
- a co-ordinated strategy is possible and implementable;
- important interests are not excluded from consideration;
- creative, integrated solutions are devised;
- decisions are reasonably transparent and have legitimacy;
- trust between people and local capacity are built up; and
- people's quality of life is improved through empowerment.

### Partners, participants and consultees

The scoping exercise should endeavour to identify who needs to participate and in what way. It is useful to distinguish between three levels of potential involvement:

*Partners* – who share the decision-making and accept responsibility for making things happen. Partnerships may involve formal contractual agreements and the dovetailing of investment programmes.

*Participants* – who actively participate in the decision-making process, but are not prime movers. Participants are likely to be involved in consensus-building processes in the context of stakeholder forums, focus groups, citizens' juries, etc.

*Consultees* – who are formally asked for their views about current problems and possible solutions but do not engage in the collaborative forums. Consultation implies the opportunity for two-way flows of information but maybe only limited dialogue. Typically all local private and public organisations would have this opportunity, plus all local people.

---

*Golden rules*

There are at least five golden rules for initiating organisations to follow in formulating a clear participation strategy:

1  *Clarity of purpose*

   – *What are you trying to achieve?*

   – *Why is consultation or collaboration needed?*

   – *Who are you targeting?*

2  *Fitness for purpose*

   – *What are the participating approaches suited to the task?*

   – *Will the approaches help deliver a co-ordinated plan?*

   – *Does the approach fulfil statutory requirements?*

   – *Have you got the capacity to see it through?*

   – *Have the other participants got the capacity to see it through?*

3  *Avoiding false expectations*

   – *Are you clear about your 'bottom line'?*

   – *Are the project boundaries explicit?*

   – *Have you got something of value to offer the participants?*

   – *Have you got on board the key agencies that can deliver improvements?*

4  *An open, inclusive process*

   – *Can you give leadership without patronising participants?*

   – *Can you share ownership of the process with the other stakeholders?*

   – *Are the channels for involvement clear and inviting?*

   – *Is information about the process as it evolves available for scrutiny?*

5  *A positive process*

   – *Have you a programme for developing a shared vision?*

   – *Can you orientate the process towards problem solving and win–win solutions?*

   – *Can you avoid the dangers of polarisation and entrenched views?*

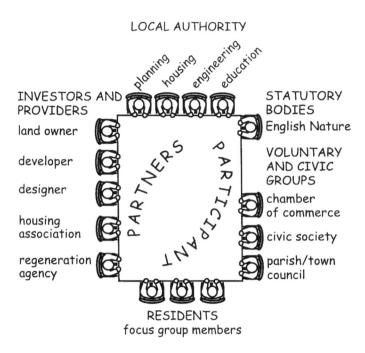

Figure 3.4
**The stakeholder forum: illustrative membership**

## STAKEHOLDERS' GROUP

For neighbourhood projects the stakeholders' group or forum is a central part of the planning process. The group meets on a regular basis (once a month, for example) and exists to

■ share ownership and engender commitment

■ exchange information and contacts

■ sort problems and develop project ideas collaboratively

■ help build a wider constituency of support; and

■ facilitate co-ordination and implementation.

The stakeholder group needs to involve all potential *partners* and those *participants* who are able and willing to give regular commitment. It may be used as a way of building towards partnership. To be effective the group needs reasonably stable membership, able to develop common understanding and momentum. Do not be tempted to use it as a catch-all for transient interests or debates.

Invite people to join in a stakeholders' group as soon as possible after the scoping exercise, with clear guidance as to the essential purpose and rationale for the plan or project. Hopefully a number of the members will have been informally consulted already, and have made their conditions for membership known. Membership is not casual but a negotiated agreement where both parties have something to gain.

Avoid premature forming of a group, except on a purely consultative basis. If the context is not clear people will come with very varied agendas and the initiative may well get derailed or meander off down a branch line.

Conversely, it is vital that the partners/participants join in soon enough to influence the shape of the project – both to engage their interest and to give the opportunity for better (more integrated) strategies to emerge. If possible the stakeholders should make an important input to the project brief.

## HORSES FOR COURSES

The participation map shows the four local partners – planning authority, investors and providers, community groups and the people – interlinked by varied participatory processes. Most neighbourhood planning exercises will need a range of participatory processes at different levels.

There is no one right way to work with local partners. Each process has specific benefits and limitations. Normally several complementary participatory processes should be running in tandem. For example

■ *A neighbourhood community plan*, led by the local authority,

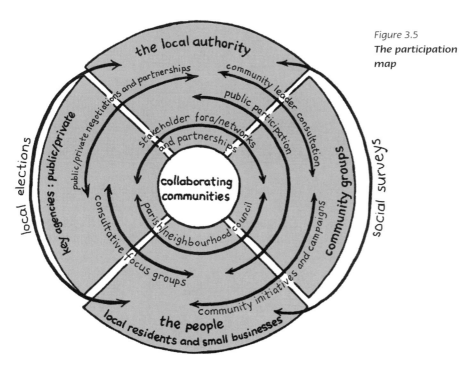

*Figure 3.5*
**The participation map**

The participation map illustrates the diversity of participatory processes on offer, from formal democratic procedures to informal consultation and focus groups. No one technique reaches all the community partners. It is vital to be clear about the participation objectives and then select the techniques that are most likely to deliver.

---

*Forging partnerships*

The experience of the Healthy Cities Movement suggests that success in collaborative, cross-sectoral projects relies on four ways of working:

1 Explicit political commitment at the highest level to the principles and strategies of the project. (Without backing from key committee chairs or the mayor of the town, ambitious schemes may be stillborn.)

2 Establishment of new organisational structures to manage change. (Formal partnerships or a Community Development Trust can help break down barriers.)

3 Commitment to developing a shared vision and plan. (Effective collaboration depends on shared ownership and consistency of purpose.)

4 Investment in formal and informal networking and co-operation, not just locally (deepening understanding and building capacity for co-operation).

Further information on the Healthy Cities approach see

• City Planning for Health and Sustainable Development – www.euro.who.int

• Twenty steps for developing a healthy cities project – www.euro.who.int

• Healthy Urban Planning (Barton and Tsourou 2000).

---

might focus on a stakeholder forum involving public-, private- and voluntary-sector membership; served by a cross-departmental officer group; with a social survey of a cross-section of residents, information to all residents at regular intervals via the local paper, and the invitation to participate in public meetings.

▨ A *major renewal project*, led by the land owners, might involve a public sector/private sector co-ordinating group at officer level, occasional public meetings with local politicians invited, and a residents' focus group meeting regularly throughout the process.

▨ A *neighbourhood action campaign*, led by a consortium of community groups, might use a public conference as a launchpad to draw in the powers that be to a stakeholder forum, and develop their popular base through direct action to improve the environment.

## BUILDING ALLIANCES

Many neighbourhood planning exercises founder because of lack of clarity about who should be actively involved: false expectations raised; key players ignored. Others founder because key agencies are unwilling or unable to participate. A central part of the participation strategy (whoever is the initiator) is therefore about trying to ensure that the appropriate partnership is brought together. The art is to woo potential collaborators successfully, and build alliances that have the practical and political clout to carry projects through.

# 3.5

### Guides to participatory working

- *Involving communities in urban and rural regeneration (DETR 1997)*

*Encyclopaedia-like coverage of ways to reach out and involve all sectors of the community in every stage of regeneration. Plenty of checklists, key points and outline case studies. Very well indexed with lists of further reading and support organisations and government departments.*

- *The Community Planning Handbook (Wates 2000)*

*Covers most aspects of how to conduct community planning. Includes how to start, about 50 techniques and 16 scenarios showing how to apply to techniques to possible situations. Checklists and full glossary.*

- *Sustainable Urban extensions – Planned Through Design (The Prince's Foundation 2000)*

*Describes and advocates a collaborative approach to new development. In-depth descriptions of case-study workshops. Supported by the CPRE, English Partnerships and the DETR.*

- *Participation works! (New Economics Foundation n.d.)*

*A guide to 21 techniques of community participation. Each technique is clearly described, together with resources required. Some advice on how to select techniques is offered.*

- *Community Participation in Local Health and Sustainable Development (WHO 2001)*

*Based on the experience of healthy city projects: www.euro.who.int*

- *Guidance on Enhancing Public Participation in Local Government (DETR 1999)*

- *Local Community Involvement: a handbook of good practice (European Foundation for the Improvement of Living and Working Conditions 1999).*

## A worthwhile investment?

Collaboration costs time and effort. It needs to be undertaken with commitment. But the investment can reap rewards later in the process if it results in barriers being lowered which allow quicker and more effective implementation. The Ashley Down case study at the end of the chapter illustrates how a false start can be turned around.

### 3.5 WORKING WITH LOCAL PEOPLE

Local residents, business people and other users are the real owners of a locality. They have a right (sometimes statutory) to be involved in major decisions that affect their environment or livelihood. But effective, inclusive participation is notoriously difficult to achieve. This section briefly sets out a range of techniques available, with special emphasis on the 'focus group'.

### AVOIDING THE PITFALLS

Sometimes participation is perceived by local people as having only marginal influence on events, so involvement is desultory, and the instigators (even if initially enthusiastic) reduce their efforts next time round. Or participation may be vociferous as people react strongly to a perceived threat, and cultured debate is squashed. Either way there is a risk of discussion being dominated by articulate minorities who are not necessarily representative. Therefore

- Don't undertake consultation as a cynical exercise in public relations.
- Value and respect the views of others.
- Raise awareness through use of the local media.
- Don't rely just on public meetings, which can be too easily hijacked.
- Engage with opponents, creating opportunities for real debate (and discovery), not rhetorical confrontation.
- Seek out and represent the views of non-joiners (both the silent majority and specific relevant minorities).

### Match purpose and method

It is all too easy to use inappropriate participatory methods. To check against this, specify the purpose of participation clearly, then match the method to the purpose. If, for example, the purpose is to find out the general attitudes of residents, then while a public meeting may be important to give people a chance of dialogue, it is not sufficient. Particular interests will be well represented but others will not. So a sample social survey should be considered as well. If the purpose is to raise public consciousness about sustainability issues, then information sheets, meetings or focus group activity will have very limited impact. Much better to work with local groups, schools or the health authority to promote a media event or competition around a highly motivating issue such as safe routes to school.

## PUBLIC PARTICIPATION TOOLKIT

A selection of techniques specifically related to development decisions and spatial strategy

| Technique | Use | Description and contacts |
|---|---|---|
| Planning for real | To let the community have creative input by identifying issues and development priorities producing options and helping to select the best scheme. | Simple models of the proposed development are used as a centre of focus. Participants are invited to be involved in design decisions by interacting with the model. This may take the form of placing stickers to indicate like/dislike/options.<br><br>FFI Neighbourhoods Initiative Foundation 01952 590777 www.nif.co.uk |
| Local design statement | To help define and protect what is particular and distinctive in an area. | A way for local people to help produce guidance for future development. Can be adopted as supplementary planning guidance.<br><br>FFI Countryside Agency 01242 521381 www.countryside.gov.uk |
| Local mapping | To reveal and record the local impression of an area by the people who live there.<br><br>Helps groups see the local area from different perspectives. | An event is organised supporting local people to map the area.<br><br>Discussions led to help compare the maps and learn more about the area, the interests of the residents in the area. Both problems and opportunities can be looked at. Can be used to map specific issues such as safety/crime or mobility/access.<br><br>FFI Common Ground 0207 267 2144 www.commonground.org.uk |
| Roadshow | To collect comments on proposals or options. | Taking the consultation exercise out and about. Allows the exercise to be re-run in several locations convenient for local people. Final central exhibition to include feedback and comments.<br><br>Travelling exhibition with provision for people to record comments. Comments then compiled and used as basis of a report. Variations include recording comments by video or staging events and entertainment at each location.<br><br>FFI Architecture Foundation 0207 839 9389 www.architecturefoundation.org.uk |
| Enquiry By Design | To produce a masterplan framework for a new development.<br><br>See case study 3b | An intensive design process usually run as workshops over a few weeks. Involves key stakeholders such as the developer, land owner and local authority as well as representatives of interest groups, and statutory consultees. With the assistance of facilitators and specialists, options and approaches to the proposed development emerge having a high degree of consensus.<br><br>Immediate output is a masterplan framework.<br><br>Development and regeneration team, The Prince's Foundation 0207 613 8500 www.princes-foundation.org |
| Round table workshops | To discuss ideas and perspectives, establish common ground and define areas of conflict for future consideration. | Workshops bringing people from a range of sectors, organisation and power bases together. Ideally providing a non-hierarchical format in which all contributions can be heard and valued.<br><br>Can be one-off workshops or linked to a series.<br><br>FFI. New Economics Foundation 0207 377 5696 www.neweconomics.org |

## FOCUS GROUPS

A focus group is a discussion group that meets regularly throughout the plan-making processes. It acts as a proxy for the local people, hopefully reflecting their consensus. It may be joined by volunteering or invitation. It should if possible include people from the diverse elements within the community.

▪ Continuity of membership is important to allow understanding and expertise to grow. At the same time open access is important to avoid the suspicion of exclusivity.

▪ The ideal number of people is 8–12. The group must be attended by key professionals involved in the whole process, who are able to speak with authority about the attitudes of the major players and fully understand the context. The professionals are there to support and enable the group, not to dominate it.

▪ The focus group serves to raise and debate issues, respond to proposals as they emerge, and generate new ideas for testing by the main agencies. While it is not a decision-making arena, the group's views need to be taken seriously by other stakeholders. If there is a positive, creative attitude by participants then innovative solutions can emerge which help to shape the final plan.

▪ The focus group process may involve a series of more specific exercises such as story-telling, visioning, or planning for real.

**Setting up a focus group**

A land owner, developer or regeneration partnership could approach this task as follows:

1   Hold an initial public meeting (widely advertised) to raise the key issues before the detailed development proposals have gelled or an architect been briefed.

2   Ask for people at the meeting to volunteer themselves to be involved in on-going discussions, giving their specific interests and skills.

3   Form a residents' focus group (preferably without pre-selection) to meet regularly and represent the local community interests. It is vital that key professionals working for the development company give this process their time and treat it seriously, without manipulation.

4   Hold subsequent public meetings as appropriate – at which focus-group members report back to the wider community on the discussions held and any solutions proposed.

5   When the plan or planning application is submitted, include a report of the focus group and public meetings, and action taken to recognise and deal with the concerns raised.

## TOP DOWN OR BOTTOM UP?

Attitudes to local government are shifting, with the growing interest in decentralised models of decision-making. Yet much community involvement in the planning of neighbourhoods is well-meaning tokenism that fails to deliver what people are led to expect, or is overtly placatory, 'managing' public opinion. Equivalently much community activism is misdirected, and fails to hit its target. Community initiatives are misconceived, because of lack of analysis about where power lies.

The 'ladder of citizen participation' analyses the relationship between the local authority and local people. It does not necessarily imply that the top rung of the ladder is 'best'. Rungs four and five – 'Genuine consultation' and 'Partnership' – may be more realistic aspirations in many situations.

*Figure 3.6*
**A ladder of citizen participation**

SOURCE: FREELY ADAPTED FROM BURNS, HAMBLETON AND HOGGETT 1994, ITSELF BASED ON ARNSTEIN 1969

| Rungs of the ladder | Neighbourhood-level characteristics | Attitude of the local authority | Comments |
|---|---|---|---|
| 7 Autonomous powers | An elected neighbourhood government with substantial powers, legally and financially independent from local authorities. | Confrontational | This is the ideal of social anarchism, and would require new legislation. Reality might fall rather short of the ideal, and be prone to NIMBYism. |
| 6 Delegated powers | Community Development Trust or parish/town council with substantial responsibilities delegated by the local authority. | Collaborative | Achievable without major legislation; can be innovative and radical. |
| 5 Partnership | Neighbourhood Forum or Management Company with power sharing between local authority, business and citizens' groups. | Collaborative | Widely practised. Relies on shared ownership and effective leadership. |
| 4 Genuine consultation | Public meetings, stakeholder groups, web votes, citizens' focus groups, planning for real, etc. – a real attempt to encourage local debate and respond to it. | Enabling | Widely practised. Local authority positive attitudes and skills are critical. |
| 3 Two-way information | Good-quality information from authority to citizens and from citizens to authority via community newspapers, local social surveys. | Technical | This is not adequate in itself, but it is a vital part of an inclusive strategy, reaching the non-joiners. |
| 2 Tokenism | Consultation too little, too late, going through the motions. | Manipulative | |
| 1 Spin and bluster | No attempt at consultation considered necessary. | Autocratic | |

53

# 3.6

# getting going

## 3.6  STAGE 1 – TAKING THE INITIATIVE

The impetus for some kind of neighbourhood plan may come from public, private, voluntary or community sectors. Whatever the trigger, however, the decision process needs to follow the same basic pathway if it is to gain the support of the local partners and have a chance of promoting sustainable development. This section shows some of sources of initiative and the mechanisms involved.

### COMMUNITY-LED PROCESSES

Community campaigns may be triggered by frustration at the lack of local facilities, by economic decline, social crisis or environmental degradation. The main purpose of such campaigning is to influence the authorities. Credibility depends heavily on the network of contacts and the level of demonstrable community support.

Community groups, voluntary organisations and small businesses are vulnerable to higher powers, but they are also able to innovate and experiment with a flexibility that big business and big government cannot match. Many of the most exciting examples of sustainable development have been launched and managed by local groups (Barton and Kleiner 2000). Often innovations are born in the localities where the key people live, but they can only flourish with public- and private-sector support.

### Winning friends and influencing people

The starting point for such a campaign is making alliances. The ambition is to form partnerships that enable effective and implementable decisions. To achieve that the community initiative group needs to

- articulate the aims and character of the initiative clearly
- attract attention by appropriate publicity
- build grassroots membership to help with the work and increase credibility with local authority/ funding organisations
- develop a pilot project (if appropriate) to demonstrate the group's capability and prepare the ground for more ambitious schemes
- build a constituency of support among local politicians, the local press, local groups and the community at large
- form partnerships with private and public sectors to undertake the project.

### INVESTOR-LED PROCESSES

Where a development site is large enough to have a significant impact of the future of a neighbourhood then the investor has a responsibility to promote a collaborative decision-making process. This is not only a question of sustainability ethics; it is also enlightened self-interest.

*Power to the people*

*The Local Government Association (2000) is calling for neighbourhood plans where local communities are empowered to take responsibility for a range of service delivery, detailed land use and development control. One model they refer to is the Village Design Statement. Transferring that idea to the much larger scale of market towns and urban townships would depend on resources, legitimacy and capacity-building.*

*Cautionary tale*

*A community forum decided to create a plan for a declining town centre. Almost everybody joined in – except for the local authority planning committee. Visions and strategies were produced, enthusiasm was high, but five years later nothing has happened.*

*Clearly something went wrong early on. Without a key partner on board the initiative was still-born.*

The potential benefits to the investor include

▪ Reducing conflict by listening to local people's concerns and responding to them appropriately.

▪ Improving the function of the scheme by early discussion with relevant transport, education, health, etc. agencies.

▪ Reaching an acceptable scheme more quickly, avoiding costly redesign.

▪ Reducing the risk of planning application refusal, and increasing the strength of any subsequent appeal if it were to be refused.

▪ Positive publicity and improved profile.

The major investors can, and should, follow the same set of planning steps as the planning authorities. The process should be thorough, inclusive and transparent.

### LOCAL AUTHORITY-LED PROCESSES

The local authority should work towards adopting an integrated approach to spatial policy in every urban township, rural town or parish, so that local plan review, LA21, economic development and regeneration projects all have a clear relationship to service department programmes, and support from local stakeholders.

There is a profusion of official initiatives affecting neighbourhoods: health action zones, housing actions zones, safe communities, traffic schemes, regeneration partnerships, development plans, etc. The risk of conflict, duplication and ineffectiveness is high. Co-ordination can occur via a number of mechanisms:

### Neighbourhood community strategies

Town or locality-based community strategies provide an opportunity for integration at the local level. Such plans are intended to promote social, economic and environmental well-being. They should include service provision, land-use and development policies, and be prepared by a broad 'community planning partnership' (DETR 2000h) within the context of local authority community strategies.

### Neighbourhood spatial frameworks

Local Plan revision gives an opportunity for neighbourhood partnerships with the parish/town councils, service providers (education, health), and the community. The locality-based spatial frameworks could give detail to broader Local Plan policies in areas of significant change.

### Development briefs

The preparation of development briefs for major redevelopment or town expansion schemes requires partnership with service providers, land and development interests, and local people.

1.3 Planning policy and neighbourhood renewal ←

*Examples of investors who should initiate collaborative processes*

● *A house builder with an option on urban fringe land.*

● *A hospital trust selling off a redundant facility.*

● *A housing association developing a major regeneration scheme.*

● *Railtrack selling unwanted sidings in the inner city.*

### Regeneration programmes

Local neighbourhood renewal strategies (see Section 1.4) involve setting up cross-sector partnerships in each renewal area, in the context of the LSP. Projects should be seen in a broad (town or township) spatial frame of reference.

### SCOPING

The purpose of 'scoping' is to set the initiative in context and review its purpose and scope before formal commitments are entered into. Effective scoping by the initiating organisation safeguards against false perceptions, blind alleys and blinkered vision. It can save time and energy, and help ensure that appropriate partners and stakeholders are identified early. Scoping typically involves

- round-table discussion/brainstorm/visioning
- informal discussion with key organisations and opinion-formers
- quick review of relevant legislation, policy documents or guidelines; and/or
- a dispassionate visual appraisal of the area involved.

Scoping seeks to answer these questions:

### What is the purpose and scope of the project?

Clarity about aims is half the battle! Scoping should identify connections with other issues, the spatial area that could be affected and the range of possible means of implementation.

### What is the organisation's capacity?

Capacity to pursue the initiative depends on commitment, time and skill. If the organisation does not have the capacity, then what key partnerships could be forged to enable effective progress?

### Is the initiative consistent with broader aims?

The original idea of the project needs to evolve in such a way that it has the potential to fit into the broad goals and strategies of the development plan and/or the Community Strategy, and also to satisfy the three criteria of sustainable development: economic viability, health/social justice and environmental sustainability. There may be links or symbiosis with other projects that can help.

### What stakeholders should be involved?

Whichever organisation is the initiator, it is vital to draw in other stakeholders as soon as possible. The potential value of a plan is as much in the process as in the product. If some of the major players are not on board then the effectiveness of any output in shaping policy will be severely hampered. Indeed it is quite possible for a LA21 or community-initiated process to sink without trace. At the outset, therefore, the strategy should be devised to reach out to sympathetic people within other groups and organisations. The intention should be to build a constituency of support, and share ownership of the project so that effective collaboration is possible.

*The scoping process should identify:*

- *Potential partners, needed to achieve a co-ordinated plan.*
- *Relevant regulatory bodies and potential sources of funds.*
- *Representatives of groups who stand to benefit.*
- *Representatives of groups who might feel threatened.*

## 3.7   STAGE 2 – DEFINING A SHARED VISION

 Effective collaboration depends on developing a common view about aims, scope and process. This takes time. A joint visioning exercise can be a means of welding disparate interests into a team. A shared vision, however, does not mean an idle dream. It is about the creation of a practical plan of campaign that can be encapsulated in a formal project brief.

### COMMUNITY VISIONING

Participation in a visioning exercise should be as open as possible. The process needs to be managed by a skilled facilitator, preferably independent of any of the main organisations. It can take a day or more. One purpose of visioning is to find and enlarge the common ground between participants; another is to get to know people; a third is to develop new, creative ideas together. All this can help engender mutual understanding, trust and enthusiasm.

### THE PROJECT BRIEF
Agreement on the project brief is a pivotal milestone in any neighbourhood planning exercise. The purpose of the brief is to set out clearly the aims and scope of the project, the process of appraisal and decision-making, and the way stakeholders and the public will be involved in that process. Joint ownership of the brief is key to partnership. Transparency of the process is key to legitimacy.

### Preparing the brief

If there has been a community visioning exercise then the participants may have allocated the task of preparing the brief. However, it is essential that the key initiating (or lead) organisation keeps a tight rein at this stage to maintain momentum. The lead organisation may prepare a first draft of the project brief on the basis of the scoping exercise and/or the visioning process. The draft should take into account the views expressed informally by potential partners. It can be used to draw other parties into engagement with the project by showing how their interests might be affected and how they could become creatively involved.

Clarity of aims is critical. The lead organisation needs to be honest and explicit about its own motives and aspirations. Fudge and waffle have no place: they can lead to misunderstanding and store up problems for later. Conversely, premature prescription must be avoided. The first draft is just that, a draft, for consultation. It is not the final version. It can therefore be short. If appropriate it may be brought back to the 'visioning' group for further joint work. The final brief, once agreed, is the basis for collaboration. If there are to be partners in the project, then the brief acts as part of the formal agreement. It is also the basis for initial publicity, and available for public scrutiny.

*Community initiatives*

*Where a community group is promoting the ideas of a neighbourhood plan it is obviously not possible to move straight to a draft brief. Instead, getting to the point where a brief can be drafted becomes a prime goal. The drafting must involve the main agency (the local authority, for example) that has the power to deliver.*

*What should the brief include?*

*The final version of the brief should be explicit about*

- *the broad policy context*

- *the purpose and scope of the exercise, with explanation*

- *how the project will be managed: leadership, resources, timescale*

- *the agreed roles of other stakeholders*

- *the process of public consultation*

- *the scope of the appraisal*

- *the process of policy-making*

- *expected outputs.*

*Community health profiles*

*Every designated healthy city in the WHO network has produced a 'city health profile' often with an explicit neighbourhood dimension. They include the full range of social, economic and environmental factors that affect health, and involve collaboration between health and local authorities.*

*Guidance is available from www.euro.who.int City health profiles: how to report the health of your city.*

# creating a strategy

**3.8 STAGE 3 – UNDERSTANDING THE LOCALITY**

**BASIC PRINCIPLES**
Neighbourhood appraisal is a systematic review of the attributes, problems and potential of an area, undertaken as an essential part of neighbourhood plan-making or a major development proposal. Detailed information on every issue is not so important as awareness of the whole sustainability agenda. Appraisal can proceed hand in hand with stage 4, 'developing ideas', as part of a progressive and collaborative learning process.

**The neighbourhood appraisal ...**

- may be tackled at different levels of sophistication depending on specific needs and resources but must encompass all the spheres of the neighbourhood model. Where time pressures and lack of resources dictate, it can take the form of a quick but comprehensive scan of all the issues, drawing on the knowledge of stakeholders. Part of the purpose of the scan is to identify where detailed research is needed.
- should build upon, and contribute to, wider review processes such as quality-of-life reports, urban capacity studies, community health profiles and local plan review.
- involves collaboration between stakeholders and this can be as important to effective action as the product itself.
- rarely occurs in a policy vacuum. Often there are already specific ideas and proposals. But it is vital to suspend judgement on those proposals and open the mind to other possibilities. The appraisal becomes, effectively, part of the evaluation process, tying in with any SEA or EIA.

## SHARING OWNERSHIP AND DEFINING SCOPE

A neighbourhood appraisal needs to be co-ordinated by one organisation (the local planning department, for example). But it should not be owned by only that organisation. Rather, the appraisal can be seen as a way of forging working relationships between a range of stakeholders. The scope of the appraisal should be defined by the stakeholder group and benefit from the specialist input they can make. For example the health authority, and the housing and education departments can each supply part of the picture. Local voluntary groups can get involved in specific surveys (such as pedestrian counts or open space surveys).

**Looking at the whole township**

Neighbourhoods cannot be treated as islands. It is vital that the appraisal encompass the areas adjacent to the neighbourhood that are locally connected, including local high streets, industrial areas, secondary schools, parks and adjacent areas of open or greenfield land. At the same time the area has to be meaningful in terms of local identity and allegiance. This broader area may be equated with the township or the country town and its immediate setting.

**Making sense of statistics**

If possible, make the area of study coincide with one or more wards or parishes. This greatly simplifies the analysis of data and links with quality-of-life indicators. It also makes clear which local councillors, parish or community councils should be involved.

**Linking with quality-of-life indicators**

Much of the neighbourhood level information should not require special surveys but be collected regularly as part of district-wide quality-of-life monitoring (often in the form of 'state-of-the-environment' reports or 'city health profiles'). Section 3.13 gives examples of indicators.

## THE USE OF AN APPRAISAL

Neighbourhood appraisal is needed when the area is likely to experience considerable change. The change might be the result of regeneration policies, new housing/commercial allocations, or progressive restructuring over a considerable period.

The appraisal is designed to assist and validate policy formulation. Its purpose is to show
- what the current problems are and how serious they are
- how effective current policies are at tackling those problems
- what the local significance is of broader trends/pressures
- how the various issues and policies are interconnected
- what the capacity or potential for change is
- who needs to be involved in policy-making.

**The political dimension**

The process is far from being value-free. The questions above imply a set of objectives and criteria. The appraisal is a means of articulating local and societal values, hopefully consistent with sustainable development. It is therefore highly politically charged. The involvement of councillors at an early stage is critical. The help of community leaders and the local press/media should be actively sought. From the outset the process needs to be seen as an opportunity not a threat.

**A holistic approach**

The typical approach to appraisal at present is based on narrowly defined problem solving. For example, there is pressure to find more housing land: so sites are identified and assessed against specific criteria. This is not adequate. The appraisal should be used to give a rounded view of the dynamics of a settlement so that individual sites are seen in context.

**Map-based systems and GIS**

The approach needs to be accessible, policy-orientated, adaptable and cheap. Much of the information can be recorded on a series of appraisal maps and commentaries which can be manually or electronically cross-referenced. This allows the incorporation of specific data on land, building, activities, social and environmental capital in a context which assists forward planning. The approach can be adopted at different levels of sophistication. It is ideally suited for Geographical Information Systems (GIS) manipulation, and consistent with both urban capacity techniques and the environmental capital approach.

## NEIGHBOURHOOD APPRAISAL – PEOPLE, COMMUNITY, ACTIVITIES

| Topics | Units and sources | Cross reference |
|---|---|---|

### PEOPLE

**Basic information**
- population levels, structure and trends
- household characteristics and trends
- socio-economic and ethnic groups
- car ownership levels

- by ward or parish
- from the Census and special sample household surveys

4.2 Population →

**Quality of life**
- poverty and employment indicators
- health and education indicators
- housing and local environmental quality indicators
- crime and community well-being indicators

- by ward or parish
- from local authority 'quality of life' or 'state of environment' reports, or city health profiles
- issues raised by residents

3.13 Indicators →
4.2 Population →

### COMMUNITY

**Community issues**
- resident perceptions of local community and support
- service provider concerns (e.g. health visitors, social services, police, housing managers, churches, youth leaders)
- stocktake of groups and activities
- facilities/places that are important for social interaction (formal/informal)

- from consultation and discussion between stakeholders
- LA21 SWOT analysis
- councillors
- sample household survey

4.3 Social capital →

**Participation**
- residents actively members of groups
- resident involvement in local policy process
- stakeholder involvement (private, public and voluntary sectors)

- base upon special sample household survey and the evidence of the processes themselves

3.5 Participation →

### ACTIVITIES

**Local services**
- issues raised by retail, transport and leisure providers
- issues raised by state service providers
- issues raised by residents and users
- use and value of local open spaces
- local facility stocktake

- from consultation and discussion between stakeholders
- LA21 SWOT analysis
- councillors
- sample household survey

4.8 Facilities →

**Economic activity**
- issues raised by local employers and entrepreneurs
- concerns of workers and residents
- extent of home working
- LETS, credit unions and informal economic activity
- economic activity stocktake: job ratio by township

- from consultation and discussion between stakeholders
- LA21 SWOT analysis
- councillors
- sample household survey

4.6 Local work →

**Movement**
- pedestrian and cycling flows, barriers, needs
- public transport services evaluated
- vehicle flows, speeds, accidents

- mapped, with commentary
- information from operators, highway department, police

4.14 Movement →

natural resources
places
local activities
community
people

## NEIGHBOURHOOD APPRAISAL – PLACE, NATURAL RESOURCES

| Topics | Units and sources | Cross reference |
|---|---|---|

### PLACE

**Basic information**
- area, net residential and gross residential densities
- land-use pattern

- survey for the National Land Use Database (NLUD)

6.8 Graded densities →
6.5 Mixed uses →

**Buildings and infrastructure**
- condition of buildings, private and public spaces
- housing stock, by tenure, type and size
- commercial and institutional building stock
- market trends, property prices and rents
- planning enquiries, applications and permissions
- infrastructure quality and spare capacity

- map at 1:2500 or 1:5000 scale
- information from land-use survey, agents and infrastructure providers (water, sewage, gas, electricity)
- planning authority records

6.4 and 6.13 Urban renewal →
6.11 Urban potential →

**Routeways and accessibility**
- pedestrian routes classified by quality, safety and connectivity
- roads classified by traffic and environmental capacity
- accessibility to bus stops and tram/train halts
- accessibility to local facilities and open space
- wider 'job search' areas by public transport access

- mapping/GIS analysis at, say, 1:5000 scale
- special visual surveys

4.14 Movement →
4.8 Facilities →

**Aesthetic character**
- local perceptions of the quality of public spaces
- townscape, and legibility analysis
- protected heritage (listed buildings, CAs, etc.)
- issues of noise, fumes, and visual intrusion

- annotated maps, relying on stakeholder/focus-group data and urban design analysis

6.3 Distinctiveness →

**Urban capacity and potential**
- potential use and density of vacant plots/fields
- potential for extra dwellings from conversion, upper storeys etc.
- potential for higher plot ratios
- environmental, access and aesthetic constraints

- analysis by land-use parcels and sampling of problematic areas – then mapped with constraints to give overall potential; should be part of local plan process

6.11 Urban potential →

### NATURAL RESOURCES

**Biophysical context**
- landform and solar aspect
- microclimate conditions and air quality
- water catchment, drainage, flood plain
- wildlife habitats and corridors
- soil quality and contamination
- tree cover and carbon sinks
- local sources of fuel or building materials

- map at 1:2500 or 1:5000 scale
- from the Local Plan or Environmental Capacity study
- supplemented by information from specialist interests (e.g. wildlife trusts, Environment Agency)

5.4 Energy →
5.7 Water →
5.18 Biodiversity →

**Ecological footprint**
- energy-efficiency in buildings, energy supply systems and transport
- water efficiency and opportunities for action
- materials recycling and re-use; opportunities
- local food production: opportunities

- commentary, with map, identifying current situation vis-à-vis best practice

5.4 Energy →
5.7 Water →
5.14 Waste →
5.10 Food →

## 3.9 STAGE 4 – DEVELOPING IDEAS

### BASIC PRINCIPLES

Policy ideas and specific development proposals may be put forward by a wide range of organisations at any stage in the process. It is likely that some proposals will proceed at a different rate to others, and with different (sometimes conflicting) objectives. This is not in itself a problem. But it lends weight to the need to agree a common approach to policy-making. There are three essential principles:

■ *Search for the best options.* Do not rely just on the first or most strongly suggested ideas, but examine other options that might do better.

■ *Evaluate alternatives systematically.* It is not only a matter of reaching agreement between key players, but also ensuring fundamental social and environmental goals are achieved.

■ *Ensure consistency.* Make sure that different policies and proposals harmonise and reinforce each other. In particular work towards an agreed spatial framework (see 3.10).

**Avoiding premature conclusions**

It is all too easy for a particular agency or a key individual to present a proposal in answer to recognised problems without adequate analysis of the situation. For example, a self-evident solution to a congested shopping street might be to ban traffic, or the answer to the question of a derelict industrial site might be a brand new business park, but such decisions need cool, dispassionate evaluation, separated from the particular financial or political issues at stake. Such evaluation relies on greater understanding through a neighbourhood (or township) appraisal, and a willingness to compare alternative solutions.

**Avoiding prevarication and delay**

At the same time as avoiding premature judgements it is also important to make progress. There is a balance to be struck between knowledge and speed. Events (including political/market pressures) often require decisions in the teeth of uncertainty. So all technical and collaborative processes need to be pragmatic, while avoiding superficiality.

■ How much do we need to know to make progress?

■ What decisions can be taken now without foreclosing desirable longer-term options?

■ What specific studies can be done to reduce key uncertainties?

### EXPLORE AND TEST OPTIONS

It is important to present real options to local people and decision-makers. This is just as vital when the options are basic ('do nothing' versus 'do something', for example) as when they are complex. Options should be compared for their likely effects using some form of sustainability assessment (see below), and testing

- desirability – fulfilling aspirations for health, sustainability and vitality

- feasibility – ensuring the mechanisms, land, finance and expertise is there to make things happen.

### Win-win-win

Policies and proposals do not normally spring from nowhere; they evolve, they respond to new pressures or opportunities. As they are doing so, it is easy to lose the sustainability focus (or miss it from the start).

The normal confrontational approach to policy debate, where one interest is pitted against another (jobs versus the environment, greenfields versus brownfields) is unlikely to lead to sustainable development. So the questions are

- How can the different interests be successfully reconciled?

- How can we devise creative policies that fulfil social, economic and environmental priorities?

It is a matter of not either/or but both/and.

The process therefore needs to be inclusive, drawing different (sometimes competing) interests into mutual engagement, forming alliances, negotiating collaborative programmes, tackling problems in the round. A committed search for solutions, together with a willingness to challenge vested interest, can lead to success. One example, in relation to transport, is the promotion of walking: creating a safe, convenient and attractive pedestrian environment is at the heart of neighbourhood planning, and has clear health, community, environmental and local economic benefits.

The real problem is not necessarily *finding* win-win-win policies, as in implementing them with sufficient coherence and dynamism to make them work. That coherence and dynamism will only happen if a common philosophy is accepted by the key interests involved.

### Synergy

Policy failure, from the sustainable development viewpoint, often occurs because *implementing* agencies are hamstrung by their institutional or financial conventions. Conversely, when agencies collaborate for mutual benefit, new doors are opened. For example, joint recreational provision by Education Authorities and Leisure or Parks Departments ('dual use') can benefit everyone and cut costs; energy-efficiency measures reduce pollution, combat fuel poverty, and create local jobs.

*Use the trefoil symbol of sustainable development as a 'quick and dirty' analytical tool. All three criteria need to be achieved. If they are not, then search for another solution that could perform better.*

*Examples of synergy later in the guide*

**4.12 Supporting health** →

**4.15 Pedestrian planning** →

**5.7 Water and wildlife** →

**5.6 Energy from waste** →

**6.5 Mixed use** →

**6.9 Green network** →

**6.15 Home-patch** →

# 3.9

---

**CATEGORIES AND CRITERIA**

**Health and well-being**

3.1   Healthy lifestyle
3.2   Social cohesion
3.3   Social inclusion
3.4   Community safety

**Economic vitality**

3.5   Local work opportunities
3.6   Good local facilities
3.7   Market buoyancy

**Social need**

3.8   Housing availability
3.9   Quality of built space
3.10  Open space
3.11  Pedestrian accessibility
3.12  Public transport accessibility

**Environmental quality**

3.13  Aesthetic quality
3.14  Cultural heritage
3.15  Biodiversity

**Resources and climate**

3.16  Food
3.17  Water
3.18  Air quality
3.19  Energy efficiency
3.20  Carbon-fixing
3.21  Land and soils
3.22  Minerals

---

*Figure 3.7*
**Sustainability appraisal**

SOURCE: THIS LIST IS DERIVED FROM DOE 1993, AND
BARTON AND TSOUROU 2000.

*This appraisal list is not too different from
lists produced by many local authorities*

## EVALUATING POLICY

A township or neighbourhood plan should be evaluated using the same approach as for development plans. The Environmental Appraisal of Development Plans good practice guide (DoE 1993) established a robust approach, which has proved its worth over the years. It is a form of Strategic Environmental Assessment (SEA).

The ODPM is encouraging local authorities to extend the scope of appraisal to encompass social and economic criteria: full sustainable development appraisal.

The evaluation exercise is ideally not an end-point test but part of the process of developing and improving policy. Policies and strategies can be assessed against a common checklist of sustainability criteria.

### Health and environmental impact

There is a very substantial overlap between the issues dealt with in health impact analyses and environmental impact analyses. The two forms of assessment should be one.

Health and environmental agencies both need to be involved, contributing their specific knowledge

### Consistency workshop

This is an essential part of sustainability appraisal. It is particularly important in relation to the spatial framework. The purpose is to establish the degree of consistency between the spatial policies being pursued by different organisations or different sections of the local authority.

The analysis can be undertaken as a workshop, with representatives from relevant agencies. The sustainability checklist provides the context against which policy combinations are evaluated. A matrix provides the agenda and mean of summarising results. The workshop is a scoping process, identifying the awkward or problematic policy interactions for subsequent work.

*Figure 3.7*
**Compatibility matrix**

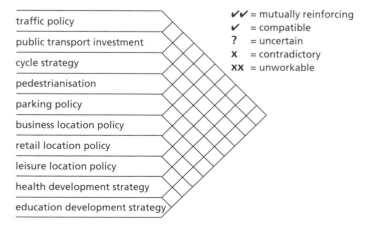

---

## 3.10 STAGE 5 – AGREEING A CO-ORDINATED PROGRAMME

 The partners should, after due consultation, aim to agree a package of commitments that encompass not only broad aims and policies but also specific mechanisms for implementing and co-ordinating change, and for subsequent management. As part of this, an agreed spatial framework working towards sustainable development is essential.

The commitment package described below could be appropriate for an area of major change: a regeneration area or urban extension. But many of the elements would be necessary, at some level, in an area of only modest change.

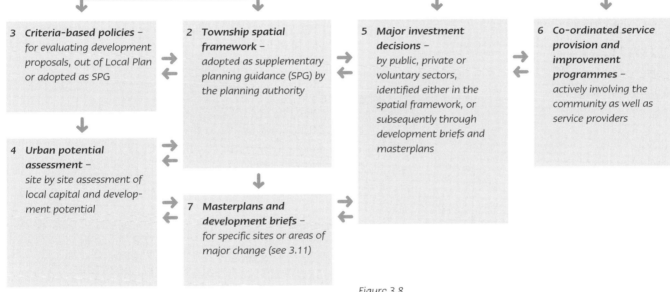

**1 Agreed vision and strategy –**
*local expression of the broader, local authority-wide Community Strategy and Local Plan*

**3 Criteria-based policies –**
*for evaluating development proposals, out of Local Plan or adopted as SPG*

**4 Urban potential assessment –**
*site by site assessment of local capital and development potential*

**2 Township spatial framework –**
*adopted as supplementary planning guidance (SPG) by the planning authority*

**7 Masterplans and development briefs –**
*for specific sites or areas of major change (see 3.11)*

**5 Major investment decisions –**
*by public, private or voluntary sectors, identified either in the spatial framework, or subsequently through development briefs and masterplans*

**6 Co-ordinated service provision and improvement programmes –**
*actively involving the community as well as service providers*

*Figure 3.8*
**Main elements of a commitment package**

## 1 AGREED VISION AND STRATEGY

The starting point for the plan should be an agreed vision for the future of the area, with a clear overall strategy on how it might be implemented. The vision and strategy should have been subject to extensive consultation. They should encompass all five elements of the neighbourhood model: people, community, activities, place and resources. Both vision and strategy must be consistent with the Community Strategy and local plan (which are for the whole local authority).

**LEGEND**

 Local Centre with basic facilities

 Higher density residential development including individual workspaces.

 Medium density residential development

 Lower density residential development.

 Existing building groups incorporated into the development.

 Structure planting & shelterbelts providing strong edges & wildlife corridors

 New formal Avenue planting to enhance approach experience.

 Greens as public open space.

 Existing drainage Rhynes giving structure to landscape.

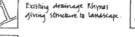 Proposed lakes to improve drainage + balancing ponds.

 Continuous frontages facing main streets & major spaces.

 Frontages alternating with walls & planting facing main streets.

 Potential Skyline interest in built form.

 Large scale Landmark Sculpture

 Major approach views of the development.

 Major new access points for the development

 Bus service extended to travel through & between the development

 Main footpath/cycle routes permeating the developments

 Exposed Ridge framing & sheltering the development

## 2 THE TOWNSHIP SPATIAL FRAMEWORK

The spatial framework is a land-use/movement strategy for township development. It needs to cover an area broad enough to provide, at least potentially, a significant degree of local autonomy. Its purpose is to articulate the intended pattern of development and activity. It should be adopted as supplementary planning guidance by the local authority. More specifically, the spatial framework should

- specify main public transport, walking/cycling and vehicle networks

- identify zones of different use-intensities, main service centres, industrial areas, etc., in relation to public transport accessibility and pedestrian connectedness

- show the greenspace system and its principal social and ecological functions.

It is not, however, a precise land-use guide. Rather, it is a broad co-ordinating mechanism, to be used in concert with the criteria-based policies (see below). The degree of site-specificity depends on levels of certainty. Firm commitments (for example an agreed site for a new health centre, or a firm reservation for a riverside park)

*Figure 3.9*
**Spatial framework for a major urban extension**

*Note: spatial frameworks for existing built up areas are illustrated in Section 6.13*

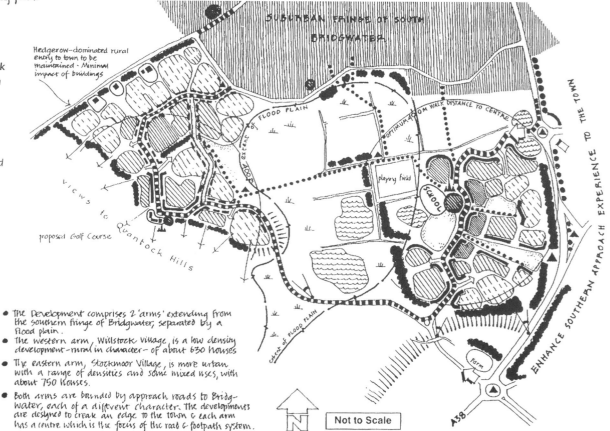

- The Development comprises 2 'arms' extending from the southern fringe of Bridgwater; separated by a flood plain.
- The western arm, Willstock Village, is a low density development-rural in character- of about 630 houses
- The eastern arm, Stockmoor Village, is more urban with a range of densities and some mixed uses, with about 750 houses.
- Both arms are bounded by approach roads to Bridgwater, each of a different character. The developments are designed to create an edge to the town & each arm has a centre which is the focus of the road & footpath system.

Not to Scale

can be shown precisely. But less certain proposals should not be prematurely identified. The framework should provide the context within which future decisions can be taken, allowing for the fact that development needs and opportunities cannot be entirely foreseen. It provides the setting for more specific masterplanning (areas of major change) and site development briefs.

The illustration opposite show a spatial framework for an urban extension. Section 6.13 shows frameworks for existing urban areas.

## 3  CRITERIA-BASED PLANNING

While future development proposals may be unpredictable, the criteria by which they will be judged should be as explicit as possible. This helps to reduce uncertainty for those making proposals, as well as for those evaluating them. Criteria can be devised for all facets of development, from location to design. They should encompass housing, commerce, open space, energy, water, biodiversity, etc. The Local Plan and Community Strategy may provide generic criteria which can be refined to reflect the specific vision and strategy of the township/town.

To be useful, the criteria should be pointed and precise. For example, the 'development code' devised for Ashton Green by Leicester City Council (1998) included the following in relation to accessibility and transport choice:

- A comprehensive network of safe, direct and attractive facilities for cyclists including cycle park provision must be provided.

- Easy access for cycle storage shall be provided for every household.

- All pedestrian routes must be well lit and overlooked by adjoining developments.

- As a minimum, public transport routes should aim to achieve accessibility standards not in excess of 250 m from trip origins to either a 'hail and ride' or formal bus stop for at least 75 per cent of the site. 250 m shall be measured 'as you walk'.

## 4  URBAN POTENTIAL ASSESSMENT

The assessment of urban capacity or potential, undertaken by the local authority, forms part of the neighbourhood appraisal but also is an important element of the plan. It involves site-by-site analysis and prescription, taking account of both the environmental constraints on development and the growth potential. Whereas the spatial framework gives a picture of the overall strategy, the urban potential assessment is much more specific. It is vital that the two are consistent with each other and with the criteria-based policies.

The site-by-site judgements give a basis for siting decisions in development briefs and developers' investment programmes.

*Chapters 4 and 5 provide specific criteria in relation to most aspects of local planning.*

*Avoid weak criteria*

*For example, the statement 'Health centres should be accessible by public transport' is open to a wide range of responses. The underlying principle should lead to a more pointed statement of criteria, such as: 'Health centres should normally be within 200 m of a regular (minimum half-hourly) public transport service giving access to nearby residential areas'.*

6.11 Preparing a spatial framework  →

6.11 Urban potential  →

*The usual suspects*

*Commitments may be needed from*
- *the Planning Department*
- *the Transport/Engineering Department*
- *the main public transport operator(s)*
- *the Health Authority*
- *the Education Authority*
- *the parks/leisure department;*

*plus, depending on context*
- *community groups and Community Development Trusts*
- *major employers/chamber of trade/house-builders*
- *the housing department and/or housing association*
- *the Police Authority*
- *Social Services and community development agencies; and*
- *Economic development/regeneration agencies.*

## 5  MAJOR INVESTMENT DECISIONS: STAKEHOLDER COMMITMENT

A plan has little value if the means of implementation are not clear. Realisation may depend on major investment decisions. An obvious example is a new tramway, without which proposals for higher density and commercial use may be invalid. The plan should be specific about commitments entered into by public, private and voluntary organisations, or, if that is premature, the process by which commitments will be made.

## 6  CO-ORDINATED SERVICE PROVISION

Collaboration between providers is an important aspiration for Community Strategies, and is likely to have local spatial manifes-tations. Secondary schools, for example, may link with community sports, swimming pool and library provision; a joint local centre for decentralised local authority services might need office/retail space; sharing of church facilities between different denominations and community groups might result in redundant buildings. The plan can facilitate and help manage such changes.

The commitment package can provide the context for reaching agreement between providers, and help to tie in investment decisions.

## TAKING THE LONG VIEW

### On-going management

It is all too easy to produce impressive schemes and policies which subsequently fail because nobody is clear how they will be implemented or managed. For example, the re-use of upper storeys above shops will often require specific grants. Similarly, the management of communal open spaces, reed-bed sewage schemes and community energy schemes is likely to require a special board or residents' management committee. The agreed programme has to anticipate these problems and be realistic in its expectations.

### Monitoring and review

A plan is not a blueprint, set in aspic and guaranteed to deliver. Rather, it is part of a continuous, evolving process – hence the circularity of the summary diagram in 3.3. Yet frequently decisions, once implemented, are not reviewed to establish whether they 'working', or what can be learnt from them. It is therefore vital to establish how monitoring and review will occur – who will do what – as part of the overall package (see 3.13).

3.11 Stage 7 Masterplanning →

3.12 Development briefs →

3.13 Learning lessons →

# making it happen

## INTRODUCTION

The process of implementation tends to be disjointed and incremental, as opposed to the neat world of analysis and strategy. Proposals come forward according to unpredictable factors from a wide range of interests. The main sets of mechanisms are

- The investment programmes of public bodies – transport, schools, health, water, leisure, etc.

- Planning applications from local households and businesses – mainly small scale but adding up to significant change over time.

- Major development proposals – from house-builders, housing associations, commercial developers.

- Projects put together by Community Development Trusts or other special voluntary sector bodies, with cross-sectoral partnerships and often local leadership.

The sections below do not attempt to cover all these mechanisms but present some tools of co-ordination: masterplanning, design codes, development briefs, and development control requirements.

## 3.11 STAGE 6 – TAKING ACTION: MASTERPLANNING

### THE IMPORTANCE OF PLACE-MAKING

A masterplan, establishing a three-dimensional framework for buildings and public spaces, is needed for any area of major change – such as an urban extension or a regeneration area. The masterplan is more detailed and prescriptive than the spatial framework or old-fashioned zoning plan. It is a tool of urban design and implementation.

The masterplan should be prepared for or by the agency which has the power to deliver. This normally means the prime land-owning or funding organisation. However, it is essential that other stakeholders are involved and preparation is seen as a collaborative exercise, with shared ownership and commitment (see Section 3.4).

There is also much more chance of a masterplan being grounded in the realities of neighbourhood planning if it is developed with the continuous involvement of the local community (see Section 3.5).

The masterplan for a regeneration area or new urban extension is likely to be a package rather than a single plan, and acts to draw together all the strands which guide and control development. It should consist of four main parts: the appraisal, the design strategy, the design code, and the implementation plan.

*Masterplans as implementation*

*Masterplans have a long and perhaps chequered history. They have sometimes been associated with overoptimistic design-led schemes unrelated to implementation mechanisms. The spatial masterplans proposed here, however, are expressly part of an implementation package.*

*The Urban Task Force report Towards an Urban Renaissance (DETR 1999i) advocates the use of masterplans and recommends that planning permission and public funding for area regeneration schemes be conditional upon the production of an integrated spatial masterplan. The Urban White Paper (DETR 2000) supports this.*

*Elements of a design code*

- *Plot size and shape (width, depth and general 'grain').*
- *Amount of building footprint on the plot.*
- *Placing of footprint on the plot (for example, terracing or distance of space between buildings, orientation for maximum solar gain, depth of front garden or yard, dependent on whether house has sunny front or not).*
- *Position of garage, car hardstanding or car court and relationship to layout.*
- *Width of pavement, verge and carriageway.*
- *Treatment of front and back boundaries, and front and rear access, planting.*
- *Number of storeys related to importance or width of street.*
- *Roof pitch related to optimum pitch of solar panels and/or achieving headroom for storage and extension.*
- *Placement of any projections in front or behind the main building lines, including potential for later extensions, conservatories.*
- *Range of building and surface materials.*
- *Proportion of windows to wall in relation to solar aspect.*

## ELEMENTS OF A MASTERPLAN

### 1  The context and site appraisal

- policy context and rationale for the project
- aims and objectives
- partners and decision-making process
- detailed site appraisals
- the site in its broader town or neighbourhood context

### 2  The design strategy

This is the heart of the masterplan and is likely to comprise notation on a map base showing use, density, routes and design features, plus indicative illustrations to aid visualisation of the proposed character of the project. It is a visual 'model' that

- determines the distribution of uses, horizontally and vertically, and the density of development
- identifies centres, nodes, sub-areas of special character or sense of place (e.g. home-patches)
- identifies landmarks, vistas, skyline treatment, hard and soft edges
- defines the network of streets and routeways for walking, cycling, public transport, cars and service vehicles
- allows us to understand what the public spaces – the streets, squares, and greenspaces – will be like and how they will be connected to each other
- delivers the general height and massing of buildings, and their relationship to public spaces in terms of access and frontage treatment
- defines key features of sustainable development such as shelter belts, water management, protected habitats, food-growing, composting and recycling spaces
- provides the context within which design codes can guide building massing, orientation, plots, street profiles and access, materials and colour.

### 3  Design codes

Design codes can be used in the context of masterplanning and are a method of street making: that is, the creation of a coherent set of streetscapes which addresses the three elements comprising a street holistically – i.e. the street, the buildings on either side, and the plots on which the buildings sit. The code aims to deliver

- a locally distinctive and attractive environment
- low crime levels and a sense of safety

■ a convivial, pedestrian-orientated public space

■ a good orientation and aspect for home and garden

■ satisfactory and secure parking arrangements; and

■ an appropriate plot-planting and biodiversity regime.

**4  The implementation plan**

■ Phasing strategy – shows the sequence of building and the allocation of development sites or parcels. It should also include a strategy regarding short term use of 'fallow' sites for future development.

■ Ownership and tenure statements – shows the projected residential tenure distribution (owner-occupied, self-build, housing association, shared equity, private rented, etc.), and the land owned by major developers/financial institutions, public ownership, and so on.

■ Management plans – these could include
– waste management plan
– biodiversity strategy
– water management plan
– energy strategy (including CHP and heat mains)
– areas likely to be covered by covenants/restrictions.

■ Development briefs – the masterplan creates a framework in which the need for more detailed guidance is identified. It is likely that the guidance will be required for the more complex or environmentally sensitive areas. See the next section.

## THE LIMITS OF MASTERPLANNING

The Taskforce report suggests masterplans should be both visionary and deliverable. Beware of glossy images where they have no clear means of realisation. Implementation relies on a supportive planning and neighbourhood context, the ownership of land and the availability of capital.

In areas of modest or unpredictable change, masterplans are not the answer. Rather it is better to rely on the spatial framework and design guidance (adopted by the local authority as supplementary planning guidance). These can provide a good basis for negotiations with developers but are intentionally robust and flexible enough to survive the extingencies of the development process. Such guidelines should identify the 'bottom line' and articulate the opportunities without being prematurely prescriptive. The process can move straight to development briefs for specific sites.

### 3.12 TAKING ACTION: DEVELOPMENT PROPOSAL

One acid test of the spatial planning process is the quality of planning applications. In the context of a collaborative approach the onus is on the prospective investors – households, firms or institutions – to come forward with appropriate schemes. The planning regime should encourage and facilitate this by requiring appraisal information and mini impact statements with applications above a certain size.

In most situations the spatial framework provides adequate guidance for investors. However, where the site is awkward or the context is complex a development brief can reduce investor uncertainties and promote an appropriate response.

### DEVELOPMENT BRIEFS: BEING AHEAD OF THE GAME

Briefs for development on specific sites should be produced by planning authorities or development companies within the context of a spatial strategy or masterplan. The main purpose of the brief is to trigger an appropriate development response. Timing is everything. The brief can invite competition in areas of high demand, or offer development incentives where demand is low.

Normally sites will be owned or available for sale as one unit. The brief sets the context for any subsequent development proposal. It interprets policy at the site level, and affects site value.

Briefs are most useful where they co-ordinate the policy and advice from various interested departments and agencies: planning, highways, utility companies, conservation agencies, for example. Objectives, site and context appraisal may be accompanied by an indicative layout and built form guidance – especially on access, desire lines across site, mix of uses, density, key building heights, views, trees, management of communal space, and so on. However, the brief should not be used as an aesthetic control tool. It is important to give freedom of interpretation to the architect/designer.

It is essential that briefs are compiled early in the development process, before sites are purchased or as a condition of purchase. At this stage the developer can assess the value of land in relation to the requirements of the brief.

A vital part of the requirements will be a Section 106 Planning Agreement, setting out expectations for contribution to public transport infrastructure, schools, parkland, off-site road junctions, etc.

### SUBMITTING AN APPLICATION

The applicant can demonstrate the logic of the proposal in its context by providing the following information in a clear and helpful way. This should apply to all development proposals over a certain size.

*The development brief*

*Typically, contents of a brief relating to a major development site might consist of*

- *a statement of the rationale of the brief*

- *status of the brief (is it adopted local authority policy or advisory?)*

- *identification of the site*

- *preferred uses and mix of uses, density, etc.*

- *context and site appraisal*

- *requirements: access, wildlife corridors, etc.*

- *urban design objectives, connections, frontages, etc.*

- *Section 106 requirements*

- *submission of information for planning application*

- *criteria for sustainability appraisal required by the local authorities; and*

- *contacts.*

*Best Practice in planning applications*

*This list of requirements is adapted from the Forest of Dean District Council's Residential Design Guide (1998). The Guide has been adopted by the Council as Supplementary Planning Guidance. All residential proposals for six or more dwellings have to conform to the requirements.*

### Application form and accompanying letter

▪ Describe what is proposed and the types of users/residents provided for.

▪ Specify the precise numbers of different types and sizes of dwellings. Give the gross site area and net and gross housing density figures.

▪ Specify by built area all the non-housing uses.

▪ State the NHER (energy-efficiency) levels achieved.

### Context map

To cover an area of at least 800 m radius from the site boundary.

▪ Show the location of nearby shops, schools, open spaces and public transport routes/stops.

▪ Identify the main potential pedestrian and cycle routes from the site to local facilities such as those above, and to the town or district centre.

▪ Indicate the walking distance in metres from key facilities to the site boundary.

▪ Mark older buildings in the vicinity which help define the distinctive character of the area.

▪ Identify nearby natural and wildlife features (such as streams, woods, railway cuttings).

### Site appraisal map

To cover the area of the development site and its immediate neighbouring sites.

▪ Show all adjacent development, as it is now.

▪ Show the form of the land (perhaps with a cross-section) and hatch any areas of north-facing slope (NW–NE) over 1:15.

▪ Show water courses and any particular ground water conditions.

▪ Mark woodlands, mature trees, hedgerows and any other specific wildlife feature.

▪ Identify all existing structures, buildings (current use and condition) and boundaries (materials, height, condition).

▪ Show potential pedestrian access points (related to routes shown on the location map) and diagrammatically indicate any likely pedestrian/cycling movement across the site.

▪ Mark existing utility routes and possible connection points.

### Site layout

To cover the same area as the appraisal map.

▪ Identify the different housing types, tenures and sizes clearly.

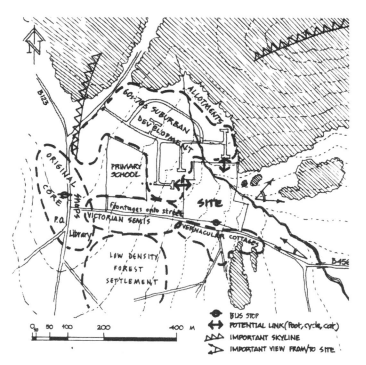

*Figure 3.10*
**Context map**

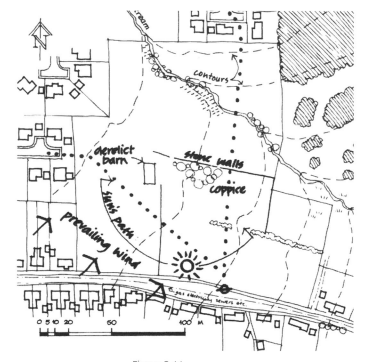

*Figure 3.11*
**Site appraisal map**

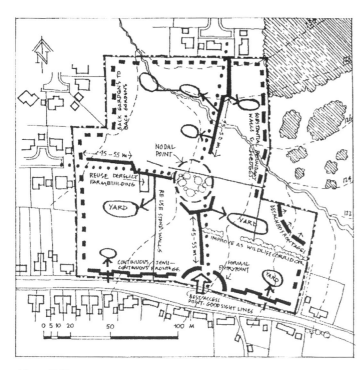

*Figure 3.12*
**Concept plan – a useful intermediary stage
between site appraisal and layout**

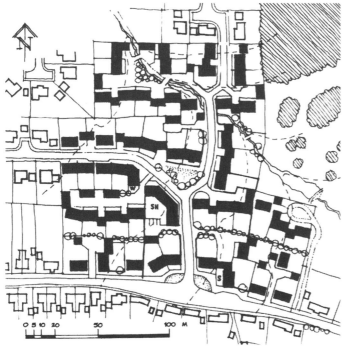

*Figure 3.13*
**Site layout**

- Show plots and curtilages clearly, distinguishing private, semi-private, semi-public and public spaces.

- Identify any work, educational or social uses (including reservations) and buildings where use flexibility would be built in.

- Highlight the pedestrian routes, any 'nodes' or concentrations of pedestrian activity, and any special public spaces.

- Identify any specific cycling facilities (other than normal access roads).

- Distinguish buildings which are oriented and designed to maximise passive solar gain.

- Show areas set aside for on-site water treatment and management.

- Show tree and shrub planting, identifying any planting intended to create a shelter belt.

- Demonstrate which structures are retained and re-used or adapted.

### MINI SUSTAINABILITY IMPACT ASSESSMENT (SIA)

All applications over a certain size (for example, 1,000 m² of built space) could be accompanied by a short 'mini-SIA' report. This would use the same checklist as the Local Plan or neighbourhood plan. It should be scoped initially by a consultation process with other stakeholders (including, of course, the planning authority), and then focus on the key issues. It should show how problems have been avoided or mitigated.

Some local authorities – such as Reading Borough Council – are already operating a mini-EIA system for some planning applications. A mini SIA is a natural extension of the idea.

### 3.13 STAGE 7 – LEARNING LESSONS

#### BASIC PRINCIPLE
Monitoring is not an optional extra. It is fundamental to the whole process – the basis on which success or failure is assessed and policy is revised. The monitoring and review process should be

- *broad ranging* – covering local quality of life, policy impacts and the effectiveness of the decision process

- *practical* – simple enough to be handled for each neighbourhood, ward or parish despite very limited resources

- *motivating* – examining the factors that matter to people with the involvement, as appropriate, of local stakeholders and decision-makers.

Monitoring occurs not only through formalised data collection by local authority officials, but also through the awareness and alertness of local community groups, and parish/town/district councillors. Local planning officers have a particular responsibility to be sensitive to the way neighbourhoods are changing physically. Effective channels of communication between local people, elected representatives and relevant agencies are vital.

## ASSESSING POLICY IMPACT

The main responsibility for assessing the direct impact of policies and development schemes rests with those who are implementing them – though others, particularly those directly affected, should be involved in the process. The key questions are:

1   *How far have policies or proposals been implemented?* For example, if the township strategy proposed new bikeways, how many have been constructed or firmly programmed? Are there mechanisms in place to ensure future progress?

2   *Have policies delivered the expected or desired results?* For example, where new bikeways have been realised, are they being used as intended? Have they led to increased cycling and less car travel? Have they proved safe? Are they approved of by residents?

3   *If there are problems with implementation, what are the causes?* For example, is there a lack of money or key personnel? Has the policy been deflected or highjacked by events? How could the barriers be overcome?

4   *If the results are disappointing where things **have** happened, then why?* For example, if the cyclists are not choosing to use the bikeways, or there has been no increase in cycling or transfer from car, then is this because of poor choice of route? Poor design? Perceived dangers? Lack of knowledge? Lack of reinforcement by other policies?

## ASSESSING HEALTH AND SUSTAINABILITY OUTCOMES

The monitoring agenda is essentially about updating and reviewing the neighbourhood appraisal on a regular basis. It is concerned with the full range of topics listed in Section 3.8: people, community, activities, place and resources. The purpose of assessment are the same.

### Practicality

While during the initial preparation of a neighbourhood strategy there may be extra resources and money to undertake detailed appraisal work, on-going monitoring is more difficult to resource. It is essential to put clear, simple mechanisms in place that are both practical and effective. For example:

3.8 Neighbourhood appraisal  ←

*Examples of possible indicators*

- *Health: mortality rates, by ward*

SOURCE: REGISTER OF BIRTHS, MARRIAGES AND DEATHS; HEALTH AUTHORITY; CENSUS. (CORE NATIONAL INDICATOR F1)

- *Housing: homes judged unfit to live in*

SOURCE: HOUSING DEPARTMENTS. (NATIONAL HEADLINE INDICATOR H7)

- *Movement: mode and distance of children travelling to school, by ward*

SOURCE: SPECIAL SCHOOL OR HOUSEHOLD SURVEYS. (SIMILAR TO CORE NATIONAL INDICATORS J1 AND J2)

- *Environment: number of days of air pollution*

SOURCE: ENVIRONMENTAL HEALTH DEPARTMENTS. (NATIONAL HEADLINE INDICATOR H10)

**Neighbourhood quality of life indicators**

Social, economic and environmental variables are routinely collected and publicised by the local authority. This menu of indicators should be designed by the local authority to be relevant to the neighbourhood level – allowing comparison between neighbourhoods and facilitating prioritisation for action. For this purpose it is normally necessary to rely on ward-based data. Neighbourhood groups, parish and town councils can then extract the data for their own wards and see their area in context.

A starting point for the identification of indicators is provided by *Local Quality of Life Counts* (DETR 2000). The Joseph Rowntree Foundation has recently piloted a more specific list geared to suburban neighbourhoods (2001).

**Social survey**

While much quality of life information is already collected by official agencies and may already be collated by local authorities and published annually, it is recommended that local authorities supplement such statistics with a sample survey of households every two or three years.

The household survey can identify trends in travel behaviour, use of local facilities, levels of satisfaction, changing attitudes and specific concerns. It acts as an objective record of actual behaviour and residents' views. It thus offers an invaluable cross-check on the views expressed by local community groups, businesses and councillors, and will in turn influence those views.

There should be at least 50 households surveyed per ward in order to provide a significant sample. Where there are very different socio-economic, ethnic or cultural groups there may be justification for sampling 50 of each group – though this may be averaged over a number of comparable wards.

**Physical trends**

It is also important to monitor physical change within the neighbourhood: renewal processes (or their absence), densities, land uses, routeways, aesthetic character. Increasingly, this information will be held on GIS software and collated as part of urban capacity or potential studies by the local planning authority. The planning officer responsible for a particular neighbourhood, town or township, working with local groups and councillors, should have a specific remit to review the evolving pattern of the area against sustainable development criteria (see Sections 6.10, 6.11 and 6.12).

**ASSESSING THE EFFECTIVENESS OF THE PROCESS**

It is important to observe and learn from the experience of a particular neighbourhood initiative both to improve that initiative itself and to pass on lessons to subsequent projects elsewhere. Has the process been effective in

▓ clarifying the best way forward towards sustainable development?

▓ reaching decisions and taking timely action?

▓ involving all relevant stakeholders, including the population at large?

▓ sorting problems and overcoming barriers?

▓ enhancing the social capital and capacity of the neighbourhood?

# Ashley Down

## BRISTOL

The City of Bristol College, part of which is located in a complex of five massive blocks of former orphanage buildings dating from the 1870s, has decided to relocate about 60 per cent of its teaching accommodation to a new purpose-built campus in Bristol's Harbourside.

The college authorities sought to finance this project by demolishing three of the former orphanage blocks and replacing them with a medium-density housing scheme. The designs were unveiled at a public meeting. The idea was to 'fast track' the project to obtain funding for the College. The local community's reaction was hostile because

- the proposals seemed alien to the locality in layout and appearance as well as being high density; and
- it meant the loss of a landmark, both in physical and social terms, when demolished, and the 'boarding up' of windows and general dereliction prior to redevelopment.

## PROCESSES

### Taking an initiative

Following the hostility of the reaction, the College and their architects decided to rethink their approach and proposed instead an 'urban village', incorporating sustainable principles as far as possible. The urban village would consist not only of housing but a focus for the wider community in the form of a mixed-use centre.

The 'Sustainable Settlements' team was approached to advise on the plan for the project. It was decided that rather than design a detailed masterplan, a brief for developers would be compiled, based on sound principles of sustainable development and urban design and with the full and continuous involvement of any interested local residents. It was also hoped that the Local Planning Authority might become positively involved in the writing of the brief, but that proved difficult to arrange.

### Working with stakeholders

A working group was established, consisting of the College Accommodation and Relocation Manager, the urban designer of the Sustainable Settlements team, backed up where necessary by other specialists in the team, a representative from the architects for the College for the initial stages, and interested residents who numbered from four to about ten at each meeting.

Others with interests in the project, such as the local planning and highway authorities, local councillors, the adjacent County Cricket Club, the Protest Group who wanted the preservation of the whole complex and buildings, were invited to participate with the group meetings at specific stages in the project.

*Figure 3.14*
**Typical 1–3 storey blocks of the nineteenth-century former orphanage**

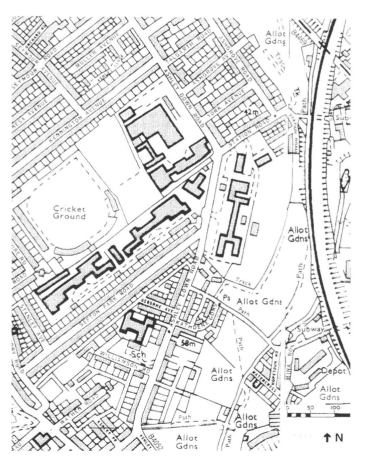

*Figure 3.15*
**Map of the neighbourhood with the college buildings outlined with a bold line. The site of a former station exists towards the northeast corner of the map.**

ASHLEY DOWN, BRISTOL

# 3.a

*This case study demonstrates that residents of a neighbourhood can make a positive contribution to neighbourhood planning if they are fully and continuously involved in the decision-making process.*

*Figure 3.16*
**Exhibition, at an interim stage of the planning and design process, reports on progress and invites local residents to 'post' their views on the exhibit boards**

The working group met fortnightly for 1½ years. The meetings were open to all with no formal committee structure. 'Chatham House Rules' forbidding disclosure of sensitive information outside the group were agreed. This meant that residents were privy to every stage of the negotiation process with planners and developers. It is a tribute to the mutual trust that was built up between members of the working group that no approach was made to the local media regarding confidential information exchanged in the development process. Consequently, residents' representatives were included in direct negotiations with prospective developers.

## Understanding the locality

The first task of the group, at the suggestion of the Sustainable Settlements team, was to conduct an audit and appraisal of the locality, involving the local knowledge of residents. A picture emerged of its character, its potentials, local issues and networks of activities, local businesses and services. The possibilities of reopening and dismantling the railway halt within 500 m of the centre of the proposed neighbourhood was explored, as was the potential to rescue the buildings and the salvage of building materials from demolished outhouses, etc.

The planners' response to local concern about the future of the college site was to recommend the listing of the buildings and the designation of a conservation area tightly drawn round the circumference of the college site.

## Creating a neighbourhood plan

Most of the time was spent in developing an urban design framework which would form the basis of a development and design brief for the site. The brief was to become both a basis for the planners to negotiate with applicants and the basis for company developers to submit bids for developing the site on sustainable urban design principles. Briefly the framework proposed that
- the listed buildings be converted
- new buildings would form streets and blocks
- the streets would have built-in traffic calming
- pedestrian routes would tie in with a local centre and bus stops; and
- the green space would be ecologically managed.

## Making it happen

Four shortlisted teams of architects and developers, complete with outline schemes based on the brief, gave presentations to a representative panel of the working group. It is interesting to note that the successful team not only produced the highest bid but most closely followed the spirit of the brief and had the most credible track record of working with communities and working with sustainable urban design principles. At the time of writing a final amended scheme, drawn up in consultation with the working group, is being assessed by the Local Planning Authority.

# Northampton

## ENQUIRY BY DESIGN

This case study describes a specific planning exercise called Enquiry By Design, which was applied on an experimental basis to the proposed south-western extension of Northampton.

The objective of the technique is to consciously plan for an urban extension to a neighbouring settlement in a way that supports sustainability of both the existing and new development.

**Working with stakeholders**

The technique brings stakeholders and urban design professionals together for an intensive period of joint work outside the normal procedural context. Using a creative design-driven process they seek to find 'win–win' solutions for sustainable development. In Northampton the participants included the landowners (English Partnerships), the Borough Council, the planning department and representatives of major house-builders. Councillors and community representatives attended the opening session and the final presentation. It was vitally important that

- all the key players were involved and accepted the principle of development, though not necessarily its scale or nature

- attendance was by invitation and application, and the process was not seen as one long, open public meeting

- the exercise was led by independent facilitators with a deep understanding of sustainable development and collaborative decision-making

- skilled urban designers were involved in developing ideas and presenting schemes graphically during the workshop.

**Understanding the locality**

One of the potential advantages of the exercise is that the inherited assumptions and positions of stakeholders may be changed as a result of working together on the problems and aspirations in the context of a thorough neighbourhood appraisal. It is essential that key parameters are understood before embarking on the exercise.

**Creating a neighbourhood plan**

The outcome of the process was a draft masterplan which changed the inherited plan in a number of ways:

- Integration of the neighbouring hospital site with the English Partnerships land to achieve more coherent development.

- Higher average densities and more developable land, so that the plan can cope with Northampton's longer-term growth.

*The exercise was carried out at a workshop organised by the Prince's Foundation 19–23 July 1999. The workshop was led by the Australian-based consultancy Ecologically Sustainable Design. For further information see Prince's Foundation 2000*

SOURCE: IMAGES REPRODUCED FROM 'SUSTAINABLE URBAN EXTENSIONS: PLANNED THROUGH DESIGN' COURTESY OF THE PRINCE'S FOUNDATION, DETR AND CPRE

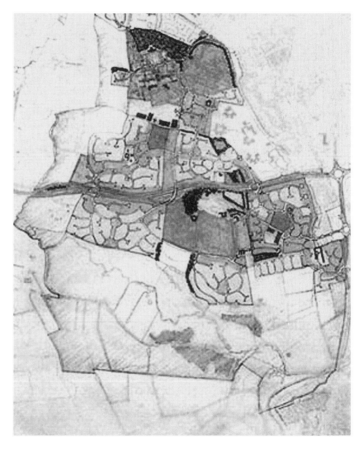

*Figure 3.17*
**The by-the-rules plan, assuming a standard masterplanning process**

■ Integrated, compact development with clear open-space strategy, rather than the previous rather fragmented pattern.

■ Mixed-use development with many more local jobs and facilities to encourage shorter trips and less car dependency.

■ Traditional street patterns replacing the previous pattern of segregated main roads and culs-de-sac.

**Making it happen**

One advantage of Enquiry By Design is that it can short-circuit years of convoluted negotiation and uncertainly. However, it cannot solve all the problems, and needs to be followed up by further appraisal and testing, which should be transparent and keep all participants involved. Follow-up roles and tasks need to be explicit before the workshop ends.

*Figure 3.18*
**The Enquiry By Design plan**

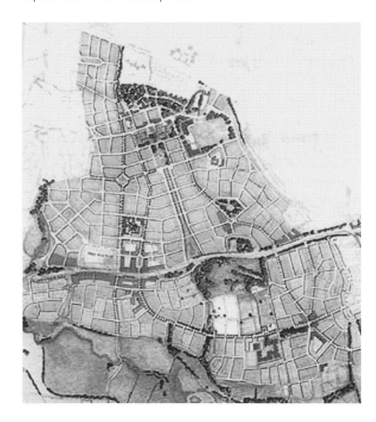

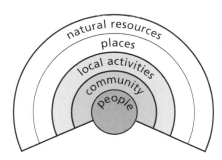

# providing for local need | chapter 4

## 4.1  PURPOSE AND SCOPE

The essence of sustainable development is providing for people's needs, now and in the future. This chapter takes the people of the neighbourhood as the starting point. It gives guidance on the way to approach questions of new housing provision and social mix. It looks at ways in which local community networks are undermined or promoted. It examines the way decisions about land use and location affect the access people have to local jobs, shops, schools and open spaces. And it introduces the planning of local movement and the public realm.

### GENERAL PRINCIPLES

The over-arching goals are *health*, *equity* and *quality of life*, now and for future generations. The 'neighbourhood design principles' set out at 2.6 are developed here from the viewpoint of providing for local need.

▢  **Stakeholder involvement**

The surest way to understand different needs and aspirations is to ask the people involved. The obligation to try to understand and then take account of different interests rests with all stakeholders – public, private and voluntary sectors. Note that the principles of participation have been elaborated in Chapter 3.

▢  **Increased local autonomy**

Neighbourhoods cannot be – and should not attempt to be – self-sufficient in work and services. But there is tremendous value in increasing the proportion of daily and weekly needs that can be satisfied locally. Surveys find that the availability or otherwise of local facilities is a key issue for residents. Where local facilities are available then people generally choose to use them, even in areas of high car ownership. Local use has benefits in terms of health, social inclusion, economic vitality and environmental sustainability; but local provision will only work if the preconditions of quality, accessibility and viability are right.

▢  **Social stability and choice**

In the face of increasing fear of violence, people are retreating behind locked doors. The goal of sustainable development is to create opportunities for social contact, social stability and 'community', which depends in part on shared local activities and life on the street. The object is to open up choice in every field: choice of housing type and location, options locally for entrepreneurs and shopkeepers, choice of means of movement. Satisfying varied needs increases the likelihood of social stability.

### ▪ Connectivity

A connected, integrated approach to provision means agencies working together to deliver shared facilities: for example, the education and leisure departments working with community groups to provide a better hall or library or hard pitch than they could separately; or small businesses and volunteer organisations sharing a serviced office space and café. Connectivity also applies to the pattern of streets: creating a permeable environment that increases accessibility.

### ▪ Diversity

Within a neighbourhood, and even more a township, choice and opportunity can be increased by achieving requisite variety: a 'balanced' population in terms of age, family status and wealth; a wide variety of housing stock; a diversity of economic niches and type of service provision. The object is to achieve/maintain what ecologists might call a 'climax culture', with maximum diversity within a stable overall pattern.

### ▪ Response to place

Place is not only important in terms of function and connectivity but also in terms of people's perceptions: the local cultural landscape. Places are valued for their history and associations, their smell, touch, sound and visual quality. As much care needs to be taken in aesthetically mundane or tawdry environments as in Conservation Areas. Each new project should make a positive contribution (see Chapter 6, Sections 2 and 3).

### ▪ Adaptability

The idea of the 'life-time neighbourhood' means adaptability to changing needs through an individual's life and to changing social/economic patterns. It means overt consideration for future generations – for example, options for second generations' homes. It means recognising the neighbourhood as providing for a dynamic community, avoiding unnecessary constraints on market and life-style innovation.

## RECOGNISING DIFFERENT NEEDS

It is important to recognisethe specific social needs relevant to any particular issue. The dimensions of difference are many, but five of the most significant in the context of local planning are

- different age groups
- varied household sizes/types
- different ethnic groupings
- income differentials and car ownership
- levels of personal mobility.

Different needs and lifestyles can be a cause of local friction. For example, in a park there may be conflicts of interest between parents with toddlers, dog walkers, old people, informal youth groups and sports people. Identifying the different needs clearly can be a helpful way for stakeholders with varied priorities to establish common ground and move forward.

# people and community

## 4.2 A BALANCED POPULATION

### BASIC PRINCIPLES

At the scale of the urban township or country town there should be a long-term, carefully monitored strategy to achieve a balanced community. This balance should be in relation to two main variables:

1. *Types of household*: young single people, young families, mature families, middle-aged and elderly singles/couples, institutional/community groupings.
2. *Income levels and socio-economic groups*: including those reliant on subsidised/rented accommodation, 'near-market' groups (such as teachers and policemen in the south-east), middle- and upper-income groups.

This variety should also be reflected at the scale of the individual neighbourhoods that go to make up the township/town, particularly in terms of income variation and provision for the elderly.

### Reasons

*Social inclusion*: the opportunity for people, whatever their income, to find accommodation in every town or part of the city, according to their specific needs.

*Life-time neighbourhoods*: providing for people at every stage of their life, so if they want to stay there they can; valuing continuity.

*Economic provision of services*: avoiding the 'leads and lags' of social provision which occur with unbalanced populations – where, for example, on a new estate there is initially a dearth of primary school places, then a lack of secondary places, and then a long-term under-provision for the elderly.

*Diversity of culture and activity*: so that children, in particular, have the chance to experience a well-rounded community, not a one-class ghetto or dormitory suburb, and learn tolerance and appreciation of difference.

*Less need to travel*: increasing the opportunity for people to find local jobs, local services, particular activities, and hence reducing the necessity to travel.

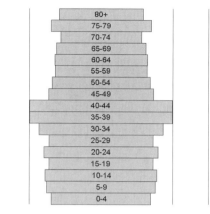

*A balanced age profile, signifying continuous, even population renewal*

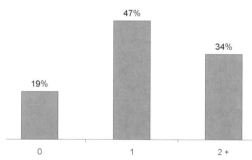

*Car ownership: cars per household*

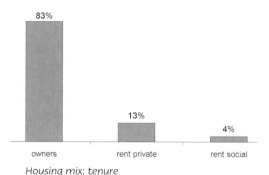

*Housing mix: tenure*

Figure 4.1
**Analysis of an urban ward**

*This well-established neighbourhood shows a reasonably balanced age/sex profile, signifying a steady process of population renewal. But the patterns of both car ownership and housing tenure suggest a skewed social mix, with lower-income groups experiencing a degree of exclusion.*

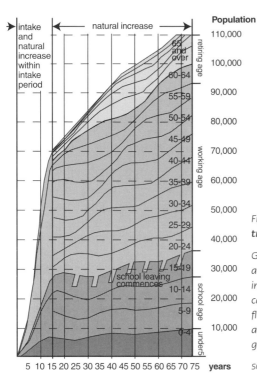

*Figure 4.2* **Peaks and troughs of demand**

*Graph showing how an unbalanced incoming population causes successive fluctuations in each age group during the growth of a town*

*SOURCE: GLC 1965*

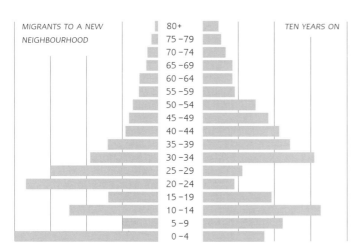

*Figure 4.3*
**Changes in age profile on a new neighbourhood**

*An unbalanced profile from a new growth area, leading to peaks and troughs of demand for local facilities. Over the next decades the peaks and troughs move up the age profile, only being slightly diluted by further migrations.*

## BUCKING THE MARKET

In large cities market trends, often reinforced by state housing and planning policies, have tended to differentiate whole urban sectors by class and age. Very high land/property values in one locality ensure continued exclusivity, while in another market demand is notable by its absence. Achieving balanced township populations in this context relies on sustained commitment and inter-sectoral co-operation. Regeneration of low-prestige zones, for example, depends on integrated strategies that tackle existing problems and create the right conditions for a change in market attitudes.

## INTER-GENERATIONAL PLANNING

The time-scale for planning balanced communities is long. In areas of major change (brownfield regeneration, greenfield urban extension or new town) the minimum time period should be a generation (about 25 years): that is, the period needed to even out peaks and troughs of demand for local facilities such as schools. Any such new development should be seen, of course, in the context of potential interdependence with adjacent neighbourhoods.

**Future-proofing** can also be promoted by building adaptability into the physical fabric so that second-generation people (or activities) have options; for example

- Incorporate building types capable of adapting to new needs: houses that can be turned into flats (or vice versa), ground floors into shops, offices into housing, etc.
- Leave some gaps in the urban framework, perhaps temporarily occupied by short-term sheds or 'soft' uses, for longer-term intensification.
- Design main routeways generously to permit later changes (such as the insertion of a tram system, or parking outside future shops).

## CREATING THE RIGHT CONDITIONS IN EACH TOWNSHIP

Each of the sub-headings below is expanded in a subsequent section of this chapter:

- **Housing** A balance of different types, sizes, tenures and affordability which allows a variety of households and flexibility over time. A central issue is the degree to which under-represented groups – such as families in the inner city, or young single people in the outer suburbs – can be attracted to the area.

- **Jobs** Diverse local economic opportunities which help maintain the attraction of the township, especially for young people and part-time workers, and support local services.

- **Retailing** Viable retail and social facilities that recycle financial resources locally and give life and vitality to the township core.

- **Quality** An aesthetically pleasing, safe and friendly environment that attracts all sectors of the population to the area and encourages them to stay.

- **Accessibility** A place that is not only easy to get around internally but is externally well connected by main roads and public transport services. This factor is absolutely key to the success of the township: good accessibility is a driver for the local economy, viable facilities and private housing development. These in turn attract and help retain diverse populations.

## 4.3 DEVELOPING SOCIAL CAPITAL

### BASIC PRINCIPLE
Investors and policy-makers have a responsibility to understand the importance of local community networks – including formal and informal social groups – and to work with local organisations to ensure that their decisions facilitate those networks. This social responsibility applies across the board – to the private sector as well as to the public and voluntary sectors.

### THE IMPORTANCE OF COMMUNITY
'Community' is generally perceived as a Good Thing, but the nature of community has changed dramatically since the mid-twentieth century. Communities of interest (linked to work, hobbies, religious or political activity, etc.) have for many people replaced communities of place. Such interest communities may have a very wide geographical spread (facilitated by car, phone and internet), but most also have a specific locus as well – school, pub, club, office, church – tying them to the locality. Poorer and less-mobile people often rely heavily on locally based networks – for example, young children in a playgroup, the elderly infirm in a day-care centre. The existence of local networks of mutual support and trust is important for health and mental well-being. Conversely, the absence of such neighbourliness exacerbates problems of isolation and social exclusion; it also increases the need to travel (with consequent environmental damage) in order to satisfy social needs.

**Social capital** is a measure of the residents' sense of community and their ability to act together to pursue shared objectives. 'It is characterised by civic identity and engagement, trust and reciprocity of actions, and networking between individuals, groups and agencies' (Health and Education Council and LGMB 1999). The approach taken by official, market and/or voluntary agencies impacts on social capital, affecting the level of engagement of local people with decision processes and their sense of power or powerlessness. According to some commentators these are significant determinants of health (Atkinson and Kintea 1998).

*Teenage capital of Europe*
*A full-page article in a national paper announced that Milton Keynes had the largest proportion (21.8 per cent) of under-14s in Europe per head of population. It continued that one in three people were aged under 20 and that schools couldn't be built fast enough (Daily Telegraph, 14 October 2000).*

*The demographic trends underlying this article have come about from building a new town that was mainly geared to a narrow age band of the population.*

*As the population matures Milton Keynes could expect a wave of derelict schools and mounting pressures for employment opportunities. Later still, it may see a peak in demand for care and retirement facilities that will be difficult to meet.*

*Caution: There is no magic wand that can create community*
*Local community links are forged by the people themselves and by the groups they form. Deterministic design solutions and governmental 'new deals' achieve little without the positive choice of residents. However, planners, developers and service deliverers have an obligation to ensure that they make it easy for people and that they remove barriers to local associations, where these exist.*

*Aspects of social capital*
- *informal networks of friends and neighbours*
- *local identity and sense of belonging*
- *norms of mutual trust and support*
- *community-level networks and pressure groups*
- *the level of civic engagement.*

*(after Putman 1993, and Atkinson and Kintea 1998)*

DEVELOPING SOCIAL CAPITAL

# 4.3

## Social esteem and the urban environment

*Townhill Neighbourhood, Swansea*

Funded by URBAN (EU), this project is set within an area of acute social, physical and environmental deprivation.

A comprehensive package of projects is involved; priorities are employment, education, training, environment, crime detection and prevention, health and housing.

The poor conditions of the front gardens of tenanted properties was taken as an indication of lack of self-esteem in the community. The poor and drab environment also affects self-confidence and self-esteem, so negatively reinforcing the problems.

Environmental projects were aimed at tackling low pride, and encouraging participation and self-realisation. Social inclusion was promoted through involving those in need in environmental projects (including training and work).

The environmental projects involved improving safety, quality of life, enhancing wildlife and landscape, and traffic-calming measures.

The involvement of local people in the improvement of their local area has resulted in an improvement also in both social capacity and health.

## ACTION TO SUPPORT LOCAL COMMUNITY

### Service delivery by public agencies

- Provision of accessible local educational facilities at primary, secondary and further-education levels. This is particularly important in smaller settlements where the primary school is a vital network-builder for both children and parents.
- Decentralised, visible provision of services, including health, housing, social services, police, job centre, library, etc.
- Co-ordinated provision across departments and agencies, for example in relation to school, library and recreational facilities.
- One-stop service provision for deprived and vulnerable groups.

### Planning and design

- Density and land-use/movement pattern planned to increase the viability of local retail, leisure and public transport facilities, hence increasing the number of places people meet.
- A permeable, safe and attractive pedestrian environment which encourages people onto the streets; convivial meeting places at nodal points.
- Mixed-use development and regeneration programmes responding to the needs of existing/potential local businesses and facilitating home-based work.
- Varied housing provision responding to the needs of different household types and cultures, and of second-generation households.
- Focus on the sense of local identity and safety within each street or home-patch – this is the scale that particularly matters for mental well-being.
- Availability of local halls/rooms for general use for public meetings, clubs, courses, competitions, etc.

### Capacity building

- A collaborative approach by the local authority to the Community Strategy and the Local Plan, encouraging effective participation by groups and individuals.
- In areas of urban regeneration, the appointment of a community development officer to connect with 'invisible' groups/interests and ease their path to involvement and joint project working ('capacity building').
- A responsive, positive attitude by official agencies and major private/voluntary-sector organisations to grass-roots initiatives.

3.2 Collaborative communities ←

3.5 Working with local people ←

## 4.4   HOUSING MIX

### BASIC PRINCIPLE: BALANCING SOCIAL NICHE WITH SOCIAL DIVERSITY

In every part of a town or city there should be a broad balance of different housing opportunities in terms of tenure, size and affordability, while at the same time safeguarding local social identity and sense of security. The strategy to achieve this needs to be agreed by the housing authority and the planning authority and fully understood by councillors.

■ At the level of the home-patch or street, housing mix is possible but not normally essential.

■ At the level of the neighbourhood it is important, but there will be differences between neighbourhoods depending on their location and density.

■ At the level of the township housing mix is critical, and within the township there should be the full range of housing options.

### Reasons

• To free up the various housing markets (social housing/rental/ first-time buyers/mid-range/'executive' housing, etc.) and allow households of all kinds the maximum opportunity to select locations convenient to their needs, which can reduce their total travel cost/distance and consequent pollution.

• To assist equity and social inclusion: normally poorer groups are particularly constrained in their search for appropriate homes; conversely, some places (certain Welsh Valleys, for example) have fewer up-market homes available.

• To avoid peaks and troughs of demand for local facilities (especially in relation to different age groups), which lead to alternating problems of shortage and surplus, with consequent extra public or private costs.

• To maintain a balance of rich and poor, growing households and shrinking households, over time – so that local shops and businesses remain viable and bus services are supported.

• To maintain or increase population levels at a time when average household size is falling, in order to bulwark local service viability, and reduce average trip length.

• To increase the potential for mutual support, surveillance, and learning between age groups – for example, real or acting grannies assisting young families; more informal surveillance of streets, imparting a sense of safety; teenage role-models for younger children; young working adult role-models for teenagers.

• To ensure the local availability of a wide range of skills and professions, easing job-filling and job-search problems, and reducing the need to travel. This is particularly important for part-time

*Figure 4.4*
**The patchwork of housing sites in Chepstow Drive grid square, Milton Keynes**

SOURCE: BARTON 2000, FIGURE 8.1, ADAPTED FROM MKDC 1992

### A patchwork of housing sites

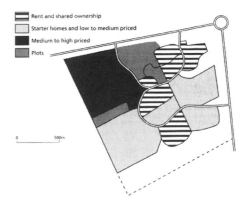

'Every grid square neighbourhood of 2000–4000 people [in Milton Keynes] has a mix of housing. The home-zones were developed by different agencies or house-builders and in the example they range from 9–130 units. The pattern of housing within the grid squares is designed to ensure that the elderly, disabled and those least likely to have cars are conveniently located at or near a local centre. To attract the more affluent residents the high-priced dwellings are located to ensure an attractive approach and the opportunity for larger gardens'. (Barton 2000: 128)

|  | Shenly Church End | Crown Hill |
|---|---|---|
| Rent/shared ownership | 388 (28%) | 383 (39%) |
| Lower priced | 484 (35%) | 370 (38%) |
| Higher priced | 422 (30%) | 139 (14%) |
| Plots (very expensive) | 93 (7%) | 90 (9%) |
| Total | 1,387 (100%) | 982 (100%) |

SOURCE: MILTON KEYNES 1992

HOUSING MIX

**4.4**

## SAFEGUARDING SOCIAL IDENTITY

There is tension between the need to provide a mix of housing and the need to safeguard feelings of security. The social identity of a local area – in terms of the social class and ethnic group residents experience or the streets near home – help to determine feelings of security. People like to live next door to people like themselves. If they feel cut off from their own social group, that can increase anxiety and fear and mental illness, and fewer local people are in a position to be able to support them (Halpern 1995).

### The patchwork neighbourhood

The important scale for this feeling of security is very local – not the neighbourhood as a whole but the street, the home-patch. The home-patch represents the safe territory or niche. There should be a limited range of housing diversity within it. This accords with the instincts of people in general and house-builders' marketing strategies in particular. Experience suggests that income types can be mixed successfully in adjacent streets (Duany and Plater-Zyberg 1991; Milton Keynes 1992).

### Pepper-potting

Government guidance enabling local authority to demand a proportion of affordable housing in every development over 25 units is desirable in that it leads to wider availability and dispersal of affordable homes. This implies a policy of pepper-potting. However, care should be taken to avoid haphazard sprinkling. Planned scatter in groups of three or four can work well (such as at the Bournville Village Trust), so long as the housing is of similar visual quality to its neighbours. The mosaic of home-patches, each with its particular character, go to make up a neighbourhood which is physically and socially diverse.

## DECONSTRUCTING THE GHETTO

Where long-established planning policies and house-price differentials are still reinforcing housing monocultures, it is important to develop an explicit strategy for diversification. Typically this is needed in affluent commuter exurbs/villages, poor inner areas, peripheral council estates, and middle-class suburbs of 'family' housing. The strategy could involve

- expressly outlawing the 'more of the same' convention, whereby social housing attracts more social housing, sheltered housing is unnaturally clustered, and up-market estates maintain exclusivity

- using local-plan density guidelines to diversify housing opportunities rather than as a covert policy of social exclusion

- redefining 'maintaining the amenity' of an area in terms of variety and quality rather than similarity

- identifying 'unbalanced' neighbourhoods in the local plan and setting targets for diversification, and not only in relation to affordable houses

- requiring every application for over (say) two new units to contribute appropriately to the diversity targets: for example, if the township lacks flats, and some local demand is apparent or suspected, then sites in appropriate locations should be devoted to providing them.

*Allaying fears*

*The sense of threat sometimes felt by home owners in relation to social housing can be reduced by discussing the spatial scale for diversification: i.e. at the neighbourhood and township level, not necessarily in each home-patch.*

**Political dynamite**

Achieving better community balance can run counter to established market practice, raise legitimate fears about lost local identity and run the gauntlet of social prejudice. Top-down imposition of quotas may be political dynamite. A collaborative *Community Strategy* approach could involve working towards a general recognition that every 'community' has a responsibility for helping to tackle housing stress across a city region. This can then be complemented by neighbourhood- or township-level analysis of need by local stakeholders.

**Market resistance**

In areas of low market potential (e.g. hard-to-let council estates or inner-city under-occupied zero-value areas), private sector development may be unprofitable – i.e. the potential sale value may be less than the cost of rehabilitation/new build. Obviously, such areas are priority for regeneration funding, which can be used to pump-prime as well as directly improve the lot of existing residents. If such pump-priming of the market is to avoid sending good money after bad then it is likely to be part of a very radical reshaping of the area, sufficient to challenge public preconceptions and the assumptions of state and private investors, and perhaps enabling unconventional/marginal housing to find a niche.

The redevelopment of Hulme in inner Manchester and of the Gorbals in Glasgow provide object lessons in comprehensive restructuring along neighbourhood lines.

## 4.5   WORKING FOR LOCAL HOUSING NEEDS

### BASIC PRINCIPLES
Regular reviews of housing need and provision in each town or township should involve partnership between the Parish or Town Council, the Local Authority, and house builders/providers. Each partner brings distinctive understanding to the table. The review should input to the Local Plan and the Community Strategy.

**Parish/Town Council**

A bottom-up appraisal of local housing needs should be instituted by the parish, town or neighbourhood council. This appraisal should encompass not only the need for social housing but identify other needs as well, as perceived by residents and local community organisations.

**The Local Authority**

The bottom-up appraisal is not, however, the whole story, but has to be married with a top-down appraisal undertaken by the local authority. This will identify needs over a wider area which are not necessarily expressed or visible locally.

**House builders and providers**

The housing developers (building firms and housing associations) have knowledge of local demands and also of developability/marketability of specific sites. As with housing land availability or urban capacity studies it is important at the township or parish level to consult the potential investors.

1.4 Community
Strategy      ←

*Government guidance*

*Circular 6/98, reinforced by PPG3 on housing, suggests affordable housing be provided in every new development over 25 units or 1 ha (whichever is the less). Up to 30 per cent affordable units may be specified.*

*In inner London the thresholds are cut to 15 units and 0.5 ha. This standard is being adopted also by other cities where larger sites are scarce (such as Bournemouth, for example).*

## RECOGNISING DIVERSE NEEDS

Local housing policy is not only a matter of the proportions of affordable homes and market homes. Each township should ideally provide for all legitimate local needs. Below are a sample of important questions:

### Variety of housing type/size/price

- Can single people (young or old) find accommodation to suit their needs and pocket – particularly are there enough flats (some with gardens/patios)?
- Can large families find large homes (not necessarily with a high price tag) to match their needs?
- Can founding families who wish to stay in the area find appropriate 'first-time' properties? Starter homes? Shared equity?
- Can successful business people/executives who want to remain in the area, or others who have work/local connections, find accommodation to match their aspirations?
- Is there a potential local demand for car-free development or for co-housing schemes, and are there appropriate sites?
- Can keen gardeners of limited means access properties with large gardens, or very close to allotments?

### Social and affordable housing

- Are there people living in the area currently sharing, or in poor housing conditions, who qualify for social housing or could benefit from shared equity homes?
- Are there households and key workers who have been forced out of the area by high prices, or others who have a local connection but cannot move in?
- Are there potentially sites available in convenient locations for households with limited car availability?

*Urban co-housing development in Stroud, with shared dining facilities and garden, solar electricity and provision for varied housing needs*

SOURCE: STROUD CO-HOUSING COMPANY

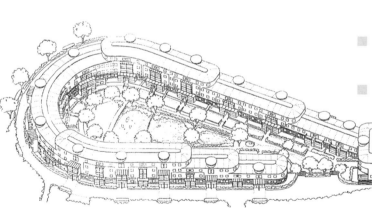

*Figure 4.5*
**Edinburgh car-free development**

*High density car-free development in Edinburgh, in an accessible inner-city location*

SOURCE: CANMORE HOUSING ASSOCIATION

### Special-needs housing

- Can local infirm elderly people gain access to sheltered housing or nursing homes in the area if they want to?
- Is there an unmet need for hostel accommodation, half-way houses or other special requirements?
- Is housing for elderly or disabled people available within (say) 300 m of general store or supermarkets, local parks, pub, church, etc., and of a bus-stop giving good access to the town centre, with a near-level gradient on the approach?

# access to jobs

**4.6  LOCAL WORK**

### BASIC PRINCIPLES

Every township should offer a good range of job opportunities generally matching the character of the local work force. Equivalently, each township should offer a range of workspaces for small businesses, located so as to maximise non-car access by employees and minimise the environmental impact of freight movement. The possibility of home-working should be actively promoted by the planning system.

**Reasons**

• The possibility of local work opens up choices to residents. This option is particularly important for those wanting part-time work – such as carers, house parents and teenagers – or those unable to afford travel.

• Local work allows some people to choose to walk or cycle, with lifestyle and health benefits, and reduced emissions.

• Local workspace increases the practicality of setting up new businesses, avoiding the need for time-consuming and polluting car trips to reach suitable accommodation.

• Home-working is a growing trend in terms of both telecommuting and sole trading. It has the potential to reduce travel, support local services and enhance local social interaction.

## OPENING UP THE JOB MARKET

There are two polarised myths about the local job market. One is that the creation of local jobs solves unemployment problems. This is an exaggeration. Employers will normally advertise vacant posts city-wide and get the best person for the job: hence the importance of training, and of public transport and road links between localities and main employment centres.

The other myth is that people do not like living near their work and that local job provision has no value. This is equally untrue. While many workers' job-search areas have increased dramatically since the 1970s, others are still very localised, for quite pragmatic reasons. There is a strong correlation between the availability of local jobs, the average length of the journey to work, and the proportion of people walking to work (Stead 1999).

The availability of local work and local workspace helps to support the viability of local shops, cafés and pubs. Many local jobs are related to local services. Local shops, schools, surgeries, pubs, police, social services, etc. provide diverse work opportunities, and can amount to 30 per cent of total demand.

*Suburban business parks rely on very heavy car use (90–95 per cent) and profligate use of land. They should not be permitted.*

***Township job ratio***

*There is some evidence of a significant threshold in local job provision. The job ratio is defined as the number of job opportunities in an area divided by the number of people available for work. A ratio of 0.7 or more is associated with shorter trips and more walking. This ratio could be a target for each town/township. (Barton et al. 1995, p. 83)*

## THE RIGHT BUSINESS IN THE RIGHT PLACE

Promoting local employment does not justify a locational free-for-all. Location should be related to likely employee catchments and the need for freight access. Scale can sometimes act as a proxy for catchment.

*Figure 4.5*
**Using scale as a proxy for catchment**

| Business | Locational criteria |
|---|---|
| **Large offices** (e.g. over 1,000 m²) | Locate only in town and township centres that have centrality in relation to public transport and good connections to intercity rail. |
| **Medium offices** (e.g. 100–1,000 m²) | Locate in neighbourhood and township centres, or along high streets, that have good public transport and good foot/pedal accessibility. |
| **Small offices** (e.g. less than 100 m²) | Locate anywhere within the built-up area – typically as home-based workplaces, subject to normal environmental safeguards. |
| **Factories/ warehouses** | Locate so as to avoid the need for lorries to go through residential and shopping areas, with good access to the national road network and to existing/potential rail or water freight possibilities. |
| **Workshops and nursery units** | Locate as for factories or in the higher intensity zones of townships where there is good access to a distributor road. |
| **Backyard workshops** | Locate anywhere within the built-up area, subject to the normal environmental and access safeguards. |
| **Other facilities** (e.g. retail, educational, leisure) | See in the relevant sections later in the chapter |

*Small workshops/offices can fit innocuously into residential areas*

## DIVERSITY OF ECONOMIC NICHE

Local economic activity creates wealth in the community. It also demonstrates the diversity and connectedness of life. The range of local activities experienced in some market towns and mixed-use inner-city districts can cause noise/disturbance problems but also delight. Progressively fewer small businesses are now real environmental hazards. For these reasons strict zoning policies should be eased. The chart above suggests a flexible approach to small offices and workshops in residential areas, while safe-guarding good neighbourliness.

Within any township/town we need to ensure diversity of economic and service opportunity. Replacing land-use zones with sustainability criteria is part of this; so also is the intentional planning of a range of economic niches:

- Small workshops caught in the interstices of residential streets.

- Double garages sold with ready-made change-of-use permission for working space.

- Ground floor space in three/four-storey terraces along neighbourhood spine roads designed for change-of-use to retail or office.

- Secondary and tertiary shopping areas (where lower rents permit more marginal businesses) allowed to switch between uses but protected from comprehensive redevelopment.

- In-town recycling muck-zones where building re-use and temporary constructions are protected by zoning from comprehensive redevelopment (and where there's muck there's brass!).

- Seedbed business premises with small size-adjustable units for subsidised rent (often in old mills or factories) and access to support services.

- Serviced community workspace for professional firms and sole traders, with shared reception/IT services/coffee room/van hire, etc.

- 'Solicitors' row': highly accessible on or adjacent to the main street, with attractive setting and buildings.

- Craft workshops in association with exhibition/meeting space and café, behind the main street frontage (rents being lower), in old school or mill building.

The suggestions here rely on local enterprise but may be facilitated by positive, non-bureaucratic official attitudes plus judicious financial support for start-ups and non-profit activities. Community networking helps create the right environment for initiative.

6.12 Spatial framework →

6.13 Regeneration strategies →

## SEEDING LOCAL GROWTH

Local economic regeneration can be promoted in a number of ways: in brief ...

**Local Agenda 21 meetings** may draw together 'movers and shakers' – perhaps as part of a community planning exercise – and create opportunities for co-operation. Often people are meeting properly for the first time. They discover shared concerns and enthusiasms. Such meetings can provide fertile ground for seeding new ideas, often serendipitously.

**Local employment policies** may be promoted by business and the local authorities. Certain jobs can be specifically advertised very locally (not across the city or county), linked to training and regeneration initiatives. For example, a publicly funded neighbourhood nursery school could employ part-time untrained parent assistants to work with an experienced childcare person. The spin-offs in such situations can by many: income for families, socialisation and shared play for children, boosted confidence in childcare for the assistants (reflected then in their own homes), social contact and parental support networks.

*ACRE*
*Support for local work in rural settlements is offered by ACRE (Action for Community Renewal and Enterprise): virtual.village@acre. ac.uk*

**Local training and adult education** is demand-responsive and will not necessarily result in local work. But the localisation of basic skills training (provided by technical colleges or special-needs charities) increases accessibility for client groups (often unskilled and/or young) and boosts local social interaction. Local space may depend on collaboration between the service provider, the local authority and secondary school or local enterprise.

**Advice and support** on business planning, funding, management and accommodation may be provided by banks, local authorities, voluntary organisations or government. It should be free, accessible and comprehensive – a one-stop shop at the centre of a district that can provide avenues to help on all fronts. This relies on co-ordination in terms both of space available and services offered.

## 4.7

*Some homeworking facts*

- *Over 25 per cent of the UK workforce carry out some of their work at home*

- *680,000 (in 1998) worked mainly from home, and this is increasing around 20 per cent per annum*

- *Women account for two-thirds of those working mainly from home*

- *60 per cent of those working at home part-time rely on telephone and computer*

- *1.5 million people telecommuted at least one day a week in 2000*

*SOURCE: DWELLY 2000*

*'Zoning the rigid separation of residential, commercial and industrial areas – is a planning system completely at odds with the new ways people live and work. Applying land-use regulations to activities carried out in single rooms in buildings, in particular, now looks preposterous.' (Dwelly 2000).*

## 4.7 HOMEWORKING AND THE INFORMAL ECONOMY

### WORKING FROM HOME

Home-based working is increasing rapidly and is a key part of any strategy for local economic diversification. It is being facilitated not only by the potential for telecommuting but also by smaller households and more space per household. The likely benefits of home-working are

- it opens up work and life-style choice for individuals
- it creates extra patronage of local services and reinforcement of local social networks
- there may be a reduced need to travel for work purposes.

ICT (Information and Communications Technology) is progressively making home-working more viable and attractive. However, the outsourcing of work by firms can lead to worker isolation, and the overall travel benefits are unproven. The promotion of 'televillages' in small settlements may indeed be counterproductive if it encourages households to move there who were previously in more accessible locations (this is based on evidence from Crickhowell Televillage – Paternoster 2000).

#### Policies for homeworking

▪ Abolish tenancy, leasing, rating and zoning restrictions which deter homeworking.

▪ Promote homeworking as part of any regeneration or new development programme, incorporating high bandwidth infrastructure alongside water, gas and electricity.

▪ Estimate housing needs (in the context of development plans or social housing provision) on the assumption of providing most households with a spare room/flexible space.

▪ Encourage provision of live-work units as part of major development projects.

▪ Support local retail/community facilities and a pleasant pedestrian environment, which can help compensate homeworkers for their working isolation.

### THE INFORMAL ECONOMY

The economic wealth of an area is not measured purely in terms of monetary income, but in terms of actual goods and services. Mutual help, barter systems and volunteering create an informal economy, often breaking down barriers between social, recreational and economic activity, and benefiting local people in many ways.

Initiatives for informal economic activity comes primarily from individuals and groups choosing to work together. However, local authorities and business can seek to support such initiative by grants, space and flexible interpretation of regulations. The essential attitude of officials is responsiveness – responding to requests for help, facilitating contact-making, co-ordinating the authority's stance.

Promoting the informal economy is a key part of any regeneration strategy. Consider

▦ The provision of, and multi-cultural access to, community halls and meeting rooms.

▦ Free or cost-rent availability of small community offices in public buildings or by local enterprises.

▦ Creating potential market space at the heart of every town or township.

▦ Safeguarding some cheap storage and workshop space within each township from renewal – for community (or small business) use – see muck-zones, etc., in 4.6.

*The informal economy takes many forms:*

- *baby-sitting circles*

- *parent and toddler groups*

- *food co-ops*

- *community gardens*

- *allotments and home-growing*

- *Local Economic Trading Systems (LETS)*

- *Environmental Improvement Action Groups*

- *Credit Unions (though also part of the formal economy)*

CATCHMENT FLEXIBILITY AND ACCESSIBILITY STANDARDS

# 4.8

# access to local facilities

## 4.8 CATCHMENT FLEXIBILITY AND ACCESSIBILITY STANDARDS

### BASIC PRINCIPLES
Localised provision of facilities to permit access by foot, bike and local bus should be encouraged in every neighbourhood. Specific standards of accessibility (detailed later) should be negotiated with service providers and, where possible, market interests. Facilities should be clustered together at locations well served by bus, bike and pedestrian routes, preferably in linear clusters akin to traditional high streets, which offer variable catchments that can adapt to changing market conditions.

### Reasons for local provision

■ The availability of local services, including schools, health services, convenience stores and post-offices, is a continuing and sometimes vociferous concern of local people.

■ The exercise involved in local walking and cycling trips – particularly for children – is important for health and well-being.

■ The meetings (casual or planned) that occur at local facilities, or on the streets getting there, reinforce local networks of support and a sense of community, which are important for psychological health.

■ Local facilities – especially retailing – are important providers of local jobs, and help recycle money locally.

■ Local provision encourages local trips, with a significant proportion of those by foot (Ecotec 1993; Winter and Farthing 1997; Barton 2000: 60), thus reducing the need for car use and helping to achieve pollution/congestion-reduction targets.

### Reasons for clustering

■ Clustering provides an opportunity for multi-purpose trips (saving people time and expense); and close association between uses reinforces their viability.

■ Clustering also increases the proportion of people using public transport rather than the private car (Cervero 1990).

percentage trips to facilities

*Figure 4.6*
**Percentage of trips made to services when they are provided locally**

*This chart is based on new peripheral estates in the Bristol sub-region – often designed primarily for car use, not pedestrians, and having very high levels of car ownership. Taking the two categories 'within the development' and 'close to the development' together, the use of local facilities is surprisingly high – for example 93 per cent of primary schools trips, 95 per cent of health centre trips and 97 per cent of supermarket trips, where these facilities are locally available.*

*SOURCE: BARTON 2000, BASED ON WINTER AND FARTHING 1997*

## FLEXIBLE CATCHMENTS

In an increasingly privatised economy it is often not possible or appropriate to define specific catchments for specific services. The principles of consumer choice, and the fact of high mobility, means that local people may or may not choose to use local facilities. Some facilities, when available locally, are very heavily used – for example supermarkets and health centres (see Figure 4.6); others much less so – for example churches and dentists. The pattern of catchment and movement must therefore be planned so as to permit ease of access between neighbourhoods as much as within them (this point is taken up in Chapter 6).

Changing patterns of service provision and of retailing also point to the need for a flexible and open system of land-use control. New commercial initiatives (e.g. 'one-stop' local shops, filling station shops, private nursery schools, local office services) which enhance provision need to be welcomed.

## REVERSING DECLINE

The general long-term pattern of decline of local facilities – caused by falling population densities as well as consumer choice and car use – is matched by increasing unit size of facilities. The result is longer trips and poorer local accessibility. In some outlying estates and rural settlements this trend has effectively disenfranchised whole sections of the population who do not possess individual mobility.

It is therefore vital to have a clear and flexible strategy for reversing the trends and for taking best advantage of opportunities that present themselves. There are potentially some powerful levers: service providers – particularly education and health – need to adopt user accessibility as a key objective. Briefs for major brownfield or greenfield residential development should specify facility provision – with the principles written into the Local Plan.

4.10 Shops  →

4.11 Schools  →

4.12 Health  →

*Figure 4.7*
***Catchment populations***

*NB: Bendy routes assume 75 per cent of the direct-line radius, giving around 55 per cent of the catchment population*

Catchment area radius

| Gross residential density | 200 m | | 400 m | | 600 m | | 800 m | | 1,000 m | |
|---|---|---|---|---|---|---|---|---|---|---|
| | Direct routes | **Bendy routes** | Direct routes | **Bendy routes** | Direct routes | **Bendy routes** | Direct routes | **Bendy routes** | Direct routes | **Bendy routes** |
| 30 ppha | 375 | **210** | 1,500 | **850** | 3,400 | **1,900** | 6,100 | **3,400** | 9,600 | **5,300** |
| 40 ppha | 520 | **280** | 2,000 | **1,130** | 4,600 | **2,500** | 8,200 | **4,600** | 12,000 | **7,000** |
| 60 ppha | 780 | **420** | 3,000 | **1,700** | 6,900 | **3,800** | 12,000 | **6,900** | 19,000 | **10,600** |
| 80 ppha | 1,000 | **500** | 4,000 | **2,260** | 9,000 | **5,100** | 16,000 | **9,000** | 25,000 | **14,000** |
| 100 ppha | 1,300 | **700** | 5,000 | **2,820** | 11,300 | **6,300** | 20,000 | **11,300** | 31,000 | **17,500** |

ppha = persons per hectare

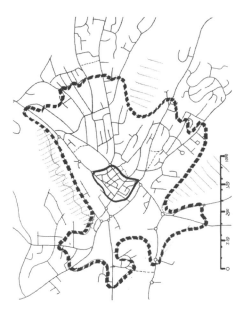

*Figure 4.8*
**Catchment analysis**

*Stroud: 800 m
'Ped-shed' measured
along pedestrian
routes from the edge
of the town centre,
revealing quirks in the
access pattern*

## MEASURING CATCHMENT POPULATIONS

Despite the fact that people often choose not to use local facilities, it remains a vital planning goal to give everybody the *option*. Policy is likely to rely on assumptions about catchment populations and appropriate accessibility standards. The accompanying tables (Figures 4.7 and 4.9) illustrate the degree of variation of catchment population with different assumptions about density, distance and route directness. Note that

- catchment population varies directly in proportion to density
- modest increases in access standard result in major changes of catchment (e.g. 600 m gives more than double 400 m).
- actual routes are not normally direct and this dramatically reduces the catchment population – if average distances are a third longer, then the catchment radius is 75 per cent of the direct-line radius, and the population is 56 per cent of the direct-line catchment.
- in reality facilities are not evenly distributed across an urban area, and the urban area itself is varied in pattern and shape. Thus in some areas it may be unpractical, for the moment at least, to set rigorous accessibility standards.

## ACCESSIBILITY STANDARDS

Accessibility standards are used to ensure facilities are as walkable as possible. Standards for common facilities are given in the table below.

*Figure 4.9*
**Accessibility standards**

| Local facility | Illustrative catchment populations (to be adapted to local conditions and policies) | Minimum reasonable accessibility standards at different gross densities (assuming bendy routes) | | | |
|---|---|---|---|---|---|
| | | *40 ppha* | *60 ppha* | *80 ppha* | *100 ppha* |
| Nursery/first school | 2,000 | 600 m | 500 m | 400 m | 400 m |
| Primary/middle school | 4,000 | 800 m | 700 m | 600 m | 500 m |
| Secondary school | 8,000 | 1,200 m | 1,000 m | 700 m | 700 m |
| Secondary school (large) | 16,000 | 1,500 m | 1,200 m | 1,000 m | 1,000 m |
| Health centre (4 doctors) | 10,000 | 1,200 m | 1,000 m | 900 m | 800 m |
| Local shop | 1,500 | 500 m | 400 m | 400 m | 300 m |
| Pub | 6,000 | 1,000 m | 800 m | 700 m | 600 m |
| Post office | 5,000 | 800 m | 700 m | 600 m | 600 m |
| Community centre | 4,000 | 800 m | 600 m | 600 m | 500 m |
| Local centre | 6,000 | 1,000 m | 800 m | 700 m | 600 m |
| District centre/superstore | 24,000 | 1,900 m | 1,500 m | 1,300 m | 1,200 m |
| Leisure centre | 24,000 | 1,900 m | 1,500 m | 1,300 m | 1,200 m |

**How to use accessibility criteria**

In major urban extensions it is reasonable for the community to expect developers and service providers to achieve good standards of local facility accessibility. Appropriate standards can be agreed and incorporated in supplementary planning guidance, built into the spatial strategy and subsequent development briefs.

In fully built-up areas the ability to achieve any standards is highly constrained by existing morphology and ownership. This is particularly the case in hilly or poorly planned settlements. Standards cannot be mandatory, but may be a starting point for negotiation.

Infill or redevelopment projects may be guided by accessibility standards, particularly through the Local/Community Plan and the long-term spatial strategy. Service providers should identify gaps and seek to fill them. Housing densities should be graded to reflect local accessibility.

## ILLUSTRATIVE CRITERIA FOR A TOWN

Accessibility criteria need to reflect

* the gross densities that are achievable
* the catchment populations of different facilities
* the degree of permeability/directness of pedestrian/cycling routes
* the propensity of users to walk to specific facilities
* the siting requirements (some facilities require more land and are therefore less locationally flexible)
* the need for some standardisation, for ease of understanding/planning.

In this example we assume a policy that all neighbourhoods should achieve a minimum gross density of 60 people per hectare (ppha). This implies that average net densities will be at least (say) 90 ppha or 40 dpha (dwellings per hectare). Using the catchments and route-bendyness assumed in the charts above, here are some suggestions for normal maximum actual distances:

6.8 Net and gross density defined →

* Within 400 m      local shop, bus stop
* Within 600 m      nursery school, primary school
                    community school
* Within 800 m      local centre, post office, pub
* Within 1,000 m    health centre
* Within 1,500 m    secondary school
* Within 2,000 m    district centre, superstore, leisure centre

Note: these generally accord with the 100 per cent standards given in Sustainable Settlements Figure 5.6d (Barton *et al*. 1995, p. 115). The groupings imply the potential for synergy between facilities.

*Recommendations*

* *Undertake a study of local conditions and spatial patterns.*

* *Collaborate with stakeholders in agreeing the principle of equitable accessibility standards.*

* *Select accessibility standards that are viable with actual routes and catchment population, not theoretical.*

* *Seek to increase permeability and reduce barriers to movement by foot and bike, making routes more direct.*

* *Seek to ensure a reasonably even distribution of facilities and avoid isolated pockets of housing.*

* *Gradually increase population densities, to increase local catchments.*

# 4.9

### Vitality and viability

*PPG6 on retailing defines vitality as a measure of how busy a centre is, and viability as a measure of its capacity to attract ongoing investment for maintenance, improvement and adaptation.*

### Shops and well-being

*'local retail services provide wider social and health benefits than simply the provision of goods'*

SOURCE: HEALTH EDUCATION AUTHORITY 1999

*Footfall measures social opportunity as well as retail viability*

## 4.9  TOWN CENTRE VITALITY

### HIGH STREETS IN CRISIS

Many town, district and local shopping centres are declining as a result of an increasingly mobile society, 'consolidation' of retail trade into fewer outlets, and the growth of out-of-town retailing. The latest major threats to the high street are from the banks, which are 'rationalising', and superstore pharmacies, which may replace their high-street competitors. In some centres, however, there is a compensating trend towards a café culture: the role of high streets is becoming more explicitly social.

### Arresting decline

The spiral of decline can only be arrested by a concerted effort on the part of all partners, not least the local residents themselves. In the case of smaller (neighbourhood) centres, community-planning exercises could provide the momentum towards a co-ordinated strategy. In larger (town/townships) centres there may need to be a formal public/private sector partnership, which would

- develop a *shared vision* in a strategy agreed by all stake-holders, based on an analysis of the competitive position, and a (usually) five-year rolling programme to secure vitality. This includes action through the Local Plan and transport investment programme.
- appoint a dedicated *town centre manager* to co-ordinate and monitor the delivery of that programme and of services provided within the centre.
- promote the centre with *effective marketing* to attract shoppers, visitors, tourists and new businesses; including the sponsorship of events and initiatives (farmers' markets, goodwill evenings, etc.).

### TOWN CENTRE HEALTH CHECK

Various indicators can be used to provide an insight into the performance of a retail centre and offer a framework for assessing vitality and viability (based on Cowley 1996):

- Footfall (pedestrian flow) – measures the number and movement of people on the streets. Footfall is a critical indicator for prospective retailers.
- Rental values – provide a measure of the relative attractiveness of different locations in-centre and between centres. Often, however, rents reflect historic expectations (from a few years back) rather than current reality, so potentially excluding more marginal users and contributing to vacancy.
- Vacancy rates – particularly street-level vacancy in prime retail areas; and, related to that, rates of enterprise turnover.
- Retailer representations and intentions, particularly as evidenced by actual investment in maintenance, window displays, refits, or redevelopment.

- Commercial yield – generally, the lower the yield (reflecting high property value) the more confidence investors have in the long-term profitability of the centre.
- Changing patterns of use – the number units and area devoted to food and durable goods, charity shops, services, social/leisure outlets, etc.
- Survey of consumers – to assess their views, attitudes and priorities.

 **RETAIL PLANNING PRINCIPLES**
Local neighbourhood and township centres should be supported by a planning strategy aimed at maximising their accessibility and attractiveness. Their location in relation to surrounding activities and transport routes is critical.

### 1 Pedestrian flows

Local shopping centres flourish on streets with the greatest connectivity to surrounding areas, where the footfall is naturally highest. Policy should work to increase pedestrian and cycle connectivity further by creating new links and overcoming severance effects (e.g. severance by heavy traffic flows).

### 2 Public transport networks

Historic centres are normally at the hub of local bus routes. New or revitalised centres should be too, giving the option of bus travel to those travelling from further away. Bus stops should be located conveniently in front of the shops and facilities clustered so as to permit access (e.g. all parts of the centre within 300 m of regular service stops).

### 3 Visibility and passing trade

Shops should not be hidden away in inward-looking neighbourhoods (where they are likely to fail), but open to general view, particularly to passing car and bus travellers: easy advertising, extended market. Local shopping centres must be close to distributor roads serving the wider residential area to permit casual purchases on the way to and from home. (This is not a cop out! The alternative is for the purchase to be made elsewhere, sometimes involving special trips rather than en route, and significantly reducing local retail viability.)

### 4 Siting flexibility

Along with catchment flexibility goes a degree of siting flexibility for small shops and businesses. In the context of a main local distributor, with a 'high street' character and regular bus services, retailers should be able to choose their location. So housing along the distributor road should be capable of converting to retail, and vice versa. Siting and catchment flexibility gives commerce more freedom to respond to changing conditions and seize opportunities. It helps ensure diversity of provision.

*Walking distances*

*'Acceptable' walking distances depend on the quality of the shops, the size of shopping centre and the anticipated length of stay of the shopper.*

*Carley and Donaldson (1997) recommend maximum distance from car park to centre according to length of stay:*

| | |
|---|---|
| *½ hour* | *100 m* |
| *1 hour* | *200 m* |
| *2 hours* | *400 m* |
| *4 hours* | *800 m* |

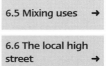

6.5 Mixing uses ➜

6.6 The local high street ➜

# 4.9

*Diversity helps vitality*

*Figure 4.10*
**The quality of the shopping environment
is key to success**

*This is an analysis of Coleford town centre by
Roger Evans and Associates*

SOURCE: GLOUCESTERSHIRE MARKET TOWNS 2000

## 5    Core retail areas

The point when residents feel they have arrived in a local shopping centre is important in relation to footfall, turnover, and perceptions of distance walked to 'get to the shops'. If at all possible, maintain active retail frontage from that point on. Continuous frontage on one side of the street is better than the same number of outlets discontinuous on both sides.

## 6    Diversity

It is important to promote diversity of retail and non-retail uses within local and township centres, making use of side streets, squares, arcades, etc. to increase the compact capacity of the centre. The reasons for this are:

- the convenience of linked journeys: i.e. fulfilling several purposes in one trip
- evidence that such convenience is valued by consumers, enhances social opportunity and boosts vitality and viability
- the reduction of journeys (due to multi-purpose trips) reduces energy use and $CO_2$ emissions
- the diversity allows mutual reinforcement between activities: for example, office workers can shop during the lunch hour and frequent the pub after work
- the spread of travel demand over a longer period of the day increases the viability of bus services, and the capacity of the road network.

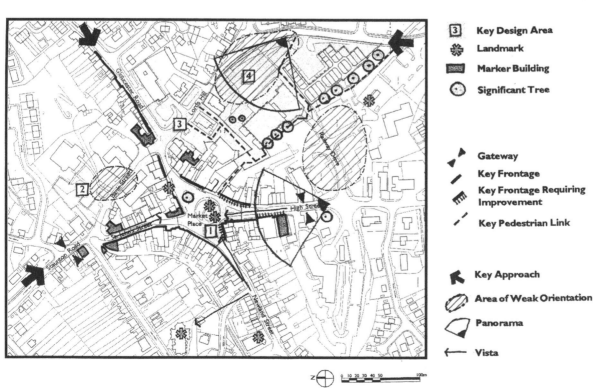

## SUPERSTORES

Large food stores are key generators of local activity. They increasingly provide a diversity of retail/service functions under one roof. They have an important social function for casual and planned meetings. In the long term, with internet shopping, their role may change, but for the moment they are vital ingredients of local culture, starting points for local food strategies. In this context the further development of supermarkets needs to be seen, not least by the retailers themselves, as an opportunity for more sustainable development.

### Township stores

Most towns, and every township within a city, should have one or more supermarkets in order to increase local consumer choice, allow pedestrian access, reduce general trip lengths and cut retail/employment leakage out of the township. Total store size should roughly match the town/township catchment. Large supermarkets poach custom from smaller shops and can kill them off. It is therefore vital that investment in new stores is used to bulwark the viability of existing/planned shopping centres.

### The sequential test

In line with Planning Policy Guidance Note 6 (PPG6) supermarkets should be located 'in centre', integrated with other retail/service facilities. Only when this is not physically possible can edge-of-centre locations be considered. Out-of-centre locations should only be contemplated as part of a planned new retail focus satisfying the essential criteria of pedestrian, bike and bus (as well as car) accessibility. Isolated stores should not be allowed.

### Integration in-centre

This should be planned so as to foster use of other shops and facilities as well as the supermarket, and facilitate access by non-car-users.

- Site the supermarket as a key 'anchor store' within the centre.
- Integrate it into the active retailing frontage, not set back behind a car park.
- Ensure the car park is available for non-supermarket users, with pedestrian access in all directions.
- Plan bus-stops close to the main entrance.
- Create an attractive frontage, with a sense of place.

## WORKING OUT SUSTAINABLE RETAIL CATCHMENT AREAS

The diagram (Figure 4.11) distinguishes three grades of catchment. Ideally, all residential areas should be within primary or secondary catchment zones: primary – within very easy walking distance (the 800 m 'ped-shed'); secondary – having the option of a modest walk/cycle (<2 km) or a frequent, accessible bus/tram service.

*Getting it wrong*

*Research on market towns and district centres shows that following the development of large edge/out-of-town-centre foodstores, the traditional convenience sector declines 21–75 per cent in market share.*

SOURCE: HILLIER PARKER 1998

*Note that where a supermarket is available locally the majority of people choose it in preference to travelling to reach other brands. One study suggests up to 90 per cent of people choose their local branch.*

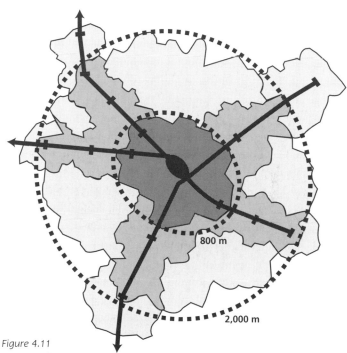

*Figure 4.11*
**Sustainable retail catchment area**

● shopping centre

✚ good bus or tram routes (400 m and 600 m catchments)

▨ primary catchment area within 800 m ped-shed

▨ secondary catchment area well served by public transport and within 2000 m ped-shed

☐ tertiary catchment area either within 2000 m ped-shed or well served by public transport

## 4.10

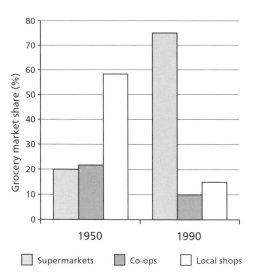

*Figure 4.12*
**The relative decline in local grocery**

SOURCE: WHO (1999)

---

### Village shop support scheme

*The Village Shop Support project, a rural project in south Norfolk, involved a package of measures aimed at helping small village shops survive, thrive and improve the service they offer; and hence the health and quality of life for people in local communities. Can we offer something similar in urban neighbourhoods?*

#### Objectives

- *To improve the shopping environment*
- *To attract more customers*
- *To improve accessibility*
- *To enhance the skills of shopkeepers*
- *To encourage the supply of more local produce*
- *To encourage greater use of shops by local people*

*The partnership included Tesco Stores plc, Rural Development Commission, Norfolk and Waveney Training and Enterprise Council, Norwich Enterprise Agency Trust.*

---

5.11 Local food →

---

### 4.10 LOCAL SHOPS AND SERVICES

### SUPPORTING LOCAL SHOPS

The neighbourhood or village shop is an important part of the social as well as the economic fabric. Strategies to support them should involve market, voluntary and local authority action.

- Retailing organisations (for example publicans, petrol companies and the post office) need to recognise a responsibility to be creative in building partnerships to maintain local viability.
- Community groups can support or run local outlets through consumer co-operatives, LETS schemes and voluntary clubs.
- Local authorities can offer rate rebates and a flexible attitude to local retail planning applications.

**The potential benefits**

- Local convenience and accessibility.

- Reduced car travel and emissions – where local shopping facilities are good most people use them; and where they are close (<500 m) most people walk to them (Saye 1999).

- Local employment opportunities.

- Opportunities for local fresh produce to be supplied.

- Informal social contact, building social capital.

- Responsiveness to particular local needs/tastes.

- Awareness/support to elderly/frail shop users and potential alertness to their health problems.

**Public houses**

Large pubs – normally part of regional or national chains – should be located in-centre, helping to bring vitality to township/neighbourhood centres, benefiting from workers and shoppers trade, and encouraging access by foot/pedal/public transport.

Small pubs are a dying breed. Many recent suburbs have none at all. The potential for new 'locals' is hampered by licensing and planning restrictions, but also by the absence of houses suitable for conversion into public houses.

An alternative approach would be to create opportunities (in a growing market) for small-scale local provision by

- ensuring over time that every neighbourhood has properties where the ground floor can be converted to pub/café/office/retail use – typically larger terraced units fronting directly onto the street at a node of pedestrian activity
- permitting small pubs/cafés (maximum customer space specified) to set up in such locations with zero or modest parking requirements
- easing the licensing regulations.

**Filling stations**

In some smaller settlements filling stations can offer the best opportunity for a local convenience store. Their location in-settlement (not outside it) is important. The retail element should be planned for local non-car access as well as for car users.

**Hairdressers**

Single practitioners (often operating from one room in their own homes) are entirely appropriate in residential areas: they diversify household income and provide a valued service within easy walking distance of local clients, part of the indigenous neighbourhood economy. Conversely, larger establishments, with several employees, benefit from the visibility, trip-purpose sharing and social opportunities of an in-centre location where access by bus is possible.

**Corner shops**

Small general stores (e.g. 50 or 100 $m^2$ ), located in residential areas outside main shopping parades, have had their viability undermined by changing shopping habits and falling population densities. However, urban intensification and renaissance could create new opportunities at points of high localised pedestrian flow. If local initiatives bubble up, then local councils should support them, with easy change-of-use regulations and, if possible, rates reduction. In new-build areas, adaptable building types are required on street corners where pedestrian flows are likely to be high.

## 4.11 SCHOOLS

**BASIC PRINCIPLES**
The provision of accessible local schools – primary and secondary – is central to the maintenance and revival of local community. Besides their prime educational functions, schools can

- contribute to and instill appreciation of local culture(s)
- foster social inclusion and tolerance
- encourage healthy lifestyle habits
- shape children's travel behaviour
- create opportunities for a flourishing school community; and
- help generate long-term networks of mutual support.

The disposition of schools across a settlement (in extreme cases, the very existence of local schools) is a central issue. The education providers and the planning authority have a shared responsibility to maximise local accessibility to schools so as to foster social inclusion, healthy child travel habits and a flourishing local school community.

*Local shops support social capital and community networks*

*The school trip*

- *Only 2 per cent of children now cycle to school compared to 60 per cent in Denmark.*

- *Less than 10 per cent of 7–8-year-olds are allowed to walk to school, unaccompanied by a parent – down from 75 per cent in 1970.*

- *Half the car journeys to primary school serve no other function.*

- *20 per cent of peak-hour traffic is associated with school trips.*

- *The average distance to secondary school has increased by a third between 1985/86 and 1994/96.*

*(Percentages apply to the UK.)*

SCHOOLS

# 4.11

## Safely to school

*This pilot project worked with nine schools in Suffolk to tackle the increasing problems associated with children's travel to and from school.*

### Objectives

*Safety – reduce child casualties, increase pupils' road sense.*

*Environment – reduce school-related car journeys, promote walking, cycling and public transport, create a safer, more pleasant environment for everyone to enjoy.*

*Health and quality of life – encourage social inclusion, increase health and fitness, give a greater sense of personal safety to pupils and parents.*

*Lessons for sustainable neighbourhoods – Consultation is at the very root of the method. Surveys and the 'planning for real' technique elicited information about local needs.*

*Involvement – Children in each school made and painted a model of the local area. This worked well when the schools mustered an army of local volunteer helpers and tackled the construction over a marathon two days.*

*The children's reaction to the model was always very touching. The older children were fascinated and very eager to locate their own houses and their routes to school. Public consultation was well attended in almost all schools and attracted a wide range of people, young and old. The result was masses of comments that were easy to understand.*

*As a way of collecting a lot of local opinion the technique works excellently.*

## WALKING/CYCLING TO SCHOOL

The declining number of children walking or cycling to school in Britain is well attested (see Figure 4.13). The decline is not only due to parental choice and longer distances to school (evidence suggests most parents still choose a school close by), it is also due to highly car-based lifestyles and the withdrawal of parental permission for children to be on the streets alone.

### Life-style and health effects

A growing number of children are missing out on the regular exercise of getting to school. The patterns of physical activity established in childhood are key determinants of adult behaviour (Kuhl and Cooper 1992). This relates particularly to cycling: only a quarter of children now use bikes (Hillman *et al.* 1991); there is almost a 'lost generation' of cyclists. More sedentary habits are leading to worrying projections of future prevalence of obesity and heart disease (Roberts 1996).

### Social effects

The children who do still walk to school see it not as a fall-back position but as having positive benefits: exercise, independence, meeting friends (Osbourne and Davis 1996). Parents walking with young children, meeting others on the way or at the school gates, create networks of mutual support. In addition the ability to walk/cycle to school reduces household travel costs: locally accessible schools are part of an equitable, inclusive society.

| Mode | 1985–86 | | 1994–96 | |
|---|---|---|---|---|
| | % trips | Average trip length (km) | % trips | Average trip length (km) |
| Walk | 53 | 1.0 | 44 | 1.1 |
| Cycle | 6 | 2.6 | 2 | 2.9 |
| Car passenger | 11 | 5.4 | 21 | 5.6 |
| Bus/rail | 21 | 5.9 | 26 | 7.2 |
| Private bus | 9 | 9.8 | 7 | 12.3 |
| Total/average | 100 | 3.4 | 100 | 4.5 |

Figure 4.13
**Journeys to and from secondary schools**

*Calculations based on Table 2 in Stead and Davis (1998), using data from DETR*

## ACCESSIBILITY POLICY

Accessibility to schools (preferably a choice of schools within easy reach) should be a significant factor determining school investment programmes and housing allocations/permission.

Appropriate standards depend on local conditions in terms of density, settlement pattern and school provision policy. Standards need to be agreed by the education authority and the planning authority and written into Local Plans following consultation with parents and the wider community.

An overall strategy could involve

- keeping schools as small as educationally/financially feasible

- using the accessibility standards to prioritise schools-investment decisions and help shape other development decisions

- gradually increasing residential densities

- ensuring a permeable neighbourhood pattern giving a choice of safe routes to school with the minimum deflection from the shortest possible route; and/or

- opening access to school sites from different directions.

### Fortress school vs. community school

The reaction of some schools to perceived 'stranger danger' has been to take stringent security precautions. The school becomes an exclusive domain, with one controlled access. This forces some children into longer journeys than necessary, with concomitant reduction in walking. It also cuts the school off from the social and economic benefits of shared local use and the sense of the school being at the heart of the community. The integration of school and community makes good use of resources and can reduce vandalism, graffiti and anti-social behaviour in and around the school.

### Remote playing fields or remote schools

Schools are sometimes shifted outside their main catchments in order to provide new classrooms and integral playing fields. The social and environmental costs of this decision – in terms of increased car reliance, pollution, congestion, lack of child exercise and loss of children's independence as well as poor community access – are significant. In situ redevelopment/reorganisation and dual school/community provision can offer viable alternatives.

*Local Education Authorities produce a School Organisation Plan in which they are required to consider accessibility and the journey to school – see DfEE 1999.*

### ■ CHECKLIST

*Education providers should*

✔ agree the objectives of schools serving their local community and being locally accessible

✔ consider the appropriate balance between economies of scale and local accessibility

✔ avoid the 'school as fortress' mentality, instead enabling access from all directions

✔ promote safe routes to school (see Planning for the pedestrian, 4.15)

✔ look at ways of reducing land-take without compromising provision – to facilitate use of smaller, accessible urban sites (e.g. two- or three-storey buildings)

✔ promote dual use of facilities with the local community (e.g. hall, swimming pool, hard pitch, library/resource centre)

✔ promote the 'community school' principle, with schools seen as a focus for training, life-long learning, voluntary activities and social events

✔ consider the degree to which 16+ provision should be integrated with local economic/ cultural activity, and colleges seen as 'permeable' on-street facilities.

4.15 Safe routes to school →

# 4.11

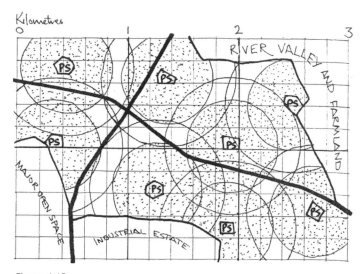

**Figure 4.15**

**Illustrative application of primary school location**

*An even distribution is important*

**Assumptions**

- *simplified straight-line catchment areas*
- *mixture of school sizes; average population served = 3,000*
- *gross density = 60 ppha (each 4 ha square = 240 people)*
- *total population = c. 26,000*
- *catchment radiuses 400 m and 600 m.*

**Secondary school admissions**

*Admission criteria used where there is over-subscription*

- *Children living in the catchment area of the school*
- *Children with medical or social needs that can only be met in the school of preference*
- *Children with brothers/sisters at the schoo.*
- *Children with the nearest available safe walking route*

SOURCE: YORK CITY COUNCIL 2000

## ACCESS TO PRIMARY SCHOOLS

Every urban neighbourhood, and every rural settlement, should if possible have one or more primary schools. The suggested accessibility standards in Figure 4.14 assume an average catchment of 4,000 people, supporting a 2-class entry school. The ideal target of 400 m actual distance means almost all children walk to school and there is an excellent choice of accessible schools. But it is only achievable where densities are high and there is an even distribution of schools across the area. The 600 m standard is achievable in more situations. Even at 800 m, a substantial majority do (still) walk, but walkable choice of school is restricted.

If one-class entry schools are the rule then of course accessibility standards are much more easily achieved, and the schools can have a more local neighbourhood catchment.

| Graded standards | Gross residential density (pph) | | | | |
|---|---|---|---|---|---|
| | 30 | 40 | 60 | 80 | 100 |
| 400 m (excellent) | ✗ | ✗ | ✗ | ✗ | ? |
| 600 m (good) | ✗ | ✗ | ? | ✔ | ✔✔ |
| 800 m (adequate) | ? | ✔ | ✔✔ | ✔✔ | ✔✔ |

| | | | |
|---|---|---|---|
| ✗ | = not achievable | | Note: if school sizes are significantly |
| ? | = difficult to achieve | | different, catchment populations |
| ✔ | = normally possible | | untypical or school distribution uneven |
| ✔✔ | = thoroughly achievable | | then these assumptions change. |

**Figure 4.14**

**Primary school accessibility standards**

*Actual home to school distance*

## SECONDARY SCHOOLS

### The significance of catchments

Studies have shown that, despite the advent of parental choice, a large proportion of children go to close schools (Farthing and Winter 1994; Stead and Davis 1998). This is often encouraged by LEA admissions policy, favouring local catchment.

The downside of this policy is that in order to ensure the school of their choice parents may move to within the catchment area so their children will get priority. Popular, successful schools are thereby affecting the pattern of residential differentiation. The system of school place allocation may exacerbate social polarisation between neighbourhoods. The solution to this is not necessarily to abolish catchments (which has social, environmental and resource implications) but to consider density, housing policy and school size policies.

### The size of schools

In a comprehensive system social polarisation is partly due to the sheer size of schools necessary to support an adequate sixth form. If schools were generally smaller then they could be located closer to where pupils live, and consequently shorten trip lengths, with more walking/cycling; and there would be greater choice of schools within a reasonable distance.

A 'sixth form college' system (often associated with a technical college and thereby offering a very wide range of subjects and training) can enable the 11–16 schools to be more 'local', on the scale of the neighbourhood rather than the township, with more local choice.

### Locational criteria

The suggested standards in Figure 4.16 are valid for areas with the potential for a reasonably even distribution of schools. Most students are willing to walk up to 1,500 m. New housing or schools should be located to facilitate this choice.

Public transport access: all secondary schools should be well located in relation to bus routes from their main hinterland areas. Clearly this is vital in dispersed settlement areas, but is also important generally to facilitate choice.

*Exemplary York*

*Stead and Davis (1998) compared pupil travel behaviour for different types of school in a number of locations. In York they found both direct grant and city secondary schools served very local catchment areas, with average trip lengths of 1 km and very few over 2 km. There was no significant change between 1987 and 1997.*

| Graded standards | Gross residential sensity (pph) | | | | |
|---|---|---|---|---|---|
| | 30 | 40 | 60 | 80 | 100 |
| 1000 m (excellent) | ✗ | ✗ | ✔ | ✔ | ✔✔ |
| 1500 m (good) | ✔ | ✔ | ✔✔ | ✔✔ | ✔✔ |
| 2000 m (sub-optimal) | ✔✔ | ✔ | ✔✔ | ✔✔ | ✔✔ |

Figure 4.16
**Secondary school accessibility standards**

*Actual home to school distance*

✗  = not achievable
?  = difficult to achieve
✔  = achievable with smaller schools (4-class entry)
✔✔ = achievable with larger schools (8-class entry)

## SIXTH FORM/TECHNICAL COLLEGE

The local college is appropriate to the scale of the whole township or market town, with a dependent population of 20,000–30,000. If colleges can be provided at this scale (rather than much bigger) then participation by less affluent/disadvantaged groups may be improved, and there is more opportunity for walking/cycling.

▪ Centrality in relation to public transport services is vital.

▪ An accessibility standard that could be achieved in most urban areas is 4 km (actual), which is a distance most cyclists are willing and able to cycle.

109

# 4.12

*Figure 4.17*
**Education catchment populations and land needs**

| Kind of school | Number of pupils | Implied catchment population | Typical land needs (range) |
|---|---|---|---|
| PRIMARY with shared classes | 50-100 | 500-1,000 | 0.3–0.6 ha |
| PRIMARY 1-class entry | 150–200 | c.2,000 | 0.5–1 ha |
| PRIMARY 2-class entry | 300–400 | c.4,000 | 1–2 ha |
| SECONDARY 11–16-year olds, 4-class entry | 500–600 | c.8,000 | 4–8 ha |
| SECONDARY 11–18-year olds, 8-class entry | 1,200–1,400 | c.16,000 | 6–12 ha |
| COLLEGE 6th-form/technical | | say 25,000 | very varied |

## 4.12 SUPPORTING COMMUNITY HEALTH

The focus of this section is on the provision of health facilities. But planning for public health involves much more than curative services. It is about a healthy human habitat and supportive social structures. Hence most sections of Chapters 4 and 5 are relevant – for example:

- the development of social capital  *§ 4.3*
- access to jobs and services  *§ 4.8*
- safe streets  *§ 4.15*
- affordable warmth  *§ 5.4*
- clean water and waste treatment  *§ 5.7*.

### LOCATING HEALTH CENTRES

Within a township of 20,000–30,000 people there should be a choice of surgeries/health centres offering together a wide range of services (e.g. midwife, district nurse, health visitor, family planning, drugs therapies, etc.) and giving accessible options to residents. The main responsibility for this rests with the Health Authority (Primary Care Group), together with GPs, reinforced by policies within the Local/Community Plan.

**Criteria**

- Is there a reasonably even spread of surgeries and health centres across the town/township to maximise the opportunity for pedestrian accessibility and interlinkages with the local community?

- Are all dwellings within 800 m (10 minutes' walk) of a health facility?

- Where local access is poor, are there plans to set up branch surgeries or to encourage more single practitioners?

*Number of people on the books*

| | |
|---|---|
| *Solo doctor* | *= 2,000–3,000* |
| *Two-doctor surgery* | *= 4,000–6,000* |
| *Four-doctor centre* | *= 8,000–12,000* |

- Are larger health centres (e.g. 3–4 doctors or more with a range of services) close to regular bus services giving good access to the whole township?

## LOCATING OTHER HEALTH SERVICES

### Dentists

People often choose to travel considerable distances to maintain contact with a dentist they trust. It is therefore important that dentists are located close to good bus routes. They should also be close to local shopping/service centres to facilitate multi-purpose trips.

### Opticians

These are health providers but also increasingly retailers of comparison goods. In-centre location permits comparison shopping and facilitates multi-purpose trips.

### Natural health clinics

Similar criteria apply as for conventional health centres. Larger facilities should locate in or close to town centres or local high streets, permitting ease of access by bus, foot and bike. However, sole practitioners should be able to operate from home (subject to normal safeguards), to hold down costs and increase client choice.

### Dispensing chemists

These should be in-centre, accessible by all modes of transport, and preferably close to health centres to maximise convenience.

### Healthy Living Centres

Healthy Living Centres is the name of a recent Government funding initiative but also a concept dating back to an experiment in Peckham opened in 1935.

Healthy living centres can take many forms but the core concept derives from a holistic view of health, recognising the relevant social determinants. This recognises that strategies to improve health require a co-ordinated and imaginative approach including health, social and leisure agencies in partnership with local communities. The traditional GPs' practice is embedded within a facility that enables people to access easily the non-medical aspects of health.

*Figure 4.18*

**The original Peckham concept: by night, by day**

*A multitude of activities provided supporting a 'healthy heart' to the neighbourhood*

SOURCE: MACFARLANE 1950

---

**Healthy Living Centres**

*St Augustine's, Norfolk*

This was the first Healthy Living Centre to open with funding from the New Opportunities Fund. The objective is to provide a one-stop shop for the wide-ranging health needs of people in King's Lynn. A large selection of facilities has been included:

- GP and primary healthcare
- childcare centre
- community café
- learning centre
- arts studio
- Citizen's Advice Bureau
- office space for community groups
- adventure playground
- garden for the disabled
- public transport, footpath and cycle links to surrounding area

*Many different funding sources have been tapped into*

- New Opportunities Fund
- Community Fund
- European Social Fund
- Department for Education and Employment
- Single Regeneration Budget
- Dow Chemicals – local sponsor

National Lottery Funding is funding a new wave of Healthy Living Centres. The funding is targeted at those suffering deprivation and the solution need not necessarily involve a single central provision building. Each Healthy Living Centre can propose a different mix of facilities and services responding to local circumstances.

### HEALTHY NEIGHBOURHOODS

The principles of healthy living centres still hold good for health provision in general. The concept can be used as an essential component of a healthy neighbourhood, pulling together some of the disparate elements of a healthy lifestyle and promoting mutual support. For example:

- Healthy neighbourhood planning: community involvement is essential to the Healthy Living Centre concept. This may be a vehicle to look at other aspects of healthy neighbourhood planning such as the provision of safe routes, access and support for local shops and affordable homes.

- Allotments, orchards and city farms: through the proved therapeutic and training benefits of horticulture and food production.

- Schools, education and libraries: through after-school care, community education careers advice.

- Shared facilities, community halls: through social events, exercise classes, space for meetings.

5.1 Allotments →

6.5 Mixing uses →

6.7 Space sharing →

*Local recreational needs*
outside the home

- *parent-supervised play*
- *playground activities*
- *informal play*
- *visiting the park*
- *picnicking/lunch hour*
- *organised sport*
- *casual sporting activity*
- *walking (including dog walking)*
- *cycling*
- *gardening in the allotment*
- *sitting and watching/reading*
- *sitting and talking.*

## 4.13 RECREATIONAL OPEN SPACE

### BASIC PRINCIPLES

Local residents – particularly children, teenagers and elderly people – should have the realistic option of walking/cycling to an appropriate range of open-space facilities, and be able to walk between spaces on the green network. As a general guide, open-space facilities should be available on the following basis

| | |
|---|---|
| Within the home-patch | toddler's playspace |
| Close to the home-patch | allotments<br>children's playground<br>local greenspace/pocket park |
| Within the neighbourhood | kick-about area<br>park, over 2 ha |
| Within the township | playing fields/tennis courts, etc.<br>adventure playground<br>access to 'natural' greenspace over 20 ha |

Note that green spaces, ranging from gardens to community forests, perform many functions within urban areas in relation to water, energy, food, pollution, biodiversity and cultural landscape as well as recreation. These overlapping functions are explored in later chapters. Here the emphasis is on recreation.

## ACCESSIBILITY AND CHOICE

Leisure is one area of life where most individuals have relatively free choice. Spontaneity and enjoyment are of the essence. Open spaces not only provide for specific recreational opportunities but also encourage healthy lifestyles and the potential for social contact. The key to local open-space provision is not therefore a set of space standards but working from an awareness of local needs to ensure everyone has access to a range of attractive and well-managed recreational facilities.

The Local Plan can be used to establish which groups, and what neighbourhoods, are underprovided, and to set targets for existing neighbourhoods and requirements for any new development areas. In this context, land allocation standards and accessibility criteria are important. They can be used to help ensure equity and comprehensiveness, to point up priorities, and give a bottom line for negotiation with developers and service providers. Any standards of accessibility or land allocation have to be judged according to local preferences and the general character of the locality, and adjusted accordingly.

## PLAYSPACE WITHIN EACH HOME-PATCH

The National Playing Field Association (1993) recommends a 'local area of play' (or LAP) for children up to five. This is a small area of open space for low-key games sited within one minute's walking time (or 100 m actual distance) of every home. As the picture suggests, this playspace may be part of the street scene but should be safeguarded from traffic, green in character, and overlooked by dwellings.

LOCAL AREA OF PLAY

*Figure 4.19*
**Local area of play**

*Some developers are incorporating the NPFA playspaces into their designs, without loss of housing space and at no greater cost, at the same time improving the estate's design quality and enhancing marketability*

BASED ON EARLY 1994

*Figure 4.20*
**Access to open space – some illustrative standards**

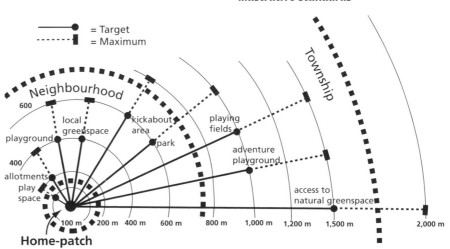

113

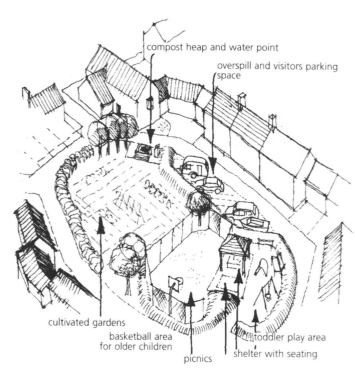

compost heap and water point

overspill and visitors parking space

cultivated gardens

basketball area for older children

picnics

toddler play area

shelter with seating

**Communal garden with playspace**

SOURCE: BARTON ET AL. 1995

*The principle of allotments very close to home has been adopted in many places, including Odense in Denmark, where allotments provide an attractive area around flats and offer an important outdoor social focus for residents. In Vancouver housing co-operatives have been surrounded by horticulture and gardens to great effect (Hopkins 2000).*

5.10 Food:
Allotments ➔

The need or appropriateness of such LAPs depends on the social mix and density of the area. Different policies for home-patch playspace may be adopted. For example:

■ **Medium-density areas:** (50 dpha)
Most back gardens are small and short excursions are necessary for toddlers/parents to gain exercise. The LAP model is ideal.

■ **High-density areas:** (100 dpha)
Few households have private gardens and where there are families communal provision is vital. If the streets are too crowded/constricted for playspace then an alternative is shared playspace within housing blocks, in the communal garden/courtyard, managed by the residents' group.

■ **Low-density areas:** (25 dpha)
There are fewer families within striking distance of any space provided, and large gardens provide ample play opportunities. There is therefore little justification for small-scale communal play spaces.

## DISPERSED ALLOTMENTS

Access to allotments is a sustainability and health issue. Local organic food production in medium–high density areas has been greatly impeded in the UK by the convention of providing allotments (if at all) in large and poorly accessed fields. Anecdotal evidence suggests that this puts people off allotment growing and increases reliance on inorganic methods. It certainly results in more vehicle use.

Allotments should be close enough to homes to permit easy access by foot, carrying tools, organic wastes or produce. The guideline maximum distance suggested is 200 m, taken as a feasible wheelbarrow or bucket-carrying distance.

Clearly this standard could vary both with topography and local attitudes. One model of allotment provision is within the home-zone in the form of community gardens, with potential for shared composting schemes and 'neighbourhood watch' over produce.

This implies a pattern of allotment provision radically different from at present. Local Plans could require all new brownfield housing development over a certain net density to include community garden space and appropriate management mechanisms. The corollary could be that there should be no net loss of allotment space within a township: sell-off of under-used allotments could then proceed no faster than alternative dispersed provision was created.

## NEIGHBOURHOOD PLAY AREAS AND GREENSPACE

Certain groups are particularly dependent on neighbourhood open-space provision – i.e. facilities within 400–600 m actual walking distance:

- parents with young children (often with pushchairs)
- young children playing, cycling, kicking around
- elderly people with limited mobility
- wheelchair users
- workers wanting a lunch break (or fag break).

The key to local provision is not the scale of specific land allocation but quality, access and safety. The needs may be met in a number of ways and often in the same or adjacent spaces. Any neighbourhood strategy is likely to involve some permutation of the following elements:

### Play street

More children's play occurs on streets than in playgrounds. Access-only, semi-pedestrianised streets can provide well-supervised opportunities for informal play.

### Playgrounds

According to the National Playing Fields Association (NPFA), equipped playgrounds for the 4–8-year-olds should be within 5 minutes' walk or 400 m actual distance of every home.

### Pocket parks

Small greens or quiet enclaves for sitting, talking, eating sandwiches and enjoying nature should be within a 300 m straight line, according to English Nature (1996). This equates with the 5-minute standard or 400 m actual.

### Kickabout areas

Informal green spaces or hard surfaces open enough for ball games with a normal minimum size of 0.2 ha.

### Local wildplace

Children love mysterious, hidden places (though parents may not), which can be allowed to develop unkempt – copses, stream bottoms, for example.

The 400 m actual walking distance is based on research showing that most young children travel less than that to play. Safety of the route is equally important. Most young children are not allowed to cross main roads or for that matter go beyond clearly defined boundaries such as railway lines. The location of playspaces must therefore recognise these limits.

*It isn't just the youngsters at play, Barcelona*

### The 'six-acre' standard

The National Playing Field Association (NPFA) adopted the 6-acre (or 2.4-ha) standard of open space per 1,000 population in 1938. It has been used by local authorities ever since. It expressly includes space for sport, active recreation and children's play, but does not include decorative parks, allotments or 'landscaping'.

| | |
|---|---|
| pitches, green and courts | 1.6–1.8 ha |
| playgrounds | 0.2–0.3 ha |
| informal play space | 0.4–0.5 ha |
| total per 1,000 population | 2.2–2.6 ha |

This standard has not been independently validated and is not achievable in many inner urban areas. However, if written into local plans it can provide a good starting point for negotiation. However, as pointed out in the main text, quality, accessibility and safety are equally important criteria.

### How not to plan local open space

'Prairie planning' of housing estates provides ample greenspace in the form of greens and wide verges. But the spaces have little recreational value and are expensive to maintain, creating open, often shapeless townscapes with little sense of place.

The other extreme is to hide the open space away, allocating land for play or for allotments on odd inaccessible corners of a development after the main layout has been worked out, without establishing who will look after it. This is called SLOAP – Space Left Over After Planning.

### THE TOWNSHIP PARKLAND

At a broader scale specific recreational provision should be seen as part of an open-space system that percolates through the urban area, creating the opportunity for greenways (foot, bike, equestrian) and round walks. Where this linkage does not currently exist then 'virtual' linkage should be established, through access, planting and pedestrian/bike priority measures.

The township strategy should seek to achieve the following standards for access:

**Parks** – or non-sports greenspaces of at least 2 ha: target maximum actual walking distance from home 600–800 m depending on local conditions. 800 m is equivalent to 10 minutes' walking time or 3 minutes' cycling.

**Playing fields** – plus other appropriate facilities such as tennis courts, bowling green and hard pitch – target actual maximum distance 1–1.2 km, i.e. 15 minutes' walking or 5 minutes' cycling, subject to topography. Note potential for 'dual use' with schools/colleges.

**Adventure playground** – activities popular with local 8–14-year-olds, such as skateboarding, cycling, climbing and football need space of at least 0.4 ha: target actual maximum distance 1–1.2 km, or 15 minutes' walking, 5 minutes' cycle.

6.13 The green
network →

These facilities should where possible provide direct access onto the parkland system, and thence to major semi-natural open space or open countryside.

# planning for movement

## 4.14 BASIC PRINCIPLES

 **STREETS ARE FOR PEOPLE**
The key to a successful strategy is reclaiming streets for people: people walking, cycling, idling, playing, sitting, drinking, talking, selling. Traffic has to be sufficiently tamed so as to pose little threat in terms of accidents, noise, fumes or space domination. This applies to all residential and shopping streets. Neighbourhood movement planning should open up choices for all groups – old and young, rich and poor – so that people have attractive options for how to get to friends, facilities and places.

### OBJECTIVES

**Accessibility:** easy access for all kinds of people to activities within and outside the locality, with a particular emphasis on non-car-users and less-mobile people.

**Exercise:** making it easy and attractive for people to gain healthy exercise by walking and cycling more – for both recreational and functional trips.

**Safety:** reducing the likelihood of road accidents and reducing the fear of assault and street crime.

**Viability:** a pattern of movement that maximises the chance of local business and social facilities being economically sustainable.

**Community:** creating streets and places where people can meet and thus foster local social networks, improving their quality of life and the sense of local community.

**Environment:** reducing transport-related levels of local air pollution and globally damaging greenhouse emissions.

Key to all these objectives is encouraging people from all sectors of society to walk. Research shows that people's propensity to walk is very significantly affected by how safe, convenient and pleasurable the experience of walking is. Safety is also a key factor in encouraging cycling, especially for children and older people. Public transport use is profoundly affected by distance to stops, reliability and the speed and comfort of service as well as frequency. Achieving the objectives requires close co-operation between transport operators, policy-makers and local planners.

### Township movement indicators

- *Percentages of people walking to key facilities (e.g. schools, supermarkets)*
- *Pedestrian casualties as a percentage of pedestrian activity*
- *Footfall in the township centre*
- *Number of Green Travel Plans adopted*
- *Number of 20 mph/home zones introduced.*

### Transport should not cost lives!

*According to the Department of Health 3,500 people are killed annually in road accidents, and 12,000–24,000 have their deaths 'brought forward' by exposure to traffic pollutants. That puts the occasional rail disasters into perspective.*

### ■ CHECKLIST

*Some groups with specific needs*

✔ *Parents with babies/toddlers (often in a buggy)*

✔ *Young children going to school/playground/ friends*

✔ *Adolescents meeting together on neutral ground; going to school*

✔ *Young people shopping, pubbing, clubbing*

✔ *People going to work by bus or tram or bike*

✔ *Local workers at lunch times and before/ after work*

✔ *Delivery vehicles to local shops/factories/ offices*

✔ *Adult carers without access to a car, using local facilities*

✔ *Infirm/disabled people meeting/using facilities*

✔ *Elderly people with limited mobility, wanting local car access*

✔ *Dog walkers, runners and others wanting round walks off road*

✔ *Allotment holders with barrows/buckets of produce/compost*

✔ *Elderly/unemployed/leisured people strolling to the park or square.*

# 4.15

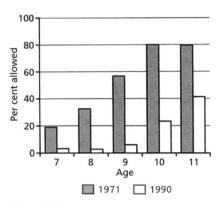

Figure 4.21
**Children allowed to use buses alone**

SOURCE: HILLMAN, ADAMS AND WHITELEGG 1991

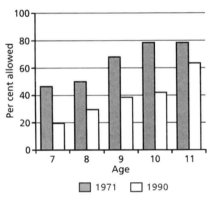

Figure 4.22
**Children allowed to go to leisure places alone**

SOURCE: HILLMAN, ADAMS AND WHITELEGG 1991

**Walking is healthy**

*For many people, walking is the best overall physical activity for maintaining and improving health and fitness, offering*

- *less risk of heart disease*
- *weight control*
- *less risk of high blood pressure*
- *less risk of diabetes*
- *less depression/anxiety*
- *less risk of cancer of the colon*
- *less risk of osteoporosis.*

## EQUITABLE ACCESS

It is important to recognise the needs of different groups, not just the dominant and ubiquitous car users, and then to plan a transport system that allows people to choose their own destinations, routes and modes with maximum freedom. This means opening up choice, and trying to ensure one person's choice does not become another person's constraint.

Designing for the most vulnerable groups (e.g. children, those who are mobility-handicapped) will normally ensure choices are opened up for others as well. For example, easily graded ramps help elderly people and parents pushing buggies as well as wheelchair users.

## PRIORITY MODES

The conventional approach in the late twentieth century was to plan the road layout first, providing for pedestrians, cyclists and particularly public transport as a secondary stage. This set of priorities can be reversed. Effective public transport routes and a permeable, safe pedestrian network should be the first considerations, with vehicle circulation second. This is not to downplay the importance of good road planning, but to reorient the focus.

## 4.15 PLANNING FOR THE PEDESTRIAN

Walking is the most common form of movement, open to almost everybody. It constitutes most trips for people who do not own a car, especially women and children. Trips by public transport and car often involve a walking element. Like cycling, walking involves minimal resources but can be a healthy and pleasurable aesthetic and physical experience. Yet the pedestrian environment in many cities is increasingly hostile, and this is being exacerbated by the car-orientated nature of much modern development. In extreme cases the pedestrian option is being effectively excluded by inconvenience, danger, fumes and ugliness.

**KEY PRINCIPLE**
Pedestrian activity is the lifeblood of the neighbourhood. Enabling free and easy pedestrian movement is therefore a very high priority. Every new development or transport investment should make a positive contribution to the pedestrian environment working to achieve the five 'Cs': connected, convenient, comfortable, convivial and conspicuous.

## CRITERIA FOR NETWORK DESIGN

The Institution of Highways and Transportation (1999) suggest there are five useful criteria for good pedestrian design, elaborated below.

### Connected
- The network should be comprehensive, serving all significant desire lines.
- It should provide good permeability, i.e. a choice of routes filtering through an area allowing pedestrians to go which way they want.
- Easy, direct access to public transport facilities is vital.
- Green spaces should be linked into the network and allow for round walks, and where possible 'green routes' to major centres of activity.

### Convenient
- Pedestrian routes should be as direct as possible in order to reduce distance to be walked and increase the pedestrian catchment of facilities.
- They should avoid steep hills, unnecessary barriers, steps or kerbs that might inhibit less agile people and those with pushchairs or wheelchairs.
- Where new routes are planned they should follow the contours, even where this does result in some route deflection. Alternative (direct) routes can be provided for the energetic. Choice is important.
- Routes should be linked by safe and convenient crossings, with minimum diversion.

### Comfortable
- Footways should be wide enough to allow easy passing and overtaking, without being pushed out into traffic – especially on heavily used roads where long vehicles on bends may be intimidating.
- Routes should be overlooked by nearby properties, giving a sense of surveillance and safety.
- The route should be well lit and feel safe, without dark corners or featureless, unconnected sections which can be intimidating.

### Convivial
- Routes should be places where people can meet casually and talk in comfort, free from excessive noise or fumes.
- They should be designed for aesthetic enjoyment, giving pleasure by the variety of prospects, spaces and landscapes.

### Conspicuous
- Main routes should be easy to 'read', distinctive, and clearly signposted. Landmark features (e.g. mature trees, public art) can help give a sense of place.

*Speed and time*
*Average walking speed = 3 mph, 5 kmph or 1.4 metres per second. Individual speeds vary widely in the 2–4 mph range*

*Walking time*

| Distance | | Time | |
|---|---|---|---|
| | 400 m | Time | approx. 5 minutes |
| | 800 m | | approx. 10 minutes |
| | 1 km | | approx. 12 minutes |
| | 1 mile | | approx. 17 minutes |

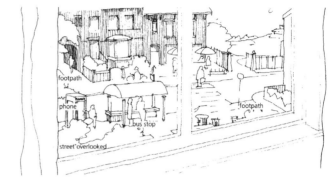

**Sketch view**

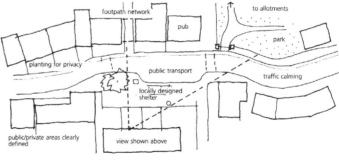

**Plan of the scene illustrated above**

*Figure 4.23*
**Clustering of facilities with natural surveillance**

SOURCE: BARTON ET AL. 1995

**How far will people walk?**
*The average walking journey is 1 km. Not many people walk more than 2 km*
- *400 m is an accepted threshold for walking to the bus*
- *800 m is a suggested threshold for walking to a town/township centre*

**Actual distances walked varies with:**
- *individual physical ability and fitness*
- *encumbrances e.g. shopping, pushchair*
- *journey purpose and availability of options*
- *topography and weather conditions*
- *perceived pleasures and/or dangers of the route*
- *individual life-style choice.*

*So while distance standards are useful they are only a starting point for local policy debate.*

PLANNING FOR THE PEDESTRIAN

# 4.15

### Standards for path design

*Gradients*
- *Normal maximum 5 per cent (1:20)*
- *Where necessary up to 8 per cent (1:12)*
- *For very short distances 12 per cent (1:8)*

*Widths*
- *Normal minimum 2 m*
- *Protected low-use routes 1.5 m*
- *Dual use with bikes 3 m.*

---

## Walking for health
## Leicester

*Promotes higher levels of awareness of the health and social benefits of walking and increases the participation in daily walking activity through increased opportunities, community action and improved environments.*

### Objectives include:

- *Developing environments and walking facilities – the focus of this is to make the links with future developmental priorities within transport and regeneration plans which seek to improve the environment in favour of pedestrians.*

- *Contributions to health improvement – reduction in coronary heart disease in Leicestershire.*

- *Providing better conditions for cyclists and pedestrians and thereby a reduction in accidents, in pollution from transport and hence in exacerbation of asthma.*

- *Regular walking for older people to strengthen their bones.*

### Urban design solutions

*Safer conditions for cyclists and pedestrians, wider footpaths, more seating and improved landscaping, slower-moving and reduced traffic, improved pedestrian street crossings, signposting walking routes.*

---

## PROBLEMS FOR WALKERS

- The absence of seating en route. This affects the distance elderly people are willing to walk.
- Poorly designed subways – the fear of lurking danger.
- Lack of toilets in local or township centres.
- Unkempt places with rubbish strewn around, e.g. dog dirt, graffiti.
- Intimidation by (possibly harmless) groups of young people/adolescents and beggars.
- Shared surfaces with cyclists – specifically for those with hearing and visual impairments.

## SAFE ROUTES TO SCHOOL: LOCAL ACTION IS NOT ENOUGH

The Sustrans 'Safe Routes to School' programme involves local authorities working with individual school communities (teachers, parents, pupils) to raise awareness and improve the safety of pedestrian routes. The approach can lead to significant short-term shifts in pupil behaviour, but the decay factor is fast. Some supposedly 'successful' schools show a substantial increase in car dependence after only a few years (Beeson 2000). In Denmark, by contrast, the shift to walking/cycling to school has been maintaining across whole cities. The moral is that a decentralised school-by-school approach, relying heavily on individual initiatives and external input being sustained, is no substitute for a city-wide integrated strategy with a comprehensive system of safe routes and high-profile political backing. The attitudes of a whole urban community have to be systematically changed.

## CRITERIA FOR NEW DEVELOPMENT PROJECTS

- **Location:** the location of new residential, commercial or social facilities should maximise the opportunity for people to walk (see sections 6.5 and 6.12).

- **Access:** every development, large or small, should have convenient and visible access for pedestrians – preferably directly off the street or square, not across extensive private car parks or grounds. Large developments should try to provide for direct pedestrian access from any approach road or path. This is particularly important for schools, supermarkets and other major trip generators.

- **Frontage:** new developments should face the surrounding routeways, presenting a friendly outlook to passers-by, inspiring confidence not fear or a sense of estrangement.

## 4.16 PLANNING FOR THE CYCLIST

### BASIC PRINCIPLES
Ordinary streets throughout the neighbourhood should be managed for bicycle use, linking directly with surrounding areas. This requires that vehicle traffic be 'calmed'. There should in addition be a network of 'safe' routes, designed for children, which may be partly on-street and partly segregated, and serve local schools/playgrounds/shopping centres.

Cycling provides excellent exercise and improves accessibility. In the United Kingdom the average cycling journey is 3 km, with a threshold of about 5 km beyond which bicycle use falls off, with a normal maximum of around 8 km. Average speed is about 15 mph (25 kph). The propensity to cycle is strongly affected by the safety and convenience of routes available. The cycling habit is best forged when young, so creating safe routes to schools, parks, local shops and around residential neighbourhoods is a priority. The challenge is to increase the amount of cycling while reducing accidents to cyclists. This is particularly difficult because cycling is a relatively anarchistic activity that is not easily regulated. Indeed, the freedom of cycling, the ability to go from anywhere to anywhere, is one of its attractions, with probable psychological benefits.

## CRITERIA FOR CYCLE NETWORKS

The criteria for designing cycle networks include access, safety, continuity, directness, comfort and cycle parking.

### Street access

General-purpose streets, which give direct access to homes and facilities, need to be bicycle friendly and traffic calmed. Segregated routes are desirable in some situations (such as greenways through parks) but are no substitute for roads on which people can cycle safely.

### Safety

Separate lanes or paths can be provided if conflict with heavy or fast-moving traffic in unavoidable. Eighty per cent of accidents are at or near junctions where cars turn across the cyclist's path. Measures to give bicycles priority at junctions are therefore especially important.

### Continuity

Main bicycle routes should be as continuous as possible, with few stops (momentum is important!). Fragmented stretches of bicycle path can actually increase overall dangers, so the process of implementation should allow for safe intermediate stages.

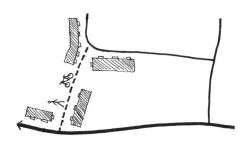

*Figure 4.24*
***Pedestrian and cycling short cuts***

*Where the road layout is indirect a well-supervised and maintained pedestrian/cycling short cut is essential, giving an advantage over motorised traffic*

*A new approach to policing may be required for a network of cycling and pedestran shortcuts. Cycle-mounted police in Bristol.*

# 4.16

Bike pow-wow in
Davis, California

Cycles and maps
provided for visitors
without cars in
Greena, Denmark

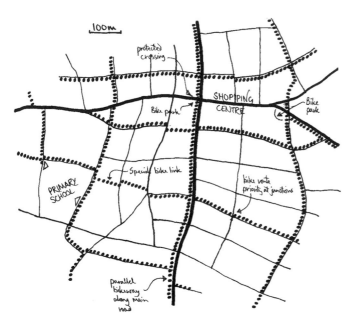

Figure 4.25
**Safe bike routes forming a complete
network across the town on a 2–400 m
grid pattern**

### Directness

Cyclists do not normally accept diversions that increase their
journey length, time and effort significantly (for example, by more
than 10 per cent). Segregated routes are sometimes impractical
since the direct route in existing urban areas is via the main road.
In new development, priorities can be reversed, giving the most
convenient route to cyclists and pedestrians.

### Comfort

Special cycling routes need to be very carefully designed in detail,
and subsequently maintained, to ensure easy gradients (normal
maximum 5 per cent), a smooth surface, protection from the
fumes from and intimidation by heavy goods vehicles and a
visually attractive experience.

### Bicycle parking

Secure end-of-journey parking in convenient locations is a factor
affecting bicycle use – at railway stations, for example.
Encouraging *bike and ride* effectively extends the catchment area
of the station.

## CREATING THE SAFE NETWORK –
## THE HIERARCHY OF ROUTE OPTIONS

1   On-street provision shared with vehicles where traffic
    volumes are low, traffic is calmed, and junctions give bike
    priority.

2   Dedicated cycleways, with kerb- or contour-separation from
    pedestrians.

3   On-street provision of cycle lanes and junction protection,
    reallocating space from road vehicles where volumes are
    moderate or high.

4   Shared surfaces with pedestrians on segregated routes.

5   On-street provision shared with vehicles where volumes are
    medium/high but traffic is effectively calmed and hazards
    (e.g. cars pulling out) are managed.

### Cycle/pedestrian shared use

The sharing of common surfaces can work when the route is well
designed and cycle and/or pedestrian flows are low. But
pedestrians with impaired hearing or sight can easily be put off
using such routes. And routes used by young families (with
unpredictable movement and lack of spatial consciousness) are
particularly inappropriate. Reliance on shared use is therefore low
down on the hierarchy of cycling provision.

## 4.17 PUBLIC TRANSPORT OPERATION

### BASIC PRINCIPLES

The pattern of bus services in a neighbourhood is too important to be left to the operators. The planners can significantly affect the viability of public transport and the route network in new areas by arranging roads, footpaths and land uses. The quality of bus and train services can be higher where the maximum number of people can reach their destination by the minimum number of routes. Linearity is therefore a key feature. The points where routes cross (nodes) then become the prime locations for local jobs and services and the focus for pedestrian and cycling routes. Public transport accessibility needs to be considered not therefore as an afterthought (left to the market) but as the starting-point for neighbourhood planning, with land uses then attached to the public transport network.

### STARTING POINTS FOR NEIGHBOURHOOD PLANNING

▓ What is the current pattern of public transport provision and use?

▓ Which routes potentially offer direct connections to important destinations?

▓ How can the viability of existing/potential routes be reinforced?

▓ Can a strong mixed-use focus for public transport services be created?

▓ Can services be concentrated on to a few high-quality public transport corridors which still reach all homes/businesses?

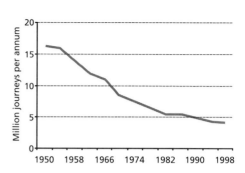

*Figure 4.26*
**The steep decline in bus journeys since the 1950s**

SOURCE: DETR 1999h

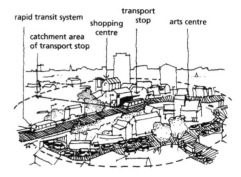

*Figure 4.27*
**Public transport magnets**

*New retail, employment and leisure facilities in town/district centres can be clustered close around public transport nodes so as to benefit customers and underpin public transport viability*

SOURCE: BARTON ET AL. 1995

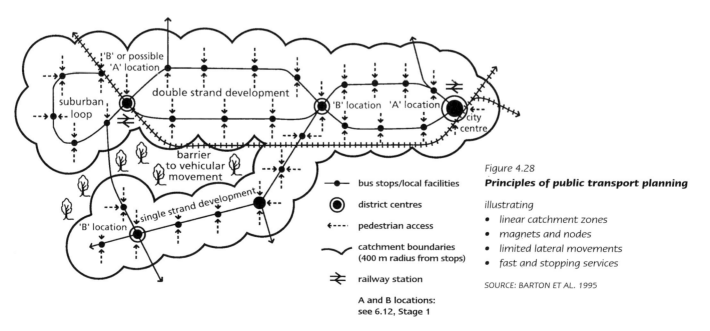

*Figure 4.28*
**Principles of public transport planning**

*illustrating*
- *linear catchment zones*
- *magnets and nodes*
- *limited lateral movements*
- *fast and stopping services*

SOURCE: BARTON ET AL. 1995

Key:
- ●── bus stops/local facilities
- ◉ district centres
- ←--- pedestrian access
- ⌒ catchment boundaries (400 m radius from stops)
- ⇌ railway station

A and B locations: see 6.12, Stage 1

## 4.17

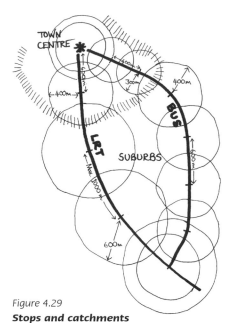

*Figure 4.29*
**Stops and catchments**

*Optimum stop-spacing and catchment vary with service quality and origin/destination*

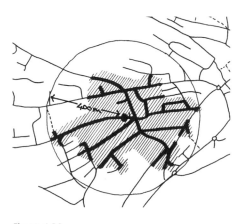

*Figure 4.30*
**Bus stop catchments**

*The 400 m zone may be smaller than you think*

### Bus priority works!

*Edinburgh's 'Greenways' cut journey times by 25 per cent and generated 250,000 extra bus trips in the first six months.*

*One Islington bus priority junction scheme saved over one and a half minutes for each bus passing through at peak times.*

6.12 The spatial framework →

## KEY PLANNING PRINCIPLES FOR EFFICIENT BUS/TRAM OPERATION

- **Directness:** provide direct routes between points of primary attraction – e.g. township centres (B locations on Figure 4.28).

- **Speed/reliability:** use bus-only lanes, junction priority and other measures to ensure that public transport vehicles are not unduly delayed by other traffic.

- **Linearity:** shape neighbourhoods so that journeys are naturally funnelled with little need for lateral trips, increasing linear demand and service quality.

- **Density:** grade densities so that the higher-density housing is close to stops, minimising the average walk distance.

- **Clustering:** locate along the route those activities that generate local trips, reinforcing visibility and potential for dual-purpose trips.

- **Environment:** ensure that the environment of the stops and main pedestrian access routes is pleasant and safe, avoiding physical or psychological barriers.

- **Shelter/information:** provide attractive bus/tram shelters with passenger information available.

## ACCESS TO STOPS AND STATIONS

All housing development should be within easy walking distance of good public transport services that give access to the main centres of urban activity. A common standard for bus access across Europe is 400 m; and this is backed by time-honoured government guidance (DoE circular 82/73) and the Confederation of British Road Passenger Transport (Addenbrooke 1981). Beyond that distance, the proportion of people willing to walk declines progressively and car dependence increases.

The 400m criterion needs to be applied with care. It is the distance people on average actually walk; if routes are indirect, the straight-line distance may be much less. Access is also influenced by gradients (especially for older people) and psychological barriers such as subways or intimidation by road traffic. Conversely, most people are prepared to walk further for high-quality metro or tram services.

### Locating new development

New housing and commercial developments must be located where they can be accessed, or are likely soon to be accessed, by public transport. This applies as much to brownfield as to greenfield development, and is the 'bottom line' of sustainable development.

## WHAT CONSTITUTES A 'GOOD' LOCAL SERVICE

The main criteria are frequency, coverage, reliability, speed, cost and comfort.

Suggested standards for frequency are

- Excellent: 5 minutes or higher. At this level of frequency travellers are able to change bus to bus with little time penalty.

- Good: 6–12 minutes. Travellers are able to wait for a bus on spec – casual use is possible.

- Regular: 13–30 minutes. Dependable timetabling is essential but the wait is not long.

- Mediocre: 40–120 minutes. Journeys have to be carefully pre-planned, but can be programmed across the day.

- Poor: over 2 hours. A residual level of service. Awkward to use.

### 4.18 PLANNING ROAD TRAFFIC

### BASIC PRINCIPLES

The key to a healthy transport strategy is taming vehicular traffic. The capacity of the road system should not normally be increased, because it simply encourages extra trips by car and compounds problems of air pollution and (sometimes) accidents, undermining the inclination to walk, cycle or use the bus. On the contrary, road capacity may be progressively reduced (allowing time for behavioural adjustment) as a direct consequence of positive planning for pedestrians, cyclists and public transport. At the same time, traffic speeds (the prime factor in accidents) should be held low by design, and parking policy used to deter unnecessary car trips.

### ROAD NETWORKS

Hierarchical road networks are compatible with sustainability because they can help keep heavy traffic out of residential areas, and well-managed main roads with limited access reduce accidents. However:

- The secondary or distributor roads act as the natural focuses of activity within or between neighbourhoods, and should be traffic-calmed and integrated into the townscape, with local facilities clustered on them (see Figure 4.32).

- The minor roads should not be a series of culs-de-sac but a network giving good vehicle, bike and pedestrian permeability through the area, yet subtly discouraging rat runs.

- The bus routes should normally follow the main distributors, so the disposition of those routes to maximise bus accessibility is critical.

*Rural bus services*

*The DETR considers that an 'adequate' service for rural settlements is an hourly service within 10 minutes' walk of homes.*

SOURCE: RURAL WHITE PAPER 2000

*Figure 4.31*
**Road accidents**

*It is not only accidents that are directly related to main roads, but also levels of air pollution and noise*

*Accidents between dates 01/01/1990 and 31/12/1998*

SOURCE: BRISTOL CITY COUNCIL

# 4.18

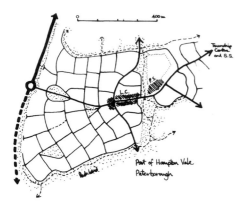

*Figure 4.32*
**Hampton Vale masterplan**

*Hierarchical road networks are compatible with sustainability*

*The Hampton Vale masterplan illustrates:*
- *A limited-access primary road.*
- *Secondary roads acting as the focus of local activity.*
- *Minor roads giving good permeability but discouraging short cuts/high speeds.*
- *A well-located linear neighbourhood centre.*
- *An open space network based around water management.*

6.b Hampton Vale case study →

## LOW CAR-USE ZONES

Vehicle access is essential for some users and for local economic vitality. It is not necessary right to exclude traffic (e.g. by pedestrianisation) unless the pedestrian flow is high in relation to street width. Nevertheless, local communities and planning authorities might consider defining existing and future home-patches by different target levels of car use.

1  **Car-free zones**

- Developments where no cars are allowed except in an emergency, with controlled access for rubbish collection, etc.
- Households pledged not to own a vehicle, relying on car rental, taxis or car pools with a limited supply of common vehicles.
- Highly accessible locations where local retail facilities are integrated/adjacent, walking/cycling is safe and pleasant, and public transport is excellent in all directions.

2  **Car-limited zones**

- Developments where car ownership is deterred – for example an ordinance or lease allowing one car only per household (as in Bermuda).
- Residents' parking limited to a maximum of one space per household.
- Accessible locations where alternative facilities (for walking, cycling, public transport) are good.
- Car pools, car clubs and car renting opportunities promoted.

3  **Car-tamed zones**

- Areas where car ownership is unrestricted but vehicle speeds are moderated by design and by law.
- Car ownership decoupled from car use by gentle deterrence and excellent provision for walking, cycling and public transport.
- Design speed 5–10 mph in a 'home-zone', and 20 mph in the wider residential area.
- Through traffic deterred and traffic volumes generally low – this could also include busier roads which function as local 'high streets'.

*Roads can create tarmac deserts and an unfriendly environment for pedestrians unless properly integrated*

## SLOWING TRAFFIC, REDUCING CAPACITY

Road capacity for ordinary traffic may be reduced as a side effect of positive planning for other modes as well as traffic-calming techniques. *The objective is not stop–start conditions, but steady, moderate, predictable, safe speeds.*

- Widen pavements and reinforce pedestrian route continuity.
- Extend pavement on corners to make bends tighter.
- Install bike lanes and bike priority on key routes/junctions.
- Insert tram-lines, bus-only lanes and priority junctions.
- Reduce sight lines at junctions (and warn motorists).
- Provide more on-street parking (and less off street).
- Enhance amenity: trees, tubs, seats.
- Install junction platforms, road cushions and rough surfaces (but make smooth routes for bikes).
- Use road humps with discretion – they are awkward for buses and cause extra pollution as vehicles brake and accelerate.

## PARKING THE CAR

- **In situ parking** is desired for convenience, car safety and car washing/DIY. For some households (with an infirm or disabled member, for example) it is a practical necessity. Where density levels allow, integral parking should be provided for most households.

- **On-street parking** has been designed-out of layouts in the late twentieth century, but acts as a very flexible, visible car store with traffic-calming attributes. The prerequisites are modest traffic speeds and overlooked streets (informal car surveillance). On-street parking is particularly appropriate for visitor parking. See the Crown Street case study (4a).

- **Parking courts** can work well but only when the design is not too big/soulless, and when natural surveillance occurs from people passing or houses overlooking. Small courts serving the immediately adjacent properties should normally be the rule.

- **Grouped car parks** away from the house can be a liability, but act as a natural deterrent to short-journey car use, and therefore may be favoured in 'car-low' developments. Normally the car park should be within 125 m of the home, with an absolute maximum of 250 m (De Knegt 1996). Distance from home needs to be compensated for by clear benefits, such as a homezone children's play area, for example. Security at the car park is paramount – preferably achieved by having services grouped around it (for example, a repair shed, washing space, bike/car hire or small workshops/offices) and a clear allocation of monitoring/locking-up responsibilities.

*Garages do not have to be eyesores*

*On street parking is sometimes a good solution!*

*Parking courts made to work at Poundbury, Dorchester*

CROWN STREET

# 4.a

*Walkways and deck construction of a now derelict shopping area in a 1960s re-development*

*Main shopping street with colonnade in a new development*

# Crown Street

## GORBALS, GLASGOW

This case study shows how a well-devised compact urban form can be used in inner-city areas to support a diverse community. Carefully constructed spaces allow a range of activities and easy social interactions.

## BACKGROUND

The Gorbals is an inner-city area just across the Clyde from the centre of Glasgow. Developed originally as four-storey tenements, it once had a thriving social and cultural life but became a byword for poverty, deprivation and crime. A 1960s regeneration scheme of high-rise towers failed to help and led to protracted community protest. The current regeneration strategy involves the re-use of tenement blocks but in a more spacious street pattern, and with mixed use and mixed tenure as an important component. 'Crown Street' is the biggest scheme in the new plan, occupying 16 ha, and is being hailed as a successful example of regeneration.

## PROCESSES

Community involvement was seen from the start as essential in creating a new image and restoring confidence in the area. Continuing involvement has also been recognised as playing an essential part in achieving a long-term solution. However, community participation was set within a very clear framework of policy goals and physical master-planning determined by the major partners:
- Glasgow Development Agency
- Scottish Homes
- Glasgow City Council
- New Gorbal Housing Association
- The local community.

## PROVIDING FOR LOCAL NEED

In as much as a key objective is to make a place 'where people want to live', the broad development partnership is attempting to provide for local need. Local need has been defined very broadly, seeing the potential role the Gorbals plays within the city as well as a whole.

### People and community

The housing mix both in tenure and form has been designed to attract a wide range of residents. Both owner-occupation and the social sector are represented (target 25 per cent of all tenure). About a fifth of residents are former Gorbals residents. Phase 1 housing has attracted families (34 per cent), singles (36 per cent) and couples without children (30 per cent). Student accommodation is planned in future phases.

### Access to jobs

Crown Street is within walking distance of a huge range of city-centre jobs. But in addition there is the promotion of local offices, workshops and services – with some of these jobs explicitly tied to local people.

### Access to local facilities

The area has been transformed by the successfully established new local centre and a new Gorbals Park. Other facilities are planned.

### Movement

The whole design is pedestrian-friendly; all forms of movement are catered for. Parking is down the middle of wide avenues between four-storey perimeter blocks.

### URBAN DESIGN

A strong urban form has been created through a masterplan relying on traditional elements of the grid, the block and the tenement. Underlying this is a concept of providing a liveable city. Together, the elements and concept have been used to create an urban form with

- a familiar scale of development;
- legible street patterns;
- a recognisable local identity; and
- housing blocks that front on to streets with semi-private open space to the rear.

Both mixed use and mixed tenure are important in the final scheme.

### Open space

Open space has been created within a hierarchy comprising the small semi-private front garden/threshold areas, communal gardens at the rear of blocks, and a new Gorbals Park.

*Strong design elements, active frontages and high density nodes*

*Protected and semi-private open space inside the perimeter blocks*

The Masterplan

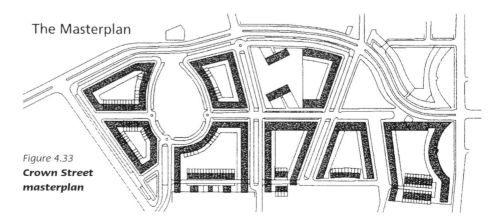

Figure 4.33
**Crown Street masterplan**

**case study**

# 4.b

'We started working
in a very holistic way'

LIN TWELL
(PROJECT MANAGER)

**St Augustine's Healthy Living Centre**

SOURCE: BARRY PULFORD, CHARTERED ARCHITECTS AND
PROPERTY DEVELOPMENT CONSULTANTS

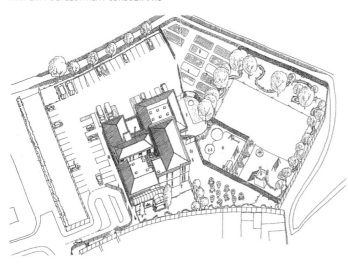

# St Augustine's

## HEALTHY LIVING CENTRE, KING'S LYNN, NORFOLK

### PROCESSES

From the start, this project has been inclusive of the local community. Evidence of local need was proven by a community survey in 1995. Grants provided market-research training for local people, a survey was undertaken and focus groups formed. The need for a local primary health care practice was established: with poor access to GPs the local population of 5,000 generated 4,000 visits to hospital casualty per year. Other needs identified were included in an SRB (Single Regeneration Budget) bid.

### PROVIDING FOR LOCAL NEED

The initiative's raison d'être is to provide for local need. Working practices and management structures have been developed to ensure that local need directs future development. By bringing together community health and social facilities under one roof synergy can be fostered. For example, the GPs are trained to pick up underlying social issues and 'refer' local residents to advice and support services.

### People and community

Formal and informal social space has been provided. A community café is at the hub of the building and from here other activities can be viewed. Childcare facilities allow access for carers to a wide range of facilities. A nursery class will link the centre to the local school.

### Access to local facilities and jobs

The centre houses a wide range of local facilities such as an arts studio, special needs activities, performance and arts spaces, GP surgery (two doctors), advice services (welfare, debt, careers, employment, single parent advice). An adventure playground is also planned for the site. Accredited training and access courses are provided.

### Movement

The main objective of the project was to reduce travel times to primary health care. The centre sits between two neighbourhoods and is accessible to a population of 5,000 within a 10-minute bus ride. For the less mobile, a community dial-a-bus scheme is operated from the same premises.

### RESOURCES AND URBAN DESIGN

Surrounding land on the 1 ha site will be used for a demonstration community garden. This provides a valuable local habitat for wildlife. Plans are to grow food that may be used in the centre's kitchens. The location of the centre is well chosen, sitting between and linking two separate neighbourhoods. The building also shows good re-use of existing redundant facility, being situated in a refurbished 1960s building.

# use of local resources | chapter 5

## overview

### 5.1 PURPOSE AND SCOPE

This chapter focuses on natural and man-made resources in the neighbourhood. It deals with each of five basic resources in turn. For each resource, an integrated strategy is outlined and issues of implementation reviewed, the key issues and solutions are summarised, design measures are looked at in more detail and opportunities for synergy are highlighted.

In order to 'get things right', we need to plan this scale very carefully. Projects at the neighbourhood scale – whether renovation, regeneration or new build – give us tremendous opportunity. At this scale we can capitalise on the synergy between objectives and reap rewards that are not available when working on individual buildings. It is also a scale with more ownership and cohesion than when working with a city: there is more scope for participative planning and management.

The basic environmental ideas involved have been around for a long time, but they are rarely implemented in a comprehensive manner. The emphasis in this publication is on the involvement of practitioners who bring a social agenda. Health, local quality of life and social goals can all be pursued through well-planned solutions to local resource use, so giving lasting environmental benefits.

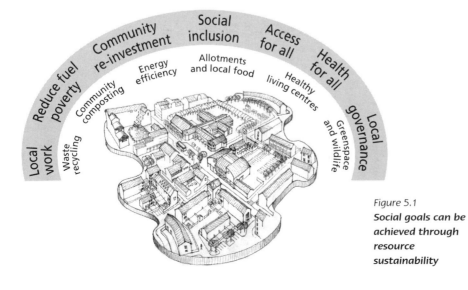

Figure 5.1
**Social goals can be achieved through resource sustainability**

'Land should be regarded as a scarce finite resource. Development projects should be as compact as possible and should enhance the environment, not just limit damage, by respecting biodiversity, harnessing natural resources and reducing the call on non-renewable resources.'

(DETR 1999i: p. 71)

131

PURPOSE AND SCOPE

# 5.1

*'Resource planning at the neighbourhood scale can give rise to benefits for developers and communities that go far beyond what can be achieved for an individual building or small site.'*

(PLANNING 1999)

### The benefits of increasing local autonomy

**Energy**
*Reducing energy costs*
*Tackling fuel poverty*
*Safeguarding future fuel flexibility*
*Reducing global warming emissions*

**Water**
*Reducing flood risk*
*Improving attractiveness*
*Enhancing wildlife*
*Adding amenity*
*Reducing scarcity*

**Food**
*Easier choice for a healthy life-style*
*Fostering social inclusion*
*Supporting local vitality – growers and shops*
*Improving access to food (resisting food deserts)*
*Reducing food transport and traffic*

**Waste**
*Providing training and local employment*
*Opportunities for fostering social capital*
*Reducing waste transport and traffic*
*Meeting waste recycling targets*

**Biodiversity**
*Creating a better-quality environment*
*Improving wildlife amenity*
*Meeting biodiversity targets*
*Buffering climate change*

6a Hammarby Sjöstad →

1.7 Neighbourhood design principles ←

## COMMON THEMES

### ■ 'Soft infrastructure'

This means people's behaviour, motivation, knowledge and support. As individuals we have lost the ability to live in a resource-efficient way. Experience has shown that merely redesigning neighbourhoods or installing the latest technology will not necessarily provide the results envisaged. Specific measures to strengthen a community's soft infrastructure and to change behaviour have to be built into a neighbourhood development initiative. Projects tackling these issues can also lead to improvements in social capital, as its support is an important component of this approach.

### ■ Social and health outcomes

When dealing with neighbourhood resource issues it is important to break out of a purely environmentally focused vision. Social and health objectives should also be pursued.

### ■ Integrated resource planning

A shift towards collaborative and integrated resource planning is needed. Use neighbourhood development to break out of the current inertia. Collaboration between social providers and private utilities may result in increased initial design and implementation costs but there will be year-on-year benefits providing payback in the medium term.

## TOWARDS AN INTEGRATED RESOURCE STRATEGY

New build, regeneration or renovation projects all need to have a clear strategy for dealing with resource issues. This strategy will be set within the wider policy context, influenced by relevant planning policy and the resource utilities and regulators. To determine the level of detail and scope, address the six principles of neighbourhood planning.

### ■ *Stakeholder involvement*
Planning more efficient resource use can be a galvanising issue for encouraging participation. Not only can people forge a better environment for themselves, but there can also be financial rewards. Additionally, raising the level of local control is *per se* good for health!

### ■ *Increasing local autonomy*
Dealing with resources in a holistic way will help to increase local autonomy; reduce the 'ecological footprint' of the neighbourhood and close resource loops. People's local, regional and global environment will benefit (see side column).

### ■ *Connectivity*
Connectivity between resource issues and social provision is the key to winning support, securing funding and long-term success. Good examples are allotments and community gardens. These can

produce local food for a community centre, they can be part of a training and employment project and also linked to the composting and recycling process.

### Diversity

Diversity results in a richer and more robust neighbourhood. Optimum use can be made of variable local conditions, of local opportunities. Locally distinctive solutions can arise.

### Response to place

For each resource there are a range of options to pursue. The appropriate choices will be determined by local conditions, such as soil types, climate, available energy sources, aspect, infrastructure. If an adequate survey is undertaken, local solutions will arise.

### Adaptability: the life-time neighbourhood

Adaptability underlies the resource approach developed in this chapter. Future flexibility of options is built in (in choice of fuel, for example).

## 5.2 IMPLEMENTING AN INTEGRATED STRATEGY

The principle of an integrated resource strategy applies at several different levels: general policy, township spatial framework, development area brief, detailed design, and ongoing management. The whole sequence is vital if sustainable resource use is to be achieved on anything more than an occasional or trial basis.

### GENERAL POLICY: THE COMMUNITY STRATEGY

The various resources are managed by a wide range of organisations, each with their own remit. Common goals, and a collaborative approach, could be agreed under the auspices of the Community Strategy, which emanates from the local authority as a whole. Unfortunately the Local Strategic Partnerships (LSPs) that produce these strategies may well not include some of the key actors. While health authorities and biodiversity groups will be members, for example, energy providers and water companies may not be, for quite practical reasons. In this situation the Local Plan review offers a way forward. The Local Plan nestles within the overall Community Strategy and effectively co-ordinates the use of resources as far as physical development is concerned.

### Recommendation

The Local Plan review should be seen by the local authority as an opportunity to form a Local Resource Partnership, under the auspices of the LSP. The Resource Partnership would aim to agree a co-ordinated programme promoting sustainable resource use. It would try to ensure that optimistic policies incorporated in the Local Plan would be reinforced by the other agencies involved in delivering and managing resources. The Partnership would provide the context within which spatial frameworks and specific development projects would produce integrated schemes.

*Figure 5.2*
**The web of resource management**

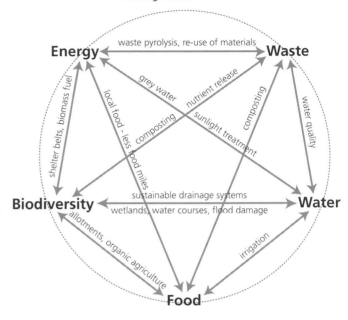

*Local resource partners*

- *Local planning and environment department*
- *Waste collection and disposal units*
- *Housing, parks and education departments*
- *Health Authority*
- *Energy supply industries*
- *Water companies*
- *Developers' representatives (such as the House Builders Federation)*
- *Wildlife interests (such as English Nature, RSPB, local trust)*
- *Environmental and recycling groups (such as Friends of the Earth)*
- *Environmental agencies*
- *Countryside Agencies and/or Regional Development Agencies*

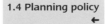

1.4 Planning policy
←

## TOWNSHIP SPATIAL FRAMEWORK

The town or township spatial framework can tie general policies to physical reality, and provide a context for the pursuit of specific projects. To have any authority the framework needs to be adopted as supplementary planning guidance by the local planning authority, and be backed by the 'local resources partners'. The 'community checklist' in Chapter 2 offers a quick set of relevant resource criteria. The framework can also point the way towards integrated resource solutions that give maximum return on land and financial investment. For example:

**2.1 Community checklist** ←

- *Safeguard a green/open space network* that preserves water courses and floodland, provides for a town farm, enhances wildlife potential, maximises tree cover, safeguards renewable potential, manages climates and pollution as well as providing for recreation; establish collaboration agreements on investment programmes and management regimes.

**6.9 The Green Network** →

**5.17 Waste parks** →

- *Plan a township waste and recycling park*, with a community composting scheme and perhaps a combined heat and power (CHP) plant using waste materials and coppice from an adjacent wildlife resource and parkland.

- *Shape the township* in terms of density, mixed use and linearity so as to enhance the long-term viability of community heating and solar power as well as public transport (see Chapter 6).

**3.10 Agreeing a programme** ←

- *Promote criteria-based policies* to foster specific resource strategies – for example, the local availability of allotments, the creation of wind breaks, the local disposal of waste water, recycling provision in home and wildlife 'threads' through development (see 3.10: criteria-based planning).

## DEVELOPMENT PROJECTS

Given a willing investment company, specific development projects (large or small) offer a tremendous opportunity to achieve sustainable resources use. The 'investor's checklist' in Chapter 2 sets out the key issues in terms of location, appraisal and design, and can be cross-referenced to material presented in this chapter. The local planning authority can, up to a point, encourage a responsible attitude from the investors by requirements in a development brief, masterplan or design guide. The limits are set by the degree to which radical or unconventional dictates are backed by the statutory local plan or supplementary planning guidance.

**2.9 Investors' checklist** ←

## 5.3   KEY RESOURCES: SUMMARY

### ENERGY – MORE FOR LESS

In this chapter, energy as it is used in homes and workplaces in the neighbourhood is the focus (local energy is also used in transport: reducing these needs are covered under movement in Chapter 4).

#### Attention to the soft infrastructure

**Local involvement** – provide training, education and advice (e.g. housing association/tenant schemes or energy clubs).

**Local control** – use energy service companies (ESCOs) as a vehicle for local involvement and investment in alternative energy sources; promote local energy solutions by the local authority.

#### Reduction in needs

**Efficient site layout and design** – design for passive solar gains; pay attention to orientation and overshadowing, use shelter belts and microclimate modification, place high levels of insulation in buildings.

**Efficient technologies** – provide neighbourhood heat infrastructure (community heating), ensure efficient generation using combined heat and power, provide future flexibility in choice of fuels (via community heating), install efficient appliances.

#### Renewable energy

**Harnessing local low-impact energy** – use (in combination) solar water heating, photovoltaic cells, small wind turbines, energy from waste, energy from biomass, heat recovery, heat pumps, small water turbines, geothermal, waste heat from industry.

**Reasons**

The extent and nature of our current energy use have resulted in rapid depletion of fossil fuels and have contributed to climate change. However, we still have winter deaths and ill-health linked to fuel poverty. Not only are we wasteful in our use of energy but we don't even bother to make use of locally available sources of energy.

Social capital can be strengthened by involving people – the consumers of energy – in new-build or regeneration schemes. This involvement is essential since life-style and behaviour have a critical impact on energy use. It has been demonstrated that local jobs can be economically provided through energy-efficiency projects.

Fuel poverty can be tackled within a long-term strategy that helps to build in future flexibility: cold living conditions increase the risk of cardiovascular illnesses; damp homes are associated with a range of respiratory and allergic conditions.

- **UK headline indicator**
  *Emissions of greenhouse gasses*

- **UK core set of indicators**
  *Electricity from renewable sources*

- **Neighbourhood QOL indicator**
  *Heat loss from buildings*
  *Household gas and electricity used*

**Energy is at the core**

*Energy is central to all three strands of sustainable development:*

- *Environmental – through climate change, pollution and ecological impacts*

- *Social – through contributing to quality of life and maintaining good health, and the eradication of fuel poverty*

- *Economic – through (literally) fuelling the economy and providing jobs*

SOURCE: LGA & LGMB 1998

5.4 Energy in
detail   →

KEY RESOURCES: SUMMARY

# 5.3

- **UK Core set of indicators**
  *Household water use and peak demand*
  *Water demand and availability*

- **UK Headline indicator**
  *Rivers of good or fair quality*

- **Neighbourhood QOL indicators**
  *Metered domestic water use*
  *Watercourse or waterbody quality*

*Smart growth*
*Creating quality developments*
*The role that water can play*

- *Reduced risk of flooding and consequential liabilities*

- *Improved quality of landscape setting and amenity through use of wetland habitats*

- *Opportunity for reduced water and sewerage charges*

- *Increase in wildlife range and quality*

- *More water available for gardens/ allotments during drought*

## WATER – THREE VITAL ISSUES

The tenets below can be applied to new build, renovation and regeneration. They can make more desirable neighbourhoods with improved market value, hand in hand with environmental benefits.

### ▪ *Involve stakeholders*

**Partnerships and participatory planning** – involve residents and businesses; form alliances between users, local authorities, water companies and the Environment Agency/Scottish Environment Protection Agency.

### ▪ *Value the asset*

**Reduce reliance on distant sources** – survey and use local sources such as rain, streams, wells and springs.

**Reduce use** – match use to water quality – use rain water and grey water where possible; collect and re-use water within the neighbourhood.

**Celebrate urban watercourses and ponds** – provide access to streams, use ponds for amenity settings and wildlife.

### ▪ *Control downstream impact*

**Reduce flood risk** – use sustainable urban drainage systems to even out the flows and improve the quality.

**Recharge aquifers** – use porous surfacing and soakaways where possible.

**Subsidiarity principle** – manage the issue as close as possible to its source.

### Reasons

We traditionally build our neighbourhoods in a way that contributes, almost negligently, to the persistent waste of this resource. We design houses to flush drinking quality water down toilets and, in the past, to pour useful rain water falling on our rooftops straight into sewers. Streams that are valuable for wildlife and our quality of life lie buried in underground pipes.

In the UK recently, we seem either to have an abundance of water or a drought. Even though most strategic water planning is by catchment, each neighbourhood has a part to play in water management – reducing flood risk, reducing scarcity, improving quality. When properly planned for in a neighbourhood, the water resource can benefit amenity and wildlife, whilst evening out glut and scarcity.

**5.7 Water in detail**
➔

## FOOD – STAPLE ISSUES

The principle for food in neighbourhoods is to assist communities in making 'local food links'; linking growing, buying, cooking and enjoying. Implementing this approach will have an effect on how we plan and develop neighbourhoods.

### Increase access for local people to food

Improve access by supporting local shops and small-scale supermarkets.

Plan safe and pleasant pedestrian and cycling routes linking retail and residential areas.

Plan for well distributed superstores in each township.

### Maximise opportunity for local food production

Maintain or provide allotment land, provide sites for locally managed organic orchards, provide back gardens/roof gardens of a size to enable food production.

Support hinterland agriculture through access to markets such as farmers' markets and local produce labelling.

### Increase community links to food

Use food projects as a focus for health, inclusion, training and employment; at the township scale, plan for city farms.

Link allotments to communities physically and through school and health projects.

### Reasons

The concept 'food miles' refers to the distance food has to travel from where it is grown to where it is purchased and then on to where it is consumed. Food transportation by road has been the fastest growing transport sector in the UK and a major contributor to air pollution and hence to ill-health. Food is often abundant in retail parks served well by cars and articulated lorries, but the term 'food deserts' has been coined to describe neighbourhoods where local grocers are disappearing. This can leave those without cars difficult access routes and little choice for their food supply. As a result, health is further damaged in those already at risk, and local producers lack small-scale local outlets.

Attention to food in local regeneration schemes can improve health, support local employment and the local economy and increase social capital and cohesion. Following wave after wave of food safety problems, we should be more aware of the quality and sources of food available in the neighbourhoods we plan, develop and live in.

### Food for health

- *local access*
- *local sources*
- *local jobs*

*Food has been recognised by WHO as a social determinant of health. The pattern and nature of food supply at the neighbourhood level can adversely affect health and the global environment.*

### Some of the range of local food initiatives

- *farmers' markets and Women's Institute markets*
- *subscription farming and box schemes*
- *community-owned farms and other investment for local food production*
- *food co-ops and community buying groups*
- *growing at home, on allotments, at school*
- *city farms and community gardens and community orchards*
- *local food directories*

*These can all be part of wider initiatives such as*
- *Healthy Living Centres*
- *Community composting*
- *LETS and credit unions*
- *Fairtrade (health for overseas food workers)*
- *Promotion of local countryside products, such as forestry, fibres, biomass*

### Food, the polluter?

*Comparison of annual $CO_2$ emissions for an average four-person household:*

- *Running a house   4.2 tonnes*
*heating, cooking, lighting, etc.*

- *Running a car   4.4 tonnes*
*20,000 km average fuel consumption*

- *Food consumed   8.0 tonnes*
*growing, processing, packing, transport and cooking*

*SOURCE: BRESCU, GIR 53, 1998*

5.10 Food in detail
→

**overview**

KEY RESOURCES: SUMMARY

# 5.3

- *Neighbourhood QOL indicators*

  *Household and local business waste arisings*
  *Recycling of household waste*

*National policy lead*

*'The rubbish bin is not the only outlet for
domestic waste. The Government and the
National Assembly are keen to see such
initiatives providing an alternative to the
rubbish bin being taken up by local
communities more widely.'*

(DETR, 2000)

*The ranking of priorities*

1  **Reduce:** *the amount of waste*

2  **Re-use:** *the item or product where possible*

3  **Recycle:** *the components or materials
where re-use is not possible.*

**Design waste management processes to
provide benefits**

- *Economic – through employment, repair
  and re-use of resources*

- *Health – through involvement, less
  transport, less incineration/landfill*

- *Environmental – reduction in material use,
  reduction in impacts.*

*Sustainable construction*
*Starting points for further information*

*Centre for Sustainable Construction at the
Building Research Establishment:
www.bre.co.uk*

*Construction Industry Research and
Information centre: www.ciria.org.uk*

*Materials Information Exchange (matching
waste supplies with potential users):
www.bre.co.uk/waste*

*National Green Specification (information and
sources for green specification for construction):
www.greenspec.org.uk*

5.14 Waste in
detail                →

## WASTE – A LOCAL RESOURCE

The maxim is reduce, re-use, recycle, but what does this mean for
neighbourhood planning? Experience from recycling schemes in the
UK indicates three basic tenets:

### Involve people

**Make recycling easy for the user**. Recycling should be the final
option after reducing waste and re-using waste have been
explored. A change in habit will come when people have to tackle
these issues in their homes, businesses and communities.

**Involve people in the community**. Effective schemes make use
of not-for-profit groups and community development: for
example, locally managed community recycling and compost sites.

### Close resource loops

**Separate waste stream materials**. Separation of materials at
source in the waste stream makes re-use through recovery more
viable and recycling more economic.

### Create local solutions

**Localise the waste facilities where possible**. There is a balance
to be struck between closing the resource loops locally or passing
sorted waste streams on to a larger spatial scale. Re-use and
recycling can provide jobs, the smaller the scale, the less transport
is required. Local examples include furniture recycling stores and
community compost sites.

**Reasons**

We need to conserve resources, reduce pollution and landfill.
Homes and businesses usually just dispose of all unwanted items
to refuse – traditionally this 'waste' gets dumped in landfill or
incinerated. Perversely, this 'waste' contains resources that we
need in order to function and we actually purchase in large
quantities: organic material to fertilise soils, jars and bottles,
metal tins, paper, clothing, furniture and appliances. Currently
almost all areas have some recycling schemes but these recover a
fraction of what could be re-used. Waste separation generates
local jobs; repair and re-use projects can be used for training and
employment.

## SUSTAINABLE CONSTRUCTION

The material in this chapter deals with the neighbourhood in use –
however, waste must also be minimised during the construction
phase. Sustainable construction includes re-use of buildings,
re-use of materials and construction waste and local sourcing of
construction materials. Best practice in this respect can deliver
better profitability and competitive advantage for developers, as
outlined in the UK strategy *Building a better quality of life:
A strategy for sustainable construction* (DETR 2000).

## BIODIVERSITY – THE BASICS

### ▨ *Build wildlife capacity – enhancement*

Seek to enhance developer's investment by providing landscapes designed to thrive as healthy habitats for local flora and fauna.

Enact Local Biodiversity Action Plans at the neighbourhood level whenever there is a significant development project.

Aim to go beyond habitat protection and provide habitat enhancement.

### ▨ *Plan access and involvement*

Provide attractive green routeways and access to natural green spaces.

Support local ownership and management.

### ▨ *Develop partnerships*

Involve local wildlife interest groups in the design and management of neighbourhood wildlife.

Involve local planners, developers and estate and parks managers in partnerships to meet Biodiversity Action Plan targets.

**Reasons**

People enjoy nature: positive effects on health and well-being have been demonstrated. But this positive interaction is less and less available: in towns and on farmland, species are in decline. The song thrush, once a common sound in towns, has shown a 59 per cent decline over 20 years.

'Nature' finds it tough in many of our urban spaces. All too often, municipal and communal green space is managed to an ethic demanding barren and costly short grass, chemically scorched earth shrubberies and wall-to-wall weed-controlled hard surfaces. Sometimes it is only private gardens and derelict sites that give succour to nature.

Even if only looking at our own needs, supporting urban biodiversity makes social and economic sense:

▨ people prefer living in neighbourhoods where nature can thrive (DoE 1996)

▨ people live healthier lives when they have contact with the natural world (Rohde and Kendle 1994).

We can benefit the planet and ourselves by considering biodiversity issues in every development scheme. There is room for more greening in cities whatever the density – from the verdant and lush of the 'garden suburb' to green roofs, from street trees and wall climbers to pocket community gardens – bringing nature and the seasons even into high-density centres.

- **UK headline indicator**
  Population of wild birds in the UK

- **EA key indicator**
  Achievement of Biodiversity Action Plan targets

**Towards an urban renaissance**

'We also need to promote the idea of the ecologically sensitive city in which humans recognise that they cohabit with nature. Trees, woodland and other open space are all important in fostering biodiversity, in enhancing human health and well-being, and in reducing noise and pollution. We can use some of our previously developed land to create new areas of urban green space.'

(DETR 1999)

**Human well-being and urban wildlife**

Contact with nature may be one of the conditions that protects individuals from a breakdown in health and supports resistance to disease. Benefits of contact with nature include

- restorative effects – reducing fatigue, 'recharging'

- cognitive effects – enhanced self-esteem, sense of peace

- behavioural effects – encourages play, exploration, adventure

SOURCE: ROHDE AND KENDLE 1994

5.18 Biodiversity in detail →

NEIGHBOURHOOD ENERGY PLAN

# 5.4

### Savings through ending fuel poverty

*The feasibility of a national 15-year energy efficiency programme for all poorly performing UK housing was assessed.*

*Total costs are outweighed by the savings when social benefits are taken into account. In particular, there are lasting health benefits.*

| | |
|---|---|
| Total programme costs | £12,612 million |
| Savings | |
|    To the NHS | £5,234 million |
|    From fuel costs | £5,630 million |
|    From jobs created | £1,405 million |
|    Others | £2,736 million |
| Total savings | £15,003 million |

SOURCE: GOODACRE, SHARPLES AND SMITH 2000

### Universal checklist: A sequential test

*For use in new build, regeneration, refurbishment and appliance replacement.*

✔ **The energy hierarchy**
1  *reduce the need for energy*
2  *use energy more efficiently*
3  *use renewable energy*
4  *any continuing use of fossil fuels to be clean and efficient for heating and co-generation (CHP)*

SOURCE: LGA 1998

### Energy Efficiency Commitment
(EESOP4 Schemes)

*The next round of OFGEM Energy Efficient targets could provide the ideal vehicle for partnerships between residents/developers/ housing association/local authorities to propose schemes for the Energy Efficiency Commitment with utilities*

# energy

## 5.4  NEIGHBOURHOOD ENERGY PLAN

 An energy plan will develop a 'best fit' between the energy demand of a neighbourhood and the energy resources of its locality. Every neighbourhood is unique: even within a neighbourhood certain measures will be best suited to specific sub-areas, certain types of house or forms of tenure.

### What opportunities exist to develop such a plan?

Major regeneration schemes as well as new build represent ideal opportunities for the comprehensive and strategic review needed for energy planning. In areas where change is incremental, processes such as Agenda 21, Community Strategies, HECA and refurbishment schemes present possibilities for energy planning.

### Who should prepare the plan?

The lead should be taken by a partnership involving the main development agent, local authority and an energy provider or Energy Service Company (ESCO – see below). The local strategic partnership, where one exists, should take the lead. It will be especially important to include residents/workers (regeneration and renovation) or make provision for their inclusion in understanding the plan later (new build). Most rewards come if the occupiers 'own' the energy approach, as occupier behaviour is a very significant factor in energy use.

## PARTNERS

### Local Authorities

Buildings and their localities are major determinants of energy intensity and supply options. Local authorities, through their policies over the years, affect most facets of energy demand and supply, and physical planning specifically affects at least 70 per cent of use (Barton 1989). Local authorities should attempt to meet pressures for a sustainable energy strategy by seeking to increase the energy-autonomy of each settlement and every neighbourhood.

### Developers

Developers can anticipate future regulations. A forward-looking response is to research and promote schemes that are innately energy efficient, both at the building and neighbourhood scale. An energy plan can offer a scheme planning and market advantages.

### ESCOs (Energy Service Companies)

An ESCO is legal partnership (public/private) formed to provide energy services for a specific scheme. In larger regeneration and new build schemes there is scope for an ESCO to be responsible for providing energy services tailored to the requirements of the scheme.

## ■ CHECKLIST FOR NEIGHBOURHOOD ENERGY PLAN

### Stage 1 – Involving stakeholders

Engage partners and potential users in a briefing workshop, define the scope, objectives and broad strategy.

3.10 Agreeing a co-ordinated programme ←

### Stage 2 – Baseline survey

Assemble basic local information. Conduct a demand and user survey, a site and energy source survey, and an institutional, management and stakeholder survey. Connect the neighbourhood with its surrounding context such as large heat producers or users – industry, swimming pools, hospitals, schools, shopping malls. The stakeholder group may need to be extended following this stage. There may now be scope for factoring in longer-term strategic issues for the area.

### Stage 3 – Develop options

Generate basic proposals and options with key actors. Carry out scoping for viability of Community Heating/Combined Heat and Power (see 5.6 Checklist for a CH/CHP scheme). Review all proposals and options at a second briefing workshop with stakeholders. Include proposals for delivering user advice/training and support during and after implementation.

- **Spatial and built measures**

*Built form:* low energy design, layout, orientation and landscape.
*Community heating:* local energy generation and fuel sources.

- **Non-spatial measures**

*Soft infrastructure:* find examples of good practice via energy efficiency agencies (see side column), such as user control, low-energy clubs, user feedback systems, energy wardens (see Beacon Energy Action).
*Buildings:* insulation, double glazing, passive solar, active solar.
*Kit:* heat-recovery equipment, and low-energy appliances and light bulbs.
*Green electricity:* consumers can opt to buy their energy from suppliers who will provide energy from renewable sources – thus reducing the global footprint of the neighbourhood.

### Stage 4 – Refining solutions and implementation

Further integrate the energy criteria into the main spatial framework for the neighbourhood. Technical consultants will usually drive the later steps of this stage, as the proposals are designed into the final scheme. Note: It is very easy to lose the investment in the 'soft infrastructure'. Ensure that users are supported during and after hand-over.

---

### Beacon Energy Action

*Tenant and residents groups and a community association save energy and improve health*

*The initiative is a good example of the benefit of forging links between health and energy. The project is situated in a Health Action Zone and part of Beacon Community Regeneration Partnership, Cornwall, an area characterised by poor housing, low incomes and high rates of respiratory disease.*

*The project is designed to improve the energy efficiency of housing, regardless of tenure, in an area. Improvements in health, reduction in fuel poverty and involving and empowering local people are all goals. As part of the project local people will be trained as 'Energy Wardens' to extend the momentum beyond the 3-year project.*

SOURCE: BEACON ENERGY ACTION OFFICE

*Tools*

*There are three standard measures for assessing energy efficiency in buildings:*

**SAP** *The Standard Assessment Procedure produces a score between 0 and 100 for domestic properties, the higher score indicating a greater level of energy efficiency.*

**NHER** *National Home Energy Rating scheme: a method of assessing domestic energy efficiency. Unlike SAP, it takes account of geographical location and other climatic variables.*

**BREEAM** *Building Research Establishment Environmental Assessment Model. This provides a score based on a number of input variables relating to environmental performance.*

*Sources of advice, training and access to funding*
*Energy Savings Trust: information for Local Authorities          www.practicalhelp.org.uk*
*Energy Efficiency Advice Centre  www.est.org.uk*
*Local environment centre:*
          *contact via the Local Authority*
*Local Groundwork Trust  www.groundwork.org.uk*
          *or www.groundworkwales.org.uk*
*Renewables                    www.etsu.com*

NEIGHBOURHOOD ENERGY PLAN

# 5.4

### Fuel poverty defined

*Severe fuel poverty: households needing to spend 20 per cent of income on heating (1.5 million homes in the UK; approximately 5 per cent of the population).*

*Extreme fuel poverty: needing to spend 30 per cent of income on heating (1 million homes in the UK; approximately 3 per cent of the population).*

*Information about best practice in energy-efficiency and fuel-poverty strategies is available from the Centre for Sustainable Energy www.cse.org.uk*

### The Energy Services Association (ESA)

*The ESA promotes dialogue and good practice – monitoring progress and tackling blockages. The Association produces briefing papers, advice and comment to key influencers in all sectors. Work involves the support for promotion of energy services including the development of local authority and housing association based energy service companies, guidelines for the provision of energy services in relevant sectors.*

*Contact via www.chpa.co.uk*

*'Base energy policy and all decisions on the principle of providing the services needed with less use of damaging forms of energy.'*

*(LGA, LGMB ET AL. 1998)*

## DRIVERS

### Global warming

A recent report by the Royal Commission on Environmental Pollution, Energy: the changing climate (RCEP 2000), calls on government to reduce $CO_2$ emissions by at least 60 per cent over the next 50 years. The government is likely to use mechanisms such as building regulations and tax controls to achieve these cuts. Future zero $CO_2$ benchmarks will become widely used in relation to energy supply and consumption.

### Fuel poverty

Combating fuel poverty is a key government objective. The approach advocated in this guide will help to make buildings cheaper and easier to heat.

### Home Energy Conservation Act (HECA) 1995

Under HECA, councils are responsible for ensuring that they achieve energy efficiency improvements for the domestic housing sector to the equivalent of 30 per cent of the 1995 levels by 2010. This should be a powerful driver for more economic use of energy in neighbourhoods.

### House buyers' survey

There is a lobby to have home energy ratings included in the information given to house buyers. The lower running costs for an energy-efficient home will then be factored in to housing choice. It is already in the interest of both private and social housing providers who are building energy-efficient housing to provide this information.

### Building regulations part L

These deal with conservation of fuel and power in all building types. They set standards for limiting heat loss, heating space, water efficiency, lighting efficiency and providing information for users. In the non-dwellings sector, additional criteria cover air conditioning, solar overheating and energy management. The regulations provide a useful source of information on 'routes to compliance', including checklists and methods of energy calculation.

## ENERGY SERVICES

*A useful concept for energy planning*

Shifting emphasis away from the 'provision of energy' to the 'provision of energy services' can assist with clearer thinking. People and businesses do not need energy supply: people need the services energy gives them (warmth, light, cooling, transport, cooking, equipment running, etc.). The delivery of some 'energy services' may not require the use of energy!

The first step in planning and design must always be to provide for energy service needs through efficient resource planning (EST 2001). The savings in lifetime fuel costs may well be greater than the extra capital cost spent in reducing energy requirements. The savings in broader terms (when including 'externalities') will be even greater.

## 5.5   ENERGY EFFICIENT LAYOUT AND LANDSCAPE

A successful neighbourhood energy strategy begins with site planning. A careful assessment of the local climatic conditions combined with layout strategies to optimise the microclimate can reduce energy costs by 10 per cent (DETR 1997a).

The aim should be to reduce wind speeds across the neighbourhood and to optimise solar access to buildings through considered design of the layout and landscape. A step-by-step method to achieve this is described below.

### STEP 1   NEIGHBOURHOOD CLIMATE

Every neighbourhood will have its own local climatic conditions. For an efficient energy layout, the designer will need the following information:

▨   *wind* – direction, strength and seasonal variations

▨   *sun incident angles* – determined by latitude

▨   *slope* – will influence solar access through lengthening shadows

▨   *landform and landscape* – dips, escarpments, frost pockets, sheltering ridges, shelter belts

*Wind rose 1*

*Understand local wind by plotting a wind rose for summer and winter*

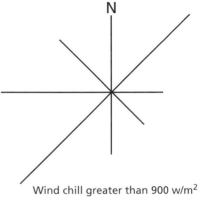

Wind chill greater than 900 w/m$^2$

Per cent for all wind directions

*Wind rose 2*

*Plot wind chill percentages for eight compass points*

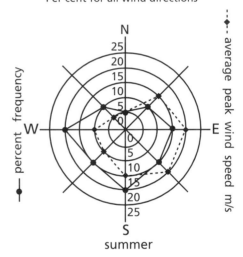

| Latitude/ typical location | | All year | 10 months (21 Jan–21 Nov) | 9 months 6 Feb–6 Nov) |
|---|---|---|---|---|
| 60°N | Lerwick | 66 m | 40 m | 25 m |
| 58°N | Ullapool | 46 m | 31 m | 21 m |
| 56°N | Edinburgh | 32 m | 25 m | 17 m |
| 55°N | Belfast | 31 m | 23 m | 16 m |
| 54°N | York | 28 m | 21 m | 15 m |
| 52°N | Milton Keynes | 23 m | 17 m | < 15 m |
| 50°N | Penzance | 19 m | 15 m | < 15 m |

Spacing between houses for a minimum of 3 hours' solar access per day. Assumes solar access to ground floor windows on a flat site of two-storey houses with 30° pitched roofs.

*SOURCE: ADAPTED FROM DETR 1997a*

*Figure 5.3*
**The feasibility of passive solar varies with latitude**

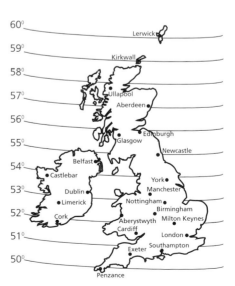

*A good source of further information is DETR 1997a*

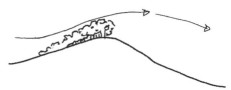

**Shelter belt on a ridge**

*Use landform to increase the windshadow*

## STEP 2  SLOPE AND ASPECT

For solar access, the building density, house design type and orientation should be informed by the degree and aspect of slope. The balance between lower densities, enabling solar access for heat gain, and higher densities, supporting other aspects of sustainability, needs careful consideration. Passive solar gain is maximised when buildings are about 20 m apart, but this could conflict with the current density requirements. To prepare an optimal density plan the slope factors must be taken together with planned facility nodes and access requirements.

Slopes within 45° (or better 30°) of south will be especially valuable for siting houses designed for solar gain. Here, higher densities will be possible without losing solar access. Buildings on slopes with a northerly aspect may need to be more widely spaced to avoid overshadowing – or use higher densities here and alternative energy service provision since passive solar is less viable.

Figure 5.4
**Zone the site for different objectives according to slope, aspect, access etc**

SOURCE: BASED ON TIBBALDS TM2

6.8 Graded densities    →

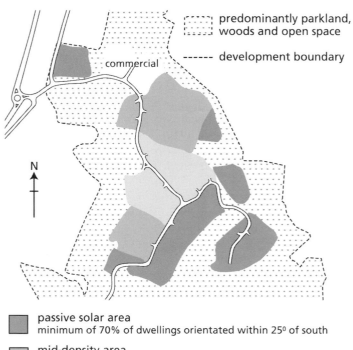

predominantly parkland, woods and open space

------ development boundary

commercial

N

■ passive solar area
minimum of 70% of dwellings orientated within 25⁰ of south

□ mid-density area
at least 60% of dwellings orientated within 25⁰ of south

□ urban development
maximise the number of dwellings orientated within 25⁰ of south

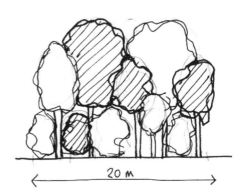

20 M

Figure 5.5
**Typical shelter belt composition**

*Use a variety of trees and shrubs to increase density*

*Further details can be found in* Energy saving through landscape planning, *Property Services Agency 1988*

## STEP 3  SHELTER BELTS

An ideal way to reduce wind speed at the neighbourhood scale is by the use of shelter belts. These should be designed to give other health benefits by providing amenity and wildlife (be careful to mainly use native species and avoid the quick-fix trap of leylandii).

| For two-storey buildings<br><br>Protection: | Shelter belt height | 'Stand-off' distance for solar access<br>(MEASURED WITHIN 30° TO THE NORTH OF THE BELT) | zone experiencing up to 50% reduction in wind speeds | |
|---|---|---|---|---|
| | | | medium belt:<br>50% porosity | dense belt:<br>20% porosity |
| up to the eaves (5 m) | 10 m | 30–40 m | 10–80 m | 0–65 m |
| up to the ridge (7.5 m) | 15 m | 45–60 m | 15–120 m | 0–100 m |
| well above the ridge (10 m) | 20 m | 60–80 m | 20–160 m | 0–130 m |
| maximum protection afforded | | | 65% reduction | 75% reduction |

Figure 5.6
**Calculating wind shadow characteristics for shelter belts**

*Design criteria for layout of neighbourhood shelter belts*

- Place the belt perpendicular to, or within 45° of, the incidence of the prevailing wind.

- The area behind the belt protected from the wind is determined by the height and degree of porosity to wind.

- A 50 per cent porosity belt should be 15 m wide (10 m minimum), with a minimum length of 20 m.

- At 50 per cent porosity wind protection is effective for a height of up to half the height of the shelter belt. Figure 5.6 gives distances and heights of protection for two different values of porosity.

- To ensure good solar access do not position a building to the north closer to a shelter belt than 3 to 4 times the shelter belt's height.

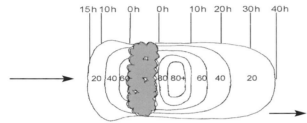

15h 10h 0h   0h 10h 20h 30h 40h

20 40 60   80 80+ 60 40   20

Figure 5.7
**Effects of a shelter belt on windspeed**

Typical percentage wind reduction for a shelter belt, height = h

→ wind direction

| Name | Porosity | | max ht (m) | Full leaf |
|---|---|---|---|---|
| | SUMMER | WINTER | | |
| Acer platanoides: Norway maple | 1 | 5 | 15–25 | mid April–mid Nov |
| Aesculus hippocast: Horse chestnut | 2 | 5 | 20–30 | early May–early Nov |
| Betula pendula: European birch | 3 | 6 | 15–25 | early May–early Nov |
| Fagus sylvatica: Common beech | 1 | 6 | 18–30 | late May–late Nov |
| Fraxinus species: Ash | 2 | 5 | 15–25 | early May–early Nov |
| Platanus acerifolia: London plane | 1 | 4 | 30–35 | late May–late Nov |
| Populus tremuloides: Aspen | 3 | 6 | 12–15 | mid April–mid Nov |
| Quercus robur: English oak | 2 | 6 | 20–30 | early May–early Nov |
| Taxus baccata: English yew | 0–1 | 0–1 | 12–15 | evergreen |
| Tilia cordata: Small-leaved lime | 1 | 4 | 15–25 | late May–late Nov |

Porosity: 0 = low (stops wind more); 6 = high (lets wind through more)

Figure 5.8
**Shelter belt characteristics for some common tree species**

SOURCE: PSA, 1988

Shelter belts can encourage wildlife and provide amenity for greenways.

5.19 Increasing wildlife capacity →

6.9 The green network →

*Design details for achieving an effective 50 per cent belt*

Porosity is determined by species composition and width – aim for 50 per cent porosity. Denser shelter belts provide more wind speed reduction but for a shorter distance.

- Use a mixture of climax and sub-climax deciduous and evergreen trees for the core. If deciduous trees are used for the main height, the solar 'stand-off' zone can be at the narrower end of the scale.

- An irregular top profile, clumps of taller trees, will further break up the air stream.

- The windward face should be fairly abrupt in the vertical plane but gently irregular in plan.

- Both faces should be well clothed with smaller trees and woodland edge/hedgerow shrubs lower down.

### Energy efficiency for sale

**Millenium Green, Collingham**

*Gusto Construction have built 22 speculative houses with special environmental features in Nottinghamshire.*

*The energy features include active ventilation with heat recovery, insulation to almost three times the 1999 building regulations, solar water heating, and low-energy fittings and appliances. Ratings of 100 for SAP and 10 for NHER have been given. It is estimated that properties will cost between 50 per cent and 70 per cent less to run than equivalent standard new homes. All properties are registered with the Energy Cost Guarantee Scheme, guaranteeing a maximum for new owners' gas bills for a 3-year period.*

*The homes have sold so well that Steven Wright, the director, will be extending the concept to future and larger phases of the development.*

GUSTO CONSTRUCTION LTD: WWW.GUSTOHOMES.COM

*Front: North elevation; 7.15 m² glazing*

*Back: South elevation; 13.2 m² glazing*

Figure 5.10
**Passive solar design can fit into the volume builder's portfolio**

*Standard house type with nearly twice as much glazing on the south elevation. Design study by Barratt (southern Counties), James and Keearns Architects funded by the DTI*

SOURCE: DETR/DTI 1999

## STEP 4  ORIENTATION

To optimise passive solar gain, housing front/back walls should be orientated to face within 25 per cent of south/north. This requirement can be fulfilled by a number of layout solutions giving rise to an interesting and varied neighbourhood character.

Figure 5.9
**A housing layout for solar access need not be constraining**

SOURCE: TIBBALDS TM2

© Tibbalds TM2

## STEP 5  BUILDING FORM

Less external wall for a given internal volume means less heat loss. With an internal living space of some 500 m³, a detached house will have an external wall area of 200 m². A semi-detached house with the same internal dimensions will have an external wall area of around 150 m², and in a terraced house the external wall area will be reduced to about 100 m². This will halve the heat losses through the walls. Reducing exposure to the external environment, for instance by setting elements of the building into the ground, should also be examined.

Maximise solar gains and minimise losses by providing 60–75 per cent of the glazing on the south elevation. This approach, often found in vernacular cottages, can provide some very desirable homes. The impact of this approach on standard estate house types and internal layout of rooms needs consideration. These aspects of building design are outside the scope of this guide, but typical layouts and further details can be found in *Passive Solar Estate Layout* (DETR 1997a). Thermal buffering (the use of an atrium or conservatory) and high levels of insulation should also be explored.

### Wind friction

Plan for additional dispersed tree planting (in addition to shelter belts) across the neighbourhood to reduce wind speeds through increasing wind friction. Tree location and groupings can be chosen that enhance character and sense of place.

> **5.21 Urban trees** →

## 5.6  SOURCING AND DISTRIBUTING ENERGY

The deregulated market provides the context for using a variety of energy sources. Using a 'private wire' system and a meter to the national grid, locally generated energy can be combined with energy bought in from the grid (this can also be renewably sourced). Excess energy generated locally can be sold back through the national grid. The details of buying and selling electricity are governed by electricity trading arrangements. This is a complex area and up-to-date advice will be required. A good starting point for social landlords is 'Selling CHP electricity to tenants' (DETR 1999c).

### SOURCING ENERGY

#### Combined heat and power (CHP)

This is a highly efficient energy-production plant. It supplies electricity and heat (often distributed by community heating schemes). Recent advances in the technology are leading to increased versatility and viability using, for example, 'micro scale' CHP: a plant little larger than a large boiler. Some plants can use a mixture of fuel sources, including waste, to generate power. Smaller good-quality plants have an exemption to the climate-change levy. The installation of a local CHP plant is the ideal catalyst for the laying of community heating distribution: see 'Distributing energy' below. This type of plant sits easily with local control and ESCOs can use this technology as part of a local solution.

*Financial and technical support for CHP*

**The Energy Saving Trust** *is supporting community heating schemes as part of its energy services programme. Grants are available for the development of plans for small CHP schemes, and in some cases to support the capital cost of a scheme.* www.est.org.uk

**Transco** *CHP Feasibility Programme helps housing providers to assess the viability of CHP/CH solutions. Grants are available of up to 90 per cent for feasibility studies.* www.chpa.co.uk

**The Combined Heat and Power Association** *is operating a programme of advice, consultancy and grants under its residential CHP development programme.* www.chpa.co.uk

*Figure 5.11*
**CHP is more efficient than conventional generation**

(ADAPTED FROM DETR 1999h)

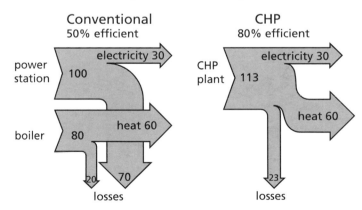

*'Buildings account for almost half the UK's energy consumption ... Combined Heat and Power schemes use waste heat and can increase fuel efficiency to 70–90 per cent (compared with 30–50 per cent with conventional electricity generation).'*

(SPACE FOR GROWTH, ENGLISH PARTNERSHIPS)

## The first community-led windfarm in the UK

*Awel Aman Tawe, Upper Swansea Valley*

*This will be the first community-led and fully community-owned windfarm in the UK. Awel Aman Tawe is a community-led project to develop a small windfarm as a major community asset providing sustainable funding for local regeneration and a source of renewable energy to UK customers. In addition, it will disseminate valuable lessons to the renewable energy industry regarding the processes of gaining community support.*

*The objective is to establish a small community-owned and managed windfarm which will generate sustainable funding to:*

- *assist in the regeneration of the Upper Amman/Swansea Valley areas; and*
- *support the implementation of Local Agenda 21 (LA21) objectives.*

*A comprehensive participatory assessment and collaborative planning process aims to explore the issues pertinent to communities, and generate a series of lessons as to how to replicate the process of community leadership in this sector.*

*Cost: £3 million*

*Projected income of windfarm: £192,000–£383,000 per annum*

*For further information, contact www.awelamantawe.co.uk*

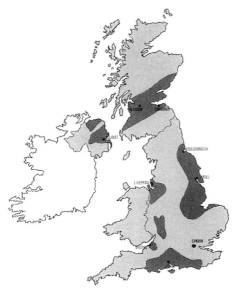

*Figure 5.13*
**Principal areas of potential geothermal aquifers in the UK**

*SOURCE: SOUTHAMPTON CITY COUNCIL*

## Small-scale wind turbines and community windfarms

Appropriate wind initiatives at the neighbourhood scale are either small wind generators for low-wattage uses or community-led windfarms. These provide an alternative to the large-scale rural windfarms. The city farm, the parks depot, the local refuse tip: these are all locations that could both use and accommodate small-scale (possibly vertical axis) wind generators. The new and developing vertical axis technology is almost silent, with very low operational wind speed. Planning policy outlined in PPG 22 (Renewable Energy) is not particularly relevant at this scale but normal planning regulations – regarding noise, visual intrusion and safety – would apply.

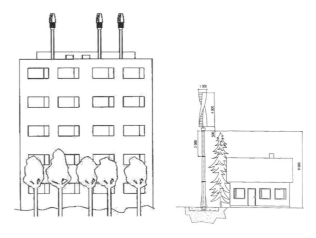

*Figure 5.12*
**Windmills in urban location**

*Vertical axis windmills (shown next to the house and on the roof of the flats) are more compatible with an urban location.
For further details of this type of windmill: www.windside.com*

*SOURCE: BASED ON MATERIAL FROM OY WINDSIDE PRODUCION LTD*

## Small-scale water turbines

In some areas small water turbines may provide a useful local power source.

## Waste

Although deriving energy from large-scale district incinerators is sometimes seen as an environmentally dirty source, on a neighbourhood scale there may be specific wastes which can be used for heat or power (tree surgery arisings, for example).

## Geothermal

Over the longer term this energy source becomes locally depleted. However, due to hot aquifers at a depth of some 1.5–2.0 km in several areas of the UK, it may be a useful and viable source to help kick-start a distributed scheme. In Southampton the local geothermal source has been successfully linked in to the community heating network.

## Biomass

Fast-growing species such as willow can be grown as a crop to feed into a boiler/CHP generator. In a neighbourhood context, the biomass production fields can be designed to fulfil additional functions. With controlled access and zoning, amenity uses, buffering from noise/roads and foul waste treatment can be accommodated. Foul waste can actually increase the growth rate of some of the biomass species. Other local sources are tree surgery arisings and forestry thinnings.

## Collective purchase

Collective purchase agreements can allow neighbourhoods to influence and support renewable energy generation. These are group contracts whereby a bulk purchase of electricity is agreed with a nominated supplier.

## DISTRIBUTING ENERGY

Community heating (CH) is the distribution of heat to users using an infrastructure of heating mains pipes. The heat can be fully controllable by the end users. End uses can be water heating, space heating or conversely, cooling (via absorption chillers).

Significant savings in fuel bills can be achieved by CH, usually in the order of 10 per cent below the cheapest other option. It has often been called district heating, though the first-generation district heating systems had less user control and gave the technology a poor reputation. An advantage is that the basic infrastructure (heat mains and a heat exchanger for each user) needs less maintenance and has a longer working life than the conventional best practice of providing every user with a high-tech (condensing) boiler.

CH systems provide future flexibility and can distribute heat from any variety of energy sources – giving opportunities for connection of renewables even when continuity of supply may not be assured. Additional power plants using different fuel sources as appropriate can be linked into the system – for example biomass, heatpumps, domestic waste, gas, 'waste' heat from industry. For the end user, a simple heat exchanger replaces the traditional boiler. The heat is controllable and can be metered.

Combined heat and power plants ( see 'Sourcing energy' above) are usually connected to CH schemes, though even in their absence there are economic and environmental benefits for CH through bulk purchase of fuel, load diversification and future fuel flexibility.

### Green heat

*A new project has got the go-ahead in the East Midlands to provide environmentally friendly heating systems using wood. The project to use wood on a commercial basis is being developed for the Forestry Commission by AEA Technology, promising to green the business environment, providing a competitive alternative to fossil fuels.*

*The project aims to provide heat from wood as a service to local customers, by using wood-powered boilers and heating systems. Customers will be able to switch from 'brown' to 'green' heating at no cost to themselves. This innovative idea aims to improve the local economy and create jobs locally, focusing initially on larger users of heat such as schools, leisure centres, factories and business parks in the region's coalfield areas.*

*'Green' heat is carbon neutral. The wood will come from the sustainable management of local woodland, where young trees are thinned out to allow space for others to mature, and from the less valuable by-products of harvesting mature trees. The thinning and replanting in turn provides much-needed diversity in the woods, which will improve their value for local wildlife, and help to ensure their long-term survival.*

*Lead partners: AEA Technology plc and the Forestry Commission.*

*For futher information, contact Forestry Commission Operations Manager East Midlands via www.forestry.gov.uk*

Figure 5.14
**Community heating idealised layout – mixed uses make infrastructure more economic**

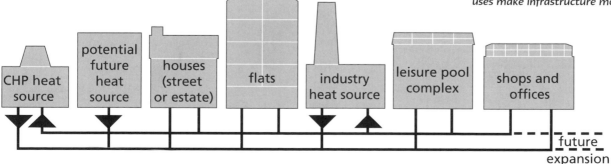

# 5.6

## ■ CHECKLIST FOR A CH/CHP SCHEME

*Basic scoping. Listed below are some indicators for a successful CH/CHP scheme (note these are not requirements for every scheme, but where four or more are present success is more likely).*

✔ *A project champion*

✔ *A core institutional user present or near by*

✔ *A social landlord or management company*

✔ *300 dwellings or more*

✔ *A medium- to high-density built form*

✔ *An existing CH scheme in the locality*

*Other factors for success. These secondary factors will also assist if present:*

✔ *An opportunity for cooling requirements*

✔ *A source of waste heat*

*A preliminary discussion with people involved in the field can help. A first point of contact is the Energy Services Association, who may be able to put you in touch with someone involved in a similar scheme.*

*Feasibility study and layout. The addition of a CH/CHP scheme is not a key determinant of the spatial framework of a neighbourhood. Following basic scoping, a full feasibility study will be needed to determine what configuration the system should have and how it could be financed. Grants may be obtainable for this. Where possible, plan to route heat pipes through 'soft' landscape and avoid major roads.*

*Sources of information for CH/CHP*

*Guide to community heating and CHP: Commercial, public and domestic applications. DETR Energy efficiency Best practice programme. Good Practice guide 234 (DETR 1998g)*

*Community heating – a guide for housing professionals. DETR Energy efficiency Best practice programme. Good Practice guide 240 (DETR 1999b)*

Community heating can be incorporated into both urban regeneration projects and new build. Laying heating pipes can be disruptive and expensive, therefore it makes sense to do this as part of area-wide infrastructure development prior to building or major refurbishment. For viability, the new consumers will have to be committed to buying their energy from the scheme: this requirement needs addressing as part of the soft infrastructure package. Community Heating and Combined Heat and Power plants are particularly compatible with mixed-use neighbourhoods for two reasons:

1    The wider spread of heat demand throughout the daily, weekly and seasonal time cycles creates a more even demand profile.

2    The closer proximity of users and plant reduces the amount of expensive heat-pipe infrastructure required.

The urban design planning implications are further developed in Section 6.7 – Space and energy sharing.

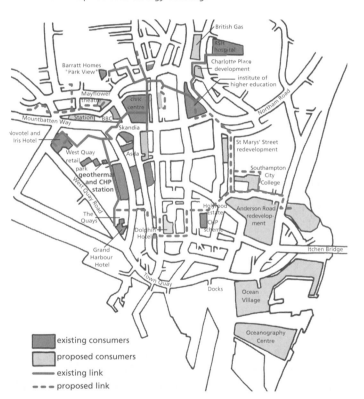

Figure 5.15
**Southampton community heating**

*The network delivering heating and cooling to buildings in the city centre, Southampton. Heat is provided from a geothermal generator and a CHP generator that also provides electric power*

SOURCE: SOUTHAMPTON CITY COUNCIL

# water

## 5.7 DEVELOPING LOCAL SOLUTIONS

 Sustainable water practice has consequences for the built form and layout of a neighbourhood. In order to be effective, the approach needs to be considered from the outset.

There are potential synergies with objectives for wildlife, movement and food. There is also great potential for environmental enhancement through using sustainable drainage systems.

A full understanding of water resources in the development area is needed as a precursor to developing low-impact solutions. Planners and designers must first take up the remit and feed it into the spatial planning process. Recognising connectivity is important.

- The neighbourhood or development site does not exist in isolation. It is influenced by discharges 'upstream' and it will in turn influence areas 'downstream'.

- The neighbourhood is embedded within the context of the basic level of water management – the catchment. Decisions at the neighbourhood level can assist in catchment management.

Widen the horizon from just thinking about mains supply to a review of all water sources, movement and possible use/re-use. Early on in the project, planners and urban designers should

- conduct a basic review of water resources in the neighbourhood, including 'hidden' water such as rainwater, culverts and storm water entering from adjoining areas.

- differentiate between the different qualities of water found both in use, after use, and in the landscape.

Once the water resources and needs are understood, adopt a sustainable water management strategy and assess options as outlined in this section.

| Water type | Source | Options for use or discharge |
|---|---|---|
| Blue | Running or standing water | Use to enhance amenity and wildlife on site |
| White | Mains water | Drinking, body washing, cooking |
| Grey | Baths, showers, washing machines | Treat then use for washing cars, watering gardens, flushing WCs Dispose to reed bed or other local biological treatment |
| Green | Captured roof rain water | Washing cars, watering gardens, flushing WCs |
| Black | Flushing WCs, kitchen sinks | Dispose to mains sewer, cess-pit or local biological treatment |

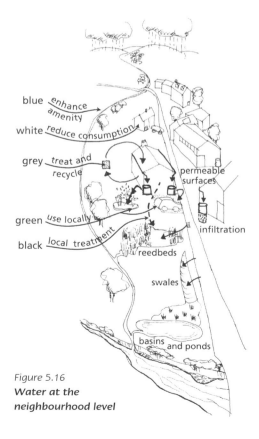

*Figure 5.16*
**Water at the neighbourhood level**

151

# 5.7

### Utilities in a proactive development role

*Hammarby Sjöstad, Sweden*

*An example of a proactive partnership where the utilities are leading the development concept for Hammarby Sjöstad – a new district 'where technology meets ecology'. The partnership is between*

- *The waste management company – Skefab;*
- *The drinking water supplier – Stockholm Vatten AB;*
- *The energy company – Stockholm Energi AB.*

*These utilities have jointly formulated a set of proposals for the energy supply, water, sewage and waste management for a city extension to the south of Stockholm.*

*The new district will be resource efficient and environmentally planned. It will exploit recycling technology and is aiming to achieve high levels of resource recovery.*

*The objectives are to close 'eco-cycles' at as local a level as possible and to minimise import of resources.*

*Further details can be found in Case Study 5.a at the end of this chapter.*
*www.hammarbysjostad.stockholm.se*

*Local Environment Agency Plans (LEAPs)*

*The Environment Agency produces LEAPs for the whole of England and Wales. The plans are non-statutory action plans based on river catchments. LEAPs operate over a 5-year cycle and are reviewed annually. They cover important issues affecting river catchments, and state how these issues might be resolved through measures set out in action tables. The Environment Agency is keen to implement these through partnerships including links to development plans, Local Agenda 21 and sustainable transport.*

## THE STAKEHOLDERS

### Environment Agency (EA)
### Scottish Environmental Protection Agency (SEPA)

These bodies have the responsibility for many aspects of the water environment, including issuing consents to abstract water or discharge water, environmental protection, water resource management and flood risk management. The Environment Agency run a National Water Demand Management Centre, they publish a series of leaflets describing practical water conservation measures in buildings.

The Environment Agency and the Scottish Environment Protection Agency have developed a concept of 'Sustainable Drainage Systems' (SuDS) to help reduce pollution, reduce flooding risk, protect aquatic habitats and help recharge ground water resources. They can provide advice, information and technical support.

### Water companies

The Environment Act 1995 placed a duty on water companies to promote the efficient use of water by their customers. This duty is enforced by the Director of OFWAT. Water companies local to a neighbourhood have been major players in sustainable neighbourhood development schemes on the continent. Water companies can reduce charges for customers implementing water-efficiency measures.

### Chartered Institution of Water and Environmental Management (CIWEM)

This professional body and its members can provide a range of expert advice and assistance in developing a strategic approach to local water resources (www.ciwem.org.uk).

### Environmental health section (Local Authority)

Local environmental health officers should be kept informed and involved in schemes dealing with issues such as local bore holes or grey water recycling. The local authority environmental health section can also be a good source of advice and regulatory information.

### Consumers

Residents will need to be involved and to understand a local water regime that may be different from conventional approaches. A sustainable approach forges (or re-forges) a closer relationship between users and water. New skills must be learnt; a certain degree of monitoring or even management may be required.

In domestic situations, for example, there may be some water that is non-potable. Inappropriate disposal of chemicals into one part of the system could lead to adverse consequences: for example, a noxious chemical disposed of in a paving gully may end up being watered on plants. In-house grey water treatment units require periodic checking and top-up of decontamination chemicals.

The installation and management of sustainable drainage systems in urban areas is in its infancy in the UK; the full management responsibilities and requirements and the consequent contractual arrangements are still being developed.

## ELEMENTS OF A WATER STRATEGY

### Reducing demand

In addition to rainwater harvesting and recycling, in new build or comprehensive refit/regeneration the developer has an opportunity to reduce neighbourhood water demand through the installation of water-efficient devices and appliances. A range of products are available – showers, water-saving baths, low flush toilets (and retrofitting water-saving 'hippos'), spray taps, more efficient dishwashers and washing machines.

In some locations significant reductions in quantity can be possible by using a dry composting toilet system.

### Working with surface water

▫ *Restore watercourses and replenish ground water*

In dense urban areas water courses can run in open channel alongside verges, walkways and roadways. Where there is more room a natural channel can be re-formed though parkland or other green space. De-culverting and restoration is closely linked to flood risk control and re-construction of natural watercourse features. The Institute of Civil Engineers considers that all urban watercourses, no matter how small, should be considered for restoration back to nature.

Recharge local aquifers where possible through use of soakaways, permeable surfaces and wetland features.

▫ *Celebrate urban watercourses and ponds*

Well-designed water 'features' can enhance the quality, amenity and values in a neighbourhood. Both ponds, lakes and moving water-courses can safely be incorporated into even the most urban of schemes. Where possible, facilitate access to water but have regard to safety. There may also be access requirements for maintenance.

Risks associated with open water features are often raised by the community. The myth of the danger is far greater than any actual risk. Once this has been dealt with by exploring the statistics with concerned stakeholders, the actual risk can be minimised by good design and community education.

### Harvesting rainwater

Rainwater can be collected from roofs. There are methods for disposing of the initial run-off or first flush, which contains most

---

**Achieving a reduced water impact**

*Reigate and Banstead Borough Council*

*An example of good practice in water strategy through planning mechanisms.*

*Supplementary planning guidance, the Horley Design Guide, relates to the expected provision of some 2,600 dwellings after 2001. Water resources, both surface water and water consumption, are dealt with comprehensively.*

*An open space, the 'Riverside Green Chain', is proposed as a location for attractive new features that are functional parts of the source control regime, such as shallow watercourses, ponds and reed beds. This will have biodiversity and amenity benefits.*

*Other measures detailed include rain water storage of 225 l per curtilage, downpipe discharge to grass swales, and wet and dry ponds.*

*Maintenance of the drainage features has also been included.*

*Environmental Policy Services
Reigate and Banstead Borough Council
www.reigate-banstead.gov.uk*

*Retrofit of green roofs on these industrial units put a stop to annual flooding of school grounds nearby* (Ekostaden, Malmö, Sweden)

SOURCE: JOHN DOLECEK

*'a typical green roof can hold 55 per cent of its volume in water, this can be as much as 110 litres per square metre'*

(BRIGHTON & HOVE COUNCIL 1998)

GREY WATER

# 5.8

### Communal grey-water use

*Shettleston Housing Association, Glasgow*

*This scheme comprises sixteen units of new-build terrace and flat development.*

*Low resource impact was designed for in both construction and management.*

*The homes are partially heated using geothermal energy from a disused mine below the site. After the heat is extracted from water pumped up from the mine, this water is then fed into a grey-water system serving all the WC cisterns in the housing.*

*For further information, contact: John Gilbert Architects www.johngilbert.co.uk*

### Grey water integrated with renovation

*Kolding, Denmark*

*The Municipality of Kolding is in the process of carrying out an urban ecology pilot project sponsored by the Danish Housing Board. This project covers ecologically orientated urban renewal in a block of flats with 129 existing flats and plans for 14 new flats. These houses lack a number of things as regards modern installations, insulation and maintenance.*

*Housing improvements in the individual properties are in progress. The owners have had the opportunity of receiving support for energy and water saving schemes, such as extra insulation, active and passive solar heating, water-saving toilet closets and fittings and recycling of rainwater for flushing the toilet.*

*Sections of the former private backyards have been fitted out as a common area with space for community purposes such as composting household waste. In the centre of this common area, a large glass pyramid, in which there is a biological purifying plant for waste water, has been built. The cleaned waste water is led outside the pyramid to permeate the soil in the area.*

contaminants. At its simplest, roof rainwater can be collected for an individual house by a rainwater butt: this is then used to water the garden. However, if integrated at a larger design scale (street, home-patch or even neighbourhood), rainwater can be fed into a communal treatment and distribution system – broadening the choice of end-uses.

Rainwater collected as run-off from paved surfaces will tend to be more contaminated than that from roofs. In some situations, though, this can be infiltrated directly into the ground or fed in to surface water systems such as reed beds or ponds.

## 5.8 GREY WATER

### TREATMENT AND RE-USE

While water recycling is a sustainable approach and can be cost-effective in the long term, the installation of grey-water systems can be initially expensive. There are public health concerns that can make it difficult to implement water recycling projects. These are not insurmountable and their remedy lies in regular system maintenance (for detailed information see Environment Agency 2000).

There are two main approaches for grey-water recycling, with differing impact on neighbourhood design and layout. Systems need to be designed with expert advice on water treatment and public health.

| Approach | Description | Pros and cons |
|---|---|---|
| Individual house systems | Grey water collected by waste pipe from appropriate sources. In-house collection, treatment header tank for use in WCs<br><br>A number of proprietary systems are on the market | **Pro**: No influence on neighbourhood spatial design<br><br>**Con**: Increase in household plumbing maintenance |
| Shared systems | Grey water collected by waste pipe from appropriate sources to central treatment facility<br><br>Distribution back to houses by secondary 'recycled water' rising main<br><br>Bespoke design at the terrace, home-patch or sub-neighbourhood scale | **Pro**: Treatment plant can be integrated with amenity uses<br>**Pro**: Central maintenance<br>**Pro**: Treatment possible to higher quality therefore more uses for the water produced<br><br>**Con**: Land required for treatment<br>**Con**: Community or residents' management company required |

## GREY WATER TREATMENT IN THE LANDSCAPE

Shared grey-water systems, using natural processes, present opportunities in terms of neighbourhood design.

### Glasshouse

At Kolding, Denmark, a specially designed glasshouse uses a combination of sunlight and vegetative processes to treat the communal grey water. The facility also provides a communal indoor garden amenity (see side box).

### Reed beds

Where space permits, a system of reed beds can be used to treat grey water. In some instances this can be designed to accept 'black water' in a fenced-off section. The reed-bed system can also be managed for biodiversity and amenity.

### Biofence

Where space is at a premium a biofence could be used. This is a proprietary 'fencing' system that contains tubes of algae which treat the water. Because this is an upright water treatment system, it is more compatible with higher-density development and also can be wall or roof mounted. The biofence treats the waste water (systems can be designed to take certain industrial waste water, from a brewery for example) and also produces a biomass product from the algae. The biomass can be used as a soil conditioner or in fish farm applications.

## 5.9  SUSTAINABLE DRAINAGE SYSTEMS (SUDS)

### BASIC PHILOSOPHY

The concept of sustainable drainage systems attempts to encompass best practice in drainage using a multitude of techniques to control quality and quality of run-off as close to the source as possible. The aim is for a developed area to mimic a natural area in terms of quantity and quality of run-off. The method, set out fully in the CIRIA design manual *Sustainable urban drainage systems* (2000) entails reviewing and modelling a number of options to find the best solution.

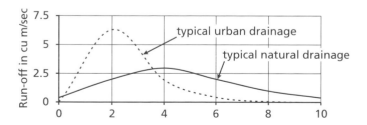

*Figure 5.18*
**Comparison between natural drainage and a developed area with no storm water retention**

SOURCE: AFTER HOUGH 1995

*Water treatment in a fence*

*A biofence at the Earth Centre*

*For further information, see: www.wastetreatmentscience.com*

SOURCE: WASTE TREATMENT SCIENCE LTD

### Retrofit of urban SuDS protects homes and school flooding

*Ekostaden, Malmö, Sweden*

*A partnership between the housing association and neighbouring industrial estate landlord (the municipal authority) is developing an innovative programme to solve problems and enhance the quality of local life. The 1 ha of flat roof on the industrial site is being retrofitted with a shallow cover of plants. This has resulted in a 60 per cent attenuation of water run-off, better insulation and longer life for the roof covering.*

*SuDS component making a strong contribution to the urban scene*

SOURCE: JOHN DOLECEK

*Downpipes in the housing area are being fed into a system of newly created open channels alongside pavement and reed beds. The aim is to relieve pressure on the combined sewer system and reduce flood risk. This is being achieved and with positive spin-offs for local amenity, biodiversity and water quality.*

*Residents and the local authority are supporting the project, which is leading to improvements in quality of life.*

*For further information, see: www.ekostaden.com*

# 5.9

### SuDS information

*An introductory video, 'Designs that hold water', is available from the Environment Agency.*

*Comprehensive design manuals for sustainable urban drainage systems are available from the Construction Industry Research and Information Association (CIRIA).*
*www.ciria.org.uk*

### Water safety
### Accident-preventative approach

*Care needs to be taken in the design of features with standing surface water to minimise risk of accidental drowning.*

*The Royal Society for Prevention of Accidents runs a consultancy and advice service. They have uncovered four links in the chain to drowning. A preventive strategy must be designed to break these links.*
1 *Ignorance, disregard or misjudgement of danger*
2 *Unrestricted access to hazards*
3 *Absence of adequate supervision*
4 *Inability to save oneself or to be rescued*

*Water bodies should be designed from the outset both to minimise the hazard (though gently shelving margins) and to reduce access to deep water (through location of paths and the use of vegetation).*

*For further information, see: www.rospa.co.uk*

## KEY OBJECTIVES

■  Attempt to control water discharge as soon as possible after precipitation (source control).

■  Slow down the speed of discharge off-site (control of quantity).

■  Use passive techniques to filter and settle suspended matter (control of quality).

■  Design the SuDS solutions as the layout plan emerges so that the components are fully integrated with development footprint, landscape character, amenity, movement and wildlife.

Additional measures may need to be taken if releasing SuDS water into sensitive environments, such as

■  bathing areas or public parks/formal areas

■  designated freshwater or shellfish fisheries. sites with statutory protection (SSSIs or Groundwater Source Protection Zones, for example).

### Maintenance

At the present time (2002), there is little experience of the long-term management of SuDS. Details of maintenance responsibility are still being resolved. The basic framework is for the local authority to adopt all above-ground works and for the water company (or authority in Scotland) to adopt below-ground structures.

Since the risks associated with flooding and silt accumulation are not yet fully understood, some local authorities may be unwilling to adopt some SuDS elements. The developer should be prepared to have the SuDS managed as a private system, handing it over to a grounds management company. There are landscape maintenance companies now specialising in this area. Some developers have also been concerned that it may be difficult to ensure the necessary high quality of landscape management and presentation once an area has been adopted by a local authority.

### SOME OF THE MAIN METHODS OF CONTROL IN SuDS

### Filter strips and swales

Vegetated surface features that drain water evenly from impermeable areas. Swales are long, shallow channels. Filter strips are gently sloping areas of ground.

They can be designed into public open space or road verges. Native grassland species can be introduced for wildlife and visual amenity.

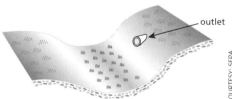
outlet

COURTESY: SEPA

## Infiltration devices

Infiltration devices drain water directly into the ground. A common examples is a soakaways, but they can also be in the form of trenches, swales and basins.

These areas can be used as playing fields and public open space. They can also be planted with trees and shrubs for biodiversity.

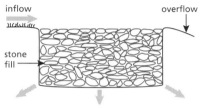

## Basins and ponds

Basins are usually dry, such as detention basins and flood plains. Ponds are designed to remain wet (for example, balancing ponds, wetlands, lagoons).

Basins can be used for sport and passive recreation. Ponds can provide public and wildlife amenity

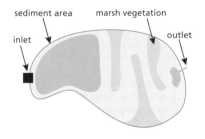

## Filter drains and permeable surfaces

Devices with a volume of permeable material below ground to store surface water. Filter drains are linear devices. Permeable surfaces are area-wide such as grass, gravel block paving or other permeable paving.

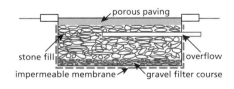

Permeable surfaces can be designed to be trafficked and used as car parks and non-adopted access roads. However, in such locations an impermeable membrane should be placed around the filtration material to prevent ground water pollution.

*SOURCE: ADAPTED FROM ENVIRONMENT AGENCY AND SOUTH GLOUCESTER COUNCIL 1999*

### Swale park storage

***North Hamilton, Leicester***

*The SuDS concept is very flexible and can be incorporated into a development scheme in various ways.*

*The urban design framework at North Hamilton uses a system of swales set in 'swale parks' as drainage channels and on-site flood storage. This provided a more attractive and cheaper alternative to the traditional solution, which would have meant a large retention pond at the bottom of the site.*

**A** *swale park serving adjacent housing areas*

*SOURCE: DAVID LOCK ASSOCIATES*

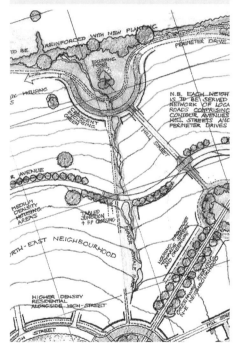

*A small swale park is shown in the illustration; a larger central swale park includes more open water and a greenway connecting the housing to the main high street.*

*The urban framework for North Hamilton was developed by David Lock Associates: www.davidlock.com*

HEALTHY LIFESTYLES: HEALTHY ECONOMY

# 5.10

# food

### 5.10 HEALTHY LIFE-STYLES: HEALTHY ECONOMY

 Food is a cross-cutting issue. It is easy to ignore the links to spatial planning, to ignore the impact that spatial designers and developers can have. For success, the widest of partnerships will need to be formed – typically involving local health groups, city farms/allotment associations, training and employment agencies, community services, environmental agencies.

### SUPPORT AND INFORMATION

#### Health Authorities

Health Authorities are starting to fund local food schemes. They are recognising that there can be positive impacts on physical and mental health through nutrition, exercise and through social contacts. Gardening and horticulture activities also assist mental health by relieving stress. Being involved in a rewarding activity, being in the open air and being in contact with nature can lower levels of stress.

---

### Food growers co-operative in Peabody estate

*This project is an example of an attempt to integrate food availability into social housing. A food growers' co-operative is planned as part of this integrated approach to mainstream low-impact living. In addition to the built development, the Beddington Zero Energy Development (ZED) project includes over 50 acres of lavender fields, wetlands, community forests and open green space on a reclaimed landfill site. This working ecology park will supply the ZED with fuel for heat and electricity generation, it will treat all its wastewater and be home to a local food growers' co-operative.*

*The developers have bought the site from the London Borough of Sutton. It is the first time that a local authority has sold land favouring a developer offering the greatest environmental benefit over one offering the most money.*

*BioRegional Development Group
www.bioregional.com*

*The Sutton Ecology Centre
www.sutton.gov.uk/el/environ/*

---

*Access to locally grown, healthy and safe food is emerging as an important consideration in urban sustainable development.*

*'A good diet is an important way of protecting health. Unhealthy diets are linked to cancer, heart disease and stroke.'*

*(OUR HEALTHIER NATION; A CONTRACT FOR HEALTH, 1998)*

---

Figure 5.19
**Food: measures and benefits**

| Measures | Access for local people | Local food production | Community action | Benefits |
|---|---|---|---|---|
| Back gardens; size and provision | ✔ | ✔ | | • increasing fitness<br>• healthy diet |
| Allotments; provision/support | ✔ | ✔ | ✔ | • healthy life-styles<br>• social inclusion and participation<br>• employment<br>• training |
| Community gardens and organic orchards | ✔ | ✔ | ✔ | |
| Healthy Living Centres (see 4.12 Healthy Living Centres) | ✔ | ✔ | ✔ | |
| Small outlets; provision in new build, support in existing areas | ✔ | | | • social inclusion<br>• supporting local economy<br>• healthy diet<br>• increasing access |
| Movement network for pedestrians and cyclists | ✔ | | | |
| Farmers' markets | ✔ | | ✔ | |
| City farms | ✔ | ✔ | ✔ | • community based regeneration<br>• life-long learning |

*Staple issues*

## Local Authorities

Food is at the heart of our well-being and is a potent Local Agenda 21 topic. Food initiatives have demonstrated

- improved physical and mental health
- opportunities for greater social cohesion; and
- potential for employment and training.

Policy ideas linking food and Agenda 21 can be found in Roundtable Guidance No. 15 *Sustainable Agriculture and Food* published by the IDEA.

## Soil Association

The Soil Association exists to support sustainable agriculture. It can offer support to food initiative partnerships involving local regeneration organisations, health promotion units and local authorities. It also offers training seminars and workshops on a number of local food issues.

The Association publishes a comprehensive outline of all local food issues relevant to local authorities and communities (Soil Association 1998): see www.soilassociation.org

## Other organisations

*National Urban Forestry Unit* – provides advice and support for wildlife and community orchards: see www.nufu.org.uk

*Common Ground* – supports community orchards, community gardens and apple day through its advocacy for the 'common-place' and 'local distinctiveness': see www.commonground.org.uk

*National Association of Farmers' Markets* – seeks to disseminate information about farmers' markets: www.farmersmarkets.net

*Federation of City Farms and Community Gardens* – offers support and advice: www.farmgarden.org.uk. See 5.13 for more details.

*Local Government Association (LGA)* – has policies to support sustainable living through a new role for allotments: www.lga.gov.uk

*Sustain* – the alliance for better food and farming. Sustain represents around 100 national public interest organisations working at international, national, regional and local levels. They provide a Food Indicators Toolkit and other information on their website: www.sustainweb.org.

### Village shop support

*South Norfolk*

The initiative shows how to use partnerships to support village shops. Could this be translated to urban estates? The project has a package of measures aimed at helping small village shops survive, thrive and improve the service they offer, and hence the quality of life for people in local communities.

The initiative is a partnership between Tesco Stores plc, the Countryside Agency, Norfolk and Waveney Training and Enterprise Council, and Norwich Enterprise Agency Trust. Objectives include

- To improve the shopping environment.
- To improve accessibility.
- To enhance the skills of shopkeepers.
- To encourage the supply of more local produce and raise the profile of local shops generally.

South Norfolk Council
www.south-norfolk.gov.uk

### Local food links

*Bristol City Council*

This project is an example of what can be achieved through an Agenda 21 food initiative. The action pack is useful as it presents a range of ideas.

The Agenda 21 group (Sustainable City Team) at Bristol City Council have set up a local food links initiative and support network. As part of this they provide a free action pack containing a briefing on 13 different projects that use food to support local sustainable development. They range from cooking clubs and community cafés to making use of excess food locally.

The pack can be viewed on the web via www.bristol-city.gov.uk

*Haringey Good Food Directory*

To support health through access to good food a directory has been produced. This lists some of the food resources that exist locally in Haringey, North London

ALLOTMENTS AND ORCHARDS

# 5.11

### New future for allotments?

*Allotments offer tremendous scope for a range of council objectives.*

*The LGA advocate that local authorities use allotments to help secure health, leisure, education, sustainability and planning objectives.*

*Using new concepts of Best Value it is imperative to integrate and harmonise the different elements of services to deliver shared goals.*

*Further reading:*
*A new future for allotments (LGA 2000a)*
*The good practice guide to the management of allotments (LGA 2001)*

4.13 Recreational
open space    ←

### Local Agenda 21: Estate allotment and leisure gardening

**QED Allotments Group, Dartford, London**

*This group promotes the sustainable development of allotment gardening. The group concentrates on ten action areas including*
- *Waste disposal and recycling*
- *Helping to meet local needs locally: for food, water, shelter and fuel*
- *People's health*
- *Access to facilities, services, goods and other people*
- *Participation in decision-making*
- *Valuing and protecting local features*
- *Satisfying employment.*

*Early successes have proved this an effective method of tackling problems common to many inner-city areas.*

## 5.11 ALLOTMENTS AND ORCHARDS

Allotments seem to send mixed messages: on the one hand, some view them as relics from 'the war', as half-derelict eyesores. On the other, rumours abound of 5-year waiting lists for those wanting to rent an allotment. Many organisations now see allotment renaissance as representing an important tool for delivering sustainability to neighbourhoods.

There are tangible benefits for planners, developers and communities in developing allotments; increasing their accessibility in regeneration and new-build schemes.

Allotments connect to social and health themes such as

- recreational activity, keeping fit

- health initiatives (healthy living centres, for example)

- urban renewal and green space provision

- community education and life-long learning.

Allotment initiatives are especially useful in increasing public participation: and helping to combat social exclusion. Allotments are accessible to all social groups, and are widely used to grow food by the elderly and other people on low incomes.

In particular for local councils, promotion of policy delivery through allotments is in keeping with Best Value and provides an integrated route to service delivery. As such allotments can have a seminal focus in Community Strategies for the promotion of well-being.

Figure 5.20
***The integrated allotment site***

*Allotment sites can underpin local access to food and open space whilst performing valuable water and biodiversity services*

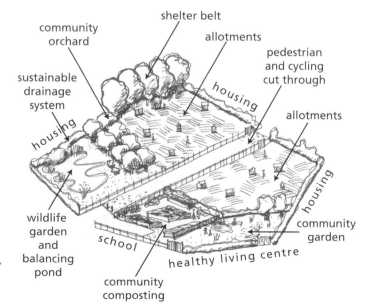

Planners and designers considering the neighbourhood spatial framework should embed new or existing allotments into the layout looking for synergy with other spatial uses. Allotment provision is particularly compatible with

- sustainable urban drainage  *§ 5.9*

- local pedestrian access  *§ 4,15*

- community recycling and composting  *§ 5.16*

- wildlife and biodiversity  *§ 5.18*

- shelter belts  *§ 5.5*

- community orchards, see below.

## COMMUNITY ORCHARDS

Community orchards can be successful in urban and rural areas. They provide many opportunities for strengthening community links through sharing knowledge, skills and activities. They can enhance the environment of housing estates, industrial estates, hospitals and schools whilst also increasing biodiversity. Community orchards can provide endless opportunities for fun events including tree dressing, blossom parties, apple-day fairs (National Apple Day is in the autumn) and apple bobbing. Land requirements are upwards from 0.1 ha for about ten trees.

### Allotments to orchards

*Blondin Orchard, London*

*Following a decline in allotment use, when consulted, the local community were keen on planting an orchard on the allotment site.*

*Local people helped to plant 46 old and local varieties of apples on a 0.5 ha site. A 50-strong Friends Group co-ordinate regular maintenance activities.*

*Project objectives:*
- *good fruit production*
- *community involvement*
- *enhancment of wildlife value*
- *use of redundant land.*

*Project partners include: London Borough of Ealing – Parks and Countryside; London Ecology Unit; Common Ground; Friends of Blondin Nature Area*

*Allotments: an accessible shared resource and a meeting place for communities*

*Common Ground provide information through a series of orchard advice notes, including sources of grant funding. www.commonground. org.uk*

# 5.12

*Farmers' markets benefit farmers, consumers, the environment, and the community*

- *They provide direct contact and feedback between customers and producers, so you can be sure how your vegetables are grown and meat is produced.*

- *They provide a secure and regular market outlet for producers, especially valuable for small-scale producers, new producers and producers in organic conversion.*

- *They cut out the middle man, allowing increased financial returns through direct selling and improved cash flow.*

- *They help bring life into towns and cities, aiding regeneration.*

- *They encourage social interaction particularly between rural and urban communities.*

- *They help to improve diet and nutrition by providing access to fresh food.*

- *They help reduce food miles and packaging.*

- *They stimulate local economic development by increasing employment and encouraging consumers to support local businesses.*

- *They raise awareness about where food comes from and how it is produced.*

*The National Association of Farmers' Markets: www.farmersmarkets.net*

**4.1 Local shops and services** ←

*The Federation of City Farms and Community Gardens (FCFCG) is the UK organisation representing groups involved in community-led development of open space through locally managed farming and gardening.*

*Advice and support is offered for the setting up and running of City Farms and Community Gardens: www.farmgarden.org.uk*

## 5.12 LOCAL SHOPS AND MARKETS

### LOCAL SHOPS

There is a strong case for supporting local shops which give easy access to food, and often supply fresh local produce. In rural villages there are several examples of shop support schemes coming to the aid of the threatened local shop. These could provide models for urban areas.

Co-operation between local producers, LETS groups, allotment associations and retailers, maybe supported by initial funding from the health authority or community/regeneration funds, could help the local store to become again a valued community asset.

### FARMERS' MARKETS

Farmers' markets sell locally produced goods to local people. The concept is obviously not a new one. Farmers have bartered and sold goods as far back in history as agriculture itself.

- Plan for or identify public open space in a local commercial centre that can serve as a market space.

- Contact the National Association of Farmers' Markets for a manual on setting up a farmers' market.

It is generally accepted by most farmers' markets that stall holders must have grown, bred, caught, pickled, brewed or baked the goods themselves. The main emphasis is to help local producers and processors to sell their goods direct to the public, near their source of origin, creating benefits to them and the local community.

## 5.13 CITY FARMS

City farms have an important role to play in urban sustainability and there is growing government recognition of their value to local communities. As a major local resource they should probably be planned for at the township scale: every township should have one. The sustainability of the surrounding neighbourhoods will benefit through

- production of fresh food and contact with food and food processes

- provision of productive, creative, safe, high-quality open space

- opportunities for people to learn new skills and abilities, either informally or on formal accredited training courses

- additions to the economic wealth of the area

- improvements to physical and mental health

▨ provision of facility that can bring people of different abilities, ages, and cultures together socially, and aid community development; and

▨ fostering community pride and independence through involving local people on management groups.

| Approximate farm size | Typical facilities | Example |
|---|---|---|
| 0.5 ha | Small herb gardens and pond areas; 22 private allotments; spinning room; dyeing area; visitors' room<br><br>Animals: poultry, cow, donkey, duck, horse, goat, pig, rabbit, sheep | Vauxhall City Farm, London<br>0207 582 4204 |
| 1 ha | Community garden, polytunnel, large adventure playground, craft and art rooms and workshop, café<br><br>Animals: poultry, goats, pig, rabbit, sheep | New Ark Adventure Playground and City Farm, Peterborough, 01733 340 605 |
| 2 ha | Kids and pensioners allotments, classrooms; run a riding programme and NVQs in horse care and animal care<br><br>Animals: poultry, cows, ducks, horses, goat, pigs, rabbit, sheep | Kentish Town City Farm, London<br>0207 916 5421 |
| 3–4 ha | Interpretation centre/ classroom, café<br>Gardens including wildlife pond<br><br>Animals: poultry, cows, ducks, donkey, goat, pigs, rabbit, sheep | City Farm Byker, Newcastle<br>0191 232 3698 |
| over 5 ha | Café, dairy, classroom, polytunnels<br><br>Animals: poultry, cows, donkey, geese, goats, pigs, pony, rabbit, sheep | Rice Lane City Farm, Liverpool (10 ha)<br>0151 530 1066 |

Figure 5.21
**Some farm sizes and facilities offered**

Figure 5.22
**Layout plans for two city farms**

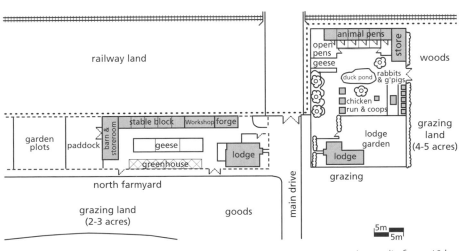

Large city farm, 10 ha – Rice Lane, Liverpool

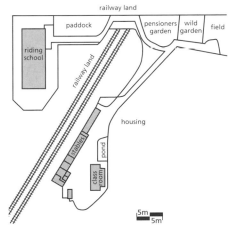

Small city farm, 2 ha – Kentish Town, London

# 5.14

### Best Value indicators for waste

- Of the total tonnage of household waste arisings
    - percentage recycled
    - percentage composted
    - percentage used to recover heat, power and other energy sources
    - percentage landfilled.

- Weight of household waste collected, per head.

- Cost of waste collection per household.

- Cost of municipal waste disposal, per tonne.

- Number of collections missed, per 100,000 collections of household waste.

- Percentage of people expressing satisfaction with
    - recycling facilities
    - civic amenity sites.

- Percentage of population served by a kerbside collection of recyclable waste, or within 1 km of a recycling centre.

SOURCE: DETR 2000k

The effluent society

The sustainable society

# waste

Material brought into the neighbourhood becomes 'waste' through being placed in the waste stream by the actions of an individual no longer requiring its use. However, much of the material in the waste stream can still perform important functions in the neighbourhood, if not in the wider economy. Therefore, when planning and designing neighbourhoods for sustainability, approach waste as a resource.

### Multiple benefits

Identifying and separating useful material in the waste stream not only releases its value for re-use but also reduces the transport required for import of new products/materials and export of waste, saves resources and reduces pollution. To determine how far waste and arisings should be transported use the proximity principle – close resource loops as close to the source as possible (see Figure 5.23).

 Policy and legislative guidelines are increasingly demanding the creation of a neighbourhood with effective re-use and recycling regimes.

■ Recognise the small but crucial space and design requirements needed in new build or regeneration of neighbourhoods for minimising waste.

■ Consult with experience in the community not-for-profit sector and with the relevant council departments.

■ Aim to provide facilities that embed re-use and recycling in the daily life of residents and businesses in the locality.

### DRIVERS

#### Local Authorities

Waste management is a key service provided by local authorities and a number of Best Value indicators have been set for waste management services (see side column). It is not only environmental and technical services who can influence the ease of meeting these targets. Planners and designers involved in neighbourhood schemes can also make a significant impact.

#### Central government

In Scotland the National Waste Strategy 1999 (SEPA 1999) and in England and Wales, Waste Strategy 2000 (DETR) set out the approach to and priorities for waste. Mandatory targets have been set for recycling and composting to be achieved by local authorities. The documents acknowledge the important role to be played by the community not-for-profit sector in providing services and raising awareness.

**EU Landfill Directive (in force from 16 July 1999)**

Mandatory targets for reduction in landfill for the next 20 years. It sets reducing targets for the amount of biodegradable waste going to landfill.

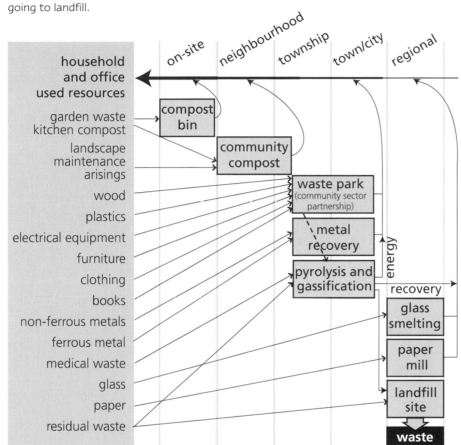

Figure 5.23
*Proximity principle*

*Close the resource loop as close to the source as possible*

## ADVICE AND ASSISTANCE

**Community waste sector**

A number of national networks and their individual members covering recycling, composting, re-use and education/raising awareness. Individual member organisations can offer advice and support to those setting up local schemes. The sector works in partnership with Local Authorities and businesses to develop best practices in all fields of sustainable waste management.

The community waste sector gives a competitive return in terms of jobs created per pound invested (see Waste Parks, 5.17). Moreover, this sector can provide good socio-economic returns, since money is reinvested in local jobs and facilities. The Community Recycling Network comprises organisations from volunteers up to businesses with turnovers of £6 million a year. Together they provide kerbside collections to over 1 million households in the UK.

*Further information*

*Community Composting Network*
*www.othas.org.uk/ccn/*

*Community Recycling Network*
*www.crn.org.uk*

*Community Furniture Network*
*www.btinternet.com/~frn/FRN/*

DOMESTIC SEPARATION

# 5.15

## Steps taken to reduce household waste in new build

*Emersons Green*

*With new build there is the opportunity to build in the systems for household recycling before the occupants arrive, making the recycling habit easier to establish. Developers assisted the local authority, South Gloucestershire, in helping to meet waste reduction targets at Emersons Green. Approximately 3,100 housing units are being built on a 150 ha greenfield site on the edge of Bristol.*

*In addition to other sustainability measures, household waste reduction will be encouraged as soon as occupants move in to their new houses, via community officer input.*

*Every house is provided with a compost bin in the garden and a recycling box linked to a new kerbside collection scheme. There is only a small sized municipal wheelie bin for residual waste, reversing the usual practice of providing a large bin.*

## Tackling issues head on

*Flemish network of re-use centres*

*Re-use centres have been set up to tackle waste, employment and environmental issues together. Waste is collected, sorted, repaired and re-sold.*

*The environmental objective is to encourage re-use and extended life of secondhand household goods. Employment is provided for low-skilled long-term unemployed people. The socio-economic objective is to provide cheap but decent products for people with lower incomes.*

*The network has 40 sites and now covers 6 million inhabitants, who produce 16,000 tonnes of waste a year: 10 per cent of this now is dealt with by the re-use centres.*

*The regional government provides start-up investment, and local authorities get grants for working with the centres.*

## 5.15 DOMESTIC SEPARATION

### STORAGE IN THE HOUSE

In many areas there is a kerbside waste collection of separated materials direct from households. These schemes should be extended to more areas in the future to meet national mandatory recycling targets. The motivation and even the ability to participate will be influenced by the provision of in-house storage for separated waste. Developers can assist through provision of storage under the sink unit for immediate storage of recyclables prior to them being taken outside the house. A number of proprietary systems are available. Designers should give thought to providing for four types of waste: organic matter, dry recyclables (glass, tins, cans, textiles and shoes), used paper and residual waste.

### STORAGE FOR RECEPTACLES OUTSIDE THE HOUSE

Separating waste in the house necessitates more than a single 'rubbish' bin outside the house. Ideally, waste streams are kept separate. Materials suitable for kerbside collection can be placed in a separate box with residual waste being put into the rubbish bin. Where wheelie bins are provided, the size can be an important factor in determining quantities sent to residual waste stream. The size of the standard wheelie bin, where provided, should be the smaller 160 l bin, with the larger 240 l bin only available on request. All new housing should have a garden compost bin provided.

### MINI-RECYCLING CENTRES FOR BLOCKS OR HOME-PATCHES

In estates or blocks of flats where there are already communal rubbish collection facilities these can be expanded to become mini-recycling centres. An effective way is to provide, in addition to the communal rubbish receptacles, storage room for separated wastes. To ensure that these are actually used there needs to be investment in the 'soft infrastructure'.

*Benefits*

▪ Can encourage high participation rates if suitable banks, bins, etc. can be located close to people's homes.

▪ Are cheaper than separate collection from households.

*Disadvantages*

▪ Badly sited banks can lead to an increase in traffic movements and may deny some people the opportunity to participate.

▪ Care has to be taken to ensure people put the right material in the right bin as contamination can damage the value of the collected materials.

### Street-scale facilities

Even in areas with a standard street layout, there is also the possibility of including a recycling facility at the home-patch scale. In some countries, a small covered and gated local enclosure is used as a local storage and collection point for large items such as fridges, batteries, furniture, other white and brown domestic goods for collection and repair/re-use (see photos below).

## 5.16 COMMUNITY COMPOSTING

In order to meet EU Landfill Directive Targets the UK needs to separate and collect household biodegradable waste (known as putrescible waste) for composting. At one end of the scale there are centralised composting sites. These are large commercial operations needing waste licences and industrial or farming locations.

At the other end of the scale is the growing network of community sites. Sites not storing over 1,000 m² (500 tonnes) at any time can apply for exemption from waste licensing regulations. Sites at this scale can be integrated into neighbourhood planning, providing local employment and community participation, in addition to recycling. Experience shows that there is scope to widen the social benefits through training schemes or, for example, working with adults with learning difficulties. In terms of physical planning, links can be made with allotments and city farms.

### Composting

*Kitchen and garden waste make up 30–50 per cent of household waste. It is valuable organic material, and none need go to landfill.*

*It is estimated that only 7 per cent of houses with gardens have a compost bin.*

5.11 Allotments ←

5.13 City farms ←

### Local effort supported by County Council

*Devon Community Composting Network*

*A network of some 25 local compost initiatives. The network itself is funded by the Devon Authorities' waste reduction and recycling committee. It provides a forum for advice and shared problem-solving, greatly assisting local organisers in setting up their own projects.*

*Projects are funded by landfill credits, sales of compost, charges for collection, grant funding and volunteer hours used as matched funding. Many sites are small but even with only a site measuring 6 m by 8 m, 50 tonnes can be processed per year. With landfill credits at £30 per tonne this is an annual income of some £1,500 (not including sales and collection charges).*

*Information on how to set up a scheme is provided in an information pack from Devon Community Composting Network: email nicompost@aol.com*

### Local recycling point in Hiriazumi, Japan

*A wide range of household items can be placed in the facility, as graphically illustrated on the notice.*

*Car batteries, sump oil, fridges, electrical goods, plastics, different types of canisters, etc.*

*Collections are twice a week.*

# 5.16

'The Government looks to community groups to

- be fully involved in Local Authority efforts to build partnerships for more sustainable waste management

- draw on the guidance on Best Value recently published by NCVO in developing partnerships with Local Authorities.

- continue their valuable work in motivating public involvement and increasing participation in recycling and composting schemes.

- take advantage of funding from the landfill tax credits scheme where possible'.

SOURCE: WASTE STRATEGY 2000, SECTION 4.32 (DETR 2000k)

Indications are that community composting schemes can be a good generator of local partnerships. Councils can pay groups recycling credits for every tonne diverted from landfill, though not all councils take up this opportunity to promote community recycling. Income can also be generated by charging for special collections/garden clearance, selling compost, education visits.

Figure 5.24
**Idealised layout for community compost facility serving 200 households**

*Note progressive reduction in size of boxes as the compost matures and shrinks in volume*

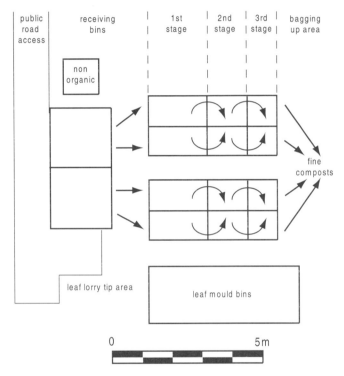

**Community compost site at Thornbury, South Gloucestershire (approx. 400m²)**

| Site | Size m² | Details |
|---|---|---|
| Chagford Old Site, Devon | 50 | 60 tonnes pa. <br><br> Comprises 6 bins, each 1.2 m x 1.2 m. Collection, and bring system, of local households' garden waste; village 1,400 pop |
| Healy City Farm Site, Sheffield | 50 | 50 tonnes pa. <br><br> Collection of kitchen waste from 200 households; city farm waste; hop waste from local brewery; commercial grass cuttings |
| Uffculme Project, Devon | 900 | 250 tonnes pa. <br><br> Bring system for village of 2,000 pop. Some use by hinterland of 10,000 pop. Charged for collection for disabled and elderly |

Figure 5.25
**Sample land requirements for community compost schemes**

## 5.17 WASTE PARKS AND PYROLYSIS

### WASTE PARKS

Local authorities provide civic amenity sites where people can bring their household waste. This consists generally of bulkier items such as furniture, DIY waste, kitchen equipment and garden waste, as well as recyclable waste.

Built at the township or whole-city scale, a waste park is like a civic amenity site but the aim is to reclaim, repair, renew and return for re-use. At its best the site will have permanent core staff and involve a partnership of organisations involved in salvage and manufacture, running workshops, craft production, training and business development. Partnerships with local business and the community sector can provide both sources of material and routes for end use.

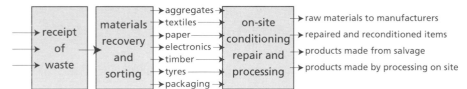

Figure 5.26
**The waste park concept**

### PYROLYSIS AND GASIFICATION

These facilities offer a clean burn waste facility. The maintenance of high temperatures is claimed to ensure that dioxins are not generated and the lack of air during the burn (in a process more akin to charcoal making than a bonfire) means a very reduced emissions quantity compared to incineration. The process can produce energy and heat (CHP). A well-designed pyrolysis and gasification plant can accept a very wide range of fuel types: household, commercial and industrial waste, clinical waste, shredded used tyres and biomass.

Unlike conventional incinerators the plant is modular; the smaller-scale units would fit on a standard town industrial estate and could sensibly be incorporated as part of a waste park. Since they burn clean and emit only very low levels of noise, they can be located nearer to centres of population and hence users for the heat output. At present they are at feasibility and pilot stages in the UK.

**Converting waste to resource**

*Sustainable Growth Park, Urban Mines Ltd*

*A proposed industrial park dedicated to reprocessing materials from the local waste stream to supply on-site manufacturers with quality secondary raw materials.*

*The concept is designed as an engine for economic development, urban renewal and job creation within an environmentally sustainable and financially self-supporting framework.*

*Principal features*

- *State of the art Materials Recycling Facility to separate materials by a combination of manual and mechanical methods.*

- *Reprocessing plant to refine the various materials to a tightly controlled quality assured specification.*

- *Units for small and medium enterprises to use the raw secondary material produced on site.*

- *Areas for aggregate treatment, composting of organic wastes and a re-use centre for refurbishment of discarded manufactured products.*

*For further information, see: www.urbanmines.org.uk*

**A different scale!**

*Compact Power's trial pyrolysis and gasification plant next to a redundant incinerator at Avonmouth. The plant can generate local heat and power. For further information see: www.compactpower.co.uk*

SOURCE: COMPACT POWER

A NEIGHBOURHOOD RESPONSE

# 5.18

'The quality of our natural environment demands that the development decisions respect the direct relationship between man and nature.' (DETR 1999: 29)

### Local Biodiversity Action Plans

The UK Biodiversity Steering Group oversees the conservation of biodiversity in Britain. It recommends drawing up local Biodiversity Action Plans to complement the national action plan. Best practice for these is to address neighbourhood biodiversity resources such as back gardens, derelict land and habitats associated with urban buildings.

### Buildings and Nature Project

This initiative provides wildlife advice for developers. Designed to be of assistance in the planning process and provide information about access to funding. It co-ordinates best practice and acts as a resource base at the Regional Development agency level.

Contact: SEEDA pilot project
email: martinbolton@seeda.co.uk

### National policy

England: Planning Policy Guidance 9: Nature Conservation (1994)

Scotland: National Planning Policy Guidelines 14: Natural Heritage (1998)

Wales: Technical Advice Note 5: Nature Conservation and Planning (1996)

Northern Ireland: PPS2: Planning and Nature Conservation (1997)

*Local wildlife trust offices can be found via www. wildlifetrusts.org.uk*

# biodiversity

## 5.18 A NEIGHBOURHOOD RESPONSE

 In the neighbourhood setting, biodiversity objectives should be pursued in tandem with social and economic objectives. Financial support can be strengthened through forming partnerships with urban regeneration, employment, training and health initiatives.

PPG 9 (Nature Conservation) sets out the framework for designation and protection of national and local sites. However, in a typical neighbourhood, the basic or 'background' level of biodiversity will not attract protection through these measures. This section sets out an approach to be followed in non-designated areas.

Policy support for biodiversity in residential or mixed neighbourhoods can be drawn from Biodiversity Action Plans, some of which are starting to address typical urban land and can and should be adopted as Supplementary Planning Guidance.

### INFORMATION AND ADVICE

**English Nature**
**Scottish Natural Heritage**
**Countryside Council for Wales**
**Environment and Heritage Service**
**Department of the Environment Northern Ireland**

These government agencies all have a statutory duty to protect the natural environment and promote biodiversity. They are a good source of advice. All have lead officers for urban wildlife.

### The National Urban Forestry Unit

Urban forestry comprises the trees and woods in towns. The National Urban Forestry Unit promotes these through publishing a wide range of literature covering many urban tree issues. Topics covered include how to develop a local urban forestry strategy, involving local people, sources of funding and design guidance.

### The local authority

Local authorities balance their statutory duties to protect the natural environment with many other responsibilities. The local plan and local Biodiversity Action Plan are essential tools in setting the policy scene for the role of the neighbourhood in nature conservation.

### Wildlife Trusts and members of the Urban Wildlife Partnership

The Urban Wildlife Partnership is a national charity devoted to promoting the well-being of wildlife and the places it lives in towns and cities. A local trust will be a valuable first point of contact for information about wildlife in the neighbourhood and is often the lead partner in preparing local Biodiversity Action Plans.

**Environment Agency**
**Scottish Environmental Protection Agency**

The EA produces Local Environment Agency Plans (LEAPs) for England and Wales; these are non-statutory action plans based on river catchments. LEAPs include local biodiversity conservation (particularly in relation to watercourses and wetlands), recreation, protection of air and water quality, water resource management, fishery management, flood protection, and treatment of contaminated land.

*Figure 5.27*
**The townscape approach**

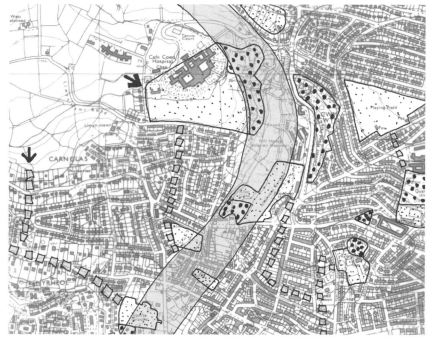

*The wildlife network at the town scale includes*

KEY

 *green wedges and countryside links* – *tracts of countryside extending into the town. The largest scale features, often associated with river floodplains or escarpment that have escaped built development*

 *wildlife corridors* – *linear tracts of habitat, sometimes connected with the surrounding countryside. Often land bordering transport corridors (especially river, canal and rail)*

 *wildlife reservoirs* – *large areas of urban green space and/or those with large biodiversity capacity. Some may have national or local designations*

 *stepping stones* – *small areas of urban green space and/or large areas of low biodiversity capacity*

 *wildlife links* – *shorter or weaker tracts of habitat linking the other features. For example hedgerows/lines of trees*

## WILDLIFE AT THE TOWN SCALE – THE WILDLIFE NETWORK

Most local authorities have a wildlife plan or local Biodiversity Action Plan. This sets out a town-wide policy framework. Current best practice for wildlife strategies is to adopt a wildlife network approach. This involves the identification of a number of key resources that are then mapped across a town or conurbation. Some of these resources will be sites that have statutory (SSSI, LNR) or local (SINC, LSNC) designation. Regulation 37 of the UK Habitats Regulations includes policies 'encouraging the management of features of the landscape which are of major importance for wild flora and fauna including links, corridors and stepping stones that are essential for the migration, dispersal and genetic exchange of wild species.'

A neighbourhood project should be set in the context of such a network and seek to strengthen it.

WILDLIFE CAPACITY

# 5.19

*As wildlife capacity increases, small-scale measures are more likely to succeed*

### Target species

*Start by identifying locally important species from the Local Biodiversity Action Plan. In general, the following species can all be assisted in gardens and allotments. They have all also been cited as of particular concern nationally by the UK Biodiversity Steering Group Report (1995)*

- *Birds: blackbird, blue tit, house sparrow, robin, song thrush, house martin, swallow, swift*

- *Several species of bat*

- *Other animals: badger, hedgehog, great crested newt.*

*Contact the local wildlife trust for further information: www.wildlifetrust.org.uk*

### Global problem; small-scale local solutions

*Modern house designs rarely offer opportunities for swifts and house martins. These can be given an opportunity by mounting nestboxes under eaves or on gable ends.*

5.21 Urban trees →

5.9 Sustainable drainage systems ←

6.9 The green network →

for more ideas see *Building Green* (Johnston and Newton n.d.)

## 5.19 WILDLIFE CAPACITY

Using the analogy of a body; the town-scale wildlife network of corridors, reservoirs, stepping stones and links provides the major arteries and organs of the urban wildlife habitat system. Missing are all the tissues, sinews and capillaries needed to make a viable entity. However comprehensive the wildlife network approach, most urban land will inevitablly fall outside all the identified areas. The biodiversity goal at the neighbourhood scale is to increase wildlife capacity on this unidentified land. The policy and tools needed for this are set out below as four mutually reinforcing measures.

At this scale, involving local people is paramount. Effective contact can be through local schools, wildlife networks, and other interest groups (see Allotments and orchards 5.11).

### NEIGHBOURHOOD BIODIVERSITY

### Measure 1  Increase wildlife capacity

Use planning and design to increase the wildlife capacity across the built environment. Aim for a very high level of biodiversity at the neighbourhood scale. This is not to say that the entire built environment must be cloaked in green, but to recognise that every development, whether renovation, enhancement or new build, has a part to play in replacing the biodiversity we have lost.

The capacity approach needs to encompass streets, commercial nodes, business parks, education facilities, health centres and all other features.

### Tools

- Plan for 10 large, native trees per ha in high-density areas, increasing to 25 in medium-density areas and 50 in low-density areas.
- Optimise elements of sustainable drainage systems for wildlife.
- Restore old hedgerows or plant new ones (even in urban areas).
- Provide green roofs and wall climbers.
- Provide bat boxes and bird boxes, garden ponds.

### Measure 2  Create threads

Use spatial framework planning to provide a wildlife network on a finer scale than the corridors of the town scale. This should comprise a fine and near continuous network of hedges, shrubs and small trees.

### Tools

- Locate, protect and enhance existing features (for example remnant countryside hedgerows).
- Consider providing hedgerows instead of fences as back garden boundaries.

- Look for opportunities for threads along boundaries to allotments and bordering open space.

### Measure 3  Local wildlife nodes

Design or improve the wildlife quality of local nodes in the urban fabric. Also remember that, in wildlife terms, two plus two equals five: the larger the habitat blocks the greater the biodiversity capacity.

### Tools

- Identify wildlife opportunities associated with urban design features, such as street corners and junctions, pocket parks, buffers, shelter belts, and sustainable drainage features.
- Combine resources: for example, combine balancing ponds from a number of developments, provide groups of large trees, use local parks.

### Measure 4  Bio-enhance greenspace

Use a comprehensive approach to both public and private greenspace, including the smallest of areas such as grass verges and private gardens. Include biodiversity requirements in the design and management of this resource.

### Tools

- Upgrade habitat – replacing some grass with native meadow or native shrubs/trees or relaxing moving regimes to encourage wildflowers.
- Use locally native shrubs and trees in landscape schemes.
- Provide residents with information about attracting wildlife to their gardens.

---

**Garden ponds, urban wasteland and allotments**

*Birmingham and the Black Country Biodiversity Action Plan (BAP)*

*This is a good example of how to include urban biodiversity in a local BAP.*

*Garden ponds, urban wasteland and allotments are the subject of habitat action plans in this BAP. The plan was prepared as a process involving a wide number of local stakeholders. The action plan recognises buildings and structures such as bridges and tunnels as valuable habitat. Species identified for protection and enhancement in the urban area are the song thrush, bats, black redstart and skylark.*

*The plan also introduced the role of different types of hard surface (permeable/tarmac) as a biodiversity concern.*

*Birmingham and the Black Country wildlife trust: www.bbcwildlife.org.uk/*

Figure 5.28
**An approach for increasing local biodiversity**

KEY
in addition to the townscape approach

Measure 1
increased capacity

Measure 2
threads

Measure 3
local node

Measure 4
enhanced greenspace

**Biodiversity**

*'biodiversity is ultimately lost or conserved at a local level'*

*'Local Biodiversity Action Plans should reflect the views, values and individual character of their area as well as the national priorities'*

(UK BIODIVERSITY STEERING GROUP 1995)

Advice on private gardens for wildlife

- RSPB: www.rspb.org
- The Centre for Wildlife Gardening: via: www.wildlondon.org.uk

*Nature conservation for developers*

*Developers should seek to optimise environmental opportunity by using this sequential approach.*

- *Identify and seek to enhance, or protect, important environmental features.*

- *Consider potential impacts on the environment of the development (direct, indirect and cumulative).*

- *Seek to improve the environment.*

- *Avoid adverse impacts, exploring all options, such as 'do nothing'.*

- *Mitigate any residual adverse impacts caused by development.*

- *As a last resort, always compensate for adverse impacts.*

SOURCE: RSPB 2000a

*Every development provides opportunities to create new habitat (Ekostaden, Sweden)*

SOURCE: JOHN DOLECEK

## 5.20 BIODIVERSITY AND THE DEVELOPMENT PROJECT

Developers, designers, planners and the community should ensure that a number of specific actions are carried out as part of every significant development project.

### 1   HABITAT AND SPECIES AUDIT

As part of the twin-track approach, advocated in Section 6.3, biodiversity survey work must be undertaken. A habitat and species audit will indicate the occurrence of species or habitats of national or local importance. Local Biodiversity Action Plans should be consulted as part of this process. In an urban area (often deficient in wildlife), local importance or non-native species assemblages may rank highly. There are standard methods for conducting surveys – a Phase 1 survey gives an assessment of the basic nature conservation interest. Local wildlife groups may already hold some of the data and can be contacted through the local wildlife trust. The audit should clearly identify neighbouring aspects of the town wildlife network.

### 2   SAFEGUARDING, CREATING AND ENHANCING HABITATS

Begin by surveying all opportunities to enhance local habitats and species. The RSPB have produced guidance on this matter for housing developments (see box). Developers can provide varied, distinctive and attractive housing whilst enhancing wildlife value through:

- retention of existing habitat;

- creation of new habitats; and

- appropriate management of all landscape areas.

The schematic layout of development projects should be influenced by these goals. Once a robust framework of habitats has been provided, simple measures such as providing bat/bird sites and using locally native species in landscape schemes will prove effective at further increasing 'capacity'.

### Making links and reversing habitat fragmentation

Linking habitats together both within the neighbourhood and to wildlife features surrounding the neighbourhood will strengthen the biodiversity value.

### Brownfield sites

Increasing pressure for development on brownfield sites must be balanced with their merits in respect of wildlife and nature conservation. In some circumstances, the species assemblages can be especially important for urban biodiversity (Shirley and Box 1998). Each site must be judged on its merits. Wildlife value does not necessarily preclude development on the whole site.

Undertaking a Neighbourhood appraisal would be a way of examining the environmental function of the site in context and in terms of human well-being (see Section 3.8).

## 3  BIODIVERSITY MANAGEMENT DURING CONSTRUCTION

Biodiversity can all too often be unwittingly damaged or destroyed during construction work. A plan for habitat asset protection during the construction phase should be developed by a Chartered Landscape Architect. A site manager with lead responsibility for habitat protection should be identified on all development sites. There is a need for training and education of contractors and sub-contractors.

Guidance for tree protection on development sites is given by BS 5837:1991 – Guide for trees in relation to construction. Many local authorities also provide guidance for contractors and developers on this and other aspects of habitat protection (a good example being Building biodiversity in Kent – a guide for clients, designers and contractors of building projects, available from Kent County Council).

## 4  SUSTAINABLE MANAGEMENT

All too often greenspace does not live up to its biodiversity capacity due to a failure to adopt sustainable greenspace management practices. Partnerships with local wildlife groups formed during the survey stage may provide a valuable links for developing a sensitive management approach.

### Key principles are:

- *Managing for people and biodiversity* – Local involvement in the management of wildlife at the neighbourhood can be seen as part of the 'closing the loops' philosophy of sustainable resource management. It is also the only way to influence the biodiversity value of private land such as back gardens. There are also direct health benefits for residents through activities and involvement in their neighbourhoods.

- *Choosing resource-efficient maintenance regimes* – Reductions in chemical inputs and labour are possible by working with natural processes. Plan for attractive swards of fine grasses with wildflowers, where possible avoiding the usual high pesticide/fertiliser/cutting turf types. Routinely use ground covers and mulches to keep weeds down instead of herbicides.

- *Recycling and closing loops* – Store and use grey water for landscape watering requirements. Chip or compost all arisings including autumn leaf fall for re-use.

**Nature conservation as urban regeneration**

*Neighbourhood Nature Programme Walsall, West Midlands*

*This is a nature conservation project that strengthens local communities whilst also improving local environments and biodiversity.*

*The project ran from 1993 to 1998 as part of an urban regeneration programme.*

*The project officer was guided by the local community and representatives of partner organisations. The project was promoted through a travelling exhibition, it included*

- *new woodland planting*

- *community-led activities/events*

- *free trees for private gardens*

- *wildlife monitoring by young people; and*

- *improving school grounds.*

*Further information can be found in Urban Forestry in Practice, available free from the National Urban Forestry Unit – www.nufu.org.uk*

*Mature tree successfully retained in difficult development circumstances by Islington Borough Council, London*

URBAN TREES

## 5.21

*Plenty of room but acute absence of trees at this nodal interchange in Kingston, London*

*Trees adding softness and seasonality to a local shopping area in Bedford*

Figure 5.29
**Tree species with berries and nuts for birds**

| Large trees | Small street trees and garden trees | |
| --- | --- | --- |
| Birch | | |
| Willow | Rowan | Elder |
| Oak | Bird cherry | Hazel |
| Ash | Yew | Holly |
| Beech | Hawthorn | Crab apple |

## 5.21 URBAN TREES

There is a national urban forestry movement with strong representation in many areas through community forests. A matrix of small woods and copses can and should be provided except in the densest urban centres. This 'urban forest' should be seen as an aid to preventative healthcare (NUFU 2000). There is also an urban design imperative for the use of trees: for outstanding specimen urban trees, for street trees, for avenues and for intimate groups of trees.

Trees in urban areas can provoke much passion and a great deal of NIMBYism. Apart from a few examples, such as new towns and the garden city movement, little strategic thought is given to the planning and planting of trees in neighbourhoods.

However, trees are an extremely important component for healthy neighbourhoods. They

- filter particulate from the air, including harmful PM10s – these fine particles are associated with mortality from cardiac and respiratory causes
- absorb pollutants such as ozone, nitrogen dioxide and sulphur dioxide – these gases can affect people with asthma and chronic lung disease
- absorb carbon dioxide and release oxygen
- give shade in the summer, from Sun Protection Factor (SPF) 6 or 10 for individual trees up to 100 in woodland – protection from the sun reduces incidence of skin cancer
- reduce stress levels (Ulrich 2000).

In terms of comfort and urban liveability, trees

- attenuate noise
- slow wind speed
- reduce the heat island effect and provide a milder climate.
- give character, soften hard urban form and provide landmarks
- provide habitats for birds and other wildlife
- add seasonal change and interest to streets
- can slow down urban water run-off after a storm, reducing likelihood of flooding.

In addition, trees

- increase property values.
- can provide energy, firewood and timber products.

Trees have been shown to promote health both symbolically and literally, bringing nature into neighbourhoods – and on such a grand scale. The problems associated with trees (root damage to structures, for example) can usually be traced to poor understanding of their needs, poor or no proper planning and poor maintenance. With proper attention to planning and management, trees are part of the solution to urban living.

## TREES IN THE SPATIAL FRAMEWORK

### Step 1 – Survey and research

▓ Using a participatory process, explore people's perceptions and views on trees.
▓ Are there important local trees or local associations with particular species?
▓ Is there professional support or local experience to draw on? (Contact the National Urban Forestry Unit, Tree Council or local Groundwork Trust.)
▓ Is there a local authority urban tree strategy?

### Step 2 – Plan tree cover as the spatial framework develops

We are used to urban areas that are denuded of trees. A local participatory process can help to generate support for a greater number and diversity of trees. There needs to be wide understanding of the range of roles that urban trees can play. It is necessary to plan deliberately for sites to accommodate the next generation of 'outstanding' urban trees. In a national survey of urban trees (DETR 1993) only 3 per cent of urban trees were recorded as providing an outstanding contribution to the visual amenity (often planes, oaks or pines). A participatory exercise such as Planning for Real can allow people to experiment with options and ideas for trees in an unthreatening way.

### Step 3 – Resolve technical issues and prepare management plan

Use professional services to liaise with stakeholders and design team members. Potential problems – such as vandalism, tree root ingress and safety – can be overcome by experienced design. For example, through early consultation, building foundation design was adapted to achieve a close physical proximity between building and trees in Milton Keynes.

### Step 4 – Plant, manage and monitor

Many planted trees die within the first 3 years of life. Newly planted trees require extra care during this time whilst they establish root systems. Involving local people can provide better results; for example, residents can help with

▓ tree planting; choose from a selected species list
▓ tree establishment; watering the street trees outside their home and reporting broken stakes/ties
▓ management of the small community woodlands in their neighbourhoods (for example, community woodlands in Reading)
▓ setting-up a tree warden scheme to encourage involvement (a scheme supported and run by the Tree Council)
▓ participatory events such as tree dressing or planting days, to encourage care and pride in local trees.

*Examples and guidance on preparing urban tree strategies can be found in* Urban Tree Strategies *(DoE 1994).*

*Trees can play a very significant role in good urban design*

- *Street trees to soften urban form.*
- *Back garden trees for seasonal interest.*
- *'Civic' trees to mark urban form.*
- *Amenity trees on open space and recreation areas.*
- *Trees along wildlife corridors.*
- *Trees in spaces where people congregate.*
- *Community orchards.*

**case study**

# 5.a

*The touchstone for this innovative project has been to 'close all ecocycles at the smallest appropriate scale'. Sponsored by both the local authority and the utilities, it represents a significant way forward in terms of resource reduction in the city.*

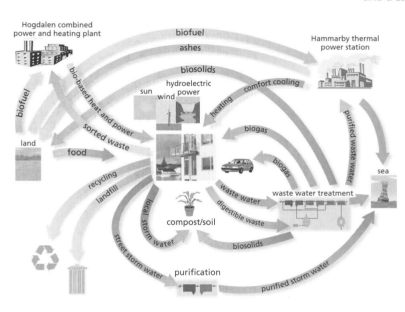

**Urban eco-cycling concept**

*This model for energy, waste and water management is known as the Hammarby model. It was developed jointly by Birka Energi, Stockholm Vatten and Skafab.*

# Hammarby Sjöstad

## STOCKHOLM, SWEDEN

### BACKGROUND

An integrated approach to resources underpins the design and planning of this new township in Stockholm, due to house 20,000 people.

The energy, water and waste utilities have worked together to formulate a new leading-edge set of proposals. The innovative and creative solutions have required new working methods with integrated collaboration between research interests, industry, national and local government organisations and environmental groups.

### RESOURCES

The environment is at the heart of the development concept. The aim is to halve the negative environmental impact, compared other modern developments. Although new technology and innovative design is seen as part of the solution, the commitment of the residents is also seen as essential. They will be provided with the ability to monitor their own energy and water consumption via the internal data network.

The three utilities leading the technical approach see it as in their companies' interests to be in the vanguard of providing the next generation of environmental-led solutions to urban resource needs. Led by a vision for a resource-efficient, environmentally planned district they aim at exploiting recycling technology and achieving the highest possible levels of recovery.

#### Energy

Demand is being reduced by district-wide efficiency in the choice of appliances and plant – lifts, fans, pumps, lights, etc. Technology will further reduce consumption: for example, lighting and ventilation are switched on only when someone enters the room.

District heating and cooling are to be provided. Energy will be generated from solar panels and heat pumps, boilers burning liquid biofuel, and combustible waste; pyrolysis is being reviewed. Residents will be able to opt for renewably generated electricity.

#### Water

The local water cycle has been integrated into the 'ecocycle' model. As such, Hammarby Sjöstad will have its own sewage treatment plant, where waste water will be treated, the heat will be recovered and any nutrients will be recycled using new technology to enable them to be returned to agricultural land.

Surface water will be cleaned locally and will not impose a load on the sewage treatment plant.

### Food

There will be provision for local food to be grown. Fertility will be improved by the use of locally produced composts.

### Waste

Household organic waste and sewage will be used to produce biogas. Residual solids can be used in agriculture: 80 per cent of nitrogen and phosphorus in waste will be returned to the ground as fertiliser. Two leading-edge technologies are being piloted – urine separation for nitrogen recovery and vacuum system waste collection.

### Biodiversity

The district will be linked to the natural environment by an 'Ecoduct': a 50m wide tree-adorned pathway that will be a conduit both for wildlife and for non-motorised movement.

## PROVIDING FOR LOCAL NEED

Municipal and commercial services will be implemented in phases. A primary school is due to open for the autumn 2001, followed by a nursery school one term later. A convenience store is expected to be ready to serve the residents at the start of 2001, and a health-care service with local facilities will be provided once the neighbourhood reaches approximately 5,000 residents.

A central library with meeting rooms is planned. There will be facilities in the larger neighbourhoods for holding meetings, throwing parties, local clubs and hobbies.

There will be low traffic volumes and speeds in residential areas. Information technology is being applied to minimise the need for transport within Hammarby Sjöstad. Public transport will take priority, with the new Tvärbanan tram service and a boat service into the city centre. A car pool is being established, and residents will be able to join this and request a car when they need one.

## URBAN DESIGN

Mixed use has been planned for within the concept based on the development of a number of neighbourhoods. There will be the development of local centres in addition to a core nucleus. Development will be based on a combination of densities from 4–6-storey inner city to more open 'outlying' layouts.

Proximity, accessibility and resident integration are important design considerations: for example, accommodation in central locations has been planned for senior citizens.

For further information see: www.stockholm.se

Mobilt sopsugsystem

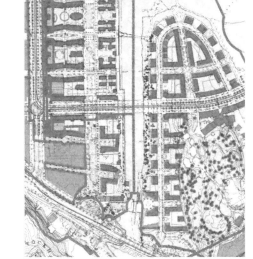

*Proposed vacuum waste collection system*

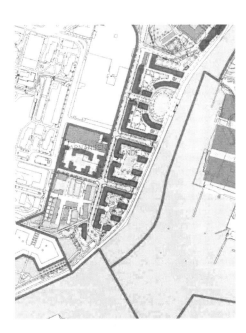

*Spatial plans for some of the neighbourhoods*

ASHTON GREEN

# 5.b

*The guiding principle is to create a quality built environment and a sustainable settlement for this urban extension.*

**Ashton Green masterplan detail**

SOURCE: EDAW LTD

*The masterplan developed by EDAW illustrates the following sustainable urban design principles:*

- *Gradation of densities from centre to periphery.*
- *Use of local public open-space nodes.*
- *Linear greenspace for movement and access.*

*For further information see: www.edaw.co.uk*

---

# Ashton Green

## LEICESTER

 Ashton Green comprises a major development to the north-west of the city. The 100 ha site will incorporate housing, workplaces, schools, open space and neighbourhood facilities. Leicester City Council, the planning authority and landowner, has developed a robust planning and design approach enabling the incorporation of a wide sustainability remit into the development.

## PROCESSES

The interesting aspect of this case study is the way in which the development process has been carefully designed so that the guiding principles of sustainability can be incorporated, refined and communicated at each stage of the development process. These 'Guiding Principles' have shaped the development of a series of design codes which then informed the spatial layout.

Community participation is being encouraged and will be carried through to the implementation and management phases.

## PROVIDING FOR LOCAL NEED

Local facilities are planned, including neighbourhood village greens, a market and local centre, and schools. Choice is a key goal in terms of the provision of routes for movement, with road layouts that reduce traffic speed being important in residential areas.

## RESOURCES

The guiding principle here is to minimise impact on the environment. The design codes set out minimum standards that will be expected from developers. Some examples are given below:

*Energy* – early involvement of a utility provider, targets set for energy efficiency.

*Water* – designed household consumption to be 30 per cent less than average.

*Food* – accessible allotment provision will be required.

*Waste* – provision for storage of separated waste in the kitchen.

*Biodiversity* – drainage features must be designed for nature conservation value.

## URBAN DESIGN

Urban design is being tightly controlled through the use of the spatial framework and design codes. It is seen as the key tool for delivery of several guiding principles. These include:

- creating a sense of place and identity.
- encompassing mixed-use development and a variety of densities and tenures.
- provision of quality open space.
- developing financial viability and market appeal.

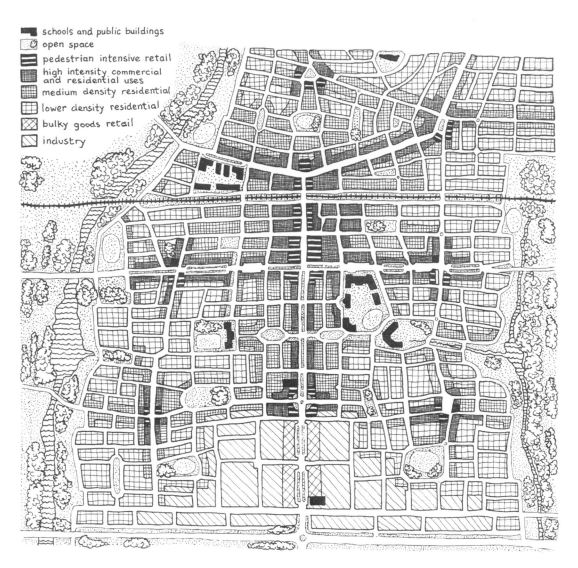

**Legend:**
- schools and public buildings
- open space
- pedestrian intensive retail
- high intensity commercial and residential uses
- medium density residential
- lower density residential
- bulky goods retail
- industry

Figure 6.1
**Township and neighbourhood structure**

*above: densities and land uses*
*right: bus services and local catchments*

BASED ON MORRIS AND KAUFMAN (1997)

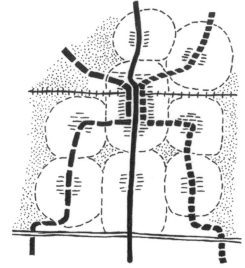

# neighbourhood design | chapter 6

## 6.1    INTRODUCTION

### SCOPE OF THE CHAPTER

This chapter provides an integrated picture of planning and design at the local level, picking up the threads from the earlier chapters. The approach is radical. It demands time and effort on the part of local authorities and developers, in responding to legitimate community, health and environmental priorities. At the same time, the guidance is pitched at a reasonably practical level. Once the essential principles and processes have been absorbed by the key local actors, and incorporated into statutory plans, then interpretation (if not implication) is straightforward and logical.

### THE GENERAL PATTERN

The plan opposite gives an idealised picture of local spatial policy. It is, effectively, a spatial framework for a township, showing one possible pattern of public transport nodes, local high streets, graded densities and pedestrian accessibility.

- For many reasons the **township** or the whole **small town** is the key scale for the provision of local services. It is large enough to offer a wide range of jobs and facilities and a fair degree of local autonomy, but small enough to be walked or cycled across and retain some sense of the locality. It also provides the interface between local people and residents or workers from other areas. The key organising principles are very important, and link back to the twin-track model in Chapter 1. The public transport network provides the rationale for residential and commercial patterns, while the watercourses and hills shape the greenspaces.

- **Neighbourhoods** are defined as the familiar, often named, localities with which people may closely identify. They are not separate functional entities but interlinked and interdependent, forming part of the urban continuum, and shaped by their relationship to the township or town as a whole.

- The **home-patch** is the street, block or enclave where people live. A successful home-patch is where residents perceive it as an extension of the home – a safe, friendly, attractive environment in which to play, move, idle, chat or debate the issues of the day if they choose to, or at least to provide a sense of security and pleasure immediately around the home.

# 6.2

# neighbourhood character

## OVERVIEW

Earlier chapters have dealt with neighbourhoods in terms of people, community, activities and environmental resources. The main themes of this section are aesthetic quality and the dynamics of change, both vital to understanding before we embark on the intentional planning of neighbourhoods. Section 6.2 assists with the analysis of aesthetic quality and local distinctiveness, 6.3 suggests policies for valuing and enhancing these qualities, while 6.4 deals with the evolutionary process of physical change, and policies for urban renewal.

## 6.2   LOCAL IDENTITY

### INTRODUCTION

Experience has shown that the design of the built environment alone cannot create a neighbourhood in the sense of a fully functioning community. However, good urban design – in other words, responsiveness to the existing context, compatible mix of uses, appropriate buildings to accommodate activities at the right rent, appropriate location and levels of accessibility, all brought together in a place which is attractive and feels safe – can create the conditions where a sense of neighbourliness and belonging is more likely to develop.

This section deals with *anchoring* and *structuring* the neighbourhood. It starts from the assumption that a major new scheme (regeneration or urban extension) is to be developed within the neighbourhood. Localities need to be 'anchored' to a place or community if they are to feel like 'neighbourhoods'. This can only develop over time. It is essential to utilise all the possible anchoring devices to generate a sense of continuity and rootedness, which gives a place character and local distinctiveness, reducing criticisms of anonymity and alienation often levelled at and experienced in so many developments.

### ANCHORING ELEMENTS IN THE EXISTING ENVIRONMENT

#### Involving the existing community

The more that the local community is involved in the design and development process of any major scheme affecting the neighbourhood, the greater likelihood there is of evolving a place that has local relevance, and where new proposals have a higher chance of acceptance through the approvals process. The process of involvement requires integrity and a continuing commitment by the design team, and inevitably points to different modes of working and communication. It is unlikely that everyone in the community will wish to be involved, but they will wish to be kept informed. If the design team can locate themselves physically within the local community (say in a vacant shop or apartment,

*Perceptions of neighbourhood*

*1   Mental maps*

*How do people define their neighbourhood? What are the key nodes, edges and centres of activity?*

*2   Access and safety*

*How safe does it feel to move about, for people of all ages and abilities?*

*3   Image*

*What images and associations do local people have of the neighbourhood; and why?*

*4   History*

*What features do people value as giving a sense of continuity with the past?*

which can be also used as a drop-in centre and meeting room), this will be of great value in creating dialogue and reducing suspicion about remote professionals.this will be of great value in creating dialogue and reducing suspicion about remote professionals.

### Re-use of existing buildings and structures

Existing redundant or vacant buildings in the scheme area are a positive resource that will lend character to the development as well as, in many cases, valuable accommodation at affordable prices or rents. Existing buildings and structures represent resources in three ways (sometimes all in the same building):

- **Cultural value**: for example, buildings of special architectural or historic interest ('listed' buildings or ancient monuments in the UK). These may be of national or local importance. More mundanely existing names (of streets, areas, fields, farms) may have local resonance and associations.
- **Locally distinctive buildings**. Their former use or function based on the local economy, and/or building materials deriving from the local geology both testify to a sense of local identity (vernacular buildings).
- **Spatial resource**. Buildings provide forms of accommodation which are likely to be more expensive to build and rent as new, especially small shop or business units. It is important to match the spatial characteristics of buildings to their proposed new use in order to reduce wasteful conversion (for example, converting a multi-cellular building to a single-cell space).

### Re-use of existing building materials or elements

If, after comprehensive appraisal of the existing buildings in the scheme area, it is proved that retention of some buildings would affect the viability of the scheme or that (exceptionally) a building is beyond repair, then the building could be dismantled carefully in order to re-use as much of the materials and other architectural features as possible. It is likely that in any building built prior to about 1920 the building materials are virtually irreplaceable as they may be 'natural' and may be from long-defunct local sources. Retention and incorporation of these into new buildings will help to reinforce local distinctiveness.

### Use of the existing land form

The main criticism of so much contemporary volume housing is that it ignores its context: that standard building forms are designed to a standard layout of roads and plots; that the resultant development is so placeless it could be anywhere.

If we want development to incorporate local distinctiveness it has to be designed as if the site really matters, so that the features, orientation, topography and location of the site have a major influence on the layout of the site and the character of the built form. This approach is of course consonant with the ecosystem view of settlements.

*Figure 6.2*
**19th century former Corn Exchange converted to a library**

*Sudbury, Suffolk*

*An excellent example of a new use matching the characteristics of the building, ie: central location,easily identifiable building, top lit main space. The new work to accommodate the library reflects good practice in conservation in that it does not pretend to be 'olde' and is largely removable.*

*Local distinctiveness*

*The organisation Common Ground has been exploring and developing the concept of local distinctiveness since the 1980s. Below is an extract from their website, outlining what they see as the four key elements of the concept:*

### 1  Detail

*We need the nourishment of detail, in things as ordinary as rumples in a field, detail in doors and windows, dialect, local festival days, seasonal variation in the goods on sale in the market, to subtly stimulate our senses and sensibilities.*

### 2  Authenticity

*The real and the genuine hold a strength of meaning for us.*

### 3  Particularity

*The point here is not to be preoccupied by difference, but by appropriateness to and expressiveness of time and place.*

### 4  Patina

*Age has to be recognised as having been gathered, hence the paradoxical vitality of patina. Local distinctiveness must be about history continuing through the present (not about the past) and it is about creating the future.*

*For further information contact Common Ground: www.commonground.org.uk*

## LOCAL DISTINCTIVENESS

Neighbourhoods in towns and cities are organic, transforming entities; they are the expression of the interaction of a number of social, economic and physical factors:

- The people (past and present) who lived and/or worked there.
- The types and pattern of activities (past and present) carried out.
- The type, size and value of the premises and their plots where people live, work and spend leisure.
- The location of the neighbourhood in relation to the centre of the urban area.
- The topography of the area.
- The age and style of the buildings.
- The distribution and type of greenspace and streets.
- The materials, whether homogeneous or diverse.
- The condition of the area.
- Ownership patterns.
- The townscape of the area: compact/enclosed/spacious, formal/informal, repetitious, hard-edged/soft-edged.

Whatever the neighbourhood characteristics, there is a sense of local identity perceived by the residents. Perhaps it is a well-established district or quarter, or it was built all at one time, or is characterised by being of a particular architectural style or by using a local building material. The neighbourhood might be physically distinct from its surroundings or just a part of the urban continuum.

## TYPES OF NEIGHBOURHOOD

Many established urban neighbourhoods are valued by their residents who wish to see that their qualities are maintained and protected against adverse development, traffic and environmental conditions. Conservation Areas provide this for certain areas but many neighbourhoods do not qualify. Below are some such typical neighbourhood categories:

- Residential villa suburbia: free-standing villas, detached or semi-detached, within relatively extensive plots and set back from the streets. Considerable vegetation (boundary hedges, trees, front gardens, etc). Usually wide, tree-lined roads.

- Terrace housing in inner suburbia: shallower but well-tended front gardens. Usually some form of grid street pattern with corner shops.

- Inner-city mainly residential area, often identified by a name. Established small-scale mixed uses – workshops and local shopping street, interspersed with terrace housing. Housing often more varied in size and age than the types above.

The next two pages illustrate the diversity of form, character and density within British settlements.

### Neighbourhood samples – character, form and density

*200 m by 200 m samples from a range of typical residential developments*

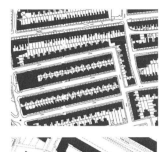

#### 90 dph 1900s terrace
*Long straight streets producing rectangular grid with shallow plots between. Narrow fronted (approx 4 m). Two-storey terraces with short rear extensions, very short front gardens (approx 1 m).*

#### 90 dph tenements
*Late nineteenth-century Scottish apartment blocks built from local red sandstone. Small one- and two-bedroom flats. The perimeter block layout surrounded courts or shared gardens. Buildings followed the regular grid of the street layout. Usually four to six storeys, types varied to suit a range of incomes.*

#### 80 dph 1970s estate
*Two-storey 'interlocking' wide frontage patio housing with informal south-west–south-east orientation. Pedestrian/vehicular separation. Mono pitch roofs. Six-storey two-person flats on north side raise the overall density.*

#### 75 dph mansions
*Mid-nineteenth-century London apartments for the prosperous. Large flats. Set back from pavement by about 3 m to allow light to semi basement floor. Often on irregular plots and usually ornate red-brick fronts.*

#### 65 dph 1950s estate flats
*Immediate post-war mixed development of eight- to eleven-storey slab blocks and four-storey terraced maisonettes informally and loosely enclosing landscaped squares. Informal road layout serving the blocks. Some retail and community uses at ground level.*

#### 50 dph Georgian square
*Georgian square. Formal square symmetrically approached by wide regular streets. Streets and square enclosed by four-storey terraces with basements. High rooms, vertically proportioned windows. Shallow rear areas with back alleys. Squares have landscaped central gardens.*

*(continued on next page)*

187

# 6.2

*200 m by 200 m samples from a range of typical residential developments*

### 45 dph 1900s terrace

*Two-storey terrace houses approx 5m wide with front bay windows and deep rear extension wings. Short front gardens (approx 2m), rear gardens of varying length due to converging street layout. Straight streets with angled corners approx 5.5m wide, parking both sides.*

### 40 dph 1990–2000 village

*Cranked street pattern with hierarchy of streets, squares and alleys with mews-style parking courts in interior of perimeter blocks. Mainly two-storey cottages in informal terraces with some three- to four-storey formal terraces and buildings. Traffic calmed by built form. Vernacular appearance.*

### 35 dph Traditional small town

*Typical small market town. Medieval street pattern centred on informal market place. Continuous frontages on the back edge of pavements. Two- to three-storey properties on narrow, long plots, shops on ground floor in the centre.*

### 35 dph 1980s estate

*Typical 1980s residential area. Individual housing estates planned either side of a distributor road with few links between. The road is designed to carry relatively fast-moving traffic. Therefore, the housing is turned inwards on a cul de sac. Most housing is two-storey, detached or linked by garages.*

### 30 dph 1930s estate

*Inter-war uniform density local authority estate. Radial road layout with wide symmetrical bisecting avenues. Semi-detached villas on relatively wide, deep plots set back approx 5–6 m from back edge of footpath. Hipped roofs. Parks, recreation grounds and shops were also provided.*

### 25 dph 1930s semi-detached

*Owner-occupied housing often developed around arterial roads and bypasses. Basic house plan was given a variety of stylistic features, such as half-timber, bay windows, 'moderne' front doors. Some short culs de sac.*

**Neighbourhood samples – character, form and density**

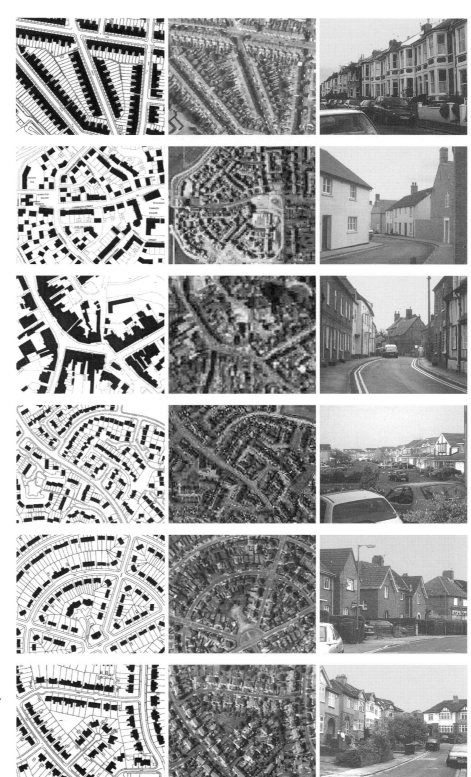

## 6.3 DEFINING AND REINFORCING NEIGHBOURHOOD QUALITIES

In order to define a neighbourhood and to identify those things that are of value, or indeed those which need replacement or improvement, it is necessary to employ various forms of appraisal.

The techniques require observation and also consultation. They require a significant input of time and human resources and therefore, as Local Authority resources in this area are severely restricted, it is likely that the only people who are willing and able to undertake those appraisals will be residents themselves (with some help and co-ordination by a facilitator trained in urban design). The act of carrying out the appraisals and importantly displaying the results and frame strategies for action usually helps in reinforcing neighbourhood identity and cohesiveness.

Appraisal is more than description: it's not just 'what is there?', but also 'why?'. It is also the estimation of the community's value of certain neighbourhood attributes:

- If we like corner shops, what are the threats to them? Are they changing, for better or worse?

- Is gentrification happening? Is it a good or bad thing?

- If the building materials are attractive/characteristic are they still available at reasonable cost?

### AREAS OF NEIGHBOURHOOD QUALITY

In order to reflect residents' concerns, in many neighbourhoods it is recommended that a new form of designation is introduced, which has a similar status to conservation areas. These Areas of Neighbourhood Quality would be defined by residents' own aesthetic judgements and community concerns and would not need to be distinguished by special (in other words outstanding or rare) historic or architectural merit.

### Designation

Designation would follow extensive neighbourhood involvement in appraising the local area to establish the qualities that are valued, the threats to those qualities and perceptions of the boundaries of the neighbourhood. The experience of parish mapping, village design statements and Conservation Area character appraisals would be valuable in forming these appraisals.

*Assessing neighbourhood quality*

*Parish mapping*

*A survey undertaken by the community in a parish to celebrate its locally distinctive character, history, culture and customs and its activities. Large-format maps often take the form of collages of detailed work contributed by individuals.*

*For further information, refer to Common Ground: www.commonground.org.uk*

*Village design statements (VDSs)*

*These are compiled with the aid of a local authority conservation officer or other facilitator. The aim is to set out the character of the local built environment and to establish guidelines for sensitive new development and alterations. VDSs can be adopted as Supplementary Planning Guidance.*

*For further information, refer to: Countryside Agency, publications ref. CCP 501 Parts I & II.*

*Conservation Area character appraisals*

*These reports should be compiled for every Conservation Area, setting out the rationale for the designation of the Conservation Area, its character and appearance, its mix of uses, its evolution, a critique of the issues facing the Area and a programme for improvements. It is undertaken by the Local Authority in consultation with the local community.*

*For further information, refer to English Heritage guidelines, English Historic Towns Forum Guidelines, Planning Policy Guidance Note No.15.*

2.8 Placecheck ←

*Placecheck*

*Using the Placecheck method is a good starting point for understanding a local area.*

*It consists of a checklist of 100 questions focusing on people, places and movement and the connections between these. For further information see Neighbourhood Checklist.*

*Figure 6.4*

**Illustrations of some of the notation symbols in Figure 6.3**

Transparency: *building users seen from street;*
Active frontage: *public entrance and human interest at street level*
*(A tailor's garment repair shop, Bristol)*

Connected/linked spaces: *new housing (foreground) connects to adjacent established area by exploiting the potential of a footpath (Friars Quay, Norwich)*

Terminated view: *building facing centre line of road 'stops' view and reinforces tight road junction*
*(Poundbury, Dorset)*

## AUDITING THE NEIGHBOURHOOD

Prior to intervening in the neighbourhood we should identify its character through an audit or appraisal (see below).

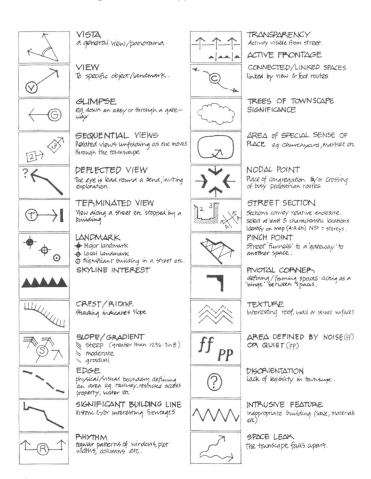

*Figure 6.3*

**Townscape and neighbourhood character appraisal notation**

*These notation symbols can be used to assist in evaluating the character of a neighbourhood. Two-person teams using a sufficiently detailed map of a locality (1:1000 or 1:1250, for example) draw the appropriate symbol on the map at the location where the feature (view, skyline, sound level, nodal point, etc.) occurs. The value of a two-person group is that the feature noted is evaluated and justified, and levels of observation are increased. The list of symbols should not be considered as exhaustive: if other features are identified, further symbols should be created.*

SOURCE: SYMBOLS DERIVED FROM GORDON CULLEN AND KEVIN LYNCH; ADAPTED AND ADDED BY RICHARD GUISE

**Measures, standards and policies**

The following modes of intervention are examples of those which might be appropriate within an Area of Neighbourhood Quality.

- Design code. This would establish patterns of plot sizes, building set-back distances, heights, boundary conditions, and so on. This would guide new development and alterations .
- Streetworks code: to inform utility agencies and highway authorities of standards on reinstatement, choice of materials, position and size of signage and street furniture.
- Community agreement, where necessary, on limits to permitted development whether through restrictive covenants or Article 4 directions (in the UK).
- Establishment of a residents' liaison group to work with officers and councillors of the Local Authority to ensure that measures are sensitively applied.

## USING DESIGN CODES

Design codes are a method of street making: that is, the creation of a coherent set of streetscapes which addresses the three elements comprising the holistic 'street' (the street itself, the buildings on either side, and the plots on which the buildings sit).

In developing new neighbourhoods, or extending or infilling existing ones, we can first determine the appropriate character for particular types of streetscapes and then, by a combination of learning from the best examples of historical precedent and including best practice based on present-day requirements, we can identify key dimensions which are likely to produce the type of streetscapes that fulfil our aims.

This may seem rather too mechanical, but it was the way in which many of our Georgian streetscapes were developed. This method is more specific in its prescriptions than the rather vague statements on street character found in many planning briefs, and yet it provides the framework or envelope within which design freedom can operate.

## 6.4  CHANGE AND RENEWAL

## NEIGHBOURHOODS AS DYNAMIC PLACES

Change is often seen locally as a threat, but neighbourhood evolution is inevitable as families and businesses grow and decline, migration alters the local balance, and the physical fabric ages and is progressively adapted to new needs. A healthy process of physical renewal is typified by

- ongoing maintenance of buildings and private open space
- minor extensions/adaptations of buildings to satisfy new needs
- modest use-changes when new compatible activities need space
- rehabilitation of outworn or outdated buildings
- redevelopment of individual or small groups of buildings
- infill development, and small-scale edge-of-town expansion.

*Controlling the critical elements*

*A design code can enhance local distinctiveness.*

- *Type and height of front of boundary hedge, railway or fence.*
- *Spacing and type of street trees and lights.*
- *Are semi basements or attic storeys (with dormers) required?*
- *Placement of any extensions or projections in front of the main building line.*

*A finer grain of local distinctiveness can be encoded in the building details:*

- *Frequency and location where gables face the street.*
- *Importance of providing a gable end oriel window.*
- *Porches and/or verandas or other modelling elements.*
- *Range of building materials.*
- *Proportion of windows*

*Figure 6.4 (cont.)*
**Illustrations of some of the notation symbols in Figure 6.3**

*Significant building line: gentle street curvature followed by new buildings
(Dutch Quarter, Colchester)*

*Design codes are an important element in masterplanning: for further information see the Neighbourhood Planning Process, Masterplanning, The importance of place making 3.11.*

3.11 Importance of place making ←

Subject to appropriate safeguards this process of gradual renewal should be welcomed. Indeed, the absence of such ongoing investment would be a serious concern. Low-key but regular monitoring of renewal processes, area by area, can give early warning of potential problems – either of decline and under-investment or of overheating and an excessive rate of change – which might exacerbate social exclusion and/or threaten aesthetic quality.

Local residents' groups, councillors and local planners should keep a watching brief on the process of gradual neighbourhood renewal.

### Symptoms of malaise

Social and economic pressures can slowly transform neighbourhoods physically in ways that compromise valued character:

- The pattern of buildings on their plots is changing: for example, infilling between buildings, creating terraces as villas become linked. Redevelopment of plots by bigger and/or taller buildings often with change of use (residential to commercial).

- Loss of trees, green verges, allotments: by householders or local councils due to simplifying maintenance or changing lifestyles.

- Environmental erosion through increased through traffic and excessive on-street car-parking or the conversion of front gardens to hardstandings and consequent removal of front boundary walls or hedges.

- Excessive alterations, replacement recladding or addition to front elevations of houses. This may be recognised as giving vitality to a street scene or as a threat to the original quality of the housing.

- Decline or loss of local facilities – libraries, surgeries, community hall, pub, primary schools, post office, and so on.

- Declining level of maintenance of street and pavement surfaces, choice of street furniture, etc.

> ### RENEWAL STRATEGIES
> Every neighbourhood (or part of a neighbourhood if appropriate) should have an identified strategy for renewal, reflecting in particular physical, social and economic characteristics. The strategy can range from containment to regeneration.

1 **Observe:** where it is evident that there is steady, on-going investment in the area, with a healthy process of gradual renewal, no special policy is needed except for a watchful eye to avoid destabilisation.

2 **Contain:** in some areas, a very active land market may be forcing physical and social change in such a way as to threaten vulnerable groups or valued environments. This may

*Figure 6.5*
**The dynamics of urban renewal**

*The object of policy should be to support ongoing gradual regeneration processes, spotting problems and taking action before the problems become severe*

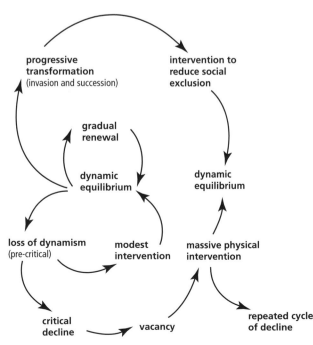

| Renewal process | Aesthetic quality | Density | Land use |
|---|---|---|---|
| **1 Observe**<br>Keep a watching brief on healthy processes of gradual renewal | **1 Observe**<br>Adopt a consciously laissez-faire aesthetic stance to encourage local taste and diversity | **1 Maintain**<br>Deter intensification (e.g. in areas where current density levels match the accessibility status) | **1 Stabilise**<br>Attempt to maintain the current mix of activities in well-established neighbourhoods |
| **2 Contain**<br>Protect vulnerable areas/groups from an over-enthusiastic market | **2 Conserve**<br>Enhance the existing neighbourhood quality, protecting and reinforcing local distinctiveness | **2 Gradually intensify**<br>Encourage gradual and progressive intensification where high accessibility status warrants it | **2 Permit change**<br>Allow uses to evolve in response to market pressures, encouraging adaptable building units and land use with minimal change |
| **3 Foster**<br>Revive a flagging but not 'critical' local economy with judicious public investment and low-key partnerships that avoid 'labelling' | **3 Enliven**<br>Promote contrast and require higher standards in areas of tawdry or tedious character | **3 Greatly intensify**<br>Radically increase densities (where public transport potential and the market will allow) to retrofit sustainability in low-density suburbs | **3 Guide change**<br>Guide market pressures by criteria-based policies and clear spatial frameworks |
| **4 Revitalise**<br>Regenerate (and maybe transform) with a major integrated regeneration programme | **4 Promote coherence**<br>Require conformity to strict design codes to link up and coalesce a disjointed, disparate townscape | **4 Reduce**<br>Gradually decrease densities and create open spaces in overcrowded zones, isolated urban enclaves, or greenspace priority areas | **4 Initiate change**<br>Promote significant change through partnerships and development briefs and masterplans in areas of major growth or obsolescence |

occur, for example, in conservation areas, or in edge-of-centre areas where low-rent zones are being invaded by high rent commercial activity. Containment implies restrictions on land use change and redevelopment.

3   **Foster**: in other areas, the problem could be one of gradual but progressive decline, with inadequate levels of maintenance and renewal. Recognising these 'pre-critical' areas in time to take modest action to trigger a turn-around may avoid the need for drastic (and expensive) state action later. Intervention may take the form of policy change (freeing the market), and public/private/voluntary sector co-operation where the purpose is seen as 'enhancing quality' rather than 'rescue' (which risks prematurely labelling the area as a failure). Judicious new investment stemming from such a partnership can help revive confidence.

4   **Revitalise**: 'critical' areas are typified by little or no reinvestment and increasing levels of vacancy, often associated with trapped populations, declining service levels and/or failing industries. Government regeneration programmes are generally targeted at these areas. The keys to success are
- effective partnerships between public, private, voluntary and local community sectors
- dynamic leadership (from any sector) and clarity of purpose
- public investment designed to trigger private/voluntary sector activity
- recognition of the needs of local people; and
- recognition of the needs for (sometimes dramatic) social and economic restructuring.

*Figure 6.6*
**Dimensions of renewal strategy**

*The renewal strategy needs to be complemented by clear policies for aesthetic quality (see previous section), density and land use (see next sections) – together making a coherent package. Note: The chart does not necessarily read horizontally*

**3.11 Taking action: masterplanning** ←

*Masterplans and development briefs have a major role to play in revitalisation*

**4a Case study Crown Street** ←

# 6.5

## Why mixed uses?

*It is generally recognised that mixed uses will*

- *reinforce the viability of centres with overlapping uses, providing multiple reasons for people to go and stay in the centre*

- *allow people to make short walking trips between facilities rather than relying on longer car-based trips*

- *create vitality and character in a place; and*

- *provide the opportunity for individuals to live and work in close proximity.*

# key structuring elements

key structuring elements

## 6.5   MIXED USES

The move towards fostering mixed-use development has become all pervading in recent urban planning policy. It is perceived as a method of reintegrating urban areas often sterilised by over half a century of zoning policies. These policies have resulted in monoculture areas generating concentrated periods of interzone traffic movement and 'dead' periods where a zone is bereft of any activity (for example, shopping centres and industrial areas 'after hours', or residential estates during weekdays).

**The need for guidance**

Whilst it is recognised that mixed uses are beneficial there is little guidance available on what constitutes appropriate mixed uses, the scale of mixed use, location and visibility of mixed uses, or critical mass of supporting population. The focus of discussion below relates these issues to retail, commercial, leisure, social and cultural activities.

*Figure 6.7*
*Mixed use considerations*

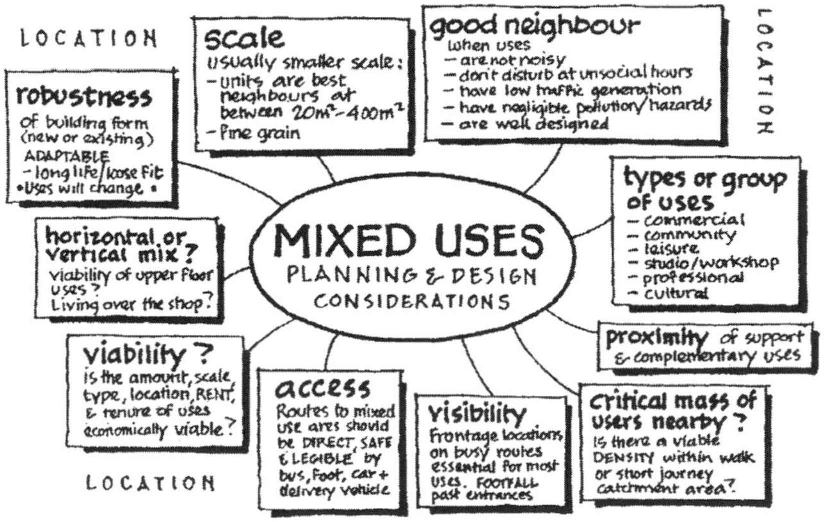

## Mixed-use advocates

*The benefits of mixed uses were advocated decades ago (for example, Jacobs 1960) but have only been absorbed into the thrust of UK policy in the last few years. Recent examples are: Francis Tibbalds/Urban Design Group 1990; PPG1 1997; DETR 1999i; Urban Task Force Report 1999; Urban White Paper DETR 2000c.*

## LOCATION OF USES

Uses have to generate vitality and thus warehousing or any low-population, large-scale and dead frontage use is unlikely to be appropriate within a mixed use area. However, small businesses, specialist shops, professional offices and restaurants are mutually supportive, with a high incidence of entrances and visibility through windows ('transparency'). Groupings of same uses reinforce trade: estate agencies, restaurants, shops, for example.

A limited number of quite specific uses can thrive on first floors (hairdressers, photographers' studios, legal practices, and so on) if they are on a busy street and their presence is obvious at ground-floor level.

Manufacturing or non-retail services can coexist if they are small scale, they have some element of transparency and do not interrupt retail frontages. Generally a large range of uses can be appropriate to coexist together if they are

- neighbourly in that they do not generate noise, fumes, vibration, undue traffic, or operate at anti-social hours
- smaller scale – say between 15 m$^2$ and 500 m$^2$.

### Visibility of commercial and social uses

Commercial and social/cultural uses often thrive on a high level of footfall past their front doors and visibility from main routes. Therefore, whilst it might be considered wise to locate mixed uses in the centre of a neighbourhood area, it may mean that these uses are only apparent to a relatively small number of people. However, if the mixed uses are located on the edge of a neighbourhood, on a main route and adjacent to another neighbourhood, the area is likely to attract a higher level of footfall and visibility. This may seem obvious but the lesson still has to be learned in quite recent developments with failing mixed use or retail areas.

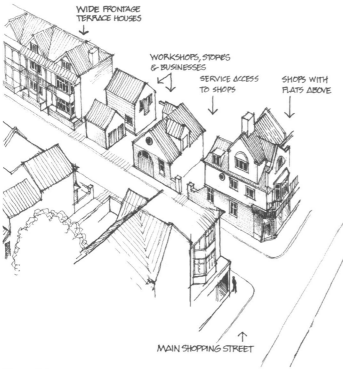

Figure 6.8
**Medium-density mixed use c.1910**

A side street off a neighbourhood high street
(still thriving), Henleaze, Bristol

*Whilst it might seem appropriate and convenient to locate the mixed use area in the centre of a neighbourhood ...*

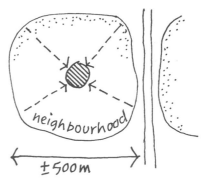

*... it may be advisable to locate it at a more visible nodal point to attract more users ...*

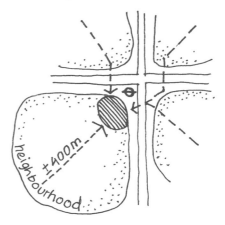

*... or even better to acknowledge and design for the fuzzy reality of neighbourhoods*

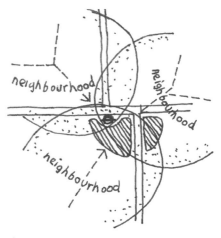

Figure 6.9
**Location of mixed use areas and neighbourhood form**

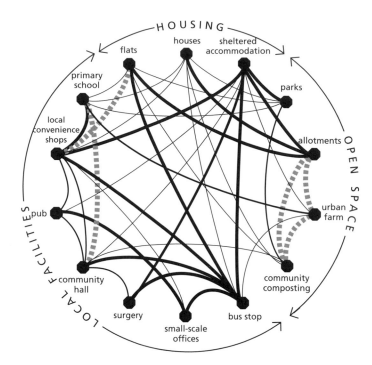

Figure 6.10
**Connectivity between local facilities**

CONNECTIVITY BETWEEN LOCAL ACTIVITIES

▪▪▪ potential dual use or combined use of space
▬▬ important 200 metres close pedestrian connections
── important 400 metres connections
── other desirable 400m metres connections

Figure 6.11
**Siting a new facility**

*This diagram, drawn from Fig. 6.10, could be used for consultation with interested parties, and subsequently for a site search and comparison*

## CRITICAL MASS

Different uses will have different catchments of users who are likely to bring their custom, given the use is visible, accessible and conveniently located. Each use requires sufficient density of population within the visibility/location/convenience criteria. Thus there are critical supporting populations for health centres, libraries, restaurants, florists, takeaways, launderette and primary schools (see Chapter 4, Sections 4.8–4.12 for use by use analysis).

As a very rough guide it is possible to have a population of 8,000–10,000 people within 400–500 m of a high street centre at an average density of 50 dwellings per hectare. This would allow not only for a resident population who would support many different uses but a wide variety of tenure-income groups adding to the diversity of uses.

It is unrealistic to expect a true diversity of mixed uses where the host population within walking distance is below, say, 5,000.

### Time to take root

It is unlikely that a mixed-use area will be functioning fully at the commencement of a new development. This does not mean that the area will be unsuccessful in 5 years' time. A 'habit of use' must be established and also it may take some time before the critical population is fully in place.

Thus it may be wise to develop some buildings which are adaptable to a variety of small-scale mixed uses but which have ground floors devoted to residential use at the outset (see Figure 6.37).

 ## CLUSTERING

Wherever possible it is desirable to group uses close to each other to achieve intensity of access, convenience and a sense of busy-ness. Clustering of uses at nodal points – intersections of routes, bus stops or shared car parks will have economic benefits. Thus convenience shops near schools, health centres and libraries will prompt visits to any of these (see A compact neighbourhood centre 6.16). Avoid 'out of sight, out of mind'. A common car park serving a supermarket (day time) with a cinema at first floor (night time) is excellent use of time management and dual use. Conversely, there are many examples of retail parks where every retail box has its own carpark requiring wasteful micro-journeys between carparks.

### Siting a new facility

In the context of clustered uses, new facilities should be carefully located to maximise accessibility to linked activities. Figure 6.11 illustrates the use of accessibility criteria to assist site search and consultations.

## 6.6  THE LOCAL HIGH STREET

The linear concentration of varied retail, social, cultural and commercial activities, plus flats and town houses, along local 'high streets' offers a way of giving coherence and flexibility to mixed-use neighbourhoods. It also ties in with the twin-track approach to town and township structure (see 6.12). Note that the high street will often be along the edge of a neighbourhood, not through the middle.*

### ADVANTAGES OF HIGH STREETS

High streets can provide varied benefits by comparison with compact centres

▦ Better access from homes to local facilities

▦ Flexibility of hinterland size for facilities

▦ Flexibility of hinterland size over time as needs change

▦ Opportunity for maximising 'footfall' and business viability

▦ A wide range of property values, permitting marginal users frontage positions

▦ A clear source of local identity and sense of place

▦ A linear, mixed-use focus for possible district heating mains.

**Policy**

Existing high streets should be maintained/ rejuvenated, and in new areas the potential for progressive development of a new high street, acting as the social focus of the community, can be planned from the outset. Keys to success:

▦ High levels of potential demand very close – i.e. the encouragement of high densities close to the high street, in line with strategies outlined in Section 6.8.

▦ A flexible approach to change of use and rebuilding along the high street, combined with insistence on a high-quality pedestrian environment.

▦ Maximum connectivity of the high street to adjacent areas by foot, pedal, bus and car.

### VARIATIONS IN ACTIVITY, INTENSITY AND VALUE

The traditional high street provides a useful model we can learn from. It typically provides the main social meeting places between residential neighbourhoods, the place for exchange of goods and services, but also where the locality meets the town and city – and the place that can give a sense of identity to the locality. The high

*The text of this section is adapted from Barton, Davis and Guise 1995.*

*Advocacy for local high streets*

- *The plan for Hook new town (GLC 1965)*

- *Sustainable Settlements (Barton et al. 1995)*

- *Sustainable Communities (Barton et al. 2000: pp.132–7)*

*Figure 6.12*
**Nodal point in high street**

SOURCE: BARTON, DAVIS AND GUISE 1995

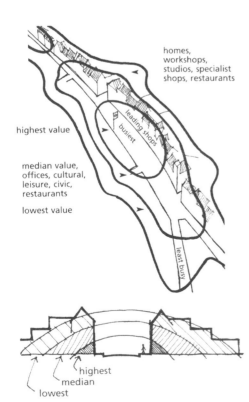

*Figure 6.13*
**Typical high street values/use contours**

SOURCE: BARTON, DAVIS AND GUISE 1995

street is a series of interlinked activity generators – bus stops, supermarkets, community/religious buildings, cafés, shops and small-scale offices. It is not uniform in use or level of activity, nor in property values. There are prime, secondary and tertiary locations, with the latter providing a habitat for more marginal users – the low-key (often charitable) office, the garage workshop, recycling shops. Housing can fill the gaps between other uses, on upper floors and in the rear of plots with courtyard arrangements.

## Variations in shape and form

In form, older high streets are rarely geometrically straight, but slightly irregular, changing direction gradually and opening out to places of congregation, typically former market places. This more organic form takes cues from the topography to give shelter and can take advantage of sunny settings for central locations.

## Vertical mixed use: living over the shop

More high streets are between three and five storeys high – at the limits of walk-up access. Living over the shop (LOTS) schemes – notably in Norwich, Ipswich, Cambridge and Stamford – show that users can be encouraged to settle in upper floors, to their advantage and to that of the centre as a whole. If living over the shop is considered at the design stage and in consultation with possible tenants, then the resistance of conventional developers/funding bodies and insurers should be overcome. Key issues are
- access to apartments (normally best from the frontage)
- car parking (reduced levels possible if public transport is good)
- noise (with respect to pubs/clubs/take-aways).

## Adaptability

The high street is an organic structure which can absorb a considerable degree of adaptation over time: some areas improving, others declining, some being renewed. The plots have surprisingly remained intact whilst the buildings on them have often been altered or rebuilt a number of times. The greatest threat to plots has been the comprehensive development area and the associated land assembly often involving blighted plots followed by large development sites which have often proved to be less adaptable to changing economic climates than the smaller plot.

## TRAFFIC TAMED BUT NOT FORBIDDEN

The drawback of the traditional high street has been its success. The combination of transport functions can range from street parking and bulk deliveries to main distributor road and public transport route. But in the same space cyclists and pedestrians want safe and convenient environments. The street acts as a series of casual meeting places, where the interests of conviviality should (but rarely do) take precedence. Pedestrianisation – even where feasible – is not necessarily the answer. The essence of the high street is that at times it is bustling with activity, the focus for residential areas that are placid by comparison. Vehicles contribute to that sense of bustle, provide access (thus supporting local services) and assist the natural policing of the street after hours. Therefore

- Only exclude traffic where pedestrian activity is high and street space at a premium

- Widen pavements at important pedestrian nodes along the street

- Allow parking where possible

- Provide safe crossings at the places convenient to pedestrians

- Traffic calmed to 20 mph through retail/social zones.

If feasible reduce traffic levels to 600 pcu per hour each way (this is the standard suggested by Buchanan in 1963 to allow easy road crossing and the ability to converse at normal volumes).

## 6.7 SPACE AND ENERGY-SHARING

### SYMBIOSIS
Social opportunity and viability can be helped by the shared use of facilities. But clear lines of management responsibility and accountability are essential, with the legitimate needs of the partners recognised.

Connections between uses can be generated and implemented though using collaborative processes to solve common problems or achieve common objectives. A meeting of the 'providers' in the community –church, youth clubs, sports facilities, school, health centre, for example – would prove a fruitful starting place. Some of the 'Healthy Living Centre' initiatives represent a good example of this approach in action.

- **Healthy Living Centre**
  The health centre can become a focus for community life, promote health and social inclusion, by forming a cluster with compatible social activities, sharing key facilities. The partnerships forged in the process of forming and managing the clusters can help build neighbourhood capacity and social capital.

- **Community pubs**
  The pub in an isolated settlement can be the common base for post office and banking services, a consumer food co-op, a function room cum village hall and recycling facilities, as well as providing food and drink.

- **Community schools**
  Secondary schools can act as the focus of community life with shared use of recreational facilities, library and hall, together with adult education out of school hours.

- **Food parks**
  In higher-density areas where gardens are small or non-existent, allotment provision could occur in the context of attractive 'food parks', with the opportunity for community composting, leisure plots and wildlife den, plus adjacent gardening/café facilities.

- **Sewage gardens**
  Local reed-bed sewage schemes, alongside SuDS (Sustainable Drainage Schemes) can offer the opportunity for community gardens, and wildlife habitats, based around water features.

*5.9 Sustainable drainage systems*
←

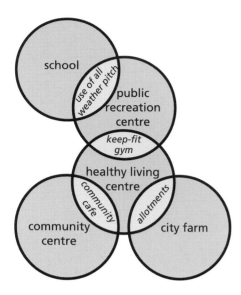

*Figure 6.14*
**Clustering of facilities allows shared use and pooling of resources**

*Figure 6.15*
**CHP plant in relation to linear concentration of heat demand**

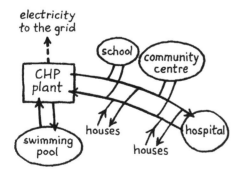

3.2 Collaborative communities ←

4.12 Supporting community health ←

4.11 Schools ←

5.11 Local food ←

5.5 Local generation and fuel sources ←

## MIXED USE AND COMMUNITY ENERGY

A mixed land-use pattern can be important for the viability of community heating schemes linked to combined heat and power (CHP). If CHP is to be a current or future energy option then the spatial organisation of activities needs to take account of the compatibility of users in terms of diurnal activity, and the base heat load that is implied. New major developments should be seen as an opportunity to initiate CHP discussions between potential local consumers.

**Partnership**
Early negotiation between developers, other potential users, the energy supply industry and the local authority are essential if the benefits of CHP are to be realised (see Chapter 5)

**Mixed use**
A general pattern of mixed use is desirable in order to even out peaks and troughs of demand. A school or factory, for example, with mainly daytime needs, is balanced with housing and a leisure centre with heavier evening demand.

**Major 24-hour consumers**
Large-scale all-day users such as hospitals or certain kinds of industry can provide the initial impetus for installing a CHP plant. Other major users then provide the rationale (and finance) for heat main connection across a neighbourhood so that smaller consumers en route can get connected.

**Linear development**
Concentration of development along a high street or similar public transport corridor, with a variety of commercial, retail and residential development along its length, is likely to smooth out demand fluctuations and reduce heat main lengths.

**Density**
Residential density is less significant a factor than the location of key users. Nevertheless, installation and embodied energy costs increase as density decreases. Any particular density figure is subject to the vagaries of fuel costs, discount rates and CH attachment rates. A minimum heat lead of 20 MWK m$^2$ has been suggested indicating a threshold residential density of 44 dph, or about 100 pph (DoE 1992).

**Heat main reservations**
The direct cost of installing heat main can be more than ten times higher along existing urban streets than for greenfield development. Indirect costs of disruption are also significant. It is therefore important in new development to anticipate possible heat main routes and allocate adequate space in common service channels or along grass verges. Development briefs can specify.

## 6.8 GRADED DENSITIES

### BASIC PRINCIPLE

The planning of density is a key part of sustainable neighbourhood strategies. In the context of mixed land use, density policy relates not only to housing but to all other urban activities as well. Levels of 'use intensity' should vary in relation to the level of public transport accessibility and closeness at prime pedestrian focuses, grading from high-intensity uses near local high streets and bus stops, to low intensity near open country, open-space wedges or major roads. The overall average density should be higher than the current suburban average. Linear bands of higher intensity are complemented by green corridors.

### Reasons

- To minimise average trip lengths and maximise the level of accessibility.

- To bulwark the viability of local shops, services and public transport.

- To permit diversity of density and character in every neighbourhood, and thus encourage diversity of household types.

- To facilitate creation of the open space network and of pedestrian access to open country.

- To facilitate an energy strategy by the distribution of main heat users and of space potential for renewables.

### MEASURES OF USE INTENSITY

Use intensity is related to people and activities rather than buildings. It can be measured in terms of resident population per hectare, workers per hectare, or visitors/clients/shoppers per hectare, also in terms of flows of pedestrians ('footfall' in retail centres) or traffic. It is the level of use intensity, combined with sensitivity to specific needs, that should ideally determine appropriate location.

However, in practice it is normally easier to use building density as a proxy – at least in residential areas.

### Different ways of calculating residential density

Residential density is usually expressed as dwellings per hectare (dph). Density can be either net or gross.

- **Net density** is the immediate housing environment (buildings, plots, access streets and playspaces). The assumption behind 'dwellings per hectare', unless specifically stated otherwise, tends to be net density.

*1 ha block*
*50 dwellings i.e. 115 people @ 2.3 persons per dwelling*

*400 m x 400 m grid*
*= 800 dwellings*
*= 1,840 people*
*(staggered junctions aid traffic calming)*

*Graded density*
*averaging 50 dph allows a wide range of choice.*

*The neighbourhood*
*3,200 dwellings*
*7,360 pop.*
*Everyone within approx. 400 m of shops.*

*This population at this density can support a school, shops and other community uses*

Figure 6.16
**Block, grid and neighbourhood**
*(diagramatic only)*

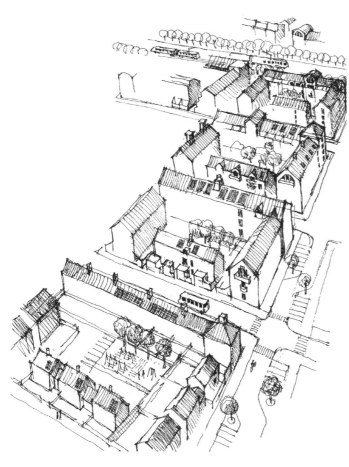

*Figure 6.17*
**Graded densities**

*Four storeys close to the main boulevard with shops and trams, two storeys and more gardens space further away. Average density c.55 dph. Note the solar collectors.*

*For further discussion of ways of calculating density see DETR 1998f*

■ **Gross density** includes the schools, distributor roads, parks, playing fields and community facilities as well as housing. It can be used to refer to the average density of a whole neighbourhood or town.

**Dwellings per hectare** can be a misleading measure because of the variation in dwelling size between, say, an area of small flats and one of large houses. However, it is widely used by planning authorities because housing need is calculated in terms of households and dwellings.

**Bedrooms per hectare** is a more accurate reflection of the residential environment, but does not necessarily reflect population levels. Many three-bedroom houses are occupied by one person.

## AVERAGE DENSITY

Average net housing density for greenfield development is currently about 30–35 dph or 70–80 people per hectare (pph), though this varies from place to place. On brownfield sites the density is often much higher. It is desirable that all areas achieve an 'urban' level of density, at least 40 dhp (90–100 pph). With falling household size, a target of 50 dph average may be reasonable – so long as it is really treated as an average, and the wide variety of needs/markets is catered for.

Beyond 60 or 70 dph, studies suggest land savings are not very great because the landtake of other uses such as schools and parks goes up in proportion to population. Exceptions might be town/city centres and inner London, where high land values justify the more complex infrastructure costs.

## RAISING RESIDENTIAL DENSITIES

Forty-five dph is the maximum a wholly two-storey dwelling environment can reach. This density means virtually total terrace housing at 5–6 m frontages with most gardens at 80–100 m2. Car parking is at a rate of 1–1.2 per dwelling, sometimes with integral garage and designed bays in the street. Gardens are about 60–70 m at rear with approximately 1.5–2 m front garden with a regular grid.

At 50 dph the same basic arrangement exists although there are likely to be some three-storey corner blocks with flats above. The home-patch street and the perimeter block shown in Figure 6.34 illustrate an approach to designing at this density. Car parking is usually no more than about 1 per dwelling. This can be accommodated in integral garages in three-storey town houses or in on-street bays.

Between 55 and 65 dph, terrace housing is narrow frontage (maximum 5 m) and organised on a strict grid pattern. Maisonettes and flats will be included in four-storey blocks. Parking will be much the same as 50 dph but might include some basement or edge of development parking provision.

## VARYING USE INTENSITY

The variations of land-use intensity may be formalised in the township/town spatial framework. In some neighbourhoods it may be practical to have the full range from high to low intensity, offering more choice and diversity. Five levels of intensity ranging form town centre situations to open space are suggested below. At each level there is a mix of use.

### Application

This is a highly stylised breakdown. Section 6.13 illustrates its application to an existing urban township. Intensity zones cannot be applied in a mechanical way; they need to respond to local conditions and reflect the need for a varied and interesting aesthetic environment as well as a convenient, resource-efficient one.

### 6.9    THE GREEN NETWORK

 The green network or greenspace system is the essential backcloth to urban life, helping to maintain the neighbourhood ecosystem in equilibrium. The value of green spaces is greatly enhanced if they are interlinked. Long-term planning and management policies can be incorporated in a Community Strategy (or equivalent) so as to

- increase the level of provision in areas of open-space deficit and progressively establish corridors and pathways between existing green spaces

- identify specific parameters of the various functions to be fulfilled by the greenspace system and maximise potential synergy between functions

- integrate nature into the neighbourhood, including places where people can experience the natural in their everyday lives

- review the long-term management implications so as to minimise possible conflicts between functions and users establishing partnerships and formal agreements where necessary.

### THE GREEN NETWORK IN NEIGHBOURHOOD LIFE

Do not leave the green network and its functions to chance but form partnerships to positively design its location, configuration and nature to perform the following vital functions.

### Quality of life

- **Public health:** trees and greenery promote better public health. They can reduce stress measurably and also aid recovery and recuperation. Woodland can filter pollutants and so

| 1 | |
|---|---|
| *Town centre activities – (A and B centres)* | *high-density flats, offices of various sizes, superstores, comparison retailers, cinemas, library, colleges, hospital, etc.* |
| **2** | |
| *Local high streets – along public transport routes* | *flats and town houses (3/4 storey), local shops and small offices (<200 m²) pubs, cafés, community facilities* |
| **3** | |
| *inner accessible zone – close to public transport services and local high streets* | *mainly terraced housing, workshops and schools, playgrounds, small parks and allotments* |
| **4** | |
| *outer accessible zone* | *mainly semi-detached housing, low-intensity industry/warehousing, schools, parks and allotments* |
| **5** | |
| *greenspace system* | *parkland and playing fields, small-holdings and neighbourhood farms, woodland, ridges, rivers* |

*Figure 6.18*
**Five levels of intensity**

**key structuring elements**

# 6.9

*The green network includes:*
*existing or proposed designed space,*
*permanently vegetated, and semi-natural and*
*natural features. There may or not be public*
*access; the spaces in the network may or may*
*not be contiguous.*

*For example: hill crests, slopes too steep for*
*development, hedgerows, watercourses and*
*their margins, fields, greensward, avenues,*
*shelterbeds, gardens and allotments, woods*
*and parks.*

### Access to greenspace

*All homes should be within 400 m actual*
*distance of a greenspace, and 800 m maximum*
*of a space on the green network, giving access*
*to round walks.*

> 4.13 Recreational
> open space ←

> 4.12 Supporting
> community health
> ←

> 5.21 Urban trees
> ←

> 4.14 Movement:
> Basic principles ←

> 4.13 Layout and
> landscape ←

> 5.20 Increasing
> wildlife capacity ←

> 5.9 Sustainable
> drainage systems
> ←

provide cleaner air; trees shade us from damaging UV radiation and give us spaces for exercise and activities that increase fitness – provide a 'green gym'.

■ **Recreation:** green spaces provide a vital resource for social recreation and relaxation that contribute to individual and community well-being. Both formally maintained parks/playing fields and semi-natural spaces are needed.

■ **Amenity:** the green network and its elements form a key facet of urban amenity and can be used as part of the palette of urban design: giving outlook, providing a setting, contributing to distinctive local character, acting as a buffer between neighbourhoods or as a link to provide a connection.

■ **Movement:** the greenspace network can increase the pleasure and choice of routes for non-motorised forms of transport, offering recreational round walks, links to open country and greenway connections to urban activities. Watercourses, hedgerows, shelter belts and playing field boundaries (among others) can offer connected linear corridors.

### Resource management

■ **Climate:** green spaces can provide cool air in the summer and warmth in the winter and thus moderate the extremes (especially of heat) to which cities are prone. They provide shelter belts for wind moderation, reducing energy needs in settlements, and tree-lined routes for shade. More broadly, the growing trees 'fix' carbon and thus help to combat global warming.

■ **Biodiversity:** green spaces are an essential habitat for the flora and fauna of urban spaces, and connect countryside and town for wildlife adaptability and migration.

■ **Water cycle:** the green network provides the neighbourhood with the capacity to mimic the water systems of undeveloped land. It should accommodate the storage, amelioration, percolation, surface conduit and discharge functions of a sustainable drainage system.

### Sustainable economy and community

■ **Woodland products:** trees and coppice can provide urban areas with local materials (for furniture, building and energy). However, local products, markets and skills may need considerable development if the potential is to be realised.

■ **Waste:** the local composting and recycling plan can involve a community compost facility, with compost or re-use for energy of all 'waste' from greenspace management, including tree surgery arisings and autumn leaf litter.

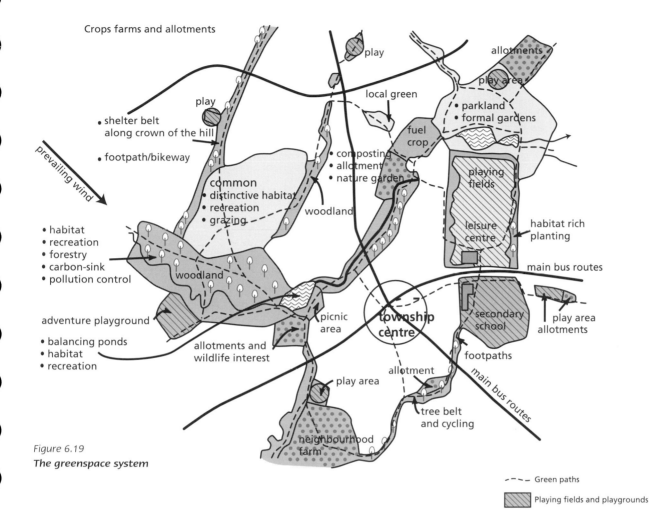

Crops farms and allotments

play

allotments

play area

local green

• parkland
• formal gardens

fuel crop

• shelter belt
along crown of the hill

play

prevailing wind

• footpath/bikeway

• composting
• allotment
• nature garden

playing fields

**common**
• distinctive habitat
• recreation
• grazing

woodland

leisure centre

habitat rich planting

• habitat
• recreation
• forestry
• carbon-sink
• pollution control

woodland

main bus routes

adventure playground

picnic area

**township centre**

secondary school

play area allotments

• balancing ponds
• habitat
• recreation

allotments and wildlife interest

footpaths

allotment

main bus routes

play area

tree belt and cycling

*Figure 6.19*
**The greenspace system**

neighbourhood farm

- - - - Green paths

▨ Playing fields and playgrounds

🌳🌳🌳 Woodland areas and tree belts

Parks and common land

▦ Crops farms and allotments

**Local food:** the network can provide for a variety of facilities including neighbourhood farms, allotments, community orchards and community gardens.

**Employment:** the integrated management of the green network provides a series of local job and training opportunities from strategic management to landscape maintenance. Ideally, the bulk of the work should be overseen, if not undertaken by a locally based ranger service. This could also provide a degree of supervision and security so often lacking. The co-ordination of local volunteers and public events would also be part of the ranger's remit.

**Local participation:** the management of the greenspace network should involve local stakeholders such as amenity groups and sports clubs. Public events (apple day, tree dressing, etc.) and active participation with maintenance (tree planting, coppicing and hedgelaying) are also part of this territory.

*5.16 Community composting* ←

*5.11 Allotments and orchards* ←

*5.13 City farms* ←

STRATEGIES FOR RENAISSANCE

# 6.10

# shaping towns and townships

## 6.10 STRATEGIES FOR RENAISSANCE

The shaping of towns/townships is pivotal to the creation of healthy and sustainable neighbourhoods. The planning process context is explained in Chapter 3.

### GETTING BOTH DETAIL AND STRATEGY RIGHT

Given effective local collaboration and a coherent broad policy context, there are two complementary approaches to shaping the physical form of towns/townships and the neighbourhoods within them. Both, at some level, are essential. One works upwards from an analysis of the characteristics and potential of individual sites and zones. The other works downwards from a consideration of sustainable urban form. This guide recommends quite specific processes in relation to each (6.11 and 6.12 respectively). The aims are, as ever, health, sustainability and vitality, but also transparency/clarity in decision-making processes.

Figure 6.20
**Quick strategy check**

The chart below sets out to assist initial recognition of the way forward

| | | DON'T | DO |
|---|---|---|---|
| 1 | Overall approach | ✘ rely on a laissez-faire stance, with disjointed project-by-project decisions, and separate consideration of each policy area | ✔ work out an integrated spatial strategy for the town/township, aimed at health, equity, economic vitality and environmental sustainability |
| 2 | Timescale | ✘ shorten the plan period to avoid awkward decisions or political embarrassment | ✔ take a long-term inter-generational view, anticipating obvious problems and keeping options open where there is uncertainty |
| 3 | Housing | ✘ allocate new housing sites purely on the basis of minimising direct environmental impact and/or political expediency | ✔ allocate new housing sites on the basis of improving the function of the township and the life chances of residents, while protecting environmental assets |
| 4 | Density | ✘ plan use intensification on every brownfield site | ✔ encourage urban intensification within identified accessible zones, with valued open space protected |
| 5 | Commercial | ✘ permit low-density single use business parks or leisure parks premised on high car use | ✔ integrate office, retail and leisure activities into mixed-use town centres and high streets |
| 6 | Landscape | ✘ treat natural features as negative constraints on the freedom of development | ✔ recognise natural landscape features as the starting point for ecological planning |
| 7 | Transport | ✘ start with a road hierarchy and vehicle access | ✔ start with a strategy for public transport and pedestrian/cycling accessibility |
| 8 | Linkage | ✘ accept parcel-by-parcel land development with separate cul-de-sac access | ✔ link developments to create a permeable, accessible environment |
| 9 | Partnerships | ✘ work in compartmentalised boxes and respond too little too late | ✔ work together in cross-sectoral partnerships and **stay ahead of the game** |
| 10 | Robustness | ✘ hold down capital costs at the expense of maintenance charges and flexibility | ✔ design to minimise the need for maintenance and facilitate adaptation and personalisation |

## 6.11 URBAN CAPACITY AND POTENTIAL

### BASIC PRINCIPLE

It is vital to the achievement of coherent town planning that 'urban capacity' studies, undertaken by local authorities in order to find urban space for housing, are extended to encompass the potential for all urban uses and accessible greenfield sites as well as brownfield sites.

Capacity studies should be seen as part of an on-going programme of gradual renewal, contributing to urban renaissance and sustainable development. As such, they are more about urban potential than about capacity.

Urban potential studies (though usually undertaken across a whole region, county or district) should involve local people in defining what is locally valued. In some situations a town, parish or neighbourhood council might itself choose to initiate a potential study to ensure local perspectives are given due weight in the wider planning game. The technique presented below is appropriate for either situation.

### Policy context

The analysis of urban capacity (or 'potential') is a core local planning requirement (PPG3 2000). There is a risk that such analysis is driven by the need to find more land for housing to the partial exclusion of other issues. The good practice guide *Tapping the Potential* (DETR 2001) bears this out. Any valid method must enable the settlement to be considered in the round. It should guide decisions on sustainable development, planning for health and quality of life, not just satisfying new housing requirements.

These latter objectives are stressed by the Urban Task Force report (1999) and the subsequent Urban White Paper (DETR 2000). 'Urban renaissance', in these documents, is seen as being about the whole dynamic process of urban renewal and change.

### AN INTEGRATED APPROACH

▨ The Urban Potential Framework advocated here is appropriate at the level of the township or the whole urban area.

▨ In common with other techniques, it estimates the capacity of specific sites and of land-use character zones. Each site or zone is categorised according to 30–40 land-use categories (typical urban areas – TUAs), allowing a sampling process within each category to reduce survey times if that is necessary.

▨ The Framework requires sites and zones to be assessed against twelve criteria of sustainable development, encompassing accessibility, environmental quality and resource management as well as the economic potential for urban intensification.

*Urban Potential Assessment*

*The Urban Potential Assessment technique is derived from the method originally put forward in the UWE/LGMB Guide Sustainable Settlements (Barton et al. 1995). The Environment Agency has revised the technique for application both at strategic and local levels. This involves a staged threshold approach which assesses environmental sustainability and offers options for development (Carroll et al. 2002, in preparation).*

*Urban Potential Assessment has been honed through a series of practitioner workshops from 1997 to 2000.*

*Quality of Life Capital*

*The Urban Potential Assessment technique is compatible with the Quality of Life (QOL) Capital approach advocated by English Nature, English Heritage, the Environment Agency and the Countryside Agency (CAG and LUC 2001).*

*The key to the QOL Capital approach is to ask: what are the benefits and services which are potentially affected by the planning process or the decision at issue? Evaluation of a specific site involves identifying*

- *the social, economic and environmental services that it offers*
- *who the services matter to, why, and at what spatial scale*
- *how important the services are*
- *whether we have enough of the services; and*
- *whether the services are substitutable.*

*The approach allows conclusions to be drawn about the future of each resource and enables management aims to be determined.*

*3.8 Neighbourhood appraisal* ←

*3.10 Agreeing a co-ordinated programme* ←

# 6.11

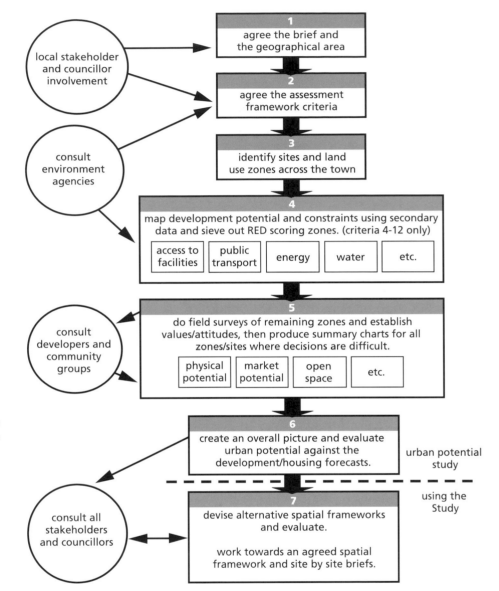

**Figure 6.21**
**The process of assessing urban potential**

### National Land Use Database (NLUD)

*The information collected for the NLUD can be incorporated within the Framework under the Physical Development Potential criteria. This cuts out unnecessary duplication of effort. NLUD sites/buildings will normally be BLUE or GREEN on the chart.*

*Main NLUD categories*

*A*
*Previously developed land that is now vacant and could be developed without treatment*

*B*
*Vacant buildings – unoccupied, structurally sound and in a reasonable state of repair*

*C*
*Derelict land and buildings – damaged by previous occupation, incapable of use without treatment or rehabilitation*

*NB. Vacant land and buildings only account for about a third of total brownfield development potential (varying between places). The rest is from windfall sites, conversions and intensification.*

▢ The assessment is for mixed-use development as well as housing.

▢ The criteria act as constraints on development in some situations, but stress the potential for development in other situations. The Framework incorporates an adapted 'traffic light' system with weighting between criteria built into the assessment (see Figure 6.22).

## NOTES ON THE URBAN POTENTIAL PROCESS

1   **The study area** may simply be of the existing built-up area, but is more valuable if it includes any neighbouring greenfield areas and assesses them on a comparable basis with the brownfield sites.

2   **The Framework** is the key tool in this process that shapes later analysis. (See a sample framework on the next page.) Its criteria ascribe values to aspects of environment capital and to social/economic variables. It is therefore highly politically charged. The pressures from special interests could be intensive, but it is important to win their support at this stage.

3   **Identifying sites and zones** may be done initially by map and memory. A sample list of various 'typical urban area' (TUA) catergories is given overleaf. The list of different TUAs need adapting to local circumstances. Both sites/zones and TUA categories can be changed later if necessary.

4   **Mapping potential and constraints** can occur before the need for field surveys. State of Environment reports and statutory consultees can supply information on, for example, land liable to flood, nature conservation and cultural heritage. North-facing slopes, pedestrian accessibility and public transport access can be assessed by Geographical Information Systems (GIS), avoiding the need for time-consuming surveys. This process acts as a sieve to cut down the need for physical surveys. It only takes one red light to stop development and those areas need not be visited.

5   **Field surveys** are undertaken for all areas where development is possible. The views of local people will be critical for some criteria, such as the value of open space, local cultural heritage, and noise levels. Parish/town councils and residents' groups must, at least, be involved. Assessing physical and market potential is highly skilled work relying on experienced planners with local knowledge, and effective consultation with market interests. It may be sufficient to sample some TUA categories (late-twentieth-century estates, for example) where different zones have very similar characteristics.

6   **Creating an overall picture.** This is the moment of truth. The process can be done using GIS software, applying a scoring or colour coding system to establish priorities, with a report setting the results in the context of housing estimates, etc. The process is likely to necessitate revisiting assumptions and judgements made previously.

7   **Using the study.** The urban potential analysis is not the be-all and end-all. Its results need to be used in a proper plan-making exercise that recognises the dynamics of change. They can also be used incrementally
    • to quickly assess windfall sites when they come forward
    • to provide site-information to potential developers (at a price)
    • to tie in with quality of life and state of the environment monitoring.

# 6.11

| CRITERIA | POTENTIAL | | | | |
|---|---|---|---|---|---|
| | *Red* – development IMPOSSIBLE | *Orange* – development PROBLEMATIC | *Yellow* – development CONDITIONAL | *Green* – development OK | *Blue* – development PRIORITY |
| 1 Physical development potential | | Contaminated land, buildings awkward to repair, steep slopes | Derelict land and buildings requiring treatment and/or rehabilitation | | Previously developed land and vacant buildings capable of easy re-use |
| 2 Market development potential | Land-locked site with no access possible | Zero/low-value site, lacking appeal or potential; owner unwilling to sell | Marketable site/ buildings depending on conditions and costs imposed | Likely to be viable irrespective of conditions or S106 costs | High-value sought-after location |
| 3 Infrastructure capacity | | Major threshold breached: shift in investment priorities required | Contribution needed to school/sewage treatment/roads/ station, etc. | No particular thresholds are breached | Spare capacity in local schools, p.t. services, road system, sewage treatment |
| 4 Pedestrian accessibility to key local facilities | No facilities within 800 m | Few facilities available within 800 m | Legal agreement could fill key gaps in facilities | Most facilities within 800 m | Choice of facilities available, most within 400 m |
| 5 Public transport accessibility to jobs/centres | No regular public transport services accessible or planned | Only poor services accessible or planned | Poor services, capable of improvement | Good-quality services within 400 m | Excellent-quality services within 300 m |
| 6 Energy use and carbon-fixing | Very exposed sites | Shelter belts, woodland, coppices | North-facing slopes, tree-replacement conditions | | Gentle south-facing slopes, spare CHP/CH capacity |
| 7 Water | Areas liable to flood every 30 years or more | Marginal flood areas; high ground-water vulnerability | Areas of medium ground-water vulnerability | Supply, treatment, drainage OK; no flood risk | |
| 8 Land, soils and local food production | Unstable land, areas prone to coastal erosion | Allotments, market gardens, organic farmland | High-quality soils; impact on farmland | | Contaminated land |
| 9 Biodiversity | SSSIs and other national designations | Locally defined valued habitats and wildlife corridors | Locally valued but common habitats, trees and hedgerows | No threat to assets | Potential to create new habitats in degraded areas |
| 10 Air quality and noise | Areas prone to unacceptable level of pollution | Source of pollution capable of correction – but who will pay? | Mitigatable noise levels | | |
| 11 Open space value or impact | Valued and well-used public open-space (POS) | Common-land, valued public access land | Inadequate local open space, contribution needed | Ample supply of accessible open space locally | |
| 12 Aesthetic and cultural heritage | Listed buildings; vulnerable landscapes of great value | Specific areas of valued landscape or great archaeological value | Conservation areas, AONBs, National Parks | | Ugly or monotonous environment needing improvement |

Figure 6.22

**The urban potential assessment framework**

Note: the specific criteria in each box need to
be negotiated in the local context

## EVALUATING INDIVIDUAL SITES

The framework can be used to summarise the situation for a specific site and pinpoint what further work might need to be done to reduce the uncertainties or overcome barriers to development.

| Site code no: Area in ha: Address | Grading | | | | |
|---|---|---|---|---|---|
| | Red | Orange | Yellow | Green | Blue |
| Development potential — Physical | | | ★ | | |
| Market | | | | ★ | |
| Infrastructure | | | | ★ | |
| Accessibility — Pedestrian | | | ★ | | |
| Public transport | | ★ | | | |
| Resources — Energy | | | ★ | | |
| Water | | | | ★ | |
| Land | | | | ★ | |
| Biodiversity | | | | | ★ |
| Air and noise | | | | ★ | |
| Place — Open space | | | | ★ | |
| Aesthetic quality | | | | | ★ |

Figure 6.23
**Illustrative chart for a derelict edge-of-town industrial site**

*In this example, poor public transport is the key factor. Unless that problem can be rectified – probably in the context of a wider plan for the area – development is inappropriate. The aesthetic and biodiversity benefits potentially achievable give urgency to the completion of an appropriate plan*

### 6.12 THE SPATIAL FRAMEWORK

It is essential to have a clear picture of the evolving shape of the whole town/township before making decisions about specific neighbourhoods or development proposals. Understanding the dynamics of urban form is critically important. Every town or township should have a spatial framework which establishes the long-term pattern of land use, density and movement. The Framework and accompanying policies can provide a key focus for cross-sectoral stakeholder debate and subsequent stakeholder commitments.

### A POSITIVE PLANNING TOOL

This 'Framework' is a vital reference for development control. But it is not primarily a negative tool, nor is it akin to old-style land-use zoning maps. Rather, it is a key stage in a positive planning

| | |
|---|---|
| • modern estate housing | 42% |
| • military sites | 7% |
| • retail stores with car parking | 6% |
| • safeguarded vacant land within settlement boundary | 5% |
| • large terraces and semi-detached town houses | 4% |
| • old industrial areas in poor condition | 4% |
| • out-of-centre offices | 4% |
| • old village cores and organic areas in towns | 3% |
| • retail road frontages | 3% |
| • derelict land | 3% |
| • mansions | 2% |
| • large/medium detached and semi-detached houses | 2% |
| • city centre mixed uses | 2% |
| • town centre mixed uses | 2% |
| • utilities | 2% |
| • community uses (not ed.) | 2% |
| • open-site parking | 1% |
| • purpose-built hotels | 1% |
| • multi-storey former industrial buildings | 1% |
| • all TUAs | 100% |

Figure 6.24
**Potential housing yield from different typical urban areas (TUAs) in south-west England**

*(TUAs yielding no gains are excluded)*

*Note: this is concerned with the re-use and intensification of sites or areas already urbanised. It excludes greenfield development*

SOURCE: BASED ON BAKER ASSOCIATES AND UWE 1999

approach which moves from clarity over goals through to clarity about context and criteria for specific projects. The zones of use-intensity should expressly avoid spurious determination of site-specific use (except where commitments have been entered into); they are intentionally mixed-use zones. Individual applications (or development briefs, etc.) are then judged against locational/design criteria.

### Inter-generational planning

The Township Framework should be designed for a generation (25 years). It should be approved either as part of the Local Plan or as Supplementary Planning Guidance in the context of a Community Strategy, with regular reviews. It is intended to be a robust expression of policy, with long-term contingencies already identified to allow effective assessment of short-term options.

### THE TWIN-TRACK MODEL

A useful starting point is the twin-track model of urban form. The two tracks are the public transport hierarchy and the greenspace/waterspace system. One provides the shaping for concentrations

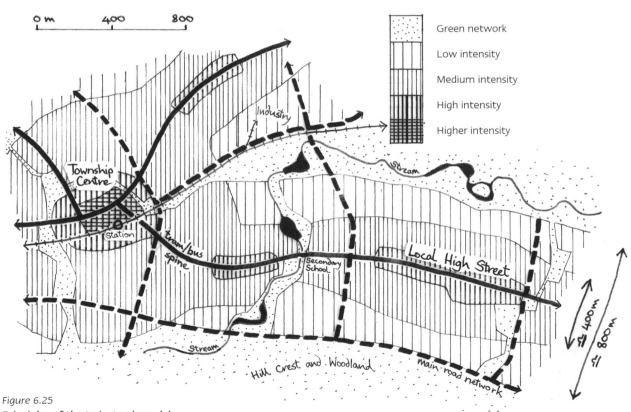

Figure 6.25
**Principles of the twin-track model**

of human activity, while the other enables the ecology of the settlement to work effectively. The whole morphology of the settlement is then defined by pedestrian accessibility: the built form, streets and public spaces flow on from that.

## A SIX-STAGE PROCESS FOR UNDERSTANDING AND SHAPING THE SPATIAL FRAMEWORK

The diagram below summarises an approach to working out a sustainable urban pattern. While current practice in defining development patterns often starts with the specific land release and the main roads, this approach starts with the public transport and greenspace systems, in line with the twin-track model. It is designed as much for existing urban areas as for urban extensions. The resulting spatial framework provides the big picture, which is then related to the disaggregated site-by-site information emerging from the urban potential study. Taken together, these two sources give an effective context for investment decisions, development briefs and development control.

*The next two pages illustrate this six-stage process in relation to a town expansion scheme.*

*Section 6.13 then shows its use for the gradual reshaping of existing urban areas.*

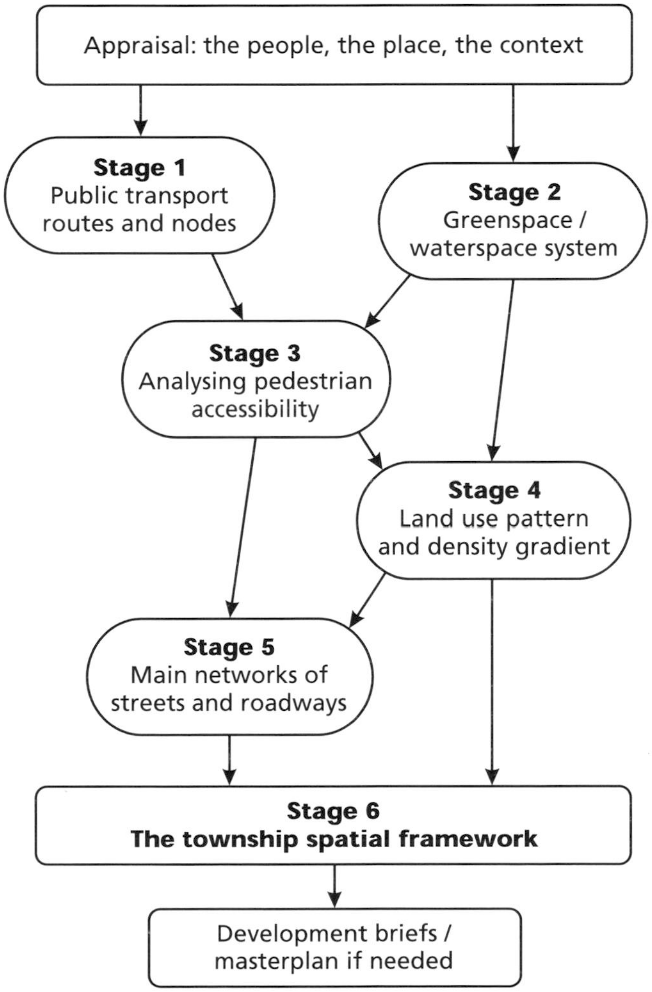

Figure 6.26
**The six-stage process**

Appraisal: the people, the place, the context

**Stage 1** Public transport routes and nodes

**Stage 2** Greenspace / waterspace system

**Stage 3** Analysing pedestrian accessibility

**Stage 4** Land use pattern and density gradient

**Stage 5** Main networks of streets and roadways

**Stage 6 The township spatial framework**

Development briefs / masterplan if needed

6a Case study → Ashton Green

## THE SIX-STAGE PROCESS IN DETAIL

The following is an example of the application of the six-stage process to a town expansion scheme.

### Stage 1
### Public transport routes and nodes

Identify the main existing public transport routes, their effectiveness, viability, and the degree of flexibility in their routing (if any).

Consult and speculate on potential improvements (or threats) to the system: for example, could an old station be reopened or a new station offer better connections (see map)?

Identify existing/potential public transport nodes, graded

'A'  intercity links and good local connections to all main areas
'B'  good local connections to all main areas
'C'  some regular connections but not comprehensive.

NB *See Section 4.17 on public transport.*

### Stage 2
### The greenspace/waterspace system

▨  Identify elements critical to local environmental capital in relation to biodiversity, landscape, water and energy/pollution management.

▨  Identify currently valued or proposed recreational open spaces and routeways.

▨  Consult/speculate on potential open-space corridors linking between existing facilities.

NB *Much of this information is equally needed by the urban potential study, and should be available from the appraisal – see Sections 3.8 and 6.11.*

### Stage 3
### Analysing pedestrian accessibility

▨  Map existing pedestrian accessibility to public transport stops and local centres, identifying barriers and other deterrents to movement.

▨  Analyse pedestrian accessibility to potential new routes or nodes/centres.

▨  Evaluate the potential local catchments of alternative routes/nodes in the light of the prime greenspace/waterspace system.

NB *The accessibility criteria applied here are critical to the emerging spatial framework. They must be robust and widely accepted. See Section 4.15.*

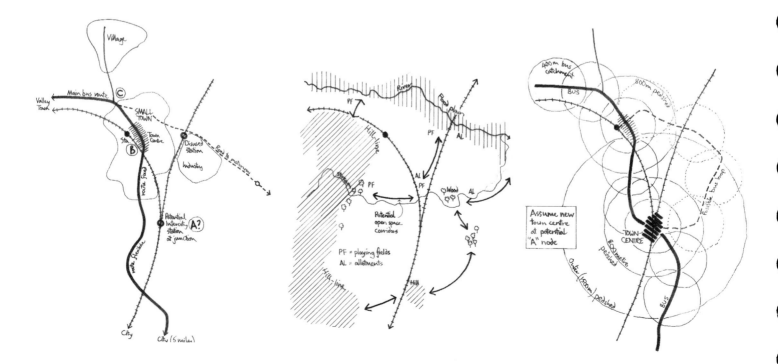

## Stage 4
### Land-use pattern and density gradient

Devise and evaluate patterns of land-use intensity, relating these patterns directly to the accessibility and open space analyses, and distinguish four levels of intensity.

1  Town-centre activities: retail, leisure, business, civic and high-density residential development.

2  Local high streets and environs: small-scale mixed uses (retail, etc.) with medium- to high-density residential development.

3  Local catchments: areas within easy reach of public transport services and nodes, mainly medium-density residential, with other uses as appropriate.

4  Greenspace system: areas dedicated to water/ecology/recreation/landscape, where new building is deterred.

NB *See Section 6.8 on density and 4.10 on local services.*

## Stage 5
### Main networks of streets and routeways

1  Devise the network of distributor roads on a modified grid basis that responds to the contours, ensures permeability, and gives natural centrality to the town/township centre.

2  Plan the cycling/walking network on about a 200 m grid, using semi-car-free 'safe routes' as well as the distributor roads (20 mph), ensuring permeability and access to nodes, etc.

3  Identify neighbourhoods, based on historic associations when they exist, or the pattern of streets and catchment when they do not.

NB *See Sections 4.14 to 4.18 on planning for movement, and Sections 1.7 and 6.2, 6.3 on neighbourhood qualities.*

## Stage 6
### The township spatial framework

The spatial framework is the combination of land-use pattern and the main networks. It should cover the whole town or township (existing/planned) and adjacent open space, showing how the settlement is linked to wider area. It should specify

1  the basic principles on which it is based – for example, criteria of pedestrian accessibility or of facility location

2  the density gradient, and specify the activities which are appropriate to each of use-intensity

3  the distributor network for walking/cycling, public transport and general traffic, but should not normally detail the minor access streets

4  specific sites for new development proposals (such as school, park, cinema) where they can be safely identified

5  spatial manifestations of policies for recreation, wildlife, water, energy/microclimate, cultural landscape

6  areas requiring a detailed masterplan and/or a development brief, with an indication of phasing where appropriate

7  neighbourhoods of function and/or character, existing and planned.

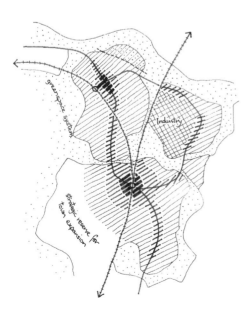

*Figure 6.27*
**Stages in preparation of a spatial framework**

*Use a reinforcement strategy when ...*

- *the existing urban form is based on pre-car patterns that still have viability: for example, market towns with strong centres and pedestrian scale; city radials with linear centres, still focused on bus/tram routes.*

- *the area is substantially built up, affords a satisfactory quality of environment, and has limited capacity for reshaping in the foreseeable future.*

## 6.13 RENEWAL STRATEGIES

The previous section demonstrated a spatial planning process for a major urban extension. The process is equally applicable to existing urban areas. The two basic strategies of reinforcement and restructuring are illustrated below. In either case, the spatial framework should guide physical planning decisions in relation to

- the use of brownfield sites
- regeneration of inner urban areas
- retrofit of outer suburban areas
- gradual renewal processes; and
- development control generally.

### STRATEGY 1
### REINFORCEMENT OF HISTORIC PATTERNS

#### Scenario

This is an inner suburb built up progressively between 1880 and 1960 around a historic tram route, which also functions as primary road, local distributor and linear shopping centre. Housing densities range from 50 dph for earlier development near the spine to 25–40 dph for the 'backlands' development later. Most surviving greenspace is in the backlands zone.

#### Appraisal

The population is relatively stable but with wide variations of wealth, class and household characteristics. There is gradual and progressive renewal of the physical structures signifying confidence in the economic future of the area. The quality of environment is humdrum but homely. Access to local facilities, and to city-wide facilities, is generally good. The existing urban form still mirrors the historic pattern of development and is for the most part well adapted to movement by foot and bus, albeit car use now dominates. The spine road acts as the main pedestrian, cycling, bus, car and service link; it is unsurprisingly both congested and polluted; however, there is no easy alternative. The greenspaces are well linked in the north but separated in the south.

#### Strategy

Reinforce the established pattern of development, concentrating higher intensity activities along the main spine while working towards reduced car reliance and greater continuity of greenspace. The numbers below refer to the map:

1   **Township centre**
    - Reinforce the main public transport node (e.g. reopen station).
    - Build on success – i.e. the existing retail 'hot-spot'.
    - Encourage/allow further intensification of 'B' centre activities.
    - Achieve improved pedestrian environment.

2   **Local high street**
    - Extend pedestrian, bike and bus priority measures, but not

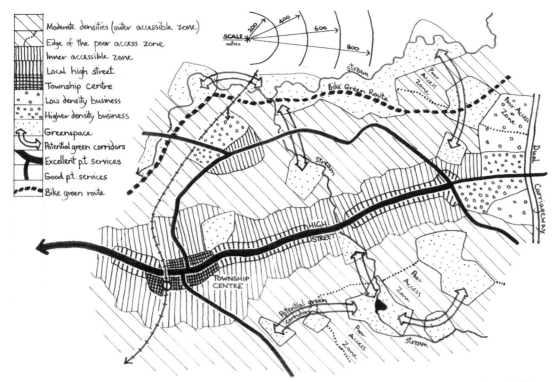

*Figure 6.28*
**Reinforcement strategy – urban radial sector**

at the expense of on-street parking where it is important for passing trade.

- Support innovation and diversity of shops and local facilities, with a flexible approach to the balance of retail and housing use along the frontage responding to changes in demand.
- Allow redevelopment of all frontage plots where this increases plot ratios, encouraging a gradual change of character from two to three or four storeys, with adaptable building types.
- Where the street narrows, apply a set-back building line to increase long-term capacity, compensating the owners/ developers with higher plot ratios.

3    **Inner accessible zone**
- Defined as areas within 200 m actual walking distance of the main street or 400 m of the township centre.
- Encourage the gradual intensification of the area, requiring three storeys minimum for any new development, and modest parking/garden provision.
- Flats and terraces predominating; aim for gross density of at least 50 dph, with average net densities of 60 or 70 dph.
- Varied uses (e.g. workshops, primary schools, pocket parks).
- Aim to extend zone by removing barriers to pedestrian access.

4    **Outer accessible zone**
- Defined as the built-up area between 200 and 400 m actual distance of a good bus route or 800 m of the township centre.

actual distance of a good bus route or 800 m of the township centre.

- Varied housing types, but aiming for at least 30 dph gross density, and at least 40 dph net density average. In some areas this implies gradual intensification.
- High-density housing not permitted.
- Industrial estates (but not office/business use) ideally form part of this zone.

5   **Poor access zone**

- Defined as built-up areas more than 400 m actual distance from a good bus route and over 800 m from the township centre.
- No intensification should be permitted, unless and until a strategy for improved accessibility is in place.
- Backland and 'infill' plots should remain unfilled, and any redevelopment should be at modest densities.
- Temporary low-intensity uses may be promoted pending public transport investment.

6   **Greenspace system**

- Includes all greenspaces including any 'waste' and linear zones of biodiversity/shelterbelt value.
- Work to increase public access open space, where needed, in the outer accessible and poor access zones.
- Increase the connectivity between green spaces with wildlife/recreational corridors, linking through inner zones as well as the outer.

## STRATEGY 2
## RESTRUCTURING OF UNSUSTAINABLE PATTERNS

### Scenario

This is an outer urban area based around two radial routes, built up mainly in the 1930s, 1950s and 1960s. The business park, however, is a more recent addition. The development is predominantly two-storey. Densities range from 20 dph to 40 dph. There is ample open space, though some of it is underused agricultural land with limited public access.

### Appraisal

- The population is stable but not particularly well off.
- There is a paucity of young professionals and young single people.
- The council estate is partially cut off from the rest of the area by the railway and open space, lacking any direct connection to the business park. It is a classic 'closed cell' design.
- The estate is socially stigmatised, lacks viable services, and has inadequate public transport connections to the wider city. There are concentrations of poverty and unemployment.
- The main residential area has better bus services (though only to limited destinations) and adequate local facilities. Car use is necessarily quite high.

*Use a restructuring strategy when ...*

- *the existing urban form is largely low-density suburban 'sprawl', premised on high car reliance, and currently lacking adequate accessibility to jobs and services.*

- *there is some opportunity for judicious intensification and infill development.*

■ The whole area lacks any township or district centre.

### The spatial framework could specify

■ Use LRT stations as focuses for development and bus services.
■ Station location is critical to creating a viable overall strategy.

### Promote a new township centre

■ This should be close to the isolated estate, acting as a functional link to adjacent neighbourhoods, drawing on wider spending power.
■ Encourage quite high density commercial, retail, leisure and residential development, maximising pedestrian, cycling and public transport accessibility.

### Intensify the inner accessible zone

■ A priority for new sites close to the station and centre should be flats aimed at young singles and couples.
■ New frontage development along potential local high streets should be three or four storeys, with use flexibility on the ground floor.
■ Gradual renewal and intensification of the low-density housing estates, with three-storey development and terracing encouraged.
■ The area of business park close to the station should be 'infilled' by developing on car parks and excess landscape areas, with three or four storeys permitted.

### Promote gradual renewal elsewhere

■ Encourage diversification of housing stock.
■ Permit small-scale commercial development on main bus routes.
■ Maintain current (medium) density levels.
■ Work to enliven and improve visual aesthetics.

### Increase connectedness

■ Create new pedestrian/cycling links between housing areas and the business park.
■ Maintain/enhance green corridors between open spaces.

### Strategy

The proposal to create a LRT (light rail transit) service with new stations along the existing railway offers the opportunity for restructuring urban form. The objectives are to

■ increase the general quality and use of public transport
■ reduce the isolation of the council estate and the business park
■ provide a new township/district centre, with a good range of jobs and facilities
■ increase population levels, particularly of under-represented groups.

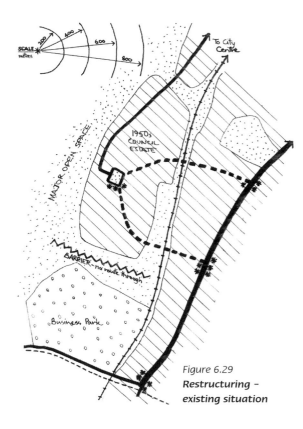

*Figure 6.29*
**Restructuring – existing situation**

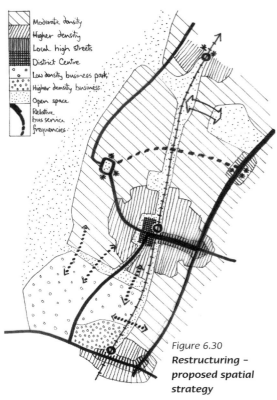

*Figure 6.30*
**Restructuring – proposed spatial strategy**

DESIGN OF THE PUBLIC REALM

# 6.14

Figure 6.31
**Making a space into a place**

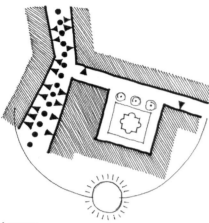

**A space**

*An interesting composition to note but perhaps not to linger. Shady, off the beaten track, dead*

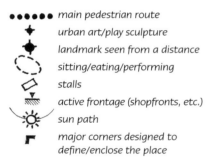

●●●●●●  main pedestrian route

urban art/play sculpture

landmark seen from a distance

sitting/eating/performing

stalls

active frontage (shopfronts, etc.)

sun path

major corners designed to define/enclose the place

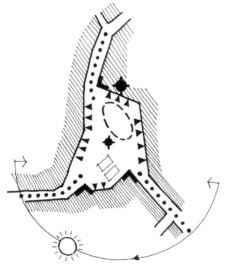

**A place**

*Somewhere to sit, to observe, to be observed. Warm, active, lively, ever changing*

---

# designing places

## 6.14 DESIGN OF THE PUBLIC REALM

### BASIC PRINCIPLES

The design of the spaces between buildings is akin to designing a complex of outdoor rooms, with different, sometimes overlapping, but well-defined functions. Good public realm design will result from a creative response to appraisals of context and site. It will be manifested in a network of sheltered, safe, accessible spaces with different functions and a clear definition between public, semi-public and private space. Existing landscape elements will be maintained to reinforce these aspects and will give the development a sense of place and local identity.

In order to achieve these principles public realm strategy must be an integral and guiding aspect of the spatial masterplan (see 3.11) and accompanying design briefs for neighbourhood development, in terms of both regeneration and new build schemes.

### AIMS OF A PUBLIC REALM STRATEGY

▨  **Aid the structuring, identity and legibility of the neighbourhood by setting out a network of linked open spaces, organised in a logical hierarchy.**

Elements of this hierarchy include major access avenues or boulevards, tree-lined streets, nodal points (the focus of foot, cycle and bus routes), structure planting, formal and informal space from domestic to civic scale and function, landmark landscape elements. Water can also be used to create similar structuring effects. It should be clear from 'reading' the spaces whether we are approaching the centre of the neighbourhood or moving from one place with a particular identity to another. Linear landscape elements such as wildlife corridors (often utilising existing and new hedgerows) or linear parks/play spaces also give a shape and structure to a neighbourhood, possible demarcating one home-patch from another.

▨  **Provide spaces appropriate to their function, in terms of size, distribution, orientation/shelter boundaries and management regimes**

Too many public spaces created in the twentieth century are often too large or open, looking empty or lacking a comforting sense of enclosure. Note how small many successful traditional urban spaces can be. It is important that the design maximises the amount of sun penetration into the space during the most useful times of day, say between 10 am and 5 pm. A focal/nodal point requires legible routes following desire lines, generators of activity and appropriate levels of enclosure.

▨  **Concentrate activities at nodal points**

It is activity and a particular mix of building or land uses that make spaces into places. Uses and activities thrive through concentration and overlapping. Increase footfall past shops, businesses and services to ensure maximum use and economic viability. Only use a zonal approach if land uses are un-neighbourly or large-scale single use.

### ◼ Ensure that non-private open spaces are accessible to all

Accessibility to all residents and visitors regardless of age or levels of temporary or permanent disability underpins legislation at national and international level in many countries. The implications are fundamental to neighbourhood planning and involve directness and length of walking routes, gradients and changes of level and shelter. Signage and other methods of information and warning should be given particular consideration. It is worth remembering that we are all susceptible to loss of full mobility at varying stages of our lives and thus what is accessible to people with disabilities is also helpful to very young children and those caring for them, and elderly people. Consideration should be given not only to wheelchair access, but also to the challenges faced by those with loss of vision or hearing, or limitations to manual dexterity.

### ◼ Increase the safety of the streets, paths, parks and squares, reducing the fear of crime

Good lighting and the overlooking of public space is an essential ingredient in the process. This provision also helps accessibility and the attractiveness of a place, and it means that they are populated over a longer time period. Lighting can be provided in imaginative ways: appropriately scaled lamp posts can be alternated with 'wall washing' and lighting of trees and shrubbery. Foot routes, where not associated with roads/bus routes, should only be contemplated if they follow a strong desire line and are as short and direct a possible, avoiding obvious ambush points by allowing good lines of sight.

### ◼ Provide opportunity in particular for teenagers to meet and chat and lark about

Whilst toddlers' and young children's needs can be catered for in well-designed play equipment, children over the age of about 10–11 years are often less well catered for. The recent concept of 'Teen-Village' may be useful in a main neighbourhood space. What is meant is the provision of open-sided shelters where youngsters can meet and chat. Siting, visibility and lighting are crucial and can perhaps best be done through community agreement, involving young people. Bikes and skateboards require more generous, often linear, provision. Skateboarding is a form of street theatre given appropriately robust, public settings, as is basketball, which could also enliven a public arena-like space. An arc of generous steps with the wall of a building as a backdrop and the right orientation suggests a performance space, but when not used as such is just a change of level.

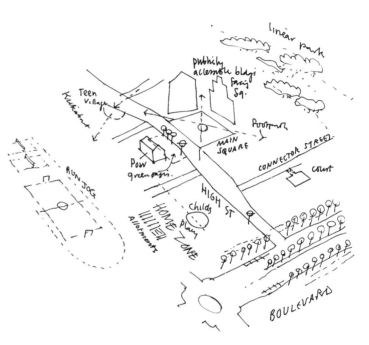

*Figure 6.32*
**The varied elements of the public realm**

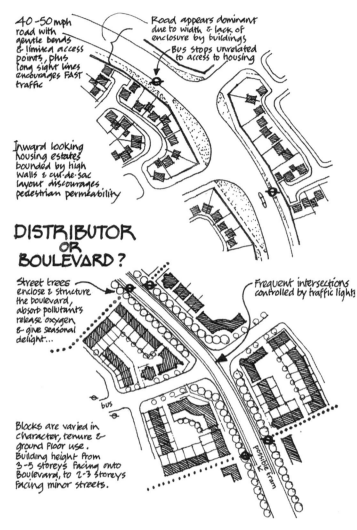

40-50 mph road with gentle bends & limited access points, plus long sight lines encourages FAST traffic

Road appears dominant due to width & lack of enclosure by buildings

Bus stops unrelated to access to housing

Inward looking housing estates bounded by high walls & cul-de-sac layout discourages pedestrian permeability

## DISTRIBUTOR OR BOULEVARD?

Street trees enclose & structure the boulevard, absorb pollutants release oxygen & give seasonal delight...

Frequent intersections controlled by traffic lights

bus

Blocks are varied in character, tenure & ground floor use. Building height from 3-5 storeys facing onto Boulevard, to 2-3 storeys facing minor streets.

possible tram

Figure 6.33
**The main road as public realm**

◼ **Foster stakeholder responsibility in the protection of the spaces immediately outside the dwelling**

The creation of zones of semi-private and semi-public space outside the dwelling overlooked by the dwelling and its neighbours can help the self-policing of groups of houses. The debate about the merits of culs de sac versus streets as to their relative safety and security has perhaps become too simplistic: neither layout is all good or all bad per se. If no one is at home in a cul de sac or a street, then the houses are vulnerable to break-in. Natural surveillance from a variety of potential and nearby sources is essential. Home-patch streets can be as safe as a courtyard if there is a feeling of ownership of the street, conveyed by its length, enclosure, number of entrances and windows, etc.

◼ **Work with the grain of the locality to enhance biodiversity, habitat, shelter, and local distinctiveness**

The characteristics of the neighbourhood location and its setting should influence decisions regarding the layout and character of open spaces. If these characteristics are not taken into consideration in the design process, the outcome can involve wasteful site engineering works, unnecessary loss of habitats, increased run-off and poor microclimatic conditions. Furthermore, standardised and stereotyped layouts that have little relationship with the locality exacerbate the familiar criticism of 'anywhere' development. Instead, the size, shape and direction of plots, the frequency of streets and junctions should influence the layout of a new development.

◼ **The main road as public realm**

Inevitably, neighbourhoods will be bounded by or directly accessed by a relatively high-volume road. This road should be considered less as a conduit for fast-moving traffic and more as a connector, where public transport, cycling and pedestrian movement (both along and across it) can be incorporated. By introducing more frequent intersections, street trees and buildings addressing the street, it becomes the interface of the neighbourhood with the rest of the urban area, it becomes a boulevard – a place in its own right, where traffic is moderated by its overall environment.

## 6.15 'HOME-PATCH' AREAS

The residential home-patch integrates blocks, plots and streets to form the home environment. This section looks in detail at how block design influences plots and streets and so the quality of the home-patch.

The home-patch concept aims to integrate all the physical elements of the built environment that are likely to foster the conditions where residents can feel that they have a stake in their immediate locality outside the home.

It is important to ensure that the sustainable home-patch is

- **attractive** – the design should create surroundings that are aesthetically pleasing in terms of touch, hearing, smell, sight and history

- **safe** – vehicular movement within the home-patch should be so controlled by the configuration of the street that vehicle speed is restricted to no more than about 15 mph (24 kph)

- **healthy** – the layout is such that walking to local facilities is the obvious option, and children can play outside in safe and attractive surroundings

- **sociable** – people can meet casually on the street and converse in sunny, informal spaces

- **convenient** – where densities permit or require, the home-patch can provide immediate access to playspace, allotments, corner shops and small office/workshop spaces

- **identifiable** – a home-patch has to have bounds where people can identify their own communal patch

- **personalisable** – the design and layout of housing and gardens should permit individual expression and local communal choice where possible

- **adaptable** – the home-patch must be capable of change and development, so that buildings may be renewed or uses can change without destroying the quality of the place

- **water-sensitive** – disposal of surface water should occur in situ, recharging ground water, and opportunities should be taken to catch rainwater and re-use grey water

- **energy-efficient** – the design should maximise the value of passive solar heat while reducing heat loss through built form and wind shelter

- **biodiverse** – the design should provide small-scale wildlife habitats, with natural vegetation and birdlife contributing to quality.

### DESIGNING FOR HIGHER DENSITIES: THE PERIMETER BLOCK

On most sites, the highest volume of accommodation at the lowest number of storeys can be achieved by locating development in a linear form around the periphery of the site. This layout also has the advantage of optimising use of external space and differentiating public and private external space. It is likely to fit into established neighbourhoods as it creates a network of streets.

### Orientation of blocks

If poorly designed, the interiors of perimeter blocks can be shady and claustrophobic. Blocks must be shaped and orientated to

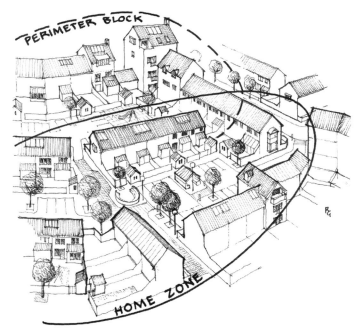

*Figure 6.34*
**Perimeter block and home zone**

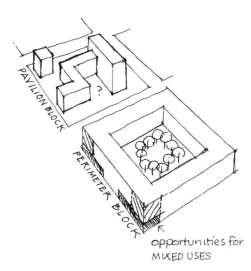

*Figure 6.35*
**Designing for higher densities without loss of quality – the perimeter block**

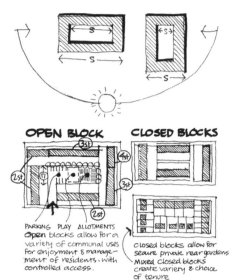

OPEN BLOCK    CLOSED BLOCKS

PARKING  PLAY  ALLOTMENTS
Open blocks allow for a
variety of communal uses
for enjoyment & manage-
ment of residents. with
controlled access.

Closed blocks allow for
secure private rear gardens
Mixed Closed blocks
create variety & choice
of tenure

### Homezones

*The UK Government is now funding pilot
implementation and research of homezones.
These are residential streets where pedestrians
and cyclists take precedence across the whole
carriageway. Communities are involved in
deciding how best to achieve this, and the change
in the hierarchy is signalled and consolidated
through alterations to the street design. The goal
is to provoke caution in the driver's mind,
leading to a change in behaviour as the road
becomes 'people' territory not 'car' territory.*

*The homezone is an emerging concept that
addresses some aspects of the home-patch,
but it is much more than just an exercise in
traffic calming. It brings residents together and
raises fundamental questions about their
shared external space – the street. Both the
processes required and resulting changes to
residential streets can bring about shifts in
communal understandings of territory,
ownership and responsibility.*

*In the UK at present (2002), we are still feeling
our way with a handful of pilot initiatives.
Problems of maintenance, liability and funding
are yet to be resolved. But experience in much
of mainland Europe shows that homezones,
when implemented widely across a township,
lead to a significant strengthening of the
home-patch. A strengthening that brings with
it social and health benefits.*

*For further information, see: www.homezones.org*

allow maximum penetration of sunlight and maximise the
number of southern elevations. Lower buildings on southern sides
can also aid sun penetration.

### Types of block

Perimeter blocks can (and should) have many variants to the basic
pattern outlined above. For instance they can be cranked or
deformed in alignment, to allow a more sympathetic relationship
to site conditions (e.g. contours, existing building patterns) or to
allow improved orientation to obtain increased sunlight. A cranked
alignment can also be used to create chicanes in a street to reduce
vehicular speeds. Variants in the basic pattern will also have the
effect of creating variety in the street scene and give each block an
identity.

Perimeter blocks, given a basic area usually ranging between 0.75
ha and 0.90 ha, have the flexibility to achieve a range of densities.

### What are the advantages of perimeter blocks?

- They are very efficient in terms of land utilisation. Higher
  densities can be achieved with the minimum number of storeys.

- They allow high levels of direct and comprehensible
  accessibility from the street to each plot.

- They are safer: there is a sharp distinction between the public
  and private side of the development with consequent
  opportunities for surveillance and enclosure of private
  gardens. Any communal space at the rear can be accessed by
  residents only.

- They are flexible: a range of densities and tenures can be
  accommodated within and between each perimeter block.
  Additionally some mixed, non-residential uses can be
  accommodated.

## THE HOME-PATCH STREET ENVIRONMENT

The home-patch incorporates the concepts of the well-established
Dutch woonerf (home street) with those espoused in the DETR
manual *Places Streets and Movement* (DETR1998d). This concept
should apply to all residential streets.

Basically, the proposal is that we should all consider the street
outside our house as the public realm of our immediate
neighbourhood – a place rather than a channel for cars. This place
is where we feel we have some ownership or stake – it is 'our'
space (belonging to us and our neighbours) – we can chat, play,
park. The street is accessible by cars and delivery vehicles but it is
so designed that it is only secondarily a route for vehicles. The
home-patch street should be a convenient route for bicycles and
pedestrians. The main home-patch street should not be designed
as a cul de sac, although there may be courts and yards accessed
from it.

## DESIGN PRINCIPLES FOR THE HOME-PATCH

Extensive tree planting is an integral part of design – street trees and trees in the blocks absorb $CO_2$ and oxygenate the atmosphere as well as aiding privacy, shade and biodiversity; trees are also attractive!

Cranked blocks allow streets to follow contours and allow greater sunlight penetration to gardens.

The communal area and toddlers' play area would be subject to residents' choice as to appropriate function and management.

Street chicane every 50–60 m to calm traffic.

High proportion of wide-frontage terrace houses – allows extension and sunny, private gardens.

Most wide frontages face south or west to optimise passive solar gain.

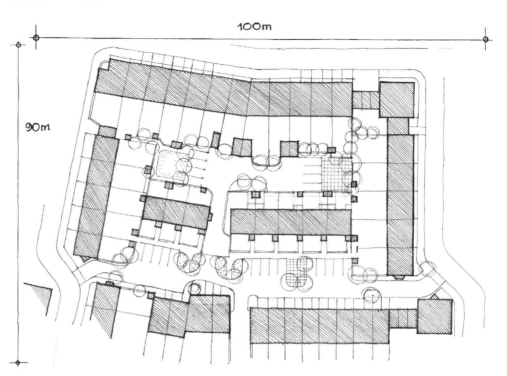

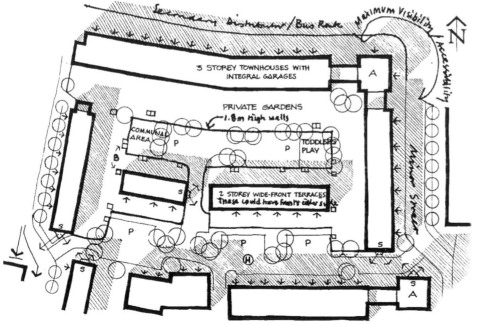

KEY

A: four-storey corner building – retail/service use on ground floor with three floors of flats above – highest building on the north-east of block reduces overshadowing (see Figure 6.37)

B: bicycle stores

H: home-patch street – access only – calmed traffic on-street parking – meeting/sitting spaces

S: passive surveillance at gateways through oriel windows on gable ends

→ house entrances

Figure 6.36
**Indicative scheme for a neighbourhood block of 50 dph**

*The framework of this block allows for a variety of house sizes, types and tenure. Virtually the same footprint could be developed at 75 or 35 dph.*

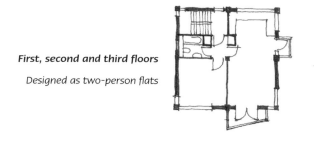

*First, second and third floors*

*Designed as two-person flats*

## FUTURE FLEXIBILITY

It is unlikely that a mixed-use area will be functioning fully at the commencement of a new development. Thus, it may be wise to develop some buildings which are adaptable to a variety of small-scale mixed uses but which have ground floors devoted to residential use at the outset.

The diagram on this page shows a possible design for the three- or four-storey corner building in the home-patch layout illustrated in Figure 6.36. It shows the ground floor and plot of the corner building. This has been designed as a flat and garden, but it might have an inbuilt permission to convert to, say, a shop, a workshop or a dentist's surgery with the garden plot convertible to a yard with some parking space or extra accommodation up to 50 per cent of the area of the garden plot.

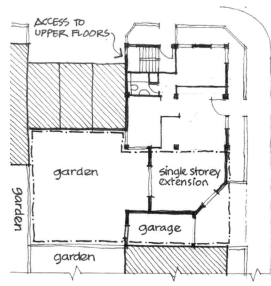

**Ground floor – option 1**

*Four-person flat*

*Extension and WC area can easily be altered for later uses*

*An alternative to option 2 if commercial/service uses are not viable in the early years*

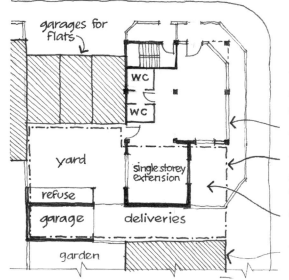

**Ground floor – option 2**

*Commercial/service use e.g. shop, bar, café, surgery, office, workshop, créche*

*Approximately 8.5 m x 8.5 m shell*

*Total external area allocated to ground-floor unit Integral permission for single-storey building/s on a maximum of 60 per cent of this area*

*Possible 'spill out' or conservatory area*

*Terrace housing*

Figure 6.37

**Three- or four-storey corner building designed for flexibility**

*The building design and planning consents ensure future adaptability for domestic, commercial or service uses*

## 6.16 CONVENTIONAL LAYOUT REVISITED

The following example illustrates how some of the urban design principles outlined in this chapter would affect the layout of an everyday small-scale residential development.

*Figure 6.38*

### A  A conventional proposal for housing on a site of approximately 1 ha (35 dph)

This consists of 35 units, mainly detached, for sale, plus an allocation of social or affordable housing, being small, narrow-frontage terraced units.

Ensure that any site plan shows its immediate context outside the site. In this case, there are influential developments such as shops, a church and school, plus a major roundabout nearby.

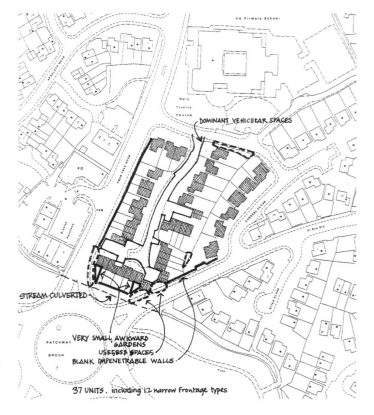

*Figure 6.39*

### B  Critique of the proposals

Is the site being used efficiently?

Is there ill-defined allocation of space?

Is it dominated by space-hungry roads and sight lines?

Are the garden sizes, shapes and orientation adequate?

How does the development address its surroundings? In other words, are there needless dead or blank frontages?

Is there an attempt to integrate the range of householders on site or is there an implied stigmatisation in the layout?

Are natural features (e.g. streams) used to enhance development?

Are pedestrian routes direct or convenient?

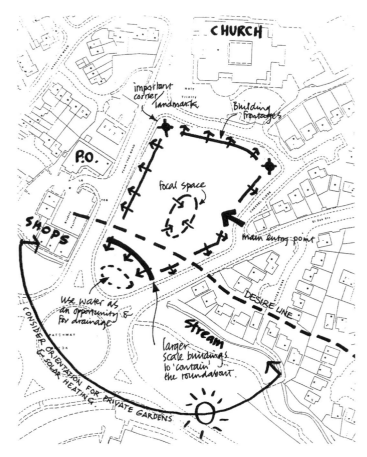

*Figure 6.40*

### C Appraisal of the opportunities offered by the site and its context

Is there a potential pedestrian desire line running across the site linking the shops and the housing to the east?

Can the stream add to attractiveness and biodiversity?

Could it be a pond, an attractive landscape element and contribute to the management of surface water on site?

Can the built form address the adjacent streets in different ways?

Can landmarks and entry points be designed to help the understanding (legibility) of the site and give it character?

Can orientation be taken into account to allow as many houses as possible to have sunny back gardens?

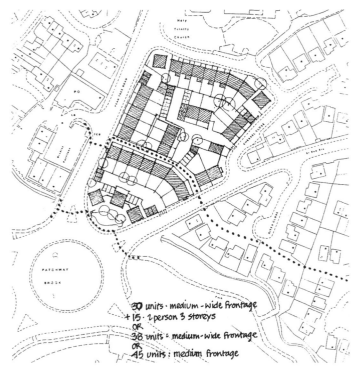

*Figure 6.41*

### D Indicative scheme

This sketch scheme demonstrates how all the points above have been addressed. It must be stressed that this is only one of many different solutions to the problem. Different solutions could be acceptable if they can demonstrate how they have fulfilled the agreed development guidelines.

Note that although density is raised, say five 3-storey individual flats included, every house can have a garden with above average area. The parking standard is one car space per property plus some overspill parking. This could be feasible in a settlement well served by public transport and with housing located close to local services.

The desire line has been incorporated into the scheme as a foot street. Similarly the stream is opened into a reedbed pond. Larger buildings face and help to contain the roundabout. Negotiations with the Highways Department might result in the reduction of the size and dominance of the roundabout.

## 6.17 A COMPACT NEIGHBOURHOOD CENTRE

The concept sketch shows a neighbourhood centre that is the focus for a wide variety of uses and activities necessary for residents' immediate requirements. It is also intended to foster the sense of a lively and sociable place.

The main influences on the design and layout are

- The centre is laid out to be at the convergence of foot, cycle and bus routes from residential streets – the point of maximum connectedness.

- It is anticipated that residents will use the centre as a single destination for all their basic requirements – making it convenient for them and economic for the enterprises and services as there will be maximum footfall across frontages.

- To ensure liveliness, sociability and safety (at night and day, weekdays and weekends) there are overlaps in the utilisation of space and time as much as possible. In particular, the school incorporates shared school/community use at its interface with the neighbourhood square. School security is ensured by using a controlled entrance in the common foyer. The cinema is located above the supermarket and shops have flats on upper floors.

- The car park is designed for maximum utilisation as it serves the cinema/supermarket, health centre and place of worship, which are located around the car park.

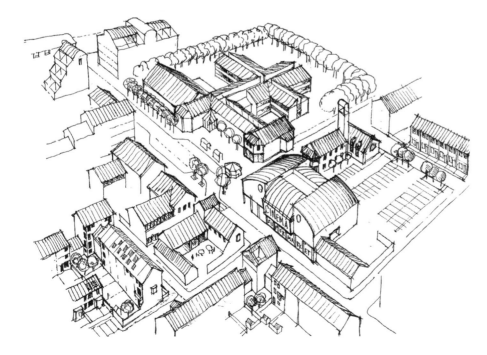

Figure 6.42
**The neighbourhood centre**

To be a place rather than just a space it has to be attractive and active. It must be a nodal point; it must be sheltered and sunny.

# 6.17

The public realm is surrounded by 'active frontages' at street/square level. Thus, there is a high incidence of entrances, windows and publicly accessible uses at street level. Blank walls facing the major public spaces are kept to a minimum.

The square is modest in size. This reduces redundant space, creates the feeling of an outdoor room and looks well peopled even when there are few people about. However, the square should be planned to accommodate bus shelters, bike-parking facilities, partially covered seating/youth hanging-out space, space for congregating, outside public venues, spill-out areas in front of shops and restaurants for display and sitting out and space for impromptu performances and market stalls.

Figure 6.43
**The neighbourhood centre in plan**

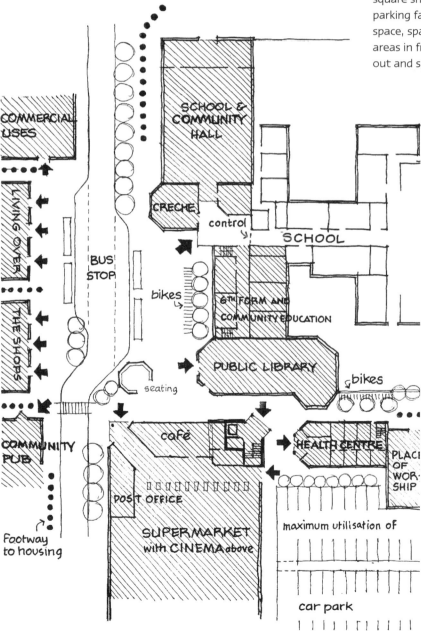

# Redcliffe

## BRISTOL

Whilst we may not design the neighbourhood in the same way today there are lessons to be learned from a neighbourhood which has stood the test of time .

## BACKGROUND

This area located between the well known St Mary Redcliffe Church and the 'New Cut' of the River Avon in Bristol, is a relatively rare example of inner city neighbourhood planning dating from the immediate post WWII period. The neighbourhood is exceptionally well located: it is within 1 km of the City Centre, well served by public transport, with a local shopping hub nearby.

From the late 1940s, neighbourhood planning in Britain was mainly concentrated on the establishment of New Towns. The early new town neighbourhoods in Harlow, Stevenage and Basildon have become attractive areas and in some cases designated conservation areas. The Redcliffe neighbourhood shows the influence of the pioneering Lansbury neighbourhood in the east end of London designed as a demonstration of progressive inner city living for the 1951 Festival of Britain.

The area of the neighbourhood is about 5.5 ha, accommodating about 375 dwellings.

Community facilities have been integrated into the design philosophy of the neighbourhood from the outset.

## PROCESSES

The neighbourhood replaced a high density mixed use working class district which was badly damaged in WWII. It was developed using the Comprehensive Development Area measures available to planners at the time.

## PROVIDING FOR LOCAL NEED

The 'estate' is relatively popular and sought after by local authority tenants. There is little evidence of damage, graffiti or general nuisance in the greenspaces. Housing is well maintained, even if the choice of replacement doors and windows is not the most sympathetic. Some shops do show signs of graffiti and have security grilles installed at night. There is a considerable movement across the site by school children at various times of the day, ensuring some life to the area and business for the shops.

The variety of building forms and the integration of tree planting helps to create pleasant surroundings.

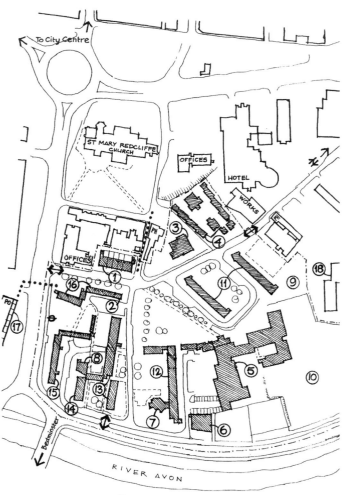

Figure 6.44
**The Redcliffe neighbourhood**

Key

1  Shops with 3 storey flats above (18 units)

2  Surgery on ground floor of flats

3  Church and church hall

4  Sheltered housing single storey (18 units)

5  Secondary school

6  Public house

7  Nursery school

8  Laundry

9  Playground

10  Playing fields

11  Blocks of 9 storey flats (2 x 54 units)

12  Block of 11 storey flats (88 units) with 3 storey wing (12 units)

13  Block of 3-5 storey maisonettes and flats (47 units)

14  Block of 5 storey maisonettes and flats (18 units)

15  Block of 3-5 storey maisonettes and flats (37 units)

16  Block of 5 storey maisonettes and flats (29 units)

17  L shaped block of 11-12 storey flats + 12 shops including post office - later phase?

18  One of 2 multi storey blocks of flats (2 x 108 units) – later phase

**case study**

REDCLIFFE, BRISTOL

# 6.a

*Shops and Somerset Square*
*From point 1 on the map*

*Nursery school in foreground*
*Point 17 on map. St Mary Redcliffe spire in background*

*Maisonettes along access road*
*Between points 2 and 12 on map*

## URBAN DESIGN

### Housing environment

Most of the housing is in 9-11 storey slab blocks with 3-5 storey terraces in a mixed development, characteristic of the time. There are also maisonettes over the shops. A communal laundry still exists and is used by the tenants. The layout is generally linear, oriented north south, but subtly opening out to the south. This allows considerable sunlight into the development. The lower blocks generally run east west thus creating informal and inter-locking green squares throughout the development. The shape of Somerset Square, a remnant greenspace from the pre-war layout, is retained and incorporated into the scheme. A group of 18 single storey houses for elderly people is located on the northern end of the site. It is important to note that this neighbourhood boundary is connected to its surroundings by streets and paths, not shut off.

### Mixed uses

The scheme not only provided homes, but on-site there is

- a secondary school with playing fields

- a nursery school

- 6 shop units, with another 12 across the road in a related development

- a church community hall

- a pub (with 2 more older ones on the periphery)

- a doctors' surgery

# Hampton Vale

## PETERBOROUGH

New urban extensions often happen without any serious thought about neighbourhood structure. Hampton is an exception, and demonstrates the value of creative partnership between the local authority and the private sector.

## BACKGROUND

Hampton is the latest new township in the expanded city of Peterborough. It is being built on a 'brownfield' site formerly occupied by extensive clay pits and brick works, four kilometres from the city centre. The township includes extensive parkland and a nature reserve (safeguarding the habitat of the great crested newt), as well as a large business park, 30,000m² of retailing space and 5,200 homes providing for about 12,000 people. The level of employment and retailing is considerably in excess of local needs, and this demonstrates Hampton's city-wide function.

## PROCESSES

Hampton provides an apt model for the process of planning and developing a major urban extension . The major land owners (O+H Group), via its subsidiary Hampton (Peterborough) Limited, are collaborating closely with the City Council to ensure quality and consistency. The development brief, provided by David Lock Associates, acts as the co-ordinating framework, adopted as supplementary Planning Guidance. It is supplemented by detailed design briefs which give O+H - as 'master developer' - control over developer proposals for each land parcel and an agreed basis for development control decisions by the City.

## PROVIDING FOR LOCAL NEED

The masterplan and development process helps to ensure a good level of provision and convenience:

- diversity of housing tenures, sizes and styles, with affordable housing well dispersed across the area

- the potential for many and varied local job opportunities, the city centre within easy cycling distance

- almost every part of the township within 400m of a local centre and 1500 metres of the township centre (Serpentine Green)

- carefully funded and programmed provision of a full range of local facilities, including well-distributed primary schools and a centrally located secondary school, with potential for dual use of leisure facilities

- excellent provision of accessible, inter-connected open spaces.

*Corner building forming gateway between two primary streets*

SOURCE: DAVID LOCK ASSOCIATES

*Development of primary street frontage giving good enclosure and connectivity*

SOURCE: DAVID LOCK ASSOCIATES

# 6.b

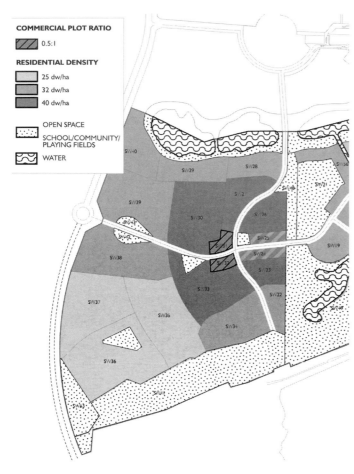

COMMERCIAL PLOT RATIO

0.5:1

RESIDENTIAL DENSITY

25 dw/ha

32 dw/ha

40 dw/ha

OPEN SPACE

SCHOOL/COMMUNITY/
PLAYING FIELDS

WATER

*Figure 6.45*
**Graded densities and development parcels**

## RESOURCES

Drainage and water management are major site issues. The masterplan makes good use of the old clay pits to create linear water features. The extensive greenspace around the lakes gives potential for biodiversity, in addition to the designation of a SSSI around the great crested newts.

However, in the first phases, other key resources (energy, materials, food, waste) are handled on conventional, and not very 'sustainable' patterns. The plan is to incorporate more sustainable approaches to several aspects of resource use in subsequent phases of the Hampton township.

## URBAN DESIGN

### The Masterplan

The masterplan successfully provides good accessibility, despite only average levels of density, and shows a very considerable advance on the estate conventions of the 1990s. The Hampton Vale neighbourhood masterplan has many helpful features:

The general shape and disposition is guided not only by the relationship to the township centre and main roads but also by the lie of the land and greenspace potential.

The 'primary streets' provide good linkage around the neighbourhood and to adjoining areas and are, as the name implies, multipurpose streets rather than simply traffic routes. Pedestrians, cyclists, buses and other vehicles all use the one network to get to the local centre, the township centre, and elsewhere in the city.

The identified bus routes (along the primary streets) give good potential for penetration and linkage, and other viability is reinforced by graded densities.

The local centre is in the form of a local high street along the main spine street of the neighbourhood, well placed at the natural focus of local trips. Mixed retail/community/commercial/educational and residential use encourages shared trip purpose.

The density levels are graded according to distance from the local centre, gradient increases the proportion of population who are conveniently close. Average density is set to increase from the original net 25dph to 32dph or even 35dph. If undertaken this would raise overall housing numbers from 5,200 to 8,000, increasing significantly the viability of local facilities and services.

Residential development parcels range between 1 and 4 hectares, and are tied to specific densities, helping to ensure some variety of character across the neighbourhood. However, the potential for unconventional, often small-scale, schemes (e.g. co-housing, low-car, zero-carbon, self-build plots, etc.) has only been partially taken up, with a small parcel set aside for seven self-build units.

*Figure 6.46*
**The street pattern: an important objective
of the plan was ease of movement by foot
and public transport**

Greenspace parkways provide round walks, wildlife corridors,
water management and an attractive landscape setting. There
could be the flexibility for local food/energy production in the
future. The standard allocation for allotments has been provided,
but the location and configuration of the plot has not been
optimised for pedestrian access or synergy with other community
facilities.

Local access streets are laid out on a rough grid, adjusted to deter
excessive speeds and rat runs, providing a permeable and flexible
system for all users.

# sources

With the ever-developing experience of sustainable design and development, no list of sources can ever be up-to-date or complete. However, the texts, organisations and websites we have listed below provided valuable sources of information and inspiration for the authors. Some are good at integrating a wide range of subjects and others provide a good starting point for further information.

## PRINCIPLES

*Achieving Sustainable Urban Form*. K Williams *et al.* (eds), Spon, London (2000).

*Building the 21st Century Home: The Sustainable Urban Neighbourhood*. D Rudlin and N Falk, Architectural Press (1999).

*Healthy Urban Planning*. H Barton and C Tsourou, Spon, London (2000).

*Planning for Sustainable Development: Towards Better Practice*. DETR, London (1998).

*Planning Guidance Notes*, DETR, London (1997–ï¿½2001), especially PPG1, PPG3, PPG6, PPG13.

*Sustainable Communities: The Potential for Eco-neighbourhoods*. H Barton *et al.*, Earthscan, London (2000).

*Sustainable Settlements: A Guide for Planners, Designers and Developers*. H Barton, G Davis and R Guise, LGMB and UWE, Bristol, (1995).

*Towards an Urban Renaissance*. Urban Task Force, Spon, London (1999).

Bedzed: An example of many principles in practice    www.bedzed.org.uk

DTLR planning policy guidance index
www.planning.odpm.gov.uk/ppg

Forum for the Future    www.forumforthefuture.org.uk

Sustainable development at DEFRA    www.sustainable-development.gov.uk

United Nations: Sustainable development commission
www.un.org/esa/sustdev

WHO Centre for Urban Health: Healthy Cities Project
www.who.dk/healthy-cities

## NEIGHBOURHOOD PLANNING PROCESS

*Participation Works! 21 Community Participation Techniques for the 21st Century*, New Economics Foundation, London, (undated).

*Planning for Communities of the Future*. DETR, London (1998).

*Preparing Community Strategies*. DTLR, London, (2000).

*Strategy for Neighbourhood Renewal*. Social Exclusion Unit, London, (2000).

*Sustainable Suburbs – Developing the Tools*. Civic Trust and Ove Arup and Partners, (2001).

*Sustainable Urban Extensions: Planned through Design*. The Prince's Foundation, English Partnerships, DETR and CPRE (2000).

Indicators for local sustainability at DEFRA
www.sustainable-development.gov.uk

New Economics Foundation    www.neweconomics.org

The Neighbourhood Initiatives Foundation    www.nifonline.org.uk

The Environment Council: Stakeholder dialogue
www.the-environment-council.org.uk

## PROVIDING FOR LOCAL NEED

*Guidelines for Providing for Journeys on Foot*, Institution of Highways and Transportation, London (2001).

*Green Spaces, Better Places*. Urban Green Spaces Task Force, DTLR (2002).

*Milton Keynes Planning Manual*. Milton Keynes Development Corporation. Chesterton Consulting (1992).

*Places, Streets and Movement, a Companion to Design Bulletin*. DETR, London, (1998).

*Rethinking the Neighbourhood Option*. in Barton *et al*. Sustainable Communities, Earthscan (2000).

*Sustainable Housing: Design Guide for Scotland*, F Stevenson and N Williams, The Stationery Office, London (2000).

*Sustainable Transport and Retail Vitality: State of the Art for Towns and Cities*. Michael Corley, HBAS and Donaldsons (1996).

Database on Good Practice in Urban Management and Sustainability
www.europa.eu.int/comm/urban

Home zones    www.homezones.org

Information network for regeneration partnerships    www.regen.net

Journal of World Transport Policy and Practice    www.ecoplan.org/wtpp

Our Healthier Nation: government database of case studies   www.ohn.gov.uk

Healthy Living Project: healthy living centres network
www.healthyliving.org.uk

Safe routes to schools    www.saferoutestoschools.org.uk

## RESOURCES

*Cities and Natural Processes*. M Hough, Routledge, London (1995).

*Designing Ecological Settlements*. M Kennedy and D Kennedy (eds), EA.UE, Dietrich Reimer Verlag, Berlin (1997).

*Developing Naturally: A Handbook for Incorporating the Natural Environment into Planning and Development*. M Oxford, Association of Local Government Ecologists (2000).

*Energy Services: A Review of the EST Residential Pilot Projects 1996ï¿½2000*, Energy Savings Trust, London (2001).

*Managing Resources Locally*. in Barton *et al*. Sustainable Communities, Earthscan (2000).

Energy Efficiency Best Practice Programme    www.energy-efficiency.gov.uk

Energy Savings Trust    www.est.org.uk

Energy Services Association    via www.chpa.org.uk

Environment Agency    www.environment-agency.gov.uk

Green Construction links    www.greenconstruction.co.uk/links.htm

HEA: Food and low incomes – database    www.food.poverty.nda-online.org.uk

National Urban Forestry Unit    www.nufu.org.uk

Scottish Environmental Protection Agency    www.sepa.org.uk

Soil Association    www.soilassociation.org.uk

Sustain: The alliance for better food and farming    www.sustainweb.org

Sustainable Construction at the DTI     www.dti.gov.uk/construction/sustain

Tree Council                                 www.treecouncil.org.uk

## URBAN DESIGN

*By Design: Better Places to Live – A Companion Guide to PPG3*. DTLR and
CABE, DTLR, London (2001).

*By Design: Urban Design in the Planning System – Towards Better Practice*.
DETR and CABE, Thomas Telford, London (2000).

*Mixed Use Development: New Designs for New Livelihoods*. W Morris and
J Kaufman, Queensland Department of Tourism, Small Business and
Industry, Brisbane (1997).

*Residential Design Guide*. Forest of Dean District Council, Coleford,
Gloucestershire (1998).

*Responsive Environments*. I Bently *et al.*, Architectural Press, London (1985).

*Sustainable Residential Quality: New Approaches to Urban Living*. Llewelyn-
Davies LPAC, London (1998).

*Urban Design Compendium*. English Partnerships and the Housing
Corporation, EP, London (2000).

*The Use of Density in Urban Planning*. DETR, London (1998).

BRE: Centre for Sustainable Construction          www.bre.co.uk/sustainable

Building Regs (DETR)                        www.safety.odpm.gov.uk/bregs

Commission for Architecture in the Built Environment      www.cabe.org.uk

Construction Industry Research and Information Association
                                            www.ciria.org.uk

Smart Growth America                 www.smartgrowthamerica.com

Smart Growth Online: Environmental Protection Agency USA
                                         www.smartgrowth.org

# bibliography

Addenbrooke P, Bruce D, Courtney I, Heliwell S, Nisbett A and Young T (1981) *Urban Planning and Design for Road Public Transport*, Confederation of British Road Passenger Transport, London.

Aldous T (1992) *Urban Villages*, Urban Village Group, London.

Arnstein S (1969) 'A Ladder of Citizen Participation', *JAIP*, XXX:4, pp. 216–24.

Atkinson R and Kintea K (1998) *Reconnecting Excluded Communities: the Neighbourhood Impacts on Owner Occupation*, Scottish Homes, Research Report 61, Glasgow.

Baker Associates and UWE (1999) *Strategic Study of Urban Housing Potential in the South West Region: Final Report*, South West Regional Planning Conference, Bristol.

Barton H (1990) 'Local Global Planning', *The Planner*, 76:42 (26 October), pp. 12–15.

Barton H (2001) *Towards a Theory of Sustainable Settlements: Integrating Health and Ecosystem Approach*, paper given to the Housing Studies Association, April 2001.

Barton H and Tsourou C (2000) *Healthy Urban Planning*, Spon, London.

Barton H, Davis G and Guise R (1995) *Sustainable Settlements: A Guide for Planners, Designers and Developers*, UWE and LGMB, Bristol.

Barton H, *et al.* (2000) *Sustainable Communities: The Potential for Eco-neighbourhoods*, Earthscan, London.

Beeson (2000) *The Effectiveness of the 'Safe Routes to School' Programme*, Unpublished MA dissertation, University of the West of England, Bristol.

Bently I, *et al.* (1985) *Responsive Environments: A Manual for Designers*, Architectural Press, Oxford.

Birmingham City Council (2001) *Places for Living: Residential Design Guide for Birmingham*, Department of Planning and Architecture, Birmingham.

Breheny M, Gent T and Lock D (1993) *Alternative Development Patterns: New Settlements*, Department of the Environment, Planning Research Programme, HMSO, London.

BRESCU (1998) *Building a Sustainable Future: Homes for an Autonomous Community*, General Information Report 53, BRESCU, Garstang.

Brighton & Hove Council (1998) *Wildlife for People: A Wildlife Strategy for Brighton and Hove*, Brighton & Hove Council, Brighton.

Bristow H (1999) 'A Fresh Approach to Local Food Supply', in *Urban Environment Today*, 22 July 1999.

Buchanan C (1963) *Traffic in Towns*, HMSO, London.

Burns D, Hambleton R and Hoggett P (1994) *The Policies of Decentralisation*, London, Macmillan.

Calthorpe P (1993) *The Next American Metropolis: Ecology, Community and the American Dream*, Princeton Architectural Press, New York.

Campbell C (1999) *Social Capital and Health*, Health Education Authority, London.

Carley M (1996) *Sustainable Transport and Retail Vitality: State of the Art for Towns and Cities*, Historic Burghs Association of Scotland, Edinburgh.

Carmona M (2001) *Housing Design Quality: Through Policy, Guidance and Review*, Spon, London.

Cervero R (1993) *America's Suburban Centres: The Land Use– Transportation Link*, Unwin-Hyman, London.

City of York Council (2000) *School Organisation Plan 2000–2005*, City of York Council, York.

Civic Trust and Ove Arup Partners (2001) *Sustainable Suburbs: Developing the Tools*, Civic Trust, London.

Dauny A and Plater-Zybeck E (1991) *Towns and Town-Making Principles*, Howard University, New York.

De Knegt (1996) *Design for Lower Car Use in Residential Areas, Planning and Transport* Research and Computation International Association (PTRC) European Transport Forum: Proceedings of Seminar C, Planning for Sustainability, Brunel University, London.

Dennis N (1968) 'The Popularity of the Neighbourhood Community Idea', in Pahl R (ed.), *Readings in Urban Sociology*, Pergamon Press, Oxford.

Department for Education and Employment (1999) *Organisation of School Places*, DfEE Circular 9/99.

DETR (1993) *Trees in Towns*, HMSO, London.

DETR (1996) *Planning Policy Guidance Notes PPG6: Town Centres and Retail Development*, DETR, London.

DETR (1997a) *Passive Solar Estate Design, Energy efficiency programme*, Best practice programme 27, DETR, London.

DETR (1997b) *Planning Policy Guidance Notes PPG1: General Policy and Principles*, DETR, London.

DETR (1997c) *Planning Policy Guidance Notes PPG7: The Countryside: Environmental Quality and Economic and Social Development*, DETR, London.

DETR (1998a) *A New Deal for Transport Better for Everyone, The Government's White Paper on the Future of Transport*, The Stationery Office, London.

DETR (1998b) *National Sustainability Strategy*, HMSO, London.

DETR (1998c) *Planning for Sustainable Development: Towards Better Practice*, HMSO, London.

DETR (1998d) *Places, Streets and Movement, A Companion Guide to Design Bulletin 32* (Residential Roads and Footpaths), DETR, London.

DETR (1998e) *Planning for the Communities of the Future*, DETR, London.

DETR (1998f) *The Use of Density in Urban Planning, Planning research programme*, DETR, London.

DETR (1998g) *Guide to Community Heating and CHP: Commercial, Public and Domestic Applications*, Energy efficiency, Best practice programme, Good Practice Guide 234, BRESCU, Garstang.

DETR (1999a) *Local Government Act* (Best Value), HMSO, London.

DETR (1999b) *Community Heating – A Guide for Housing Professionals*, Energy efficiency programme, Good practice guide 240, BRESCU, Garstang.

DETR (1999c) *Selling CHP Electricity to Tenants – Opportunities for Social Housing Landlords*, Energy efficiency programme, New practice report 113, DETR, London.

DETR (1999d) *New Deal for Communities*, DETR, London.

DETR (1999e) *Opportunities for Change*, DETR, London.

DETR (1999f) *Quality of Life Counts: Indicators for a Strategy for Sustainable Development for the UK: A Baseline Assessment*, Government Statistical Service, London.

DETR (1999g) *School Travel Strategies and Plans: A Best Practice Guide for Local Authorities*, DETR, London.

DETR (1999h) *From Workhorse to Thoroughbred: A Better Role for Bus Travel*, DETR, London.

DETR (1999i) *Towards an Urban Renaissance*, E&FN Spon, London.

DETR (1999j) *Planning Policy Guidance Notes PPG12: Development Plans*, DETR, London.

DETR (2000a) *Local Government Act*, DETR, London.

DETR (2000b) *Our Countryside: The Future – A Fair Deal for Rural England* (The 'Rural White Paper'), The Stationery Office, London.

DETR (2000c) *Our Towns and Cities: The Future – Delivering an Urban Renaissance* (The 'Urban White Paper'), The Stationery Office, London.

DETR (2000d) *Planning Policy Guidance Note 13: Transport*, DETR, London.

DETR (2000e) *Planning Policy Guidance Note 3: Housing*, DETR, London.

DETR (2000f) *Planning Policy Guidance Notes PPG13*, DETR, London

DETR (2000g) *Planning Policy Guidance Notes PPG3*, DETR, London.

DETR (2000h) *Preparing Community Strategies*, draft guidance, DETR, London.

DETR (2000i) *Transport Statistics. Travel to School*, URL: www.transtat.detr.gov.uk/facts/nts/pt2_99/school99.htm accessed 12/7/00.

DETR (2000j) *Encouraging Walking: Advice to Local Authorities*, London.

DETR (2000k) *Waste Strategy 2000*, The Stationery Office, London.

DETR/DTI (1999) *Planning for Passive Solar Design*, Building Research Establishment, Garstang.

DETR and CABE (2000) *By Design: Urban Design in the Planning System*, Thomas Telford Publishing, London.

Dodd JS (1988) *Energy Saving through Landscape Planning*, Property Services Agency, London.

DoE (1973) *Circular 82/73*, HMSO, London.

DoE (1993) *Reducing Transport Emissions Through Planning*, HMSO, London.

DoE (1994) *Urban Tree Strategies*, HMSO, London.

DoE (1996) *Greening the City: A Guide to Good Practice*, The Stationery Office, London.

DoH (1998) *Our Healthier Nation*, The Stationery Office, London.

DoH (1999) *Saving Lives: Our Healthier Nation*, The Stationery Office, London.

DTLR (2001) *Preparing Community Strategies*, DLTR, London.

Dwelly T (2000) *Living at Work: A New Policy Framework for Modern Home Workers*, Joseph Rowntree Foundation, York.

Early D (1994) 'The National Playing Fields Association', in *Planning Practice and Research*, 9:1, pp. 71–7.

ECOTEC (1993) *Reducing Transport Emissions Through Planning*, DoE/HMSO, London.

English Partnerships (n.d.) *Space for Growth*, EP, London.

English Partnerships and the Housing Corporation (2000) *Urban Design Compendium*, EP, London.

Environment Agency (2000) A *Study of Domestic Greywater Recycling*, EA, Bristol.

Environment Agency and South Gloucester Council (1999) *Sustainable Drainage Systems: A Guide to Developers*, Interim advice note C10, South Gloucester Council, Thornbury.

EST (2001) *Energy Services: A Review of the EST Residential Pilot Projects 1996–2000*, Energy Savings Trust, London.

EU Expert Group on the Urban Environment (1995) *European Sustainable Cities Report: Part Two*.

Fairlie S (1996) *Low Impact Development*, Jon Carpenter, Oxfordshire.

Forest of Dean District Council (1998) *Residential Design Guide*, Forest of Dean District Council, Coleford, Gloucestershire.

Frey H (1999) *Designing the City Towards a More Sustainable Urban Form*, E&FN Spon, London.

Garnett T (1999) *City Harvest: The Feasibility of Growing more Food in London*, Sustain, London.

Gilchrist A (2000) 'Design for Living: the Challenge of Sustainable Communities', in Barton H, *et al. Sustainable Communities*, Earthscan, London.

Girardet H (1999) *Creating Sustainable Cities*, Green Books, London.

GLC (1965) *The Planning of a New Town* (The 'Hook Book'), GLC, London.

Gloucestershire Market Towns (2000) *Market Towns Health Check 2000*, Gloucestershire County Council, Gloucester.

Goodacre C, Sharples S and Smith P (2000) *Integrating Energy Efficiency with the Social Agenda in Sustainability*, paper presented at the Second Sustainable Cities Network Conference, 12–13 September, Manchester.

Hall P and Ward C (1998) *Sociable Cities*, John Wiley, Chichester.

Halpern D (1995) *Mental Health and the Built Environment*, Taylor and Francis, London.

Harris R and Larkham P (1999) *Changing Suburbs: Foundation, Form and Function*, E&FN Spon, London.

Hass-Klau C, *et al.* (1992) *Civilised Streets: A Guide to Traffic Calming*, Environment and Transport Planning, Brighton.

Haughton G and Hunuter C (1994) *Sustainable Cities*, Regional Studies Association, London.

HEA (1999a) *Deprived Neighbourhoods and Access to Retail Services*, Health Education Authority, London.

HEA (1999b) *Promoting Community Health – Developing the Role of Local Government*, Health Education Authority, London.

HEA (2000a) *Beacon Community Regeneration Partnership – The Beacon Energy Action Area*     www.hea.gov.uk accessed 03/10/00.

HEA (2000b) *Safely to School Pilot Project*,     www.hea.gov.uk accessed 03/10/00.

HEA (2000c) *Town Centre 2000 Regeneration Scheme*,     www.hea.gov.uk accessed 03/10/00.

HEA (2000d) *Walking for Health – Specific Benefits*     www.hea.gov.uk accessed 03/10/00.

Hertfordshire County Council (1995) NB Accessibility isochromes

Hillier Parker (1998) *The Impact of Large Food Stores on Market Towns and District Centres*, HMSO, London.

Hillman M and Whalley A (1983) *Energy and Personal Travel: Obstacle to Conservation*, Policy Studies Institute, London.

Hillman M, Adams J and Whitelegg J (1991) *One False Move*, Policy Studies Institute, London.

Hopkins R (2000) 'The Food Producing Neighbourhood', in Barton H (ed.), *Sustainable Communities*, E&FN Spon, London.

Hough M (1995) *Cities and Natural Processes*, Routledge, London.

Howard E (1902) *Garden Cities of Tomorrow*, Faber, London.

Hulme Regeneration Limited (1994) *Rebuilding the City: A Guide to Development in Hulme*, Hulme Regeneration Ltd, Manchester.

ICE (2000) *Returning Roads to Residents*, Institute of Civil Engineers, Thomas Telford, London.

IHT (2001) *Guidance for Providing for Journeys on Foot*, Institution of Highways and Transportation, London.

Jenks M, *et al.* (1996) *The Compact City: A Sustainable Urban Form?* E&FN Spon, London.

Johnston J and Newton J (n.d.). *Building Green*, London Ecology Unit, London.

Joseph Rowntree Foundation (1995) *Made to Last: Creating Sustainable Neighbourhoods and Estate Regeneration*, Joseph Rowntree Foundation, York.

Kennedy M and Kennedy D (eds) (1997) *Designing Ecological Settlements*, EA.UE, Dietrich Reimer Verlag, Berlin.

Kuhl D and Cooper C (1992) 'Physical Activity at 36 Years: patterns and children predictors in a longitudinal study', *Journal of Epidemiology and Community Health*, 46, pp. 114–19.

LGA (1998) *Energy Services for Sustainable Communities: The Local Government Position*, Local Government Association, London.

LGA (2000a) *A New Future for Allotments*, LGA, London.

LGA (2000b) *Local Spatial Development Strategies*, LGA, London.

LGA (2000c) *Reforming Local Planning: Planning for Communities*, LGA, London.

LGA (2001) *Growing in the Community: Good Practice Guide to the Management of Allotments*, LGA, London.

LGA and LGMB (1998) *Energy Services for Sustainable Communities: The Local Government Position*, LGA, London.

Llewelyn Davies (1998) *Sustainable Residential Quality – New Approaches to Urban Living*, LPAC, London.

Local Agenda 21 *Roundtable Guidance No. 15 'Sustainable Agriculture and Food'*, IDEA, London.

LUC & CAG (2001) *Quality of Life Capital*, English Nature, English Heritage, the Environment Agency and the Countryside Agency, London.

Lynch K (1981) *A Theory of Good City Form*, MIT Press, Cambridge MA.

Macfarlane S (1950) 'Peckam', *Plan 7 – Journal of the Architectural Student's Association*, pp. 22–7.

Making Cities Liveable (1996) *Newsletter*, MCI.

Marmot M and Wilkinson R (eds) (1999) *The Social Detriments of Health*, Oxford University Press, Oxford.

Marvin S and Guy S (1997) *Creating Myths rather than Sustainability: The Transition Fallacies of the New Localism*, Local Environment, 2:3, pp. 311–18.

McGill J (2001) *Planning for Efficient Natural Resource Use in the Housing Sector*, unpublished thesis, Faculty of the Built Environment, University of the West of England, Bristol.

McLoughlin B (1968) *Urban and Regional Planning: a Systems Approach*, Faber, London.

Milton Keynes Development Corporation (1992) *The Milton Keynes Planning Manual*, Chesterton Consulting, Milton Keynes.

Mollison B (1998) *Permaculture: A Designers Manual*, Togari Publications, Australia.

Morris W and Kaufman J (1997) *Mixed Use Development: New Designs for New Livelihoods*, Queensland Department of Tourism, Small Business and Industry, Brisbane.

NAHB (1999) *Smart Growth: Building Better Places to Live, Work and Play*, National Association of Home Builders, USA.

NPFA (1992), *The Six Acre Standard: Minimum Standards for Outdoor Playing Space*, National Playing Fields Association, London.

NEF (n.d.) *Participation Works!: 21 Techniques of Community Participation for the 21st Century*, New Economics Foundation, London.

NUFU (2000) *Sustainable Urban Forestry: Benefiting Public Health*, National Urban Forestry Unit, Wolverhampton.

Odum H (1971) *Environment, Power and Society*, Wiley-Interscience, New York.

Osborne S and Shaftoe H (1995) *Safer Neighbourhoods? Successes and Failures in Crime Prevention*, Safe Neighbourhoods Unit, London.

Osbourne P and Davis A (1996) *Safe Routes to School Demonstration Projects*, PTRC Education and Research Services Ltd, London.

Owen S (1991) *Planning Settlements Naturally*, Packard Publishing, Chichester.

Oxford M (2000) *Developing Naturally: Handbook for Incorporating the Natural Environment into Planning and Development*, Association of Local Government Ecologists.

Paternoster N (2000) *Trip Generation of Crickhowell Televillage*, Unpublished postgraduate study, University of the West of England, Bristol.

Peabody Trust (2000) *Bedzed: Building a sustainable future*, Peabody Trust, London.

Peterborough Development Corporation (1970) *Greater Peterborough Master Plan*, PDC, Peterborough.

Pharoah T (1993) *Traffic Calming Guidelines*, Devon County Council, Exeter.

Planning (1999) 'Development wide ecology is possible', *Planning*, 19 November 1999, p. 2.

Plato (1952) *Timaeus, Critias, Cleitophon, Menexenus, Epistles* (trans. R. Bury), Harvard University Press.

Prince's Foundation (2000) *Sustainable Urban Extensions: Planned Through Design*, The Prince's Foundation, London.

PTRC (1996) *Planning for Sustainability*, Proceedings of Seminar C of the PTRC European Transport Forum, Brunel University.

Putnam R (1993) 'The Prosperous Community: Social Capital and Public Life', *America Prospect*, 13, pp. 35–42.

Roberts I (1996) 'Safety to School', *Lancet*, 347 (15 June), p. 1642.

Rohde C and Kendle A (1994) *Human Well-being, Natural Landscapes and Wildlife in Urban Areas, A Review*, English Nature Science 22, English Nature, Peterborough.

Royal Commission on Environmental Pollution (1994) *Eighteenth Report: Transport and the Environment*, HMSO, London.

Royal Commission on Environmental Pollution (1997) *Transport and the Environment: Development Since 1994*, HMSO, London.

Royal Commission on Environmental Pollution (2000) *Energy: The Changing Climate*, HMSO, London.

RSPB (2000a) *Good Practice Guide – Housing*, RSPB, Sandy.

RSPB (2000b) *Planning for Nature Conservation*, RSPB, Sandy.

RSPB (1999) *Planning for Biodiversity: Good Practice Guide*, RSPB, Sandy.

Rudlin D and Falk N (1999) *Building the 21st Century Home: The Sustainable Urban Neighbourhood*, Butterworth-Heinemann, Oxford.

Russell H (2000) *Public Health and Regeneration: Making the Links*, LGA and HEA, London.

Saye N (1999) *A Comparison of Different Neighbourhoods to Determine the Extent to which Neighbourhood Structure may Reduce the Need to Travel*, Unpublished dissertation, Faculty of the Built Environment, University of the West of England, Bristol.

Scottish Environmental Protection Agency (2000) *Watercourses in the Community: A Guide to Sustainable Watercourse Management in the Urban Environment*, Stirling, SEPA.

Selman P (1996) *Local Sustainability*, Paul Chapman Publishing, London.

SEPA (1999) *National Waste Strategy 1999*, Scottish Executive Publications, Edinburgh.

SEPA (2000) *Watercourses in the Community: a Guide to Sustainable Watercourse Management in the Urban Environment*, Scottish Executive Publications, Edinburgh.

Shankland, Cox and Associates (1968) *Ipswich Draft Basic Plan*, Ministry of Housing and Local Government, HMSO, London.

Sherlock H (1990) *Cities are Good For Us*, Transport 2000, London.

Shirley P and Box J (1998) *Biodiversity, Brownfield Sites and Housing*, The Urban Wildlife Partnership.

Sibley P (n.d.) *The Sustainable Management of Greenspace*, Institute of Leisure and Amenity Managers, London.

Social Exclusion Unit (2000) *National Strategy for Neighbourhood Renewal*, HMSO, London.

Soil Association (1998) *Local Food for Local People*, Soil Association, Bristol.

Speller V (1999) *Promoting Community Health: Developing the Role of Local Government*, Health Education Authority, London.

Stead D (1999) *Planning for Less Travel – Identifying Land Use Characteristics Associated with More Sustainable Travel Patterns*, Unpublished PhD thesis, University College, London.

Stead D and Davis A (1998) 'Increasing the Need to Travel? Parental Choice and Travel to School', in *Proceedings of Seminar C: Policy Planning and Sustainability*, 26th PTRC European Transport Forum, Uxbridge.

Stevenson F and Williams N (2000) *Sustainable Housing: Design Guide for Scotland*, The Stationery Office, London.

Thomson R (ed.) (1996) *Environmental Design: An Introduction for Architects and Engineers*, E&FN Spon, London.

Tjanllingii, S (1995) *Ecopolis: Strategies for Ecologically Sound Urban Development*, Backhays Publishers, Leiden.

Tolley R (ed.) (1997) *The Greening of Urban Transport*, Wiley, Chichester.

Ulrich R (2000) 'Stress, patient recovery and trees', in Proceedings of Trees and Healthy Living National Conference, National Urban Forestry Unit, Wolverhampton. Urban Task Force (1999) Towards an Urban Renaissance, Spon/DETR, London.

Urban Green Spaces Task Force (2002) *Green Spaces, Better Places*, DTLR, London.

Wates N (2000) *The Community Planning Handbook*, Earthscan, London.

Whitehead M and Dahlgren G (1991) 'What can we do about inequalities in health?', *The Lancet*, 338, pp. 1059–63.

WHO (1946) *Constitution of the World Health Organization*, WHO, Geneva.

WHO (1999) *Urban Food and Nutrition Action Plan* – Oct99 draft, LVNG 030102, WHO, Europe.

Williams K, *et al.* (2000) *Achieving Sustainable Urban Form*, Spon, London.

Williams S (1995) *Recreation in the Urban Environment*, Routledge, London.

Winter J and Farthing S (1997) 'Co-ordinating Facility Provision and New Housing Development: Impacts on Car and Local Facility Use', in Farthing S (ed.), *Evaluating Local Environmental Policy*, Aldershot, Avebury, pp. 159–79.

WCED (World Commission on Environment and Development; the 'Brundtland Report') (1987) *Our Common Future*, Oxford University Press, Oxford.

York City Council (2000) *School Organisation Plan*, September 2000–2005, City Council, York.

# index and key terms

In the following index, page numbers in bold indicate a definition and in italics indicate a figure

243